George Barnett Smith

Leaders of modern Industry

Biographical Sketches

George Barnett Smith

Leaders of modern Industry
Biographical Sketches

ISBN/EAN: 9783743333383

Manufactured in Europe, USA, Canada, Australia, Japa

Cover: Foto ©ninafisch / pixelio.de

Manufactured and distributed by brebook publishing software (www.brebook.com)

George Barnett Smith

Leaders of modern Industry

CONTENTS.

	PAGE
THE STEPHENSONS	1
CHARLES KNIGHT	73
SIR GEORGE BURNS	133
SIR JOSIAH MASON	189
THE WEDGWOODS	231
THOMAS BRASSEY	301
THE FAIRBAIRNS	335
SIR WILLIAM SIEMENS	379
THE RENNIES	421

THE STEPHENSONS.

THE courage and perseverance of Englishmen under difficulties have become proverbial, and these admirable qualities were never shown to greater advantage than in the lives of George and Robert Stephenson. The father was vigorous in mind and body, strong and self-reliant in character, always keeping his end steadily in view, and yet with a strain of tenderness running through his nature which rendered him humane and sympathetic towards struggling merit wherever he found it. Similar in gifts and disposition was the son; and the names of both are indissolubly connected with that mighty engine of modern progress, the locomotive. Their hardships, disappointments, and final triumphs form one of the most interesting chapters in the fairy tales of science.

George Stephenson's father, Robert Stephenson, was the son of a Scotchman who came into England in the capacity of a gentleman's servant. Robert was a collier, and married Mabel Carr, the daughter of a dyer, whose family had long been settled at Ovingham. The young couple lived at a village near Wylam, eight miles from Newcastle, and here six children were born to them, of whom George was the second. The poverty of the Stephensons will be understood, seeing that the father had to maintain his family on twelve shillings a week. The future engineer's first employment was herding cows at twopence a day, from which he was advanced to hoeing turnips at fourpence, and then to driving a gin-horse at eightpence. As a boy he had all his wits about him, being full of fun and tricks, and he was generally foremost in all the sports and pastimes of youth. A strong love of birds and animals was a characteristic he inherited from his father. Young birds, and even blackbirds, he would feed and tame until they would fly in and about the cottage, and roost upon the head of his bed at night. George's ambition was to be an engineman, and great was his delight when at fourteen years of age he was appointed assistant fireman at a shilling a day. At fifteen he was at Throckley Bridge, with a salary of twelve shillings a week, which sum seemed almost dazzling in its proportions. 'I am now a made man for life!' he exclaimed triumphantly to his companions.

It was at this period that Stephenson began to develop the industry and dogged perseverance for which he was famous. At seventeen he had not yet learned to read, and as it was only in books that he could find a description of the wonderful engines of Boulton and Watt of which he had heard, he bent himself to the acquisition of knowledge. For this purpose he devoted out of his humble gains the sum of fourpence weekly for lessons in reading, writing, and arithmetic, which were conned over at night and mastered by the light of his engine fire. He also used the practical means at hand for acquiring experience and information; and as fireman he applied himself to a diligent study of the steam-engine, taking his machine to pieces during his leisure hours. He was at this time working at the Water-row Pit. Pastime was not forgotten in study, however, and the big and bony youth delighted in feats of strength. At throwing the hammer he had no compeer, and he was equally strong and agile in lifting heavy weights off the ground from between his feet. Dr. Smiles, in his *Life of George Stephenson*, gives one very interesting glimpse of him touching his favourite animals. 'Like his father, he used to tempt the robin-redbreasts to hop and fly about him at the engine fire, by the bait of bread-crumbs saved from his dinner. But his chief favourite was his dog—so sagacious that he almost daily carried George's dinner to him at the pit. The tin containing the meal was suspended from the dog's neck, and, thus laden, he proceeded faithfully from Jolly's Close to Water-row Pit, quite through the village of Newburn. He turned neither to left nor right, nor heeded the barking of curs at his heels. But his course was not unattended with perils. One day the big strange dog of a passing butcher, espying the engineman's messenger with the tin can about his neck, ran after and fell upon him. There was a terrible tussle and worrying, which lasted for a brief while, and, shortly after, the dog's master, anxious for his dinner, saw his faithful servant approaching, bleeding but triumphant. The tin can was still round his neck, but the dinner had been spilt in the struggle. Though George went without his dinner that day, he was prouder of his dog than ever when the circumstances of the combat were related to him by the villagers who had seen it.'

While at Black Callerton Colliery in 1801 Stephenson employed his off-time in mending shoes and cleaning watches, by means of which he managed to save his first guinea. On accepting the charge of the engine on Willington Ballast Hill at an increased wage, he also determined to marry. He had given his affections to Fanny Henderson, servant to a small farmer, and a young woman of considerable personal attractions and amiable character. George was twenty-one, and had managed to put by a small hoard; this, together with Fanny's little savings, enabled him to take a cottage dwelling at Willington Quay, on the north bank of the Tyne, about six miles below Newcastle. The young couple were married at Newburn Church on the 28th November, 1802. After paying a visit to old Robert Stephenson, 'the bridal party prepared to set out for their new home at Willington Quay. They went in a style which was quite common before travelling by railway had been invented. Two farm horses, borrowed from a neighbouring farmer, were each provided with a saddle and a pillion, and George having mounted one, his wife seated herself behind him, holding on by her arms round his waist. The bridesman and bridesmaid in like manner mounted the other horse; and in this wise the wedding party rode across the country, passing through the old streets of Newcastle, and then by Wallsend to Willington Quay—a long ride of about fifteen miles.'

It is stated that in his little cottage during the winter evenings Stephenson was usually occupied in studying mechanical subjects, or in modelling experimental machines. Like many others before him, he indulged the dream of being able to discover perpetual motion. At other times he would employ himself for a few hours in casting ballast out of the colliery ships, thus earning a few additional shillings weekly. Sir William Fairbairn informed Dr. Smiles that 'while Stephenson was employed at the Willington Ballast Hill he himself was working in the neighbourhood as an engine apprentice at the Percy Main Colliery. He was very fond of George, who was a fine hearty fellow, besides being a capital workman. In the summer evenings, young Fairbairn was accustomed to go down to Willington to see his friend, and on such occasions he would frequently take charge of George's engine for a few hours, to enable him to take a two or three hours' turn at heaving ballast out of ships' holds. It is pleasant to think of the future President of the British Association thus helping the future railway engineer to earn a few extra shillings by over-work in the evenings, at a time when both occupied the rank of but humble working men in an obscure northern village.' In shoe-making and clock-cleaning George also became quite an expert, and his neighbours found him profitable overtime in these capacities.

At Willington Quay, on the 16th of October, 1803, Stephenson's only son was born. He was christened by the name of Robert, and from the first his father was wrapped up in him, making him the cherished companion of his evening hours. About the end of 1804, Stephenson became brakesman at West Moor Colliery, Killingworth. He had not been in his new post two years before a severe calamity befell him. His young wife, the bright and affectionate and ministering spirit of his home, and the sharer of his joys and sorrows, died of consumption, leaving him desolate and alone, save for the little child Robert. For a twelvemonth George now superintended the working of a Boulton and Watt engine at Montrose, and so profitable was the engagement that when he returned to Killingworth it was with £28 in his pocket. His father having met with a serious pit accident, by which he was reduced to the severest poverty, George paid his debts and found a little cottage for his parents near his own home, where he supported them for years. Yet at this time the working-classes suffered much from heavy taxation and the serious cost of provisions, while they were in constant dread of being drawn for the militia—George Stephenson himself was so drawn, and in order to save his work and avoid service, he had to spend the whole of his savings, and a further sum of £6 which he borrowed, in finding a substitute. His biographer says of his position at this time: 'He was almost in despair, and contemplated the idea of leaving the country, and emigrating to the United States. Although a voyage thither was then a much more formidable thing for a working man to accomplish than a voyage to Australia is now, he seriously entertained the project, and had all but made up his mind to go. His sister Ann, with her husband, emigrated about that time, but George could not raise the requisite money, and they departed without him. After all, it went sore against his heart to leave his home and his kindred, the scenes of his youth and the friends of his boyhood; and he struggled long with the idea, brooding over it in sorrow. Speaking afterwards to a friend of his thoughts at the time, he said: "You know the road from my house at the West Moor to Killingworth. I remember once when I went along that road I wept bitterly, for I knew not where my lot in life would be cast." But his poverty prevented him from prosecuting the idea of emigration, and rooted him to the place where he afterwards worked out his career so manfully and victoriously.'

In pursuing his avocations Stephenson effected various little economies in colliery working, which benefited both masters and men. He also improved the pumping apparatus to such an extent that his master presented him with a gratuity of £10, and further appointed him engineman at the High Pit at good wages. The result of George's success as an engine-doctor was that he was soon called upon to prescribe remedies for all the old wheezy and ineffective pumping machines in the neighbourhood. In 1812 he was appointed enginewright to the Killingworth collieries at a salary of £100 a year. Stephenson spent many of his evenings with John Wigham, at the Glebe Farm at Benton. Wigham taught his friend the Rule of Three and the higher branches of arithmetic. He was an excellent talker, no mean thinker, and an extensive reader; and as George was a good intellectual absorbent he gained much from Wigham, which he ever afterwards gratefully acknowledged.

Meanwhile George Stephenson's son Robert was now growing up. He was active and intelligent, and deeply interested in his father's mechanical experiments. George Stephenson determined that his son should have those educational advantages he had himself been deprived of. In a speech, delivered long afterwards at Newcastle, the great engineer said: 'In the earlier period of my career, when Robert was a little boy, I saw how deficient I was in education; and I made up my mind that he should not labour under the same defect, but that I would put him to a good school and give him a liberal training. I was, however, a poor man; and how do you think I managed? I betook myself to mending my neighbours' clocks and watches at nights, after my daily labour was done, and thus I procured the means of educating my son.' There was great shrewdness in his method of saving. Having, by extra labour, managed to save a sum of £100, which he accumulated in *guineas*, he sold each of these coins to Jews, who went about buying them up (gold coins being then dearer than silver) at twenty-six shillings apiece; and he lent out the proceeds at interest. As his son was to be a director of labour as well as an engineer, he must not be beaten back by defective knowledge; and it was in this spirit that, among other things, he was put to learn French.

Robert Stephenson went to school first to a man named Rutter, parish clerk of Long Benton, and in the summer of 1815 he was transferred to Mr. Bruce's school in Percy Street, Newcastle. Dressed in a suit of homely grey stuff, cut out by his father, Robert rode into Newcastle daily on a donkey. He spoke the broadest dialect of the pitmen, and was full of all kinds of pranks and fun. In his *Life of Robert Stephenson*, Mr. Cordy Jeaffreson observes: 'Up to the time when he left Bruce's school Robert did not exhibit any marked enthusiasm for the pursuits in which his father was most warmly interested. Possibly George Stephenson was too urgent that he should prosecute the study of mechanics, and by continually goading him to work harder and harder "at his books" gave him a transient distaste for subjects to which he was naturally inclined. As a member of the Literary and Philosophical Society of Newcastle, Robert brought home standard popular works and encyclopædic volumes treating of natural science and of inventions. These books his father read, and compelled him to read, but the labour went very much against the boy's grain.

'The earliest "drawing" by Robert Stephenson's hand of which there is any record was that of a sun-dial, copied from *Ferguson's Astronomy*, and presented by the lad to Mr. Losh, in the year 1816, in token of his gratitude to him as his father's benefactor. This drawing set the father and son on another work—the construction of a real sun-dial, which, on its completion, was fixed over George's cottage door, where it still remains, bearing the date "August 11th, MDCCCXVI."

'A good story is told of "the hempy boy," who dearly loved mischief. From the meadow before the West Moor cabin he sent up his enormous kite, reined in by copper wire instead of string, the copper wire being insulated by a piece of silk cord. Anthony Wigham's cow, peacefully grazing in the meadow, was first favoured with a smart dose of electricity, one end of the copper wire being brought down to the tip of the animal's tail. Standing at his cottage window, George Stephenson watched the discomfiture of his neighbour's cow in high glee. But when the operator, ignorant whose eyes were upon him, relinquished the torture of the "coo," and proceeded to give his father's pony a fillip with the subtle fluid, George rushed out from his cottage with upraised whip, exclaiming, "Ah! thou mischeevous scoondrel, aal paa thee!" It is needless to say that Robert Stephenson did not wait to be paid.'

In the year 1854 Dr. Smiles accompanied Robert Stephenson on a visit to his old home and haunts at Killingworth. Here is one of the reminiscences of his youth recalled by the engineer during that visit: 'While Robert was still at school his father proposed to him during the holidays that he should construct a sun-dial, to be placed over their cottage door at West Moor. "I expostulated with him at first," said Robert, "that I had not learnt sufficient astronomy and mathematics to enable me to make the necessary calculations. But he would have no denial. 'The thing is to be done,' said he; 'so just set about it at once.' Well, we got a *Ferguson's Astronomy*, and studied the subject together. Many a sore head I had while making the necessary calculations to adapt the dial to the latitude of Killingworth. But at length it was fairly drawn out on paper, and then my father got a stone, and we hewed, and carved, and polished it until we made a very respectable dial of it; and there it is, you see," pointing to it over the cottage door, "still quietly numbering the hours when the sun shines. I assure you not a little was thought of that piece of work by the pitmen when it was put up, and began to tell its tale of time." The date carved upon the dial is "August 11th, MDCCCXVI." Both father and son were in after-life very proud of their joint production. Many years after George took a party of savans, when attending a meeting of the British Association at Newcastle, over to Killingworth to see the pits, and he did not fail to direct their attention to the sun-dial; and Robert, on the last visit which he made to the place, a short time before his death, took a friend into the cottage, and pointed out to him the very desk, still there, at which he had sat when making his calculations of the latitude of Killingworth.'

The subject of the locomotive engine began to engage George Stephenson's attention at Killingworth as early as 1813. Before recounting his success, it will be convenient here briefly to refer to the early history of the use of tractive power on roads. In the construction of tramways stone or wood was first used, but towards the close of the eighteenth century iron was substituted on lines laid down in collieries and quarries. Attempts were made in various countries to utilise steam-power for locomotion on ordinary roadways, but the credit of producing the first practical working engine is awarded to Nicholas Joseph Cugnot, a native of Void, in Lorraine. In 1769 he constructed in the French National Arsenal, at the cost of the Comte de Saxe, a carriage which ran on three wheels, and had two single-acting cylinders turning the front wheel. Oliver Evans, a citizen of the United States, constructed in 1804 a steam dredging-machine which propelled itself on wheels to the river adjacent, a distance of a mile and a half. James Watt's improvements in the steam-engine led to better forms of locomotives, and successful models were produced respectively by William Murdoch, William Symington of Dumbarton, and Richard Trevithick. Trevithick made experiments with the first railway locomotive on the Merthyr Tydvil tramroad in 1804; but he was discouraged by the breakage of the plate rails of cast-iron, and the locomotive was not given an adequate trial. The invention was subsequently exhibited in London. Trevithick's experiments had much to do with the development of the high-pressure engine. Mr. Blackett, of Wylam, near Newcastle-on-Tyne, was the first colliery owner in the North who displayed an active interest in the locomotive. He made experiments on Trevithick's lines, but was compelled to abandon them in the first instance. Then Mr. Blenkinsop, manager of the Middleton collieries, near Leeds, took up Trevithick's idea. Although the engine which he constructed was clumsy and slow, it was fairly successful, and was long regarded as one of the wonders of the neighbourhood. It travelled at a speed of ten miles an hour, did the work of sixteen horses in twelve hours, and its cost was £400. William Hedley—encouraged and assisted by Mr. Blackett—constructed and patented in 1813 the *Puffing Billy*, which is now to be seen in the Museum of the Patent Office, and to this steam-carriage 'must be ascribed the honour of being the progenitor of the enormous stud of iron-horses now existing in all parts of the world. In previous experimental lines, rack rails and toothed wheels had been provided under the mistaken notion that the adhesion of a smooth wheel to a smooth rail would not be sufficient." After various trials and alterations, *Puffing Billy* was set to work at the Wylam Colliery in 1813, and this venerable locomotive was kept in constant use until 1872, when it was purchased by the Government. It lacked advantages afterwards discovered by Stephenson, but it was successful up to the point anticipated.

Meanwhile, George Stephenson was studying the question of the locomotive for himself. At the same time he economised labour in the haulage of coal by facilitating the means of transit by inclined planes and other methods. With regard to the Blackett and Blenkinsop engines, he made himself thoroughly acquainted with their principles and working. He then addressed himself to the task of making his first locomotive, or 'travelling engine' as he called it. Lord Ravensworth, the principal partner in the Killingworth Colliery, found the money for the experiment, and was counted, by many, a fool for his pains. Stephenson had to contend with imperfect tools and workmen poorly skilled in mechanics. He constructed an engine, however, somewhat after Blenkinsop's method, in the workshops at the West Moor, his leading mechanic being John Thirlwall, the colliery blacksmith. The engine was placed on the Killingworth tramway on the 25th of July, 1814, and its powers were tested the same day. The wheels were smooth, and, on an ascending gradient of 1 in 450, the engine succeeded in drawing after it eight loaded carriages of thirty tons weight at about four miles an hour. The *Blutcher*, as it was named, was kept regularly at work for some time, but it was a somewhat cumbrous and clumsy machine, and lacked springs; and when it had been tried for a considerable period, it was ascertained that steam-power and horse-power were as nearly as possible equal in point of cost.

Robert Stephenson, in giving an account of his father's later and successful efforts to produce an economical working locomotive, says:—

'In 1815 my father had succeeded in manufacturing an engine which included the following important improvements on all previous attempts in the same direction: simple and direct communication between the cylinder and the wheels rolling upon the rails, joint adhesion of all the wheels, attained by the use of horizontal connecting-rods, and, finally, a beautiful method of exciting the combustion of fuel by employing the waste steam which had formerly been allowed uselessly to escape. It is, perhaps, not too much to say that his engine, as a mechanical contrivance, contained the germ of all that has since been effected. It may be regarded, in fact, as a type of the present locomotive engine.

'In describing my father's application of the waste steam for the purpose of increasing the power of the engine without adding to its weight, and while claiming for this engine the merit of being a type of all those which have been successfully devised since the commencement of the Liverpool and Manchester Railway, it is necessary to observe that the next great improvement in the same direction, the " multitubular boiler," which took place some years later, could never have been used without the help of that expedient *the steam-blast*, by which power only the burning of coke was rendered possible.

'I cannot pass over this last-named invention of my father's without remarking how slightly, as an original idea, it has been appreciated, and yet how small would be the comparative value of the locomotive engine of the present day without the application of that important invention!

'Engines constructed by my father in the year 1818 upon the principles just described are in use on the Killingworth Colliery Railway to this very day (1856), conveying, at the speed of perhaps five or six miles an hour, heavy coal trains, probably as economically as any of the more perfect engines now in use.'

It was George Stephenson's grand improvement of the 'steam-blast' which enabled him to carry his locomotive experiments to a triumphant issue. On this point Dr. Smiles observes: 'The invention of the Steam-Blast by George Stephenson, in 1815, was fraught with most important consequences to railway locomotion, and it is not saying too much to aver that the success of the locomotive has been in a great measure the result of its adoption. Without the steam-blast, by means of which the intensity of combustion is maintained at its highest point, producing a correspondingly rapid evolution of steam, high rates of speed could not have been kept up, the advantages of the multitubular boiler (afterwards invented) could never have been fully tested, and locomotives might still have been dragging themselves unwieldily along at little more than five or six miles an hour.' The invention of the steam-blast has been the subject of much controversy, and it has been claimed for Trevithick in 1804, Hedley in 1814, Sir Goldsworthy Gurney in 1820, and Timothy Hackworth in 1829. But as Dr. Smiles has shown, the statements in the first edition of Mr. Nicholas Wood's *Practical Treatise on Railways* (1825) made it 'perfectly clear that George Stephenson invented and applied he steam-blast for the express purpose of quickening combustion in the furnace by increasing the draught in the chimney. Though urged by Wood to abandon the blast, Stephenson continued to hold by it as one of the vital powers of the locomotive engine.' Its usefulness was further developed by the sagacity of Timothy Hackworth, of Darlington.

The next great invention by George Stephenson—that of the 'Geordie' safety-lamp—brought his name prominently before the public, and led to a long discussion between the partisans of Stephenson and those of Sir Humphry Davy. Moved by the terrible calamities which ensued from the explosions of firedamp, Stephenson devised his colliery safety-lamp. Dr. W. R. Clanny, of Sunderland, had already contrived the first lamp which would safely burn in an explosive mixture of gas and air, but it was unfit for ordinary use. It is stated that both Clanny and Stephenson applied wire-gauze cylinders to their lamps after Davy had made a communication to the Royal Society about his own lamp, though before he produced his own lamp to the public. Stephenson's lamp had a glass cylinder inside the wire-gauze, the former having a cap of perforated copper. Small orifices below the glass admitted the necessary air, and when the air became highly explosive the light went out, so that the lamp did not get overheated. To enable it to burn well, the lamp required to be either held or suspended. Dr. Smiles gives this interesting account of the rival Davy and Stephenson lamps :—

'An angry controversy took place as to the respective merits of George Stephenson and Sir Humphry Davy in respect of the invention of the safety-lamp. A committee was formed on both sides, and the facts were stated in various ways. It is perfectly clear, however, that Stephenson had ascertained *the fact* that flame will not pass through tubes of a certain diameter —the principle on which the safety-lamp is constructed— before Sir Humphry Davy had formed any definite idea on the subject or invented the model lamp afterwards exhibited by him before the Royal Society. Stephenson had actually constructed a lamp on such a principle, and proved its safety, before Sir Humphry had communicated his views on the subject to any person, and by the time that the first public intimation had been given of his discovery, Stephenson's second lamp had been constructed and tested in like manner in the Killingworth Pit. The *first* was tried on the 21st of October, 1815, the *second* was tried on the 4th of November; but it was not until the 9th of November that Sir Humphry Davy presented his first lamp to the public. And by the 30th of the same month Stephenson had constructed and tested his *third* safety-lamp.

'Stephenson's theory of the "burnt air" and the "draught" was no doubt wrong; but his lamp was right, and that was the great fact which mainly concerned him. Torricelli did not know the rationale of his tube, nor Otto Gürike that of his air-pump; yet no one thinks of denying them the merit of their inventions on that account. The discoveries of Volta and Galvani were in like manner independent of theory; the greatest discoveries consisting in bringing to light certain great facts, on which theories are afterwards framed. Our inventor had been pursuing the Baconian method, though he did not think of that; his sole object being to invent a safe lamp, which he knew could only be done through the process of repeated experiment. Hence his numerous experiments on the fire-damp at the blowers in the mine, as well as on carburetted hydrogen gas in his cottage by means of original apparatus. By experiment he distinctly ascertained that the explosion of the fire-damp could not pass through small tubes; and he also did what had not before been done by any inventor—he constructed a lamp on this principle, and repeatedly proved its safety at the risk of his life. At the same time, there is no doubt that it was to Sir Humphry Davy that the merit belonged of elucidating the true law on which the safety-lamp is constructed.'

Stephenson received a public testimonial of £1,000 for

his discovery, and Davy received £2,000 from those who regarded him as the inventor of the safety-lamp. The undoubted fact is that both inventors arrived at the same result independently of each other. As Robert Stephenson well put it, 'If George Stephenson had never lived, Sir Humphry Davy could, and most probably would, have invented the safety-lamp; but again, if Sir Humphry Davy had never lived, George Stephenson certainly would have invented the safety-lamp, as I believe he did independently of all that Sir Humphry Davy had done in the matter.' As might naturally be expected, the Clanny, Davy, and Stephenson lamps have all been practically superseded by later improved safety-lamps. The Final Report of the Commissioners on Accidents in Mines, published in 1886, showed that there were four lamps in which the quality of safety, in a pre-eminent degree, was combined with simplicity of construction and with illuminating power at least fully equal to that of any of the lamps hitherto in general use. These were Gray's lamp, Marsant's lamp, the lamp of the latest pattern proposed by Evan Thomas, and the bonneted Mueseler lamp. Of these four lamps, the one which has become the favourite, and which has passed into most general use, is the lamp constructed by M. Marsant, of the Bessèges Collieries, Gard, France. Made with three gauzes, it will not cause an explosion in so strong a current as fifty feet per second, or even when the inner gauze is at a bright red heat, unless the glass cracks. With two gauzes its light is three and a half times greater than that of a Davy lamp.

George Stephenson proceeded with his improvements, both in mining and locomotion, and he was one of the first to introduce steam machinery underground for the purpose of winning and raising the coal. The Killingworth mines, indeed, came to be regarded as the models of the district. A system of improved transit was also devised for conveying the coals aboveground from the pit-head to the shipping-place. Even when persons regarded his travelling engine as little better than a dangerous curiosity, he predicted that the locomotive would yet supersede every other traction-power for drawing heavy loads. To avoid jerks and shocks, and to avert the overturning of the engine, Stephenson devised the half-lap joint, by means of which the rails extended a certain distance over each other at the ends. These ends, instead of resting on the flat chair, were made to rest upon the apex of a curve forming the bottom of the chair. The new system contributed largely both to efficiency and smooth action. A patent was taken out for this improved form of rail and chair, in the joint names of the inventor and Mr. Losh, an ironfounder of Newcastle. This gentleman had a great belief in Stephenson, and guaranteed him a salary of £100 per annum, with a share in the profits arising from his inventions, conditional on his attending at the Walker Ironworks one day a week—an arrangement which the Killingworth Colliery owners cordially sanctioned.

Dr. Smiles observes that Stephenson's 'endeavours having been attended with such marked success in the adaptation of locomotive power to railways, his attention was called by many of his friends, about the year 1818, to the application of steam to travelling on common roads. It was from this point, indeed, that the locomotive had started, Trevithick's first engine having been constructed with this special object. Stephenson's friends having observed how far behind he had left the original projector of the locomotive in its application to railroads, perhaps naturally inferred that he would be equally successful in applying it to the purpose for which Trevithick and Vivian had intended the first engine. But the accuracy with which he estimated the resistance to which loads were exposed on railways, arising from friction and gravity, led him at a very early stage to reject the idea of ever applying steam-power economically to common road travelling. In October, 1818, he made a series of careful experiments in conjunction with Mr. Nicholas Wood, on the resistance to which carriages were exposed on railways, testing the results by means of a dynamometer of his own contrivance. The series of practical observations made by means of this instrument were interesting, as the first systematic attempt to determine the precise amount of resistance to carriages moving along railways. It was then for the first time ascertained by experiment that the friction was a constant quantity of all velocities. Although this theory had long before been developed by Vince and Coulomb, and was well known to scientific men as an established truth, yet at the time when Stephenson made his experiments the deductions of philosophers on the subject were neither believed in nor acted upon by practical engineers.'

Robert Stephenson records that the following were the principal arguments which influenced his father 'to work out the use of the locomotive in a directly opposite course to that pursued by a number of ingenious inventors, who, between 1820 and 1836, were engaged in attempting to apply steam-power to turnpike roads. Having ascertained that resistance might be taken as represented by 10 lb. to a ton weight on a level railway, it became obvious to him that so small a rise as 1 in 100 would diminish the useful effort of a locomotive by upwards of fifty per cent. This fact called my father's attention to the question of gradients in future locomotive lines. He then became convinced of the vital importance, in an economical point of view, of reducing the country through which a railway was intended to pass to as near a level as possible. This originated in his mind the distinctive character of railway works as contradistinguished from all other roads,— for in railroads he early contended that large sums would be wisely expended in perforating barriers of hills with long tunnels, and in raising low ground with the excess cut down from the adjacent high ground. In proportion as these views fixed themselves upon his mind, and were corroborated by his daily experience, he became more and more convinced of the hopelessness of applying steam locomotion to common roads,—for every argument in favour of a level railway was an argument against the rough and hilly course of common road. He never ceased to urge upon the patrons of road steam-carriages that if, by any amount of ingenuity, an engine could be made which could by possibility traverse a turnpike road at a speed at least equal to that obtainable by horse-power, and at a less cost, such an engine, if applied to the more perfect surface of a railway, would have its efficiency enormously enhanced. For instance, he calculated that if an engine had been constructed, and had been found to travel uniformly between London and Birmingham at an average speed of ten miles an hour, conveying, say, twenty or thirty passengers at a cost of one shilling per mile, it was clear that the same engine, if applied to a railway, instead of conveying twenty or thirty people would have conveyed 200 or 300 people, and instead of a speed of ten or twelve miles an hour a speed of at least thirty to forty miles an hour would have been obtained.'

But while there was to be seen at Killingworth in daily use a system of road locomotion which was destined to revolutionise England, Stephenson was for a long time unable to bring it to the notice of the English public. Indeed, there seemed so small a prospect of introducing the locomotive into general use, that Stephenson recurred to an old idea he had indulged of emigrating to the United States. He thought the great lakes of North America presented a splendid field for introducing steam-power into navigation. Happily this was averted by the authorities of the Hetton Coal Company stepping in and engaging George Stephenson to lay down the Hetton Railway—the longest locomotive line that had hitherto been constructed in the district. The line was successfully laid, and on the 18th of November, 1822, it was opened in the presence of thousands of spectators. Five locomotives were seen at work, with a speed of about four miles an hour, and each engine drew after it a train of seventeen waggons weighing about sixty-four tons.

While this was going forward in 1819 Robert Stephenson left school, and was put apprentice to the head viewer at Killingworth, to learn the business of the colliery. This he did for three years, and then he was sent for a brief course of instruction to the Edinburgh University. He attended the Chemical Lectures of Dr. Hope, the Natural Philosophy Lectures of Sir John Leslie, and the Natural History Class of Professor Jameson; while he devoted several evenings a week to the study of practical chemistry under Dr. John Murray. He made careful notes of the lectures, which he afterwards read over to his father. During his stay at the University, Robert Stephenson was one of a band of pupils whom Professor Jameson took on a geological and botanical excursion along the Great Glen of the Highlands, in the line of the Caledonian Canal, as far as Inverness. This tour made an impression upon him which was never effaced. The young student gained a prize for mathematics at the University. He was glad to return home, however. Two years before he had found a true mother in his father's second wife, Elizabeth Hindmarsh, the daughter of a respectable farmer at Black Callerton.

The first *public* Railway Act—says Stephenson's biographer—was that passed in 1801, authorising the construction of a line from Wandsworth to Croydon, under the name of 'The Surrey Iron Railway.' Its object was to furnish a more ready means for the transport of coal and merchandise from the Thames to South London, and at the same time to enable the lime-burners and proprietors of stone-quarries to send their lime and stone to London. The line was afterwards extended, but it never paid, and was dismantled by the projectors of the London and Brighton line, who bought it in 1837. The Wandsworth, Croydon, and Merstham Railway 'was a beacon to warn capitalists against embarking in railways; and many years passed before another was ventured upon.' However, further projects were put forward, both with regard to land-ways and water-ways; but nothing was done in the matter of public railways until the construction of the Stockton and Darlington line, which was the parent public locomotive railway in the United Kingdom. After several abortive movements in favour of a canal instead of a railway, a survey was at length made in 1818 for a railway, the Peases of Darlington being the most prominent supporters of the scheme. So many other members of the Society of Friends ultimately joined them that the railway became known as 'the Quakers' Line.'

An Act was obtained for the construction of the line in 1821. The Directors of the Stockton and Darlington Company appointed George Stephenson their engineer, and adopted his recommendation that a railway be formed instead of a tram-road. The first rail was laid near Stockton, on May 23rd, 1822; but even at this time Stephenson's predictions as to the eventual success of locomotive engines were regarded as mere speculations. Having paid a visit to Killingworth, however, and seen the engine in action there, Edward Pease and his friend Thomas Richardson—the leading promoters of the Stockton and Darlington line—became strong supporters of the locomotive engine. On Stephenson's urgent recommendation, an amended Act of Parliament was obtained, containing a provision for working the railway by means of locomotive engines, as well as a clause—the first of the kind in any railway Act—empowering the employment of the engines for the carriage of passengers as well as of merchandise. Stephenson occupied himself closely in making the working survey of the line, starting very early in the morning, and getting his meals how, when, and wheresoever he could. Here is an entertaining anecdote of him at this time:—

'After the day's work was over, George would drop in at Mr. Pease's, to talk over the progress of the survey and discuss various matters connected with the railway. Mr. Pease's daughters were usually present, and, on one occasion, finding the young ladies learning the art of embroidery, he volunteered to instruct them. "I know all about it," said he; "and you will wonder how I learnt it. I will tell you. When I was a brakesman at Killingworth, I learnt the art of embroidery while working the pitmen's buttonholes by the engine fire at nights." He was never ashamed, but, on the contrary, rather proud of reminding his friends of these humble pursuits of his early life. Mr. Pease's family were greatly pleased with his conversation, which was always amusing and instructive: full of all sorts of experience, gathered in the oddest and most out-of-the-way places. Even at that early period, before he mixed in the society of educated persons, there was a dash of speculativeness in his remarks, which gave a high degree of originality to his conversation, and he would sometimes, in a casual remark, throw a flash of light upon a subject, which called up a train of pregnant suggestions.'

With the assistance of Messrs. Pease and Richardson, George Stephenson established a manufactory at Newcastle for the building of locomotive engines. This was in 1823, and the firm was instituted in consequence of a rupture between Stephenson and his old co-patentees and employers, Losh, Wilson, & Bell. The name of the firm which acquired great celebrity as manufacturers of locomotive engines was Robert Stephenson & Co. George Stephenson thus put his brother Robert in the forefront, and made his own son Robert the chief engineer, as well as an actual member of the firm, while he himself kept in the background. One of his main objects was to obtain good and skilled workmen, capable of carrying out various improvements in detail which he contemplated. Stephenson recommended malleable rails for the new line, although he was interested in the patent for cast-iron rails. But he had demonstrated the vast superiority of malleable rails. They were very expensive, however, and the directors would only allow half the rails to be malleable, the other half being cast-iron. The line was constructed with a gauge of about four feet eight and a half inches; but the press and the public were against the 'new-fangled roads.' The *Whitehaven Gazette* ridiculed the idea of steam-carriages ever travelling 'at a rate almost equal to the speed of the fleetest horse!' The *Tyne Mercury*, of Nov. 16, 1824, asked, 'What person would ever think of *paying anything* to be conveyed from Hexham to Newcastle in something like a coal-waggon, upon a dreary waggon-way, and to be dragged for the greater part of the distance by a roaring steam-engine?' But the courageous railway directors ordered three of Stephenson's locomotive engines, at a cost of several thousand pounds, in view of the opening of the line. The first engine, the *Locomotion*, was duly delivered, weighing about eight tons. In a conversation with his son and a helper named John Dixon, George Stephenson, in drinking success to the line, predicted that the time would come when railways would supersede all other methods of conveyance, and when it would be cheaper for a working-man to travel on a railway than to walk on foot. As the opening of the first railway in England is a memorable historical event, I will quote Dr. Smiles's description of the ceremony:—

'Tuesday, the 27th of September, 1825, was a great day for Darlington. The railway, after having been under construction for more than three years, was at length about to be opened. The project had been the talk of the neighbourhood for so long that there were few people within a range of twenty miles who did not feel more or less interested about it. Was it to be a failure or a success? Opinions were pretty equally divided as to the railway, but as regarded the locomotive the general belief was that it would "never answer." However, there the locomotive was—"No. 1"—delivered on to the line, and ready to draw the first train of waggons on the opening day.

'A great concourse of people assembled on the occasion. Some came from Newcastle and Durham, many from the Aucklands, while Darlington held a general holiday, and turned out all its population. To give *éclat* to the opening, the Directors of the Company issued a programme of the proceedings, intimating the times at which the procession of waggons would pass certain points along the line. The proprietors assembled as early as six in the morning at the Brusselton fixed engine, where the working of the inclined planes was successfully rehearsed. A train of waggons laden with coals and merchandise was drawn up the western incline by the fixed engine, a length of 1,960 yards, in seven and a half minutes, and then lowered down the incline on the eastern side of the hill, 880 yards, in five minutes.

'At the foot of the incline the procession of vehicles was formed, consisting of the locomotive engine, No. 1, driven by George Stephenson himself, after it six waggons loaded with coals and flour, then a covered coach, containing directors and proprietors, next twenty-one coal waggons, fitted up for passengers (with which they were crammed), and, lastly, six more waggons loaded with coals.

'Strange to say, a man on a horse, carrying a flag with the motto of the Company inscribed on it, *Periculum privatum utilitas publica*, headed the procession! A lithographic view of the great event, published shortly after, duly exhibits the horseman and his flag. It was not thought so dangerous a place after all. The locomotive was only supposed to be able to go at the rate of from four to six miles an hour; and an ordinary horse could easily keep ahead of that.

'Off started the procession, with the horseman at its head. A great concourse of people stood along the line. Many of them tried to accompany it by running, and some gentlemen on horseback galloped across the fields to keep up with the train. The railway descending with a gentle incline towards Darlington, the rate of speed was consequently variable. At a favourable part of the road, Stephenson determined to try the speed of the engine, and he called upon the horseman with the flag to get out of the way! Most probably deeming it unnecessary to carry his *Periculum privatum* farther, the horseman turned aside, and Stephenson " put on the steam." The speed was at once raised to twelve miles an hour, and at a favourable part of the road to fifteen. The runners on foot, the gentlemen on horseback, and the horseman with the flag were consequently soon left far behind. When the train reached Darlington it was found that four hundred and fifty passengers occupied the waggons, and that the load of men, coals, and merchandise amounted to about ninety tons.

'At Darlington the procession was re-arranged. The six loaded coal-waggons were left behind, and other waggons were taken on, with a hundred and fifty more passengers, together with a band of music. The train then started for Stockton—a distance of only twelve miles—which was reached in about three hours. The day was kept throughout the district as a holiday, and horses, gigs, carts, and other vehicles, filled with people, stood along the railway, as well as crowds of persons on foot, waiting to see the train pass. The population of Stockton turned out to receive the procession, and after a walk through the streets, the inevitable dinner in the Town Hall wound up the day's proceedings.'

But the Directors and their engineer were still filled with anxiety as to the success of the line. It had been opened, but would the traffic grow, and prove profitable? Yes; ultimately the results amazed even the projectors. It appears that in 1827, the first year in which the coal and merchandise traffic was fully worked, the revenue from coal was £14,455; from lime, merchandise, and sundries, £3,285; and from passengers, £563. But in 1860, when the original line of 25 miles had become extended to 125 miles, and the original capital of £150,000 had grown to £3,800,000, the quantity of coal carried was 3,045,596 tons, producing a revenue of £280,375; while 1,484,409 tons of ironstone and merchandise were also carried, producing £63,478; and 687,728 passengers were conveyed, producing £45,398. During the last thirty years these figures have been further considerably enlarged, so that it is impossible to estimate the services to English industry rendered directly and indirectly by the first railway constructed by George Stephenson.

The first railway passenger carriage designed by Stephenson was 'a somewhat uncouth machine, more resembling a showman's caravan than a passenger-coach of any extant form.' It had a row of seats on each side with a long deal table in the centre, and the door was at the hinder end, as in an omnibus. The engineer dubbed it the *Experiment*, and it formed part of the opening procession. Contrasted with the luxurious Pullman cars of to-day it would appear a very primitive conveyance indeed. The speed of the first railway engine, the *Locomotion*, was considered marvellous, although in a race with the ordinary stage-coach between Stockton and Darlington it only came in first by about one hundred yards. The engine was, after many years, placed as a curiosity upon a pedestal in front of the railway station at Darlington. Dr. Smiles points out that one of the most remarkable results of the Stockton and Darlington Railway was the creation of the now flourishing and populous town of Middlesbrough.

In 1821 another great project was mooted—this was the scheme for the Liverpool and Manchester Railway. The causes which lent strength to this were the rapid growth of the trade of South Lancashire and the unpopular management of the Bridgewater Canal. Owing to a variety of reasons, it sometimes occupied a longer time to convey cotton from Liverpool to Manchester by canal-boat than it had taken to bring it from New York to Liverpool by sailing ship. Considering the vast commercial interests at stake, these delays became intolerable. Consequently, Mr. Joseph Sandars, a warm advocate of tramroads, got together a committee of Liverpool gentlemen to consider the matter. Mr. William James, of West Bromwich, also an enthusiastic advocate of tramways, made a trial survey of the ground to be covered, meeting with much hostility from the inhabitants on the route. This was carried to such a pitch that Mr. James was unable to complete his survey in time to allow of an application to Parliament in the ensuing session. He paid a visit to Killingworth, and saw at a glance that there was a great future in store for Stephenson's locomotive. Robert Stephenson, who had acquired some practical knowledge of surveying, accompanied Mr. James on his return to Liverpool, and a second survey was begun. Obstacles sprang up thick and fast, however, and among the landowners opposed to the scheme were Lords Derby and Wilton, Mr. Bradshaw (canal agent to the Duke of Bridgewater), and the Strafford family. The agents were driven off the land, and farmers set men at their gates with pitchforks to resist their progress. Only two landowners, Mr. Legh and Mr. Wyrley Birch, supported the project and took shares in the undertaking. Mr. James's funds fell short, and the survey again failed.

Mr. Sandars now applied to George Stephenson, and the Committee unanimously appointed him engineer of the projected railway. But before formally setting the undertaking on foot, the Committee appealed to the Duke of Bridgewater's representative to increase the means of conveyance by the canal and to reduce the charges. They were not only met by a definite refusal, but the agent ridiculed the proposed railway as a chimera, and said he should oppose it with all his power. A deputation was now appointed to visit Darlington and Killingworth, and its report was so satisfactory that a company of proprietors was formed for the construction of a double line of railway between Liverpool and Manchester. These original promoters included such well-known men as the Lawrences, Gladstones, Potters, Birleys, Ewarts, and Croppers. One member of the Committee, Henry Booth, afterwards became secretary and manager of the line. That competition in transport was obviously necessary was shown by the fact that shares in the Old Quay Navigation, of which the original cost was £70, had been sold as high as £1,250 each. The first estimated cost of the new railway line was put down at £400,000, and this was subscribed immediately, although it afterwards proved to be quite inadequate. A third survey was made, under great difficulties, and Stephenson and his assistants were driven off the Earl of Derby's Knowsley property by the keepers, who threatened them with personal violence. The Duke of Bridgewater's agent actually declared that he would order the keepers to shoot or apprehend any persons attempting a survey over his Grace's property; but a survey was effected one moonlight night by an ingenious ruse. Such was the general animosity manifested towards the project, that the Company's solicitors wrote to Mr. Sandars that the country was up in arms against it; and, with the exception of Mr. Trafford, the whole of the great proprietors along the entire line were dissentient. The press was also called into requisition by the canal proprietors to denounce the scheme.

Nevertheless, the projectors prepared their case for the House of Commons. But, as showing the prevailing scepticism with regard to steam locomotion, Mr. William Brougham—one of the counsel for the promoters,—on being told by Stephenson that he expected to attain a speed of twenty miles an hour, replied that if he did not moderate his views, and bring his engine within a *reasonable* speed, he would 'inevitably damn the whole thing, and be himself regarded as a maniac only fit for Bedlam.' Civil engineers generally rejected the notion of a locomotive railway, and Stephenson stood practically alone. A scientific writer in the *Quarterly Review*, while admitting the necessity for the railway, scouted the idea of travelling at a greater speed than eight or nine miles an hour; and, with regard to a projected railway to Woolwich, remarked, 'We will back old Father Thames against the Woolwich Railway for any sum.'

On the 21st of March, 1825, the House of Commons went into Committee on the Liverpool and Manchester Bill. There was a great array of legal talent on both sides. The opening evidence for the necessity of the line was conclusive, and it was shown that locomotive travelling was not dangerous. Then the engineering evidence—the most vital part of the case—was taken. George Stephenson was examined, and his testimony subjected to the severest scrutiny. Eight or ten barristers set themselves to the task of bewildering him, while one member of the Committee asked if he was a foreigner, because of his Northumbrian burr, and another hinted that he was mad. But he held to his guns, and stated that he was prepared to prove the safety of working high-pressure locomotives on a railroad, and the superiority of this mode of transporting goods over all others. As to speed, he recommended eight miles an hour with twenty tons, and four miles an hour with forty tons; but much more might be done—even to the rate of twelve miles an hour—with safety. One of the most interesting parts of Stephenson's cross-examination is thus given by Dr. Smiles:—

'It is not necessary to state that to have passed through his severe ordeal scatheless needed no small amount of courage, intelligence, and ready shrewdness on the part of the witness. Nicholas Wood, who was present on the occasion, has since stated that the point on which Stephenson was hardest pressed was that of speed. "I believe," he says, "that it would have lost the Company their Bill if he had gone beyond eight or nine miles an hour. If he had stated his intention of going twelve or fifteen miles an hour not a single person would have believed it to be practicable." Mr. Alderson had, indeed, so pressed the point of "twelve miles an hour," and the promoters were so alarmed lest it should appear in evidence that they contemplated any such extravagant rate of speed, that immediately on Mr. Alderson sitting down Mr. Joy proceeded to re-examine Stephenson, with the view of removing from the minds of the Committee an impression so unfavourable, and, as they supposed, so damaging to their case. "With regard," asked Mr. Joy, "to all those hypothetical questions of my learned friend, they have been all put on the supposition of going twelve miles an hour; now that is not the rate at which, I believe, any of the engines of which you have spoken have travelled?" "No," replied Stephenson, "except as an experiment for a short distance."—"But what they have gone has been three, five, or six miles an hour?" "Yes."—"So that those hypothetical cases of twelve miles an hour do not fall within your general experience?" "They do not."

'The Committee also seem to have entertained some alarm as to the high rate of speed which had been spoken of, and proceeded to examine the witness further on the subject. They supposed the case of the engine being upset when going at nine miles an hour, and asked what, in such a case, would become of the cargo astern. To which the witness replied that it would not be upset. One of the members of the Committee pressed the witness a little further. He put the following case: "Suppose, now, one of these engines going along a railroad at the rate of nine or ten miles an hour, and that a cow were to stray upon the line and get in the way of the engine, would not that, think you, be a very awkward circumstance?" "Yes," replied the witness, with a twinkle in his eye, "very awkward—*for the coo.*" The honourable member did not proceed further with his cross examination; to use a railway phrase, "he was shunted." Another asked if animals would not be very much frightened by the engine passing at night, especially by the glare of the red-hot chimney? "But how would they know that it wasn't painted?" said the witness.'

Stephenson was severely cross-examined on the practicability of forming a road on so unstable a foundation as Chat Moss; and when it was found also that since the depositing of the plans a more favourable line had been discovered, this told against the scheme. Then the scientific evidence called by the opponents of the Bill was felt to be strong, though read now in the light of subsequent events it appears supremely ridiculous. Mr. Alderson, the leading opposition counsel, in summing up, declared Stephenson's plan to be 'the most absurd scheme that ever entered into the head of man to conceive'; and he protested 'against the despotism of the Exchange at Liverpool striding across the land of this country.' The counsel for the canal companies stigmatised Stephenson's evidence as 'trash and confusion,' and otherwise heaped abuse upon the far-seeing engineer. The Committee passed the preamble of the Bill by a majority of one only—thirty-seven to thirty-six; but when the first clause, empowering the Company to make the railway, was lost by nineteen to thirteen, and the next clause, empowering the Company to take land, was likewise rejected, the promoters withdrew the Bill.

The loss of the scheme pressed upon Stephenson for a time as a personal calamity. But in this case, as in others, the darkest hour came just before the dawn. The Committee of Directors met and determined to renew their application to Parliament in the ensuing session. A new survey was resolved upon, but it was deemed advisable for many reasons, and especially to disarm criticism as much as possible, that George and John Rennie should be appointed engineers instead of Stephenson, and Mr. Charles Vignoles was appointed on their behalf to prepare the plans and sections. The new line adopted was somewhat different from the old. It entirely avoided Lord Sefton's property, and passed through but a few detached fields of Lord Derby's, at a considerable distance from Knowsley. The principal parks and game preserves in the district were likewise avoided, while the crossing of certain streets in Liverpool was averted, and an entrance devised by means of a tunnel and an inclined plane. The Marquis of Strafford, who was chiefly interested in the Bridgewater Canal, was won over to subscribe for a thousand shares in the undertaking. Being now more hopeful, the survey was completed and the promoters again went before Parliament. On the 16th of March, 1826, the preamble of the Bill was declared proved by forty-three to eighteen votes. What followed has been thus described:—

'On the third reading in the House of Commons an animated, and what now appears a very amusing discussion took place. The Hon. Edward Stanley (afterwards Earl of Derby and Prime Minister) moved that the Bill be read that day six months. In the course of his speech he undertook to prove that the railway trains would take *ten hours* on the journey, and that they could only be worked by horses, and he called upon the House to stop the Bill, "and prevent this mad and extravagant speculation from being carried into effect." Sir Isaac Coffin seconded the motion, and in doing so denounced the project as a most flagrant imposition. He would not consent to see widows' premises and their strawberry-beds invaded; and "what," he would like to know, "was to be done with all those who had advanced money in making and repairing turnpike roads? What with those who may still wish to travel in their own or hired carriages, after the fashion of their forefathers? What was to become of coach-makers and harness-makers, coach-masters and coachmen, innkeepers, horse breeders and horse dealers? Was the House aware of the smoke and the noise, the hiss and the whirl, which locomotive engines, passing at the rate of ten or twelve miles an hour, would occasion? Neither the cattle ploughing in the fields nor grazing in the meadows could behold them without dismay. Iron would be raised in price 100 per cent. or more, probably exhausted altogether. It would be the greatest nuisance, the most complete disturbance of quiet and comfort in all parts of the kingdom, that the ingenuity of man could invent."

'Mr. Huskisson and other speakers, though unable to reply to such arguments as these, strongly supported the Bill, and it was carried on the third reading by a majority of eighty-eight to forty-one. The Bill passed the House of Lords almost unanimously, its only opponents being the Earl of Derby and his relative the Earl of Wilton. The cost of obtaining the Act amounted to the enormous sum of £27,000.'

The Directors appointed George Stephenson principal resident engineer to the line, at a salary of £1,000 per annum. He selected three assistant engineers—Mr. Joseph Locke, Mr. Allcard, and Mr. John Dixon, and to the last named was assigned the unenviable task of subjugating Chat Moss. This immense and dreary peat bog was about twelve square miles in extent, and Michael Drayton—three centuries before—had conjectured that it had its origin at the Deluge. Mr. Dixon nearly lost his life on one occasion in the Moss. But Stephenson adhered to his conviction that Chat Moss could be overcome. He was warned that the task was hopeless, yet he persevered, and enjoyed a great triumph. He laid branches of trees and hedge cuttings—and in the softest places rude hurdles interwoven with heather—on the natural surface of the ground, containing intertwined roots of heather and long grass; a thin layer of gravel was then spread above all, and on it the sleepers, chairs, and rails were laid in the usual manner. Drains were at the same time cut on both sides of the line, and in the central part of the Moss a conduit was formed beneath the line of railway of old tar-barrels placed end to end. So, notwithstanding difficulties which everyone but himself regarded as insuperable, Stephenson eventually constructed this portion of the line, and, strange to say, at a smaller expense than any other part of the railway. The whole cost of the Chat Moss portion of the line was £28,000, whereas an estimate had been given by one well-known engineer of £270,000. During the progress of the works the wildest rumours were set afloat, such as that the Moss had been blown up, that hundreds of men and horses had sunk in the bog, that the works were abandoned, that the engineer himself had been swallowed up, and that railways were at an end for ever.

Before the whole line was completed the battle of the locomotive engine was fought. All existing engines being unsatisfactory, the Directors of the Company—who were desirous of settling the method of traction for the new line—offered a prize of £500 for the best locomotive engine. The conditions laid down were: That the engine must effectually consume its own smoke; that if of six tons weight it must be able to draw after it daily twenty tons weight at ten miles an hour, with a pressure of steam on the boiler not exceeding fifty pounds to the square inch; that the boiler must have two safety-valves; that the engine and boiler must be supported on springs and rest on six wheels, the height of the whole not exceeding fifteen feet to the top of the chimney; that the engine might be either of six or four and a half tons, and if the latter it might be put on only four wheels; that a mercurial gauge must be affixed to the engine, showing the steam-pressure above forty-five pounds per square inch; that the engine must be completed by Oct. 1st, 1829, and that its cost must not exceed £550. The Stephensons complied with these conditions, and constructed the now famous engine, the *Rocket*. It comprised, among other things, the following advantages: A requisite draught to the surface; the utilisation of waste steam as a blast to stimulate combustion; the principle of the multitubular boiler invented by Mr. Henry Booth; a direct communication between the cylinders and the wheels, and the joint adhesion of all the wheels by the use of horizontal connecting rods.

The competition—which excited great interest—took place at Rainhill in October, 1829, when the superiority of the *Rocket* over its rivals was at once made manifest. It drew a coach with thirty passengers along the prescribed course at the rate of thirty miles an hour. The engine—which went into regular service on the opening of the railway—weighed, with its supply of water, only four and a half tons; and long after it had been superseded by heavier engines, it ran on one occasion four miles in four and a half minutes. It is a remarkable fact that the numerous changes which have since been effected in the appearance and size of the locomotive have been more matters of detail than of principle. 'The 75-ton express passenger-engine, which runs at a speed of a mile per minute for miles together, does not differ materially in construction from George Stephenson's pioneer engines.' During its trial trip the *Rocket* attained a maximum speed of twenty-nine miles an hour. This made an eminent Liverpool citizen, Mr. P. Ewart, look rather foolish, for he had declared it to be impossible to make a locomotive engine go at ten miles an hour, and had gratuitously added that if this was ever done he would undertake to eat a stewed engine-wheel for his breakfast! At the close of the *Rocket's* successful run the locomotive system was safe; and Mr. Cropper—one of the Directors favourable to the fixed-engine system—lifted up his hands and exclaimed, 'Now has George Stephenson at last delivered himself!' After being of service for many years, the *Rocket* was at length deposited in the Museum of Patents at Kensington, where it may now be seen.

In the construction of the Liverpool and Manchester Railway, Stephenson encountered many difficulties besides those at Chat Moss. He had to form the tunnel under Liverpool, 2,200 yards in length; then there was the Olive Mount cutting to be made, about two miles long, through red-sandstone rock; thirdly, he had to provide for the ascent and descent of the Whiston and Sutton Hills by means of inclined planes of 1 in 96; fourthly, a viaduct had to be built over the Sankey Valley, and fifthly, sixty-three bridges required to be constructed in a line of only thirty miles in length. The second of these undertakings was almost as formidable as any which have since been encountered. But he was served by men whom he had admirably trained, 'whose handiworks will be the wonder and admiration of succeeding generations. Looking at their gigantic traces, the men of some future age may be found to declare of the engineer and of his workmen that "there were giants in those days."'

The Company had its pecuniary difficulties, but these were overcome; and tunnels, cuttings, and bridges having all been successfully completed, and Stephenson's well-nigh overwhelming labours been brought to a triumphant conclusion, the line was ready for opening, and a complete trial trip between Liverpool and Manchester was made on the 14th of June, 1830. The public opening—which was viewed as a national event—was fixed for the 15th of September ensuing, and on that date there was an imposing gathering at the Liverpool terminus, among those present being the Duke of Wellington, then Prime Minister; Sir Robert Peel, Home Secretary; Mr. Huskisson, Colonial and War Secretary, and many other public personages. The memorable proceedings of that day, as well as the lamentable accident which occurred to Mr. Huskisson, have been thus graphically described by Dr. Smiles:—

'Eight locomotive engines, constructed at the Stephenson works, had been delivered and placed upon the line, the whole of which had been tried and tested, weeks before, with perfect success. The several trains of carriages accommodated in all about six hundred persons. The *Northumbrian* engine, driven by George Stephenson himself, headed the line of trains; then followed the *Phœnix*, driven by Robert Stephenson; the *North Star*, by Robert Stephenson, senior (brother of George); the *Rocket*, by Joseph Locke; the *Dart*, by Thomas L. Gooch; the *Comet*, by William Allcard; the *Arrow*, by Frederick Swanwick, and the *Meteor*, by Anthony Harding. The procession was cheered in its progress by thousands of spectators—through the deep ravine of Olive Mount; up the Sutton incline; over the great Sankey viaduct, beneath which a multitude of persons had assembled—carriages filling the narrow lanes, and barges crowding the river; the people below gazing with wonder and admiration at the trains which sped along the line far above their heads at the rate of some twenty-four miles an hour.

'At Parkside, about seventeen miles from Liverpool, the engines stopped to take in water. Here a deplorable accident occurred to one of the illustrious visitors, which threw a deep shadow over the subsequent proceedings of the day. The *Northumbrian* engine, with the carriage containing the Duke of Wellington, was drawn up on one line in order that the whole of the trains on the other line might pass in review before him and his party. Mr. Huskisson had alighted from the carriage, and was standing on the opposite road, along which the *Rocket* was observed rapidly coming up. At this moment the Duke of Wellington, between whom and Mr. Huskisson some coolness had existed, made a sign of recognition, and held out his hand. A hurried but friendly grasp was given, and before it was loosened there was a general cry from the bystanders of "Get in, get in!" Flurried and confused, Mr. Huskisson endeavoured to get round the open door of the carriage, which projected over the opposite rail; but in so doing he was cut down by the *Rocket*, and falling with his leg doubled across the rail, the limb was instantly crushed. His first words on being raised were, "I have met my death," which unhappily proved true, for he expired that same evening in the Parsonage of Eccles. It was cited at the time as a remarkable fact that the *Northumbrian* engine, driven by George Stephenson himself, conveyed the wounded body of the unfortunate gentleman a distance of about fifteen miles in twenty-five minutes, or at the rate of thirty-six miles an hour. This incredible speed burst upon the world with the effect of a new and unlooked-for phenomenon.

'The accident threw a gloom over the rest of the day's proceedings. The Duke of Wellington and Sir Robert Peel expressed a wish that the procession should return to Liverpool. It was, however, represented to them that a vast concourse of people had assembled at Manchester to witness the arrival of the trains; that report would exaggerate the mischief if they did not complete the journey, and that a false panic on that day might seriously affect future railway travelling and the value of the Company's property. The party consented accordingly to proceed to Manchester, but on the understanding that they should return as soon as possible and refrain from further festivity.

'As the trains approached Manchester, crowds of people were found covering the banks, the slopes of the cuttings, and even the railway itself. The multitude, become impatient and excited by the rumours which reached them, had outflanked the military, and all order was at an end. The people clambered about the carriages, holding on by the door-handles, and many were tumbled over; but, happily, no fatal accident occurred. At the Manchester station the political element began to display itself; placards about "Peterloo," etc., were exhibited, and brickbats were thrown at the carriage containing the Duke. On the trains coming to a stand in the Manchester station the Duke did not descend, but remained seated, shaking hands with the women and children who were pushed forward by the crowd. Shortly after, the trains returned to Liverpool, which they reached, after considerable delay, late at night.

'On the following morning the railway was opened for public traffic. The first train, of one hundred and forty passengers, was booked and sent on to Manchester, reaching it in the allotted time of two hours; and from that time the traffic has regularly proceeded from day to day until now.'

Mr. Huskisson, who was fated to be the first person who lost his life by accident on the English railways, lingered for some hours in the Vicarage of Eccles suffering great agony. He was remarkably composed, however, and exhibited extraordinary firmness of mind. The doctors present decided that it was impossible to venture upon the amputation of the crushed limb. In the course of the evening the patient expired, having shown all through the most unshrinking fortitude and Christian resignation. On the following day an inquest was held, when a verdict of 'Accidental death' was returned. The remains of the distinguished statesman were laid to rest in the new burial-ground at Liverpool on the 24th of September, the funeral ceremony being of a most imposing character.

The railway proved completely and speedily successful.

Besides its enormous goods traffic, it began almost at once to carry 1,200 passengers daily, and in five years from the open- it carried nearly 500,000 persons annually.

I must now recur for a time to Robert Stephenson, whom I have long kept waiting. Although only a young man, he had gained great experience, both of a scientific and general character, in the locomotive manufactory, when the prospect of a new career suddenly opened up before him. A company was set on foot under the title of the Colombian Mining Association, which proposed to recommence working the disused gold and silver mines of Spanish America. One of its chief projectors was Mr. Thomas Richardson, a partner in Robert Stephenson & Co., and the founder of the famous discount house of Richardson, Overend, & Gurney. It was expected that the firm of Stephenson & Co. would receive large orders from the Association for engines and iron goods, and George Stephenson was appointed to select miners, artisans, inspectors, and implements. The Directors sounded his son Robert as to whether he would like to go out with the expedition as engineer, and he was delighted with the project. He was to receive an annual salary of £500, with allowances for travelling expenses. Robert was the more ready to go out to Colombia as he was threatened with serious pulmonary disease, and the climate would, in all likelihood, prove beneficial to him. Before leaving England he went down into Cornwall, and made a careful investigation of the mining industry of that district in all its branches. Then, having formally accepted the post of engineer-in-chief to the Colombian Mining Association, he went to London to purchase stores and implements and to engage workmen for the expedition. In June, 1824, he set sail from England, but before doing so he wrote an affectionate letter to his mother, explaining that he had directed Messrs. Herring, Graham, & Powles to pay £300 per annum—that is three-fifths of his salary—to his father. On July 23rd he landed off La Guayra, on the Colombian coast. The principal mines of the Colombian Association were situated near Mariquita, and he reached this ill-starred city towards the close of January, 1825. He then had twelve miles to go to the mines. By the following October sufficient miners had been collected to begin extensive operations, but a band of Cornish miners who arrived on the scene caused great trouble by their excesses. He was also called upon to quell riots and disturbances which broke out. Then a short acquaintance with the country convinced him that he was at the head of an enterprise projected by visionary speculators, while the factory at home was suffering from his absence. But feeling bound in honour to stay at the mines, he resolved to fulfil the stipulated period of three years unless he could obtain a release from his engagement. Mr. Jeaffreson states that 'from Dec. 30, 1824, to Dec. 31, 1827, the entire expenditure of the Colombian Mining Association had been little short of £200,000. A large portion of this sum had been wasted by maladministration in London, but the great operations carried on with the remainder had been directed by Robert Stephenson—a mere boy, between twenty-one and twenty-four years of age. And for everything in which he could be individually held accountable the expedition had been successful. Had he worked the mines, as the Spaniards worked them, with the cheap labour of slaves, they would have yielded as much profit as preceding engineers had extracted from them. As it was, on bidding official farewell to the Directors, he was in a position to tell them that their property, under economical management, and with the agency of proper machinery, could be made to pay them a handsome, though not an enormous, dividend.'

At Carthagena, on the return journey to England, Stephenson encountered Trevithick the inventor—half-starved, but self-reliant, daring, and burning as ever for knowledge. They voyaged together to New York, and were nearly lost during a storm at sea; but, eventually they found themselves in New York, minus their luggage, and with little money. Here they parted and Stephenson visited Canada. Stephenson stated after his return to England that what he had seen of licence and venality in Colombia made him a more pronounced Conservative than ever, and a strong supporter of vigorous monarchical government. But he had gained a great variety of experience in other ways, and when his father welcomed him at Liverpool in November, 1827, the raw Northumbrian youth had been transformed into a travelled polished gentleman.

Robert Stephenson soon became immersed in the business of his firm, but he had also time for other things, and he became engaged to Miss Fanny Sanderson, the daughter of a gentleman of good repute in the City of London. The young couple were quite in love with each other, and, though neither could lay claim to wealth, they were married in the parish church of Bishopsgate on June 17th, 1829. Those who knew the many admirable qualities of his wife said that Stephenson had made a wise and happy selection. After a brief wedding-trip Stephenson and his bride settled down in their new home, Greenfield Place, Newcastle, though it was destined to be not for long.

Robert Stephenson soon began to make a position for himself. The Canterbury and Whitstable line, constructed under his supervision, was opened in the spring of 1830; and the same year saw the Bill for the Warrington Railway safe through both Houses of Parliament. He immediately began to construct this line as engineer-in-chief. Other projects were in the air, and there was plenty of work for the locomotive factory of Robert Stephenson & Co. The young engineer was next given the charge of the projected line from Leicester to Swannington. While the railway was in progress he came to the conclusion that there were seams of coal under the Snibston Estate, and, as the estate was for sale, he explained his views to his father, who prevailed upon two friends to join him in purchasing it. Robert's foresight was rewarded; for, after great labour, the coal was found at a depth of two hundred yards, and the venture proved most lucrative. By the opening of the Leicester and Swannington Railway the price of coals in Leicester fell nearly forty per cent., and the town was saved about £40,000 a year.

Great improvements in the locomotive engine were effected both by George Stephenson and his son after the public opening of the Liverpool and Manchester Railway. Power, speed, economy, and regularity were the objects they always had in view. It is pointed out that in the *Planet* engine, delivered on the Liverpool line soon after its inauguration, all the improvements which had up to this time been contrived by the two Stephensons 'were introduced in combination—the blastpipe, the tubular boiler, horizontal cylinders inside the smokebox, the cranked axle, and the fire-box firmly fixed to the boiler. The first load of goods conveyed from Liverpool to Manchester by the *Planet* was eighty tons in weight, and the engine performed the journey against a strong head-wind in two hours and a half. On another occasion, the same engine brought up a cargo of voters from Manchester to Liverpool, during a contested election, within a space of sixty minutes. The *Samson*, delivered in the following year, exhibited still further improvements, the most important of which was that of *coupling* the fore and hind wheels of the engine. By this means, the adhesion of the wheels on the rails was more effectually secured, and thus the full hauling power of the locomotive was made available. The *Samson*, shortly after it was placed upon the line, dragged after it a train of waggons weighing a hundred and fifty tons, at a speed of about twenty miles an hour; the consumption of coke being reduced to only about a third of a pound per ton per mile.'

Owing to the success of the Stockton and Darlington Railway, the triumph of the locomotive, and the approaching completion of the Liverpool and Manchester line, in 1830 an old project was revived for a railway between London and Birmingham. George and Robert Stephenson were employed as engineers to make the surveys and plans and to carry the line through Parliament. It was Robert, however, who made the surveys; and when the Bill was obtained he was appointed engineer-in-chief to the line. The railway was constructed by Robert Stephenson alone, and to him must be awarded the praise for having overcome obstacles apparently insurmountable. Not only was opposition shown by all classes and by the press, but scientific authorities affirmed that the line could not answer. After a severe struggle, the Bill passed the Commons in 1832, but it was lost in the Lords. Robert Stephenson was so chagrined at its rejection that Lord Wharncliffe, the Chairman of the Committee, took him aside, and said, with much kindness, 'My young friend, don't take this to heart. The decision is against you; but you have made such a display of power that *your fortune is made for life.*' The recollection of these sympathetic words often cheered the engineer in his later years. Powerful supporters soon came forward on behalf of the projected London and Birmingham Railway, and in the Session of 1833—after a third survey of the line by Robert Stephenson—a Bill was obtained authorising the formation of the line. The total cost of carrying the Bill through Parliament amounted to no less than £72,868, and the compensation paid to landowners—which was originally estimated at £250,000—actually reached the enormous sum of £750,000.

On becoming engineer-in-chief to the London and Birmingham Railway, Robert Stephenson left Newcastle, and removed, with his wife, to a house on Haverstock Hill, London, which they continued to inhabit for many years. As it has been justly pointed out, Robert Stephenson had now undertaken a stupendous task, for, up to 1833, no railway of similar magnitude had been attempted. Compared with this new line from London to Birmingham, that from Liverpool to Manchester was a trifling work. The latter was little more than a quarter of the length of the new road, and its most important works could not vie for a moment with the Kilsby tunnel, the Blisworth cutting, and the Wolverton embankment and viaduct.

The engineer was by no means a strong man, and the prospect before him must have caused him much solicitude. It was stipulated that the 112 miles of the proposed railway between Camden Town and Birmingham were to be completed within four or five years. There were no great contractors in those days, so that the line was divided into sections, for each of which one contractor, or firm of contractors, was responsible. Stephenson made the most perfect and minute plans of every portion of the line, and he had to keep an exact account of every portion of the work done. Fortunately, he had able assistants, and reserving for his own special supervision a district of nine miles from Maiden Lane, Camden Town, he divided the remaining 103 miles into four districts, each district having an assistant engineer to superintend it, and each assistant engineer being supported by a staff of three sub-assistants.

The chief contracts originally entered into—viz., those for the tunnel at Primrose Hill, the Kilsby tunnel, and the Blisworth cutting—were returned to the hands of the Company unfinished, and the works were perfected by the Company without the intervention of contractors. The brickwork of the Primrose Hill tunnel was eventually made so much higher than the first estimate, that the total cost of the tunnel was £280,000 instead of £120,000. The Blisworth excavations were to have displaced 800,000 cubic yards of earth and stone, but they were not finished till nearly 1,000,000 cubic yards had been removed. Some 700 or 800 men were continually employed, and there was a weekly consumption of 2,500 lb. of gunpowder. Many disasters attended the formation of the Wolverton embankment, and litigation had to be resorted to against the interference of the Grand Junction Canal Company, before the work could be completed. But the most difficult and costly undertaking of all was the Kilsby tunnel, about six miles from Rugby. Stephenson's original plan was to construct the line by way of Northampton through Rugby, but the foolish people of Northampton successfully opposed this. At a later period, when their folly was made manifest, they petitioned for a line, and obtained it. But as the result of their original action, Stephenson was compelled to bore a way through the Kilsby ridge at the enormous cost of £320,000. The tunnel constructed was 2,400 yards in length; 36,000,000 bricks were used in its formation; and at one time 1,250 labourers were employed upon the tunnel. Dr. Arnold, of Rugby, prophesied that the cutting of the tunnel would give great trouble, and his forecast was justified. The men were frequently in danger through the irruption of water and the discovery of quicksands, and the works were again and again seriously obstructed. However, all difficulties were at length overcome. The Directors of the Company obtained a supplementary Act of Parliament, allowing them to extend their line in London to Euston Square, which became the terminus. On account of the steep ascent from Euston to Camden Town, that portion of the railway was for some years worked by ropes and stationary engines, which involved an outlay of £25,000. The trains were drawn up the incline at the rate of twenty miles an hour by an apparatus consisting of 10,000 feet of rope—six inches in circumference—and two stationary engines. This continued until 1844, when locomotives were first employed for the work.

The first sod of the London and Birmingham Railway was cut at Chalk Farm, on June 1, 1834, and the line was opened to the public on September 15, 1838. Throughout those four years, Robert Stephenson's army of workmen numbered on the average 12,000, or rather over 107 men to each mile. Lieutenant Lecount, R.N., one of the assistant engineers of the line, and 'the historian of the works,' says with regard to the labours of the 12,000 workmen:

'The Great Pyramid of Egypt, that stupendous monument which seems likely to exist to the end of all time, will afford a comparison. After making the necessary allowances for the foundations, galleries, etc., and reducing the whole to one uniform denomination, it will be found that the labour expended on the great pyramid was equivalent to lifting fifteen thousand seven hundred and sixty-three million cubic feet of stone one foot high. This labour was performed, according to Diodorus Siculus, by three hundred thousand, and according to Herodotus, by one hundred thousand, men, and it required for its execution twenty years. If we reduce in the same manner the labour expended in constructing the London and Birmingham Railway to one common denomination, the result is twenty-five thousand million cubic feet of material (reduced to the same weight as that used in constructing the pyramid) lifted one foot high, or nine thousand two hundred and sixty-seven million cubic feet more than were lifted one foot high in the construction of the pyramid. Yet this immense undertaking has been performed by about twenty thousand men in less than five years.'

The successful completion of the London and Birmingham line was celebrated in the way immemorial with Englishmen, namely by a dinner, held after a run along the line, and a second banquet was given to Stephenson at Dunchurch in Warwickshire, when the acting and assistant engineers presented the engineer-in-chief with a silver soup-tureen and stand worth 130 guineas, as an expression of their affectionate admiration. Robert Stephenson maintained his connection with the railway up to the time of his death, acting as its consulting engineer with a salary of £100 per annum, and his expenses when called to attend on the line. 'It was the first of our great Metropolitan railroads,' observes Mr. Jeaffreson, 'and its works are memorable examples of engineering capacity. They became a guide to succeeding engineers; as also did the plans and drawings with which the details of the undertaking were plotted in the Eyre Arms Hotel, St. John's Wood. When Brunel entered upon the construction of the Great Western line he borrowed Robert Stephenson's plans, and used them as the best possible system of draughting. From that time they became recognised models for railway practice. To have originated such plans and forms, thereby settling an important division of engineering literature, would have made a position for an ordinary man. In the list of Robert Stephenson's achievements such a service appears so insignificant as scarcely to be worthy of note.'

One undertaking was a source of grave uneasiness to Robert Stephenson, and it nearly brought him to pecuniary ruin. This was the Stanhope and Tyne Railway, a line entered upon by certain Durham speculators without duly considering the nature of the country through which it passed. Stephenson was appointed engineer, and he was to receive £1,000 for his remuneration. Instead of taking cash, he accepted ten shares in the Company's stock. It was soon discovered that the line could never pay, and as the Company was on the old unlimited liability principle, calls were repeatedly made on the shareholders. The consequence was, that instead of holding £1,000 worth of stock in a flourishing company, Stephenson found that his shares were a perfect drug in the market, and that they rendered him personally liable for an enormous sum of money. After causing terrible anxiety and loss to Stephenson, the Company was eventually dissolved, and a new one formed on a more satisfactory basis. We learn that for speculation of all sorts Stephenson had a decided repugnance, believing that a high rate of interest was only another name for bad security. He took a keen delight in horse-racing, but he was never known to bet at Epsom or Ascot.

Railway projects were as thick as blackberries between 1830 and 1840. Mr. Francis Giles undertook the line between London and Southampton; the younger Brunel the Great Western line from London to Bristol; and Mr. John Braithwaite that from London to Colchester. As for George Stephenson, he was overwhelmed with projects. In the three years ending with 1837, he was principal engineer on the North Midland, York and North Midland, Manchester and Leeds, Birmingham and Derby, and Sheffield and Rotherham Railways.

During the year 1836 alone, 214 miles of railway were put under his direction, involving a capital of £5,000,000; and he would sometimes dictate reports and letters for twelve continuous hours. As a central spot of action, he made his home at Alton Grange, near Leicester, while occupied in carrying out the vast network of railways which soon stretched over the country. The Grand Junction Railway, projected by George Stephenson, but executed by Joseph Locke, had already connected the Liverpool and Manchester line with the London and Birmingham line, thus establishing a communication between Liverpool, Manchester, and London. Robert Stephenson was the acting engineer for the North Midland line, but he was obliged to suspend his work there and cross over to the Continent. He was called upon to superintend the lines from Ostend to Liège and from Antwerp to Mons; and he was also invited to visit France, Switzerland, and Italy, to advise on lines contemplated in those countries. On returning to England in July, 1839, he resumed all his arduous duties, flying about from town to town, and attending at intervals before Parliamentary committees. He likewise acted as arbitrator in disputes between contractors and companies, and so highly esteemed were his services in this capacity that a number of gentlemen invited him to a banquet at the Albion Hotel, Aldersgate Street, London, and presented him with a service of plate valued at £1,250.

Some entertaining facts are given by the biographers of the Stephensons in connection with the North Midland line. The Littleborough tunnel, for example, was a giant undertaking. More than a thousand men were engaged for nearly four years in its construction. The arch was excavated out of the solid rock, and 23,000,000 of bricks and 8,000 tons of Roman cement were used in the building of the tunnel. Thirteen stationary engines and about 100 horses were employed in drawing the earth and stone out of the shafts. The entire length of the tunnel was 2,869 yards, or nearly a mile and three-quarters—thus exceeding the Kilsby tunnel by 471 yards. Dr. Smiles notes that the Midland Railway was a favourite line of George Stephenson's, and, although it 'was only one of the many great works of the same kind executed at that time, it was almost enough of itself to be the achievement of a life. Compare it, for example, with Napoleon's military road over the Simplon, and it will at once be seen how greatly it excels that work, not only in the constructive skill displayed in it, but also in its cost and magnitude, and the amount of labour employed in its formation. The road of the Simplon is 45 miles in length; the North Midland Railway 72½ miles. The former has 50 bridges and 5 tunnels, measuring together 1,338 feet in length; the latter has 200 bridges and 7 tunnels, measuring together 11,400 feet, or about 2¼ miles. The former cost about £720,000 sterling, the latter above £3,000,000. Napoleon's grand military road was constructed in six years, at the public cost of the two great kingdoms of France and Italy; while Stephenson's railway was formed in about three years, by a company of private merchants and capitalists out of their own funds, and under their own superintendence.'

It is stated that during the three busiest years of George Stephenson's life he travelled by post-chaise alone upwards of 20,000 miles, and yet not less than six months out of the three years were spent in London. Then, his correspondence was such that he had little leisure left for himself. But in the midst of all this absorbing business he preserved a youthful spirit, and he would steal some time for his old recreations. He would take a day's rest now and then for birds'-nesting, gardening, or nutting at Alton Grange, or at his country seat, Tapton House, near Chesterfield. There he kept his favourite old pony, 'Bobby,' who died at upwards of twenty years old. Here is a pathetic little story related by Dr. Smiles:—

'During one of George's brief sojourns at the Grange, he found time to write to his son a touching account of a pair of robins that had built their nest within one of the empty upper chambers of the house. One day he observed a robin fluttering outside the windows, and beating its wings against the panes, as if eager to gain admission. He went upstairs, and there found, in a retired part of one of the rooms, a robin's nest, with one of the parent birds sitting over three or four young—all dead. The excluded bird outside still beat against the panes; and on the window being let down, it flew into the room, but was so exhausted that it dropped upon the floor. Stephenson took up the bird, carried it downstairs, and had it warmed and fed. The poor robin revived, and for a time was one of his pets. But it shortly died too, as if unable to recover from the privations it had endured during its three days' fluttering and beating at the windows. It appeared that the room had been unoccupied, and the sash having been let down, the robins had taken the opportunity of building their nest within it; but the servant having closed the window again, the calamity befell the birds which so strongly excited the engineer's sympathies. An incident such as this, trifling though it may seem, gives a true key to the heart of a man.'

King Leopold of Belgium summoned the Stephensons to Brussels in May, 1835, to advise him as to the construction of a complete system of railways for his kingdom. On that occasion the elder engineer was awarded the decoration of the Order of Leopold. Two years later they again visited Belgium, to attend the opening of the railway between Brussels and Ghent; and in 1841 the King conferred on Robert Stephenson the same distinction that he had conferred on his father. Between 1835 and 1837 the younger Stephenson was engaged in many railway projects. It is curious that Robert Stephenson concurred with his father in giving emphatic testimony as to the hazard of setting fire to towns by driving steam-carriages through them. Although, as Mr. Jeaffreson remarks, there is danger of fire from passing locomotives, the fears indulged by the Stephensons were excessive. 'At the present date, when the ropes and stationary engines with which the Blackwall line was long worked have been for years discontinued, and when locomotives are shooting to and fro through every quarter of London at every variety of distance above the level of the streets, and passing through every description of property, a person of the humblest intelligence would smile at an assurance that London ran any risk of being destroyed by sparks thrown out from the chimneys of locomotives. That the Stephensons so miscalculated on a point relating to the locomotive, is a matter worthy of reflection; that their error was on the side of *caution*, is a fact that illustrates one of their principal characteristics, and points to the cause of a large part of their success.'

In 1837, Robert Stephenson made arrangements with Professor Wheatstone for the use of the electric telegraph from Euston to Camden Town; and the London and Birmingham line thus gave the first successful exhibition of the working of Wheatstone and Cooke's marvellous invention.

Some idea of the ramifications of English railway enterprise may be gained from the statement that before the year 1840 dawned 321 miles of railway—exclusive of the London and Birmingham line—had been constructed under George Stephenson's superintendence, at a cost of upwards of £11,000,000. After a time, railways came to be regarded as great blessings, and even Colonel Sibthorp, who had once described them as 'infernal,' was obliged to recognise their utility. Dr. Arnold regarded the London and Birmingham line as a great step accomplished in the march of civilisation. 'I rejoice to see it,' he exclaimed, 'and to think that feudality is gone for ever: it is so great a blessing to think that any one evil is really extinct.' Yet the Duke of Wellington would not trust himself behind a locomotive again, after the opening of the Liverpool line, until the year 1843, when he took his first trip by the South-Western Railway in attendance upon the

Queen. The Prince Consort had long travelled alone by rail, and in 1842 Her Majesty began to use the same mode of conveyance in her journeys between Windsor and London.

Robert Stephenson's railway projects in the North were carried on with vigour between 1841 and 1844. Five miles of the disastrous Stanhope and Tyne line—now known as the Pontop and Shields Railway—were made into a connecting-link between the Durham Junction Railway and the Brandling Junction Railway, and were used for conveying passengers between Newcastle, Gateshead, South Shields, Sunderland, and other important towns. These five miles became a part of the Great North of England Railway, which was to unite Newcastle with London and the South. George Hudson, afterwards known as the 'Railway King'—whose fall was as sudden and dramatic as his rise—was appointed Chairman of the Newcastle and Darlington Junction line, and Robert Stephenson became its engineer. 'To connect London and Newcastle by railway communication had long been a favourite object of Robert Stephenson's ambition, and now he was called upon to construct the last link of the chain.'

While he was busy upon this task, the engineer was fated to endure the heaviest calamity of his life. On the 4th of October, 1842, Mrs. Stephenson died of malignant cancer, and the sorrowing husband made this entry in his diary: 'My dear Fanny died this morning at five o'clock. God grant that I may close my life as she has done, in the true faith, and in charity with all men. Her last moments were perfect calmness.' Robert Stephenson had no child even to cheer him in his loneliness, for it had been the one sorrow in the lives of the otherwise happy couple that they were childless. Work was his only resource, and he turned to this with redoubled energy. The line in which he was deeply interested, the Newcastle and Darlington Junction—the link between the North of England and the Metropolis—was duly completed and opened with great rejoicings on the 18th of June, 1844.

A banquet was given in the Town Hall, Newcastle, at which George Hudson and John Bright, among many others, were present, and, in addition to the health of Robert Stephenson, that of George Stephenson was proposed as 'the father of the railway system,' both toasts being most enthusiastically received.

After his wife's death, Robert Stephenson could no longer bear the house at Haverstock Hill, so he removed to one in Cambridge Square, Hyde Park. As regards his labours, we have now come to the parting of the ways. Mr. Jeaffreson well says with regard to this matter: 'The year 1844 is a conspicuous landmark in the career of Robert Stephenson. For twenty years he had been at work without intermission, and as the result of his exertions he found himself, while he was still only forty years of age, in the first rank of his profession. Had he, however, died then, he would have left nothing to which history could point as the monument of original and distinctive genius. He had raised the locomotive by a series of beautiful improvements from the ill-proportioned and ineffective machine of 1828 almost to its present perfection of mechanism. He had, in conjunction with his father, so fixed the English railway system in continental countries, that throughout Europe his name was identified with the new means of locomotion. His engineering achievements were beyond all cavil works of great ability—but not of distinctive genius. Hitherto he had, in the manner of a master, carried out the principles and developed the conceptions of previous teachers, of whom his father was the most important. The time, however, was now come for him to take a higher position, and accomplish works altogether without precedent.

'The next six years of Robert Stephenson's life—years memorable in the annals of social folly, crime, and suffering—witnessed the exertions by which his influence and name will reach future generations. They saw the atmospheric contest, the battle of the gauges, the construction of the tubular bridge, and the completion of the High Level Bridge.

'It is impossible to record the labours of the engineer during the interval between the opening of 1844 and the close of 1850 without contrasting them with the intrigues of adventurers who regarded railway enterprise as gamesters regard a gambling-table. The triumph of these adventurers was brief. Just as the worker reached the fulness of his fame the chief speculator dropped from his eminence, to be scouted by those who had fawned on him in prosperity, and to be despoiled by those whom he had benefited even more than by those whom he had wronged.'

There was great fluctuation in the number of Parliamentary schemes for new railways between 1825 and 1846. The Stockton and Darlington line having inspired public confidence, in 1826 ten schemes were introduced; but in consequence of the commercial panic of that year there was only one Bill in the Session of 1827. In 1828 there were five schemes, and the number went on increasing annually until 1836, when there were 29. Then the railway speculation mania suffered a temporary decline, and the number of Bills fell until 1840, when there was not one. Construction began again in 1842; and in 1844 Bills were passed authorising 48 new lines, extending over 700 miles, at an estimated cost of £14,793,994. In 1845 there were 120 new lines, measuring 2,883 miles, with an expenditure of £43,844,907. But in view of the Session of 1846, by the 30th of November in 1845—the latest date on which the Board of Trade would receive plans for new railways—there had been lodged 1,263 Bills, with plans and sections for new railways, representing a capital of £563,000,000, and requiring the deposit of a total sum of £59,000,000. The amount required for payment of the deposit exceeded by more than £20,000,000 the whole amount of gold and coin in the Bank of England, and notes in circulation. As soon as these figures were published there was a great revulsion of public feeling, and of the 1,263 companies promoted only 120 survived the ordeal of Parliament. It was now that the great railway panic occurred, with its concomitant evils of bubble companies and corrupt practices. When the frenzy was at its height, Robert Stephenson and George P. Bidder received one morning cheques from various companies amounting to more than £1,000. They at once returned them, intimating that their evidence was not to be bought and sold; and other honourable engineers behaved in the same way. Before leaving this subject of the railways of Great Britain, it may be stated that in 1875—when the jubilee of the railway system was celebrated—there were 16,449 miles of railway in the United Kingdom, representing a capital cost of £600,895,000, and producing from traffic a revenue of £56,898,000, of which £24,893,000 was received from passenger fares, and £32,005,000 from the conveyance of goods and minerals. At the close of the year 1890 there were 20,073 miles of railway open for traffic. The authorised capital for the construction of railways was £1,004,529,164, being nearly double the whole amount of the 2¾ per cent. British Consols. The total receipts of these railways were £79,948,000, which was only £10,000,000 less than the actual receipts paid into the National Exchequer from all sources of revenue for that year.

Robert Stephenson made a series of careful investigations into the system of atmospheric pressure as a propelling force. He showed the defects of the system in certain classes of working, though he admitted that it was capable of being applied to somewhat steeper gradients than the locomotive system, and that on such gradients a greater speed might be maintained than with locomotive engines. But on lines of railway where moderate gradients were attainable at a reasonable expense, he held the locomotive engine to be decidedly superior, both as regarded power and speed, to any results developed or likely to be developed by the atmospheric system. As to the cost of the atmospheric system, taking as an example the London and Birmingham Railway, with its 111 miles, he demonstrated that the cost of the atmospheric apparatus would amount to £1,221,000, whereas the capital expended on locomotives and all their contingent outlay was only £321,000 making a difference of £900,000 against the atmospheric system. With regard to the cost of working, taking the London and Birmingham line again as an example, Mr. Stephenson was of opinion that the expense would be greater by the atmospheric than the locomotive system in the proportion of £74,000 to £64,000 per annum. From the point of view of certainty of action, the locomotive possessed even greater advantages still. Yet many engineers were in favour of the atmospheric system, and a Committee of the House of Commons reported favourably upon it in 1845. Several railways were worked by it, but in course of time the objections urged by Stephenson began to prevail, and eventually the system was abandoned, chiefly on the grounds of its inflexibility, its inconvenience, its want of adaptability, and its expense.

Another question of great interest which arose was the dispute between the respective advocates of the narrow gauge and the broad gauge system. On all the lines built by the Stephensons, and indeed by most other leading engineers, the narrow gauge of 4 feet 8½ inches was adopted; but in 1838 Brunel, desirous of obtaining double the attained speed and capacity, determined upon a 7 feet gauge for the Great Western Railway. This led to the famous battle of the gauges. In consequence of the serious difficulties arising from breaks of gauge, the matter was eventually investigated by a Gauge Commission appointed for the purpose, and Robert Stephenson's evidence on behalf of the narrow gauge had great effect. In favour of the narrow gauge were thirty of the best engineers and railway authorities in the kingdom, including Bidder, Braithwaite, Hawkshaw, Hudson, Huish, Locke, Stephenson, Whitaker, and Wood. In favour of the broad gauge there were only Brunel and three others, all connected with the Great Western Railway. The Commissioners reported in favour of the narrow gauge, and in August, 1846, an Act was passed making it unlawful in future to construct any railway for the conveyance of passengers on any gauge other than 4 feet 8½ inches for Great Britain and 5 feet 3 inches for Ireland. The Great Western continued to use the broad gauge, but finding the difficulties of the system press upon them, in 1869 the Directors began gradually to discontinue the system, and on the 20th of May, 1892, the broad gauge was abolished altogether.

Some further passages in George Stephenson's career now demand attention, as well as his enlightened views on the development of England's prosperity. He perceived that the strength of Britain lay in her coal and iron beds, and that the locomotive was destined above all other agencies to bring those treasures forth and convey them to the required destination. He was the first to point out the practicability of establishing a profitable coal trade by railway between the northern counties and the Metropolis. But, even before this was achieved, he desired to see an effective passenger service. With the aid of friends he established collieries and lime-works in various places, thus finding labour for thousands of workmen. He supported Mechanics' Institutes as a great benefit to those who in youth had been deprived of education, and he took the principal part in founding one of these institutes at Newcastle. When the British Association met at Newcastle in 1838, a gratifying tribute was paid to him as one who had achieved an almost world-wide reputation as a public benefactor.

Stephenson matured his invention of the carriage-brake, and when he was examined before the Select Committee on Railways in 1841, he expressed his conviction that if self-acting brakes were put upon every carriage, scarcely any accident could take place. He regarded this brake, indeed, as the most important arrangement that could be provided for increasing the safety of railway travelling. Stephenson was not in favour of too great a velocity of speed, which he thought a positive danger, and he held that no railway ought to exceed forty miles an hour on the most favourable gradient. He had, indeed, constructed for the Great Western Railway an engine capable of running fifty miles an hour with a load, and eighty miles without one, but he deprecated a hurricane speed of this kind. There was a point, he urged, at which both rails and tyres must break, and every increase of speed increased the strain upon the road and the rolling stock. Fifty miles an hour or more might be run with safety on a level railway, but only if perfect iron, perfect rails, and perfect locomotives could be ensured. He further strongly opposed the theory that an undulating railway was much better than a level one for purposes of working, and his judgment proved correct.

When the railway mania was at its height, Robert Stephenson's offices in London were crowded every day with men of all ranks and conditions, eager to strengthen their prospectuses by the weight of his name or that of his father. But their integrity was above reproach, and on no single occasion did a bubble scheme ever receive their imprimatur. Neither father nor son cared for money obtained without honour, or without legitimate service. Before the mania of 1845-6 came to a climax, George Stephenson warned the public against the prevalent disposition towards railway speculation, but the frenzy unfortunately seized upon all classes of the community.

In the middle of September, 1845, George Stephenson left England to visit Belgium and Spain, in connection with the West Flanders Railway and the Royal North of Spain Railway. The latter was to pass through Irun, St. Sebastian, St. Andero, and Bilbao. Stephenson carefully surveyed the whole of the proposed route, working from break of day until darkness again set in, and frequently resting at night on the floor of some miserable hovel. After being engaged in the district for ten days he proceeded across the province of Old Castile towards Madrid, surveying as he went. Finding that formidable tunnels and other expensive works would be necessary, he recommended that the line should be constructed from Madrid to the Bay of Biscay. But Sir Joshua Walmsley, the contractor, found his negotiations with the Spanish authorities most unsatisfactory. Instead of giving him an answer, they invited Walmsley and his friend Stephenson to a bull-fight, which they politely declined. The railway project was ultimately abandoned, owing to the engineer's unfavourable opinion of its possibilities.

Stephenson's labours, and the privations he endured in Spain, told severely upon his health, and on the return voyage from Havre to Southampton pleurisy developed itself. From this he gradually recovered after several weeks' rest at his country seat, but he was never the same man again. During the few years which yet remained to him, he practically withdrew from the engineering profession, and although he still gave some attention to his collieries and lime-works, his life for the most part was that of a simple country gentleman. He interested himself in fruit-growing and in cultivating exotics, and he built extensive pineries, melon-houses, and vineries. Farming operations, and the rearing of animals and birds, also occupied his leisure. For books he cared little, as he had always led an outdoor life, but he enjoyed conversation. When he found intelligent auditors he delighted in 'fighting his battles o'er again.' The marvels in creation and in science he always revelled in, and he found keen enjoyment in the microscope. He never forgot his humble origin, but took pleasure in the society of his early companions, with whom he would discuss the old times and all their hard struggles. Sir Robert Peel frequently invited him to Drayton Manor, but it was some time before he could bring himself to accept an invitation. Dr. Smiles gives the following amusing anecdote:—

'Stephenson's strong powers of observation, together with his native humour and shrewdness, imparted to his conversation at all times much vigour and originality. Though mainly an engineer, he was also a profound thinker on many scientific questions: and there was scarcely a subject of speculation, or a department of recondite science, on which he had not employed his faculties in such a way as to have formed large and original views. Mr. Sopwith, F.R.S., has informed us that the conversation at Drayton, on one occasion, turned on the theory of the formation of coal, in the course of which Stephenson had an animated discussion with Dr. Buckland. But the result was, that Dr. Buckland, a much greater master of tongue-fence, completely silenced him. Next morning, before breakfast, when he was walking in the grounds deeply pondering, Sir William Follett came up and asked what he was thinking about? "Why, Sir William, I am thinking over that argument I had with Buckland last night! I know I am right, and that if I had only the command of words which he has, I'd have beaten him." "Let me know all about it," said Sir William, "and I'll see what I can do for you!" The two sat down in an arbour, where the astute lawyer made himself thoroughly acquainted with the points of the case; entering into it with the zeal of an advocate about to plead the interests of his client. After he had mastered the subject, Sir William said, "Now I am ready for him." Sir Robert Peel was made acquainted with the plot, and adroitly introduced the subject of the controversy after dinner. The result was, that in the argument which followed, the man of science was overcome by the man of law. "And what do you say, Mr. Stephenson?" asked Sir Robert, laughing. "Why," said he, "I say this, that of all the powers above and under the earth, there seems to me to be no power so great as the gift of the gab."

In June, 1847, Stephenson was present at the opening of the Trent Valley Railway, which was originally designed by himself, and the first sod of which had been cut by the Prime Minister. 'What a change had come over the spirit of the landed gentry since the time when George Stephenson had first projected a railway through that district! Then they were up in arms against him, characterising him as the devastator and spoiler of their estates; whereas now he was hailed as one of the greatest benefactors of the age. Sir Robert Peel, the chief political personage in England, welcomed him as a guest and a friend, and spoke of him as the chief among practical philosophers. A dozen Members of Parliament, seven Baronets, with all the landed magnates of the district, assembled to celebrate the opening of the railway.' The clergy were there to bless the enterprise, which enabled them to carry on their religious operations with greater facility; the army, through one of its Generals, acknowledged the vast importance of railways, as tending to improve the military defences of the country; and the representatives of municipal bodies gratefully confessed the immense benefits which railways conferred upon the inhabitants of our towns and cities. George Stephenson married his third wife, who was considerably younger than himself, in January, 1848. In the spring of the same year, at the house of his friend and former pupil, Mr. Swanwick, Stephenson met Emerson, and so struck was that distinguished American with his conversation and bearing, that he afterwards said 'it was worth crossing the Atlantic were it only to have seen Stephenson—he had such force of character and vigour of intellect.'

The last public appearance of George Stephenson was at a meeting of the Institute of Mechanical Engineers at Birmingham, July 26th, 1848, when he read a paper 'On the Fallacies of the Rotatory Engine.' Soon after his return to Tapton he was seized with intermittent fever. He was apparently recovering from this, when a sudden effusion of blood from the lungs proved fatal, and he expired on the 12th of August, 1848, in his sixty-seventh year. His remains were laid to rest in Trinity Church, Chesterfield, the body being followed to the grave by a large number of his work-people, between whom and himself a deep sympathetic feeling ever existed. Their physical, mental, and moral welfare had been with him a subject of constant solicitude. A statue of Stephenson, commissioned by the Liverpool and Manchester and Grand Junction Companies, was placed in St. George's Hall, Liverpool, and another full-length statue of him, by Baily, was erected in the vestibule of the London and North-Western station in Euston Square. The movement for this statue was set on foot by the Society of Mechanical Engineers, and the subscribers included 3,150 working-men, who were voluntary donors of two shillings each. The best artistic tribute to George Stephenson, however, was the statue erected at Newcastle-upon-Tyne in 1862, after the design of John Lough. It was fitting, perhaps, that the noblest monument to the great engineer should be raised in the vicinity of his early struggles and triumphs. George Stephenson was a type of the honest, kindly, shrewd, and capable Englishman— a man of the people, and one with all the instincts of the true gentleman.

Again resuming the sketch of the labours of Robert Stephenson, it is to be noted that, contemporaneously with his triumph over his rival Brunel with regard to the East Coast railway to Scotland, he began his important work of constructing magnificent bridges. The Royal Border Bridge of Berwick was one of his fine structures. The first two Stuart Kings had built a bridge of fifteen arches across the Tweed at Berwick. It occupied more than twenty-four years in building, and cost £15,000, which amount was paid out of the national resources. Now in 1844-7 Stephenson built a bridge for the railway company, at a much higher level, with twenty-eight arches, the cost being £120,000. It was finished in three years and four months from the laying of the foundation-stone. The total length of the work was 2,160 feet, and each arch was 61 feet 6 inches in span, the greatest height above the bed of the river being 126 feet. Another and still more important bridge in connection with the East Coast route was the High Level Bridge over the Tyne at Newcastle. This is regarded by many as the masterwork of Robert Stephenson, who had, as his co-designer, Mr. T. E. Harrison. The idea for this bridge originated with R. W. Brandling, an early friend of George Stephenson's, in 1841, and a prospectus of a High Level Bridge Company was issued in 1843, with the names of Stephenson and George Hudson attached, but nothing was done. Ultimately, the Newcastle and Darlington Railway Company took up the project, and an Act for the construction of the bridge was obtained in 1845. The first pile was driven on the 6th of October, 1846, under the direction of Robert Stephenson. The piles were driven by Nasmyth's gigantic steam-hammer, this being one of the first cases in which it was used. The total quantity of masonry in the bridge when completed was 686,000 cubic feet, and the weight of ironwork was 5,050 tons. The cost of the entire work, including that of the temporary bridge, was £243,000. The breadth of the Tyne at the point of crossing is 515 feet, but the length of the bridge and viaduct between the Gateshead station and the terminus on the Newcastle side is about 4,000 feet. 'It springs from Pipewellgate Bank, on the south, directly across to Castle Garth, where, nearly fronting the bridge, stands the fine old Norman Keep of the New Castle, now nearly 800 years old; and a little beyond it is the spire of St. Nicholas Church, with its light and graceful Gothic crown; the whole forming a grand architectural group of unusual historic interest. The bridge is a unique structure in cast iron, a fine example of the bow-string arch. It passes completely over the roofs of the houses which fill both sides of the valley, and the extraordinary height of the upper parapet, which is about 130 feet above the bed of the river, offers a prospect to the passing traveller the like of which perhaps is nowhere else to be seen.' The arches of the bridge—each of which is complete and independent in itself—are six in number, with a span of 125 feet each; and the whole structure is unrivalled for massive solidity. The High Level Bridge was formally opened by the Queen on the 15th of August, 1849; and in the following year her Majesty inaugurated the extensive stone viaduct across the Tweed, thus completing the last link in the continuous line of railway between London and Edinburgh.

Stephenson's next magnificent undertakings were in connection with the Chester and Holyhead Railway. It was necessary to cross the estuary of the Conway, and the Menai Strait; and the bridges proposed involved spans of 400 feet and upwards. As cast-iron had been found unsuitable for bridges of very large span, the question was raised of the sole employment of wrought-iron. After much thought, Stephenson resolved upon wrought-iron tubes for crossing the Conway River and the Menai Strait in large spans, through which railway trains were to be conducted. Sir William Fairbairn, who carried through the preliminary experiments, discovered that rectangular tubes had the advantage in point of strength, and a model beam was therefore constructed to a scale of one-sixth of the proposed bridge. This bore the test most satisfactorily, and showed that the proposed tube could be made self-supporting over the desired span of sixty feet. Upon this it was determined to proceed with the erection of the colossal structure itself. Mr. D. K. Clark, the civil engineer, in his article on 'Bridges' in *Chambers's Encyclopædia*, gives the following interesting description of the Britannia Tubular Bridge, which is so called because of the Britannia Rock on which the central pier rests :—

'It consists of two independent continuous wrought-iron tubular beams, 1,510 feet in length, weighing 4,680 tons each, independent of the cast-iron frames inserted at their bearings in the towers. They rest on two abutments and three towers of masonry at a height of 100 feet above high water. The middle, or Britannia tower, 230 feet high, is built on a rock in the middle of the strait. The bridge is thus in four spans, of which there are two spans of 460 feet over the water, and two spans of 230 feet over the land. The weight of one of the longer spans, single tube, is 1,587 tons, and that of one of the shorter spans, 630 tons. The average weight of a single tube is over three tons per lineal foot of advance. The chief mass of the material is placed at the top and the bottom, represented by the upper and lower flanges or tables of an ordinary beam, the two sides serving to connect the top and the bottom. Constructed of plate-iron, the top requires more metal than the bottom, in order to resist the buckling stress to which it is subject. But, instead of putting the metal into one thick plate, or into several plates laid one on another, it is constructed to form a set of small tubes or cells, which give additional stiffness and strength to the whole tube. The floor, in like manner, contains cells. Each tube is straight on the lower face, and slightly curved on the upper face, insomuch that the height of the tube externally is 30 feet at the middle in the Britannia Tower, and 26 feet internally, and 22 feet 9 inches and 18 feet 9 inches at the extremities in the abutments. The width of each tube externally is 14 feet 8 inches, and 13 feet 5 inches clear inside. The side plates are from $\frac{1}{2}$ inch to $\frac{5}{8}$ inch in thickness; the top plates are from $\frac{3}{8}$ inch to $\frac{3}{4}$ inch, for resisting compression; and the bottom plates are from $\frac{7}{16}$ inch to $\frac{9}{16}$ inch thick, for resisting extension. The tubes repose solidly on the centre tower, but on the land towers and abutments they repose on roller beds, thus permitting free expansion and contraction, according to the temperature. The daily variation of length is from $\frac{1}{2}$ inch to 3 inches for the whole length of the tube, the extremes of the movement being attained at about 3 p.m. and 3 a.m. The effect of sunshine in deflecting the Britannia Bridge, as observed by Mr. Edwin Clark, is very curious. A short spell of sunshine on the top of the tube raised it on one occasion nearly an inch in half an hour, with a load of 200 tons at the centre, the top plates of the bridge being expanded by increase of temperature, while the lower plates remained at constant temperature by radiation to the water beneath them. In like manner, the tube was drawn sideways to the extent of an inch by the sun shining on one side, and it returned immediately to its normal position as clouds passed over the sun. The tubes sometimes move as much as $2\frac{1}{2}$ inches vertically or horizontally when the sun shines on them. The tube is, in fact, a most delicate thermometer in constant motion, both vertically and laterally. The Britannia Bridge was opened in March, 1850, by the passage through it of three powerful locomotives with tenders. The second experimental train that went through consisted of twenty-four heavily-laden coal-waggons, aggregating 300 tons weight. The train was drawn through the tubes at leisurely speed. During the passage a breathless silence prevailed, and when the train emerged at the other end the event was announced by great cheering, mingled with the reports of pieces of ordnance.'

The Britannia Bridge cost Stephenson many a sleepless night. Describing his feelings afterwards to Mr. Gooch, he said: 'It was a most anxious and harassing time with me. Often at night I would lie tossing about, seeking sleep in vain. The tubes filled my head. I went to bed with them and got up with them. In the grey of the morning, when I looked across Gloucester Square, it seemed an immense distance across to the houses on the opposite side. It was nearly the same length as the span of my tubular bridge!' When the first tube had been floated, a friend observed to him, 'This great work has made you ten years older.' 'I have not slept soundly,' he replied, 'for three weeks.' But when the work was done, he was found sitting calmly, smoking a cigar, on a platform overlooking the suspended tube. It may be added that in fitting the Britannia tubes together, no fewer than 2,000,000 bolts were riveted, weighing some 900 tons. Each length of tube constituting the main span is twice as long as the London Monument is high; and if it could be set on end in St. Paul's Churchyard it would reach nearly 100 feet above the cross. The cost of this remarkable engineering work was £234,450. 'On the occasion of raising the last tube into its place, Mr. Stephenson declared, in reply to the felicitations of a large company who had witnessed the proceedings with intense interest, that not all the triumph which attended this great work, and the solution of the difficult problem of carrying a rigid railway across an arm of the sea at such a height as to allow the largest vessels to pass with all their sails set beneath it, could repay him for the anxieties he had gone through, the friendships he had compromised, and the unworthy motives which had been attributed to him; and that were another work of the same magnitude offered to him with like consequences, he would not for worlds undertake it!'

The Conway tubular bridge consisted of two tubes, each of one span of 400 feet. It was opened for traffic in May, 1848. The Victoria Railway Bridge over the St. Lawrence River at Montreal, Canada, was another of Robert Stephenson's stupendous works. Like the Britannia Bridge, it is tubular in design. It is 9,144 feet, or nearly a mile and three-quarters in length, in 24 spans of 242 feet, with a central span of 330 feet. The total length of each tube is 6,592 feet, and there are 9,044 tons of iron in the tubes. There is a total painted superficies equal to 32 acres. The river is 8,660 feet, or about one mile and two-thirds, wide at the crossing, where it descends at the rate of seven miles per hour. The bridge is chiefly remarkable for its ice-breaking piers, which are constructed with large bows at the up-river ends to resist the enormous pressure of the ice in spring. The rails are sixty feet above the level of the river. The Victoria Bridge is longer than the Forth Bridge, and, indeed, it is the longest bridge in the world with the exception of the Tay Bridge, which is 10,780 feet in length as compared with 9,144 feet, the length of the Montreal structure. The Victoria Bridge was begun in 1854, and finished in 1859. It was formally opened for traffic by the Prince of Wales on the 25th of August, 1860. Among other works of various kinds, Stephenson also designed two tubular bridges which were built across the Nile, near Damietta, in Lower Egypt.

In 1847 Robert Stephenson was returned to Parliament as Conservative member for Whitby, which borough he continued to represent until his death. Like his father, he declined the honour of knighthood. He took a deep interest in the Institution of Civil Engineers, of which he was elected a vice-president in 1848. This office he held until 1855, when he was elected to the presidential chair, which he occupied for the years 1856 and 1857. Elected a Fellow of the Royal Society in 1849, he subsequently sat on the Council of that learned body. In politics he was violently antipathetic to Earl Russell, and to Cobden, Bright, and other representatives of the Manchester School. He voted steadily with his party in all important divisions, but otherwise he was not regular in his attendance at the House of Commons. He only took part in the debates when special scientific questions were brought forward, but he was a member of the Sewage and Sanitary Commissions and of the Commission which sat on Westminster Bridge. He was an ardent Protectionist, and remained so even after the advantages of Free Trade had been conclusively proved. Among his chief speeches in Parliament were those on the cleansing of the Serpentine and against the Suez Canal. He considered that the latter scheme was impracticable; that it would not justify the expenditure necessary to complete it, and that if ever executed it would prove a commercial failure. Stephenson proved to be wrong on all points. The Suez Canal was made, and proved a magnificent success, and the great engineer's predictions only show that a man may be fallible, even in things on which he may be justly considered a distinguished expert.

Stephenson was very sociable, and at his London residences there were frequent gatherings of men celebrated in science, literature, and art. He was a charming companion, and was famed for his liberality towards his professional brethren. Even rivals like Brunel found in him a chivalrous friend. His fame was at its zenith in 1850 and 1851, and in those years he acted as a member of the Executive Committee and Building Committee for the Exhibition Building of 1851, and also as one of the Commissioners for carrying out that great project. One of his favourite recreations was yachting; and, among other excursions, he made voyages to Egypt and Norway. He was unfortunately addicted to the use of narcotics, which prejudicially affected him.

Invited by the King of Sweden to visit that country, for the purpose of advising as to the railway between Christiania and Lake Miösen, he was decorated with the Grand Cross of the Order of St. Olaf in consideration of his services. He further visited Switzerland, Piedmont, and Denmark, to consider the system of railway communication best adapted to those countries. The Emperor Napoleon conferred upon him the Legion of Honour at the Paris Exhibition of 1855, and the University of Oxford gave him the honorary degree of D.C.L. Notwithstanding all his successes, however, both social and public, Robert Stephenson experienced much sorrow in his later years. Mr. Jeaffreson draws this pathetic picture of him as the sands of life gradually ran out:—

'He had reached the period of life when men who have no children confess to themselves that the glory of their days is only a shadow. To those that enjoyed his inmost confidence, he more than once revealed his sadness, and he was counselled to rouse himself against despondency.

'His health was irreparably broken; but to the last he was so full of animation when in society that men found it difficult to imagine him other than he appeared. His hair had indeed turned white without long warning, but it was remembered that George Stephenson had a snowy head while he was still in the prime of manhood. There were those also who could tell how the amiable and gentle-tempered man began to manifest a passing peevishness and irritability on trivial provocations. Those who knew him thoroughly saw in these and other symptoms the conclusive proofs of serious mischief affecting health. But few suspected how he struggled against melancholy, and how he looked forward to death. The quiet of his house, when it was without guests, he could not endure. Often he walked about the lonely rooms, and sat down to yield to sorrow which in the presence of others he courageously suppressed. In these last days he used to look regretfully on the scenes of his early professional triumphs, and of his wedded joy in the little house in Greenfield Place, Newcastle.

'"The Robert Stephenson of Greenfield Place is the Robert Stephenson I am most proud to think of!" he once said to a lady. He was at all times very fond of the mechanical department of engineering, and to the last no part of his cares afforded him more pleasure than the direction of the Newcastle factory. His admiration of "really good, honest, mechanical labour" was enthusiastic. If he railed paradoxically at new-fangled notions for educating workmen, he did so from a lively sense of the comparative worthlessness of superficial education. For the "skill of artisans" he had a strong poetic sympathy, and as his career drew to a close, his affectionate appreciation of the class from which his father had sprung manifested itself in many pleasant ways.'

In the autumn of 1859 Stephenson sailed for Norway. He was then in shattered health, but it was hoped the voyage would have a beneficial effect. He was worse, however, when he returned to England in September. He landed at Lowestoft, and at once returned to London. After reaching home he seemed to revive for a time, but early in October obstinate congestion of the liver set in, and this was followed by dropsy of the whole system. On the 12th of October he expired, being only in the fifty-sixth year of his age. Regret was expressed by all ranks of the community, and he was accorded a public funeral in Westminster Abbey, where his remains were interred by the side of Telford.

Like his father, Robert Stephenson was of a kindly and benevolent disposition, and his services were much sought after in the settlement of disputes. The difference between him and Brunel, Dr. Smiles illustrates by an anecdote. Brunel complained that his contractors were always quarrelling with him. 'You hold them too tightly to the letter of your agreement,' said Stephenson; 'treat them fairly and liberally.' 'But they try to take advantage of me at all points,' remarked Brunel. 'Perhaps you suspect them too much,' said Stephenson. 'I suspect all men to be rogues,' said the other, 'till I find them to be honest.' 'For my part,' said Stephenson, 'I take all men to be honest till I find them to be rogues.' 'Ah, then I fear we shall never agree,' concluded Brunel. Robert Stephenson loved and admired his father deeply. He would openly and proudly confess that he owed all to him. 'It is my great pride to remember,' he once observed in public, 'that whatever may have been done, and however extensive may have been my own connection with railway development, all I know and all I have done is primarily due to the parent whose memory I cherish and revere.' And he confided to Lough the sculptor that he had never had but two loves—one for his father, the other for his wife.

Unobtrusive, and manly and gentle in demeanour, Robert Stephenson was a favourite with all who came in contact with him, whether men, women, or children. He was princely in his generosity, both public and private. To the nation such men are invaluable, their great and enduring achievements conferring glory and stability upon the country. As the poet is honoured for his song, so must the man of invention be honoured for those marvellous works which advance the material interests and the prosperity of the human race.

CHARLES KNIGHT.

CHARLES KNIGHT.

THE printing industry is one of the greatest and most beneficent enterprises associated with the history of the human race. Milton's noble plea for the liberty of unlicensed printing —the most splendid argument to which the world had as yet listened on behalf of intellectual liberty—has been abundantly justified by the developments of the past two centuries and a half. Of all the arts which make for peace, printing has been the most effective and wide-reaching, notwithstanding those momentary periods of aberration when its influence has been cast upon the side of war. If it were not for the gigantic industry of printing, with all the trades affiliated with it, it is not too much to say that England would not be the England of to-day, the majestic mother of free peoples.

In selecting for this biographical sketch one of the pioneers of popular literature, it is not with the intention of exalting Charles Knight above others who have rendered perhaps equal service in the extension of printing, such as William and Robert Chambers and John Cassell; while as regards those great benefactors who have done so much towards the mechanical perfection of the printing press, we cannot fail to remember with gratitude the names of König, Cowper, Walter, Clowes, Hoe, Marinoni, and others. I have chosen Charles Knight because there is a good deal in his character that is typically English—for example, his energy, perseverance, straightforwardness, and his courage under difficulties. Then, again, his career has a double interest, because he was thrown into contact with most of his eminent contemporaries. Knight may be viewed in a triple capacity, as author, printer, and publisher. His life was a long, useful, and honourable one, and his name and services eminently deserve to be perpetuated.

Some entertaining facts concerning book-producers and the book-trade antecedent to the time of Knight may be cited before I pass on to the record of his own labours. Bookselling as a trade was of little moment until the invention of printing. Before that most books were lent, not sold, for they were not within the means of any but the wealthy. Caxton's labours soon led to a change, but the first real impetus given to bookselling was the great demand for Bibles caused by the Reformation. Yet on the Continent books had become such an important feature of commerce that in 1450 a guild of booksellers, copyists, and allied trades was formed at Antwerp, while four years later the guild acquired a footing at Bruges. Gutenberg's partners, Fust and Schöffer, conveyed the productions of the Mainz press to Paris and Frankfort. The earliest printers were generally learned men, and in some cases they were the authors of the works produced. They acted both as printers and booksellers, but in the fifteenth century the two branches of the industry began to be divided. Mr. Robert Cochrane, who has compiled statistics on the book-trade, notes that the founder of the Stephens family of printers and publishers settled in Paris in 1502; Louis, the first of the Elzevirs, was settled as a bookseller and bookbinder in Leyden in 1580; the Aldine Press printed 908 different works between 1490 and 1597; and the Plantin Press of Antwerp, 1514-89, had sometimes twenty presses at work. In England, the early booksellers were known as *stationarii*, or stationers, from taking their stand or station at a fair. In the sixteenth century the restriction as to giving the price of a book on the last page was frequently enforced by Government. Between the years

1476 and 1600, 350 printers were at work in England and Scotland, and at least 10,000 distinct works were printed during that period. From 1623 to 1664 only two editions of Shakespeare were issued, but there was so much religious and political controversy between 1640 and 1660 that the British Museum is able to boast of more than 2,000 tracts — embracing 30,000 separate publications—issued during that period. It is computed that the loss to booksellers in the vicinity of St. Paul's, in consequence of the great fire of 1666, was no less than £200,000—an enormous sum for those days.

The book-trade was greatly harassed by legislation, royal patents, and proclamations, by ordinances of the Star Chamber, and by the granting of monopolies. The Stationers' Company of London, constituted by Royal Charter in 1557, exercised an arbitrary censorship of the press. An Act called the Licensing Act, passed in 1673, gave to the Crown control over the issue of books; but this Act, with its renewals, ultimately expired in 1694. In 1710 the first Copyright Act afforded protection to authors, and absolved both them and the publishers from the authority of the Stationers' Company. Power was given to certain high public functionaries, however, to regulate the prices of books, and to fine those who sought higher prices. These provisions remained in force until 1738, when an Act was passed which made the book-trade free. Among famous booksellers and publishers, who were either authors or intimately associated with authors, may be mentioned Thomas Guy, founder of Guy's Hospital; John Dunton, whom the Pretender threatened to hang if he ever came to the throne, 'for having writ forty books to prove him a Popish impostor'; Jacob Tonson, Dryden's publisher, and the populariser of Shakespeare and Milton; Lintott, the publisher of Pope's editions of the *Iliad* and the *Odyssey*; Curll the notorious and the pilloried; Samuel Richardson, novelist and printer; Cave, the founder of the *Gentleman's Magazine*; Millar, the publisher for Fielding, Thomson, and Hume;

Newbery, who was associated with Goldsmith; Griffiths of the *Monthly Review;* Dodsley of the *Annual Register;* and Joseph Cottle, of Bristol, the friend of Coleridge, Southey, and Wordsworth. The names of at least a hundred enterprising English and Scotch publishers in the nineteenth century— worthy successors of the best of those above-mentioned— instinctively rise to the mind, but they are so well-known as to need no recapitulation.

School-books, encyclopædias, educational and religious publications, maps, atlases, etc., indicate further important developments in the book-trade. Excellent cheap editions of popular works were inaugurated by an Edinburgh publisher named Donaldson about 1760-70, and he was closely followed in London by John Bell, who issued his *British Poets* in 1777. This led to a meeting of the book-trade, and the publication of Johnson's *Lives of the Poets.* Then came C. Cooke's admirable cheap reprints at the close of last century, which were succeeded by Suttaby's, Sharpe's, Walker's, and Dove's pocket editions. Many cheap periodicals and newspapers appeared between 1800 and 1820, a considerable number of them leading to prosecutions for seditious libel. The *Mirror*, an illustrated weekly sheet of another type, issued in 1822, achieved a permanent success. Five years later the Society for the Diffusion of Useful Knowledge began to publish its popular scientific treatises, while Archibald Constable inaugurated his valuable series of works under the title of *Constable's Miscellany.* A short time afterwards Messrs. Chambers began their *Chambers's Edinburgh Journal*, the Society for the Diffusion of Useful Knowledge followed with the *Penny Magazine*, and the Society for Promoting Christian Knowledge with the *Saturday Magazine.* Then came in rapid succession various popular ventures by Charles Knight, W. & R. Chambers, and John Cassell.

At this point I take up the story of Charles Knight. He was the son of a Windsor bookseller, and was born in the year

1791. The house in which he first saw the light was close to the great entrance to the lower ward of Windsor Castle—called, after its builder, Henry the Eighth's Gateway. He has recorded how, as a boy of nine, he went to bed on the night of the 31st of December, 1800, expecting to find the house shaken to its foundations by the boom of artillery. Not only was the next morning the beginning of a new year, but the beginning of a new century—one of the most momentous in the history of the world. There was no boom of artillery, however, for the King had forbidden it, lest the new painted window by Mr. West, at the east end of St. George's Chapel, might be broken by the concussion. But the bells in the belfry of St. George's Chapel and the bells of the parish church rang out a merry peal. On the morrow, the sun shone brilliantly on the new Standard of England raised over the Round Tower. The arms of France had disappeared from the Standard, for the King's title now ran, 'George the Third, by the Grace of God, of the United Kingdom of Great Britain and Ireland, King, Defender of the Faith.' Some said the change was ominous of the departing glory of Old England, but Britain still stands where she did. On that memorable 1st of January, 1801, the bells of Windsor, as of many other towns and cities, hailed the commencement of the legislative Union between Great Britain and Ireland.

When only two years of age Charles Knight had lost his mother. She was the daughter of a wealthy yeoman named Binfield, of Iver, in Buckinghamshire. The boy was the sole companion of a somewhat moody and eccentric father, though one withal of an enlightened mind, and who consequently fostered in him studious habits. Young Knight was educated at the school of the cultured Dr. Nicholson, of Ealing. Writing of his pupil to Mr. Knight in 1804, Dr. Nicholson said : 'With an excellent disposition and good temper, he has very superior abilities, and will shine in a learned profession. I wish particularly to call your attention to his Latin verses and

English themes, in which I am confident he goes much beyond your expectations. It would be a pity to bury such talents in an office or a counting-house.' Compositions executed by Charles Knight at thirteen show a singular maturity of thought and expression. From eight years of age Knight was a frequent attendant at that smallest of playhouses, the Theatre Royal of Windsor; and in his *Passages of a Working Life* he gives an amusing picture of the visits paid by 'Farmer George' and his Queen to the theatre :—

'That honoured playhouse no longer exists. The High Street exhibits a dissenting chapel on its site, whose frontage may give some notion of the dimensions of that cosy apartment, with its two tiers of boxes, its gallery and its slips. It was not an exclusive theatre. Three shillings gave the entrance to the boxes, two shillings to the pit, and one shilling to the gallery. One side of the lower tier of boxes was occupied by the Court. The King and Queen sat in capacious armchairs with satin play-bills spread before them. The orchestra, which would hold half a dozen fiddlers, and the pit, where some dozen persons might be closely packed on each bench, separated the Royal Circle from the general parties in the opposite tier of boxes. With the plebeians in the pit the Royal Family might have shaken hands, and when they left there was always a scramble for their satin bills, which would be afterwards duly framed and glazed as spoils of peace. As the King laughed and cried " Bravo, Quick ! " or " Bravo, Suett ! "—for he had rejoiced in their well-known mirth-provoking faces many a time before—the pit and gallery clapped and roared in loyal sympathy; the boxes were too genteel for such emotional feelings. As the King, Queen, and Princesses retired at the end of the third act to sip their coffee, the pot of Windsor ale, called Queen's ale, circulated in the gallery. At eleven o'clock the curtain dropped. The fiddles struck up "God save the King," their Majesties bowed around as the house clapped, and the gouty manager, Mr. Thornton, leading the way to the entrance (carrying wax-lights and walking backward with the well-practised steps of a Lord Chamberlain), the flambeaux of three or four carriages gleamed through the dimly-lighted streets, and Royalty was quickly at rest.'

During one of his holidays Knight was taken to call upon Mr. Stratford Canning, afterwards the distinguished diplomatist Lord Stratford de Redcliffe. He was managing editor of *The Miniature*—a successor after a long interval of the Eton *Microcosm*—which the elder Knight was printing and publishing. This is an interesting glimpse of Stratford Canning, as well as of some other persons whose names became well known to the world : 'How well I remember his tall figure and handsome face, with the down upon his chin. Some forty years afterwards, at an entertainment given upon a trial-trip of a frigate that had been built for the Sultan, I was introduced to Sir Stratford Canning. I had much talk with the great diplomatist about the progress of education and of popular literature, in the efficacy of which he did not appear to have any confident belief. He talked, too, of that literary production of his boyhood with which he associated my name. Of course he spoke slightingly of it, as men who have made their mark in the world generally do of their juvenilia. There were, however, some literary matters of more importance arising out of the forgotten Eton periodical. "Your father," said Mr. Murray to me once after dinner, "helped to make my fortune. When I kept a little trumpery shop in Fleet Street, Dr. Rennell, the Master of the Temple, told me one day that his son and young Canning owed an account for printing *The Miniature* to their publisher, who held a good many unsold copies. I took the stock, paid the account, made waste paper of the numbers, brought out a smart edition which had few buyers, got the reputation of being a clever publisher, was introduced to George Canning in consequence of the service I had rendered to his cousin, and in a few years set up the *Quarterly Review*."'

Knight was taken away from school in 1805, and put to learn printing and bookselling. He resented this, for he was desirous of being a scholar. However, his father indulged him during his apprenticeship, for we read of his often galloping his pony along the glades of the forest; or watching his little boat, hour after hour, from the Thames bank at Datchet or at Clewer; or wandering, book in hand, by the riverside. He read old novels and poems, the classics, Scott's new poems, the newspaper, and anything in the shape of literature he could lay hold of. Before he was seventeen he had become quite a book hunter. On one occasion he so pleased an old bibliopole, for whose library he was negotiating, that he was rewarded by the gift of a first-folio Shakespeare—a sadly defective copy, it is true, but still a first-folio. When in his eighteenth year, the youthful enthusiast drew up a list of ambitious works he intended composing himself, and actually produced various essays, poems, and sketches. He seems to have been of a devotional temperament, and frequently prayed for strength to shake off the allurements of sloth and to despise the seductions of idleness. An 'Arrangement of Study for a Month,' which he drew up, left the mornings for original composition, with allowance of an hour for chronology, geography, logic, or rhetoric; the evenings were to be devoted to reading aloud history, voyages, etc., or works in polite literature, with one hour for Greek, Latin, Italian, or French. The Old Testament in English was to be read on Sunday mornings, and in the evenings the New Testament in Greek; the rest of the Sunday being spent in reading moral and religious authors, or in studying natural religion, etc. Knowledge was to be systematised, and in order to acquire it he rose before six o'clock in the morning. It was his settled conviction that 'he that leaves his studies or occupations to chance, suppresses his memory and darkens his judgment, by giving too much leisure to the imagination.' Knight had a sharp temper but a sensitive heart, and in his diary there are such entries as the following, relating to a fellow-workman :—' This day has been disgraced by some excesses towards Meyrick. Let me keep in mind that a want of understanding demands our pity, not our contempt; and though I may inwardly despise vain ignorance and obstinacy, let me not commit myself by vulgar railing and harsh invective.'

When only eighteen, Charles Knight began a Reading Society in Windsor, and read an address before it on the use of such institutions. He also invented two new printing-cases, and collected materials for a life of Bartholomew Las Casas, and other works. He was further commissioned by the Countess of Orkney, who occupied Cliefden, to make a catalogue of a large collection of books which had long been neglected. In the year 1812 he founded, with his father, the *Windsor and Eton Express*, a weekly newspaper, which he edited for fourteen years. In addition to this he became editor of the *London Guardian*, a literary and political paper. The *Windsor and Eton Express* of the 3rd of December, 1814, contained a paragraph which Knight had copied from *The Times* of the 29th of November. It had strongly excited his wonder and curiosity, as to the probable consequences of what *The Times* described as 'the greatest improvement connected with printing since the discovery of the art itself.' Well knowing the great bodily exertion hitherto required of two men, working at the common press, to produce two hundred and fifty impressions of one side of a newspaper in an hour, Knight might well be surprised when he read as follows :—' The reader of this paragraph now holds in his hand one of the many thousand impressions of *The Times* newspaper which were taken off last night, by a mechanical apparatus. A system of machinery almost organic has been devised and arranged, which, while it relieves the human frame of its most laborious efforts in printing, far exceeds all human powers in rapidity and despatch.' The process was then briefly described, and it was added that 'the whole of these complicated acts were performed with such a velocity and simultaneousness of movement, that no less than eleven hundred sheets were impressed in one hour.' The printing machine thus inaugurated was the one invented by König. But as the machine was complicated, expensive, and liable to derangement, Mr. Walter did not relax his efforts until he had still further perfected and simplified his printing machines. These new processes were destined to have a marked effect upon Charles Knight's future, for he was always ready to avail himself of any new ideas on the subject of printing.

Knight was sufficiently successful in his business career as to enable him to marry at a comparatively early age. But while he was very much attached to the domestic fireside, he was deeply interested in public affairs, working also energetically at parish affairs, and infusing a new spirit into them. He further found time to compose poems, some of which gained the warm commendation of Leigh Hunt, and which may even now be praised for their smooth versification and placid yet poetic spirit. As for his continued devotion to study, he remarks : ' I may truly say—and I say it for the encouragement of any young man who is sighing over the fetters of his daily labour, and pining for weeks and months of interrupted study—that I have found through life that the acquisition of knowledge, and a regular course of literary employment, are far from being incompatible with commercial pursuits. I doubt whether, if I had been all author or all publisher, I should have succeeded better in either capacity.' Knight and other friends of the drama built a new theatre at Windsor, at a large cost, and with consequently small dividends to the shareholders, of whom the elder Knight was the principal. It was opened in August, 1815 ; and Charles Knight wrote a Prologue, which was not conciliatory to the bigoted opponents of the stage, who regarded their proceedings as criminal. The time was still far distant when Shakespeare would be quoted in the pulpit. The new Windsor Theatre was commodious ; but the manager, like many succeeding ones, could not draw audiences without stars. Here is a reminiscence of the famous Edmund Kean :—

'In 1817 I became acquainted with Edmund Kean, on his visit to Windsor at our Christmas season. I was an enthusiastic admirer of his genius; and wrote most elaborate criticisms on his Othello and Shylock, his Sir Giles Overreach, and Sir Edward Mortimer. I had often then what I considered the great privilege of supping with him after the play. He was always surrounded by two or three followers who administered to his insatiable vanity in the coarsest style; applauded to the echo his somewhat loose talk; and stimulated his readiness to "make a night of it." My unbounded admiration for the talent of the actor was somewhat interrupted by a humiliating sense of the weakness of the man. Nevertheless the attraction was irresistible as long as he strove to make himself agreeable. How exquisitely he sang a pathetic ballad! The rich melody, the deep tenderness, of his "Fly from the World, O Bessie, to me," were to live in my memory, in companionship with the exquisite music of his voice in his best days, when he uttered upon the stage, in a way which no other actor has approached, the soliloquy ending with "Othello's occupation's gone."'

Charles Knight was very active as a promoter of popular education, but a severe check to this and other reforms which he advocated was administered in 1819, as the result of the political tumults of the time. The effect which the serious events of the period had upon his thoughts and aspirations he has thus described: 'There were riots and arrests; and at length came what is called "The Manchester Massacre." The country was thoroughly frightened. Parliament was called together to make new laws; and it produced what Lord Campbell describes as "the unconstitutional code called the Six Acts." At the Christmas of 1819 every journalist went about his work under the apprehension that, if he wrote what, by the uncertain verdict of a jury might be construed into a seditious libel, he would not only be subjected to very terrible fine and imprisonment, but, if convicted a second time, would be liable to be transported beyond the seas. I looked with dread towards a struggle which would end either in anarchy or military government. Like Sydney Smith, I regarded democracy and despotism as equally dangerous results of a contest between power and mob violence: "In which of these two evils it terminates is of no more consequence than from which tube of a double-barrelled pistol I meet my destruction." The effect of these circumstances upon my political opinions, during several succeeding years, is not altogether satisfactory to look back upon. In my hatred and contempt of the demagogues and profligate writers who were stirring up the ignorant masses to revolt and irreligion, I turned somewhat aside from regarding the injustice that was at the root of a desire for change. I panted for improvement as ardently as ever. I was aspiring to become a popular educator. But I felt that one must be content for a while to shut one's eyes to the necessity for some salutary reforms, in the dread that any decided movement towards innovation would be to aid in the work of lopping and topping the sturdy oak of the constitution till its shelter and its beauty were altogether gone. I believe this was a common feeling, not only with public writers who did not address the passions of the multitude, but with statesmen who were not subservient partisans. Thence ensued a reticence in writing and in speaking, which looked like a distrust of the progress of improvement even with many of decided liberal opinions. I think this was amongst the worst results of those evil days in which we had fallen in the last months of the reign of the old King. I had to drag this chain of doubtful timidity in my first attempt to address the humbler classes.'

However, Knight resolved to do something towards stemming the tide of evil caused by the numerous injurious cheap publications; and his first venture as editor and publisher into the region of popular literature is to be traced to a paper which he wrote in the *Windsor Express* of December 11, 1819, entitled 'Cheap Publications.' Cobbett's *Twopenny Register*, Wooler's *Black Dwarf*, and even worse publications, were having it all their own way; and Knight set forth, as one of the most fearful signs of the times, the excessive spread of publications whose chief aim was to inspire hatred of the Government and contempt for the religious institutions of the country. It ought to be said here that Cobbett and his friends were not originally to blame, for England was really suffering at this juncture under one of the most oppressive and tyrannical of Governments. However, Knight saw chiefly the excesses to which their reactionary policy had led, and this is the way in which he sought to overcome them by the diffusion of useful literature :—

'Knowledge must have its worldly as well as its spiritual range; it looks towards Heaven, but it treads upon the earth. The mass of useful books are not accessible to the poor; newspapers, with their admixture of good and evil, seldom find their way into the domestic circle of the labourer or artisan; the tracts which pious persons distribute are exclusively religious, and the tone of these is often either fanatical or puerile. The "two-penny trash," as it is called, has seen farther, with the quick perception of avarice or ambition, into the intellectual wants of the working-classes. It was just because there was no healthful food for their newly-created appetite, that sedition and infidelity have been so widely disseminated. The writers employed in this work, and their leader and prototype, Cobbett, in particular, show us pretty accurately the sort of talent which is required to provide this healthful food. "*Fas est ab hoste doceri.*" They state an argument with great clearness and precision; they divest knowledge of all its pedantic incumbrances; they make powerful appeals to the deepest passions of the human heart. Let a man of genius set out upon these principles, in the task of building up a more popular literature than we possess; and let him add, what the seditious and infidel writers have thrown away, the power of directing the affections to what is reverend and beautiful in national manners and institutions —tender and subduing in pure and domestic associations— sacred and glowing in what belongs to the high and mysterious destiny of the human mind—satisfying and consoling in the divine revelations of that destiny,—and then, were such a system embodied in one grand benevolent design supplementary to the Instruction of the Poor, National Education, we sincerely think it would go on diffusing its blessings over every portion of the land, and calling up a truly English spirit wherever it penetrated. Neglect this provision, and we fear that no penal laws will prevent the craving after knowledge from being improperly gratified, and then—but the evidence of the danger is before us.'

Translating his ideas into action, Charles Knight began the issue of *The Plain Englishman*, in February, 1820. He had the assistance of his friend Edward Hawke Locker, Commissioner of Greenwich Hospital, who thoroughly sympathised in Knight's objects, and wrote for the new periodical 'Lectures on the Bible and Liturgy.' Other contributors included Dr. John Bird Sumner (afterwards Archbishop of Canterbury), who wrote a series of articles called 'Conversations with an Unbeliever'; Mr. John Cole, a well-known surgeon, wrote on 'Cleanliness and Ventilation'; Mr. John Steer, on 'Popular Law'; the Bishop of Calcutta, on 'Naval Victories'; while Knight himself contributed a 'Monthly Retrospect of Public Affairs.' Selections were also given from the best writers under such headings as 'The Christian Monitor,' 'The British Patriot,' and 'The Fireside Companion.' It is rather amusing to note this sentence from one of the health articles written by Mr. Cole—the forerunner of Southwood Smith and Chadwick: 'Those who can be brought to venture on *so unheard of a thing* as to wash the whole of their bodies, will generally be induced to repeat the experiment from the comfort it affords.' The contemporaries had heard that there was 'Death in the Pot,' and they evidently believed also that there was 'Death in the Bath.' 'You have killed my mother,' said a good housewife of the Lake District to Miss Martineau ; 'she had never washed her feet till you persuaded her, and this is the end on't.' Mr. Cole gave very good advice on such subjects as Ventilation, Cooking, and the Management of Infants, and Sanitary Dwellings.

During the summer and autumn of the first year's issue of *The Plain Englishman*, Knight occupied a cottage on the bank of the Thames. But in the ensuing winter he settled in a house at Windsor which was most interesting in its connexion with the dim antiquity of the Castle. Its entrance was in the smaller cloisters to the north of St. George's Chapel, but its principal rooms were over the great cloister on the east of the chapel. In his study, which had a richly-carved ceiling, he could frequently hear the swelling tones of the organ. Yet, beautiful and unique as the dwelling was, the want of free air made it unfit for healthful existence. A daughter was born to him there, but there also he unfortunately lost a son, Charles James. His dear friend Matthew Davenport Hill passed some happy hours with him at Christmas. But before Easter, Knight had to record his first grief :—

'I was then, as I am now, as little disposed as Coriolanus was, to show my wounds in the market-place ; but my feelings overflowed into a paper which I printed in *The Plain Englishman*. Two sentences will be sufficient to mark this passage in my life. "Until I had reached my thirtieth year I had known nothing of what I can properly term sorrow. The evils of mortality had not begun to come home to me. The wings of the destroying angel had rested upon the dwellings of my neighbours ; but death had never yet crossed my threshold, and sickness seldom. I had heard the voice of misery like the mutterings of a distant storm, but the thunder had not yet burst over my head—I had not covered my eyes from the passing lightning" .... "I now knew, for the first time, what it is to have death about our hearths. The excitement of hope and fear in a moment passes away; and the contest between feeling and reason begins, with its alternation of passion and listlessness. It is some time before the image of death gets possession of the mind. We sleep, perchance, amidst a feverish dream of gloomy and indistinct remembrances. The object of our grief, it may be, has seemed to us present, in health and animation. We wake in a struggle between the shadowy and the real world; and we require an effort of the intellect to believe that the earthly part of the being we have loved is no more than a clod of the valley."

While believing in the regenerating power of the press, Knight dreaded the advent of cheap scurrilous newspapers and periodicals. His forebodings proved unfounded, and years afterwards he frankly admitted that he 'could scarcely have imagined that some distant age of cheapness would have been an age when the impure, seditious, violent, intolerant, and libellous writer would have become a rare exception amongst journalists.' On the 3rd of March, 1821, Knight created a new department of newspaper literature, by publishing in *The Guardian* the first of a series of monthly articles, entitled 'Magazine Day.' Nearly two years later he sold the above newspaper, and took up his position as a publisher in Pall Mall East.

Knight had some time before been thrown into contact with many choice literary spirits, for in 1820 he had brought out *The Etonian*, which had for its editors Walter Blunt and Winthrop Mackworth Praed. The other contributors included William Sidney Walker, a youth of brilliant promise, John Moultrie, and Henry Nelson Coleridge. The publication continued for about two years, and then it was succeeded in 1823 by *Knight's Quarterly Magazine*. In addition to the writers above-named, the new periodical counted among its contributors De Quincey, Macaulay, Derwent Coleridge, and Henry Malden. Praed's opening article in the magazine was called 'Castle Vernon,' and Knight's only prospectus of his new periodical was this very whimsical extract from the article:—

'To the Lady Mary Vernon, the Mistress of all Harmony, the Queen of all Wits, the Brightest of all Belles, we, the undersigned, send greeting: "We, the undersigned, are a knot of young men, of various forms and features—of more various talents and inclinations; agreeing in nothing, save in two essential points—a warm liking for one another, and a very profound devotion for your Ladyship.

'" Some of us have no occupation.

'" Some of us have no money.

'" Some of us are desperately in love.

'" Some of us are desperately in debt.

'" Many of us are very clever, and wish to convince the public of the fact.

'" Several of us have never written a line.

'" Several of us have written a great many, and wish to write more.

'" For all these reasons we intend to write a book.

'" We will not compile a lumbering quarto of Travels, to be bound in Russia, and skimmed in the *Quarterly*, and bought by the country book-clubs;—nor a biting Political Pamphlet, to be praised by everybody on one side, and abused by everybody on the other, and read by nobody at all;—nor a Philosophical Essay, to be marvelled at by the few, and shuddered at by the many, and prosecuted by His Majesty's Attorney-General;—nor a little Epic Poem in twenty-four books, to be loved by the milliners, and lauded in the *Literary Gazette*, and burnt by your Ladyship.

'" But a book of some sort we are resolved to write. We will go forth to the world once a quarter, in high spirits and handsome type, and a modest dress of drab, with verse and prose, criticism and witticism, fond love and loud laughter; everything that is light and warm, and fantastic, and beautiful, shall be the offering we will bear; while we will leave the Nation to the care of the Parliament, and the Church to the Bishop of Peterborough. And to this end we will give up to colder lips and duller souls their gross and terrestrial food; we will not interfere with the saddle or the sirloin, the brandy-bottle or the punch-bowl;—our food shall be of the spicy curry and the glistening champagne; our inspiration shall be the thanks of pleasant voices, and the smiles of sparkling eyes. We grasp at no renown—we pray for no immortality; but we trust that in the voyage it shall be our destiny to run, we shall waken many glowing feelings, and revive many agreeable recollections; we shall make many jokes and many friends; we shall enliven ourselves and the public together; and when we meet around some merry hearth to discuss the past and the future, our projects, and our success, we shall give a zest to our bottle and our debate by drinking a health to all who read us, and three healths to all who praise."'

Amid many lighter things in the magazine was an article by Macaulay on West Indian Slavery, in which he sternly combated the evil which his father, Zachary Macaulay, and other philanthropists, did so much towards abolishing. To later numbers Macaulay contributed his 'Ivry,' and other fine lyrics, 'Dante,' 'The Athenian Orators,' and other prose articles. There were likewise fine contributions by other writers, but the periodical was a loss and a trouble to its conductor, and its career closed with the sixth number. Another venture of a similar character, *The Brazen Head*, edited by Knight and Barry St. Leger, was brought out in the Spring of 1826, but it only lasted for four weeks. Nevertheless, those few numbers contained poems by Praed which have acquired a permanent fame. In one of them, 'The Chaunt of the Brazen Head,' occur these well-known lines :—

' I think that friars and their hoods,
    Their doctrines and their maggots,
Have lighted up too many feuds,
    And far too many faggots;
I think while zealots fast and frown,
    And fight for two or seven,
That there are fifty roads to town,
    And rather more to Heaven.

   .   .   .   .   .

' I think that very few have sigh'd
    When Fate at last has found them,
Though bitter foes were by their side,
    And barren moss around them;
I think that some have died of drought,
    And some have died of drinking,—
I think that naught is worth a thought,
    And I'm a fool for thinking!'

Charles Knight's *Plain Englishman* continued to appear for three years, faithfully supporting the Constitution in Church and State, and supplying pure and wholesome literature. But the patronage of the public at large not being such as would enable its conductors to continue the work without serious loss, the venture was given up. The freedom of the press was an unknown quantity early in the century. John and Leigh Hunt were prosecuted in 1812 for libelling the Prince Regent in the *Examiner*. They had simply called him ' an Adonis in loveliness ' and ' a corpulent gentleman of fifty,' yet for these mild phrases they were fined £1,000 each, and imprisoned for two years in separate prisons. Again, in May, 1821, John Hunt was prosecuted for a libel on the House of Commons, and sentenced to two years' imprisonment. Charles Knight himself was the subject of vexatious actions on grounds for which he would be applauded now. The actions arose out of articles published in the *Windsor Express*, and Knight, writing about the affair in 1865, remarks :—

' Imagine, at the present day, the Lord Chief Justice of the Court of Queen's Bench trying an action for libel,—with two leaders, such as Mr. Denman for the prosecution, and Mr. Scarlett for the defence,—the alleged libel being the report in a country newspaper of a flagrant case of cruelty which was a notorious subject of local indignation. The libel consisted in terming that "a brutal assault" upon which the assailants were held to bail. Imagine that the persons whose characters were thus defamed were a pig-keeper and his wife, who let lodgings to poor people; and having a dispute with a family of which the mother had only been confined a week, threatened to pull the bed from under her, and turn her into the street. Imagine a London jury finding a verdict for the plaintiff with £50 damages. Imagine a second action for the same libel being brought by the wife. Imagine ten several actions against ten London papers, for reporting the trial in the King's Bench with a few words of just comment upon the scandal of such litigation, when there was no "private malice" or "gross negligence." Imagine a hungry attorney, prowling for prey, at the bottom of all these actions, who had no object to attain but the heavy costs which he pocketed. These verdicts cost me £500 in 1825. Is not the newspaper press in a better condition than it was in, forty years ago?'

At the time of Lord Byron's funeral, Knight was involved in a matter of public interest connected with the deceased poet. Five days before he witnessed the poet's funeral procession, on the 12th of July, he was served with a Chancery injunction to restrain him from publishing certain letters of Lord Byron. It appears that Robert Charles Dallas, who was connected by marriage with the family of the poet, prepared a volume with the object of presenting a faithful delineation of Byron's character as he had personally known it. After the poet's death, Dallas remodelled his memoir into *Correspondence of Lord Byron*, and this work Charles Knight purchased for a large sum. It was already advertised for publication, when Mr. Hobhouse and a friend called upon Knight and protested against the issue of the work. Although Knight assured the family and the executors that they need feel no apprehension as to the character of the work—which was intended to elevate Lord Byron's moral and intellectual character,—legal proceedings ensued. The Vice-Chancellor granted an injunction upon the affidavits of Mr. Hobhouse and Mr. Hanson, co-executors, that such contemplated publication was 'a breach of private confidence and a violation of the rights of property.' There was an appeal, and after two months of anxiety for Knight, Lord Chancellor Eldon gave judgment to the effect that the owner of the letters had no right of publication in them. However, after the death of Dallas, in 1824, Knight published a trustworthy and authentic volume entitled *Recollections of Lord Byron*, edited by Dallas's son, the Rev. Alexander Dallas. Besides the annoyance and loss to Knight, it was not a pleasant thing for him to see Moore reap the full advantage of the suppressed correspondence, by filling many pages in 1829 with the letters of Dallas and Byron which the executors had thought fit to suppress in 1824.

Brougham was busily engaged in organising the Society for the Diffusion of Useful Knowledge in the autumn of 1826, when M. D. Hill informed him of Charles Knight's scheme for the issue of popular books. An interview was speedily arranged between the great lawyer and the publisher. That interview was indelibly impressed on Knight's memory, and it had also much to do with moulding his future. Knight gives this graphic picture of their first meeting :—

'There was an image in my mind of the Queen's Attorney-General, as I had often beheld him in the House of Lords, wielding a power in the proceedings on the Bill of Pains and Penalties which no other man seemed to possess—equivocating witnesses crouching beneath his withering scorn ; mighty peers shrinking from his bold sarcasm ; the whole assembly visibly agitated at times by the splendour of his eloquence. The Henry Brougham I had gazed upon was, in my mind's eye, a man stern and repellent ; not to be approached with any attempt at familiarity; whose opinions must be received with the most respectful deference; whose mental superiority would be somewhat overwhelming. The Henry Brougham into whose chambers in Lincoln's Inn I was ushered on a November night was sitting amidst his briefs, evidently delighted to be interrupted for some thoughts more attractive. After saluting my friend with a joke, and grasping my hand with a cordial welcome, he went at once to the subject upon which I came. The rapid conception of the features of my plan; the few brief questions as to my wishes; the manifestation of a warm interest in my views without the slightest attempt to be patronising, were most gratifying to me. The image of the great orator of 1820 altogether vanished when I listened to the unpretentious and often playful words of one of the best table-talkers of 1826,—it vanished, even as the full-bottomed wig of that time seemed to have belonged to some other head than the close-cropped one upon which I looked. The foremost advocate of popular education made no harangues about its advantages. He did not indoctrinate me, as I have been bored by many an educationist before and since, with flourishes upon a subject which he gave Mr. Hill and myself full credit for comprehending. M. Charles Dupin said to Mackintosh, after a night in the House of Commons, "I heard not one word about the blessings of liberty." "No, no," replied Mackintosh; "we take all that for granted." So did Henry Brougham take for granted that he and I were in accord upon the subject of the Diffusion of Knowledge. He was then within a few days of the completion of his forty-seventh year; full of health and energy—one who had been working without intermission in literature, in science, in law, in politics, for a quarter of a century, but one to whom no work seemed to bring fatigue; no tedious mornings of the King's Bench, no sleepless nights of the House of Commons, able to "stale his infinite variety."'

Under the auspices of the Society for the Diffusion of Useful Knowledge, Knight began the issue of the *British Almanac* in

1827, which was soon followed by the *Companion to the Almanac*, and he continued the work for thirty-seven years, writing many original articles himself. Up to this time almanacs had been of a very inferior type, but Knight now supplied useful and trustworthy information. He had gathered together a number of scientific men, who were able to deal with such subjects as Astronomy, Meteorology, Tides, Eclipses, etc. Knight was not so successful, however, with his scheme for a *National Library*. It was at first taken up by the Society, but difficulties arose, and Knight finally arranged with Murray the publisher to carry out the idea for a series of cheap volumes, which should condense the information only to be found in voluminous and expensive treatises. The Prospectus set forth that 'the divisions of Popular Knowledge in which the *National Library* is arranged will comprehend, in distinct Treatises, the most important branches of instruction and amusement. They will present the most valuable and interesting articles of an Encyclopædia in a form accessible to every description of purchaser.' But various things soon began to militate against the undertaking; differences of opinion arose about the editorial responsibility for the series; no satisfactory arrangements could be made regarding the projector's old stock and copyrights; and Murray became frightened at the magnitude of the plan. The scheme was consequently abandoned, to Knight's great loss. In fact, he was absolutely crippled for a time. A private trust administered his affairs, whose only concern was to realise, at any cost, land, houses, newspapers, stock, copyrights, etc. In the end he walked forth from his business homes in London and Windsor a poor man, and one who had to begin the battle of life afresh.

Finding a home at Brompton, with his wife and four little girls, he soon began to look hopefully on life again, though under changed circumstances. He obtained an engagement as a writer on James Silk Buckingham's new paper, *The Sphinx*, but his course of journalism under Buckingham was not agreeable, and he soon abandoned it. Buckingham was not only difficult to work with owing to his conceit, but he at length disgusted Knight by proposing an amended scale of remuneration for literary criticisms, which began at half-a-crown and rose to a guinea, according to the length of the article. Happily a more worthy course of industry was soon to open out for Charles Knight, though before the time arrived he had a little experience in producing *Friendship's Offering*, one of the numerous Annuals which were then so much in vogue. For this periodical, Praed wrote his fine poem, 'The Red Fisherman.'

Before the work of the day commenced, Charles Knight was fond of taking a walk through Kensington Gardens. He did this frequently during the summer of 1827—when all Nature had put on the garb of loveliness—and in the course of one of these walks he witnessed a peaceful and happy scene in which the Princess Victoria, the future Queen of these realms, was the central though youthful attraction. 'In such a season,' he wrote in his *Passages of a Working Life*, 'when the sun was scarcely high enough to have dried up the dews of Kensington's green alleys, as I passed along the broad central walk, I saw a group on the lawn before the Palace, which, to my mind, was a vision of exquisite loveliness. The Duchess of Kent, and her daughter, whose years then numbered nine, are breakfasting in the open air—a single page attending upon them at a respectful distance,—the matron looking on with eyes of love, whilst the "fair, soft English face" is bright with smiles. The world of fashion is not yet astir. Clerks and mechanics passing onward to their occupations are few, and they exhibit nothing of that vulgar curiosity which I think is more commonly found in the class of the merely rich, than in the ranks below them in the world's estimation. What a beautiful characteristic it seemed to me of the training of this royal girl, that she should not have been taught to shrink from the public eye—that she should not have been burthened with a premature conception of her probable high destiny—that she should enjoy the freedom and simplicity of a child's nature—that she should not be restrained when she starts up from the breakfast table and runs to gather a flower in the adjoining parterre—that her merry laugh should be as fearless as the notes of the thrush in the groves around her. I passed on and blessed her, and I thank God that I have lived to see the golden fruits of such training.'

A new departure of great importance to Charles Knight was initiated on the 26th of July, 1827. On that date there was a general meeting of the Committee of the Society for the Diffusion of Useful Knowledge, with James Mill in the chair, when Knight was appointed to undertake the superintendence of the Society's publications. At that time the only publications of the Society were the treatises in the *Library of Useful Knowledge*, issued fortnightly in sixpenny numbers. Brougham had most successfully opened the series with his 'Discourse on the Objects, Advantages, and Pleasures of Science.' It was intended to follow this up with manuals for self-education—clear, accurate, but not to be mastered without diligence and perseverance. Those which were issued made it clear that there was a great body of students—whether in colleges or Mechanics' Institutes, in busy towns or quiet villages—to whom such guides were welcome. Knight was general editor and manager of the series, as also of the *Almanacs* of the Society, to which reference has already been made. Throughout England and Scotland a great number of unstamped almanacs were surreptitiously sold by pedlars and hawkers, as well as privately in shops. Knight prepared a report on the subject which led to the total repeal of the Almanac Duty. In March, 1828, Knight became part proprietor of the *London Magazine*. To the first number of a new series, begun in April, he contributed an article on the 'Education of the People,' distinguished for its liberality and breadth of view.

In the interest of the Society's publications, Knight visited the principal towns of the kingdom—Birmingham, Liverpool, Manchester, Leeds, Sheffield, York, Nottingham, etc. The progress of humanising and elevating efforts on behalf of factory workers, and the working-classes generally, he thus describes in connection with a visit paid to Manchester: 'When I visited Manchester in 1828, five years were to elapse before children and young persons working in factories would be protected by law from working an unreasonable number of hours, and when Government Inspectors would watch over the preservation of their health and enforce the necessity for their education. The first Factory Act did not come into operation till January, 1834. It may well be imagined, therefore, that in the mills I looked upon male and female children, from seven years of age till seventeen (the employment of children under nine years was not then prohibited), who, scarcely coming under the cognisance of the masters,—for such children were subject to the control of the spinners,—were growing up in bodily weakness, in ignorance, and in vice. There was then little of kindly intercourse between the employers and the employed. The means of mental improvement for adults were very limited. A Mechanics' Institute and a Mechanics' and Apprentices' Library were indeed established in 1826. The "Athenæum" was built several years later. It was remarked in 1842 that there was no public park or green in which the labouring population could enjoy healthy exercise and recreation. "The Peel Park," the first of those free pleasure-grounds which have removed this disgrace from Manchester, was not opened till 1846. So rare was any endeavour to advance the condition of the workers, to promote their innocent enjoyments, to cherish and instruct their children in the spirit of a common humanity, that when two letters to Mr. Horner, printed in a periodical work of 1840, recorded what had been done in a new mill in 1832, erected near Manchester by Messrs. Greg, there was a good deal of incredulity as to the probable results of such a deviation from the usual course of neglect. These gentlemen had built cottages for the operatives; they had attached a garden to each house; they had Sunday-schools; they had arranged outdoor exercises for the hours of leisure. They had provided hot and cold baths; they had evening parties, to which the young people were invited by their employers. This solitary example soon had its imitators. A factory, whether for cotton, linen, or woollen fabrics, is not now a region especially suited for the cultivation of all the suspicions and hatreds that in former times made the relations between the capitalist and the labourer the most dangerous aspect of our social state.'

By Midsummer, 1829, Knight was again established in Pall Mall East as a publisher, though still retaining his connection with, and preparing works for, the Society for the Diffusion of Useful Knowledge. The Society included on its committee or among its members, Henry Brougham, Lord John Russell, William and Thomas Tooke, James Mill, Henry Hallam, Admiral Sir Francis Beaufort, Henry Bellenden Ker, Matthew Davenport Hill, Dr. Roget, Charles Bell, Dr. Neil Arnott, Dr. Maltby (afterwards Bishop of Durham), William Allen, the philanthropic Quaker, John William Lubbock, Lord Wrottesley, George Long, A. de Morgan, Leonard Horner, Herman Merivale, George Cornewall Lewis, Spring Rice, George Denman, Lords Auckland and Althorp, and Sir Henry Parnell. The reader will recognise among these many steadfast friends of education, as well as men who became eminent in various spheres. After the Reform era, it was no uncommon thing for five Cabinet Ministers to sit down at the Society's monthly dinner. George Lillie Craik was one of the most valuable writers connected with the Society, and his work entitled *The Pursuit of Knowledge under Difficulties* did great service among the working-classes, and attained a large sale. During the spring of 1830, Charles Knight vigorously pushed forward the monthly issue of the *Library of Entertaining Knowledge*—a series of half volumes which began in 1828, and to which

Knight himself contributed two volumes on 'The Menageries,' and Craik other two on 'Paris and its Historical Scenes.' Brougham, although he had been appointed Lord Chancellor in December, 1830, prepared an edition of Paley's *Natural Theology*, with Notes and an Introductory Discourse. The Society began the issue of a small series of shilling volumes, entitled *The Working Man's Companion*. Knight wrote a volume on *The Rights of Machinery*, for which he received the special thanks of the Useful Knowledge Committee. The book achieved a wonderful amount of good in convincing workmen, infuriated by the introduction and multiplication of machinery, of the groundlessness of their fears. It was a sober and argumentative little treatise, which contained no appeals to the passions, but rested the strength of its assaults against long-cherished prejudices upon a battery of facts. Printers and bookbinders were amongst those who long opposed the improvements in machinery, and *The Times* had great difficulties to encounter when its proprietors first made use of machinery.

The Useful Knowledge Society began the issue of the *Quarterly Journal of Education* in January, 1831. Charles Knight, as publisher, bore the risk of the undertaking. Professor Long was the editor, and the *Journal* was regularly continued for five years. It numbered among its contributors men of such eminence as Dr. Whately, Dr. Thirlwall, and Dr. Arnold, and it is scarcely necessary to add that the 4,000 pages of which the work consisted embraced a mass of information of original value and general interest. 'There was a great work to be accomplished to take the education of all classes out of the hands of incompetent and prejudiced instructors, and to free the young, upon whose judicious training the welfare of another generation would depend, from that discipline which united the extremes of laxity and severity, and that routine which, relying upon forms, so constantly neglected essentials.' In 1831, Knight again directly addressed himself to workmen in a volume which he wrote under the title of *The*

Rights of Industry, which had for its second title, Capital and Labour. This book exhibited the rights of workmen in connection with their duties, by proving that the interests of every member of Society, properly understood, were one and the same. It was ready for publication when the fatal riots at Bristol occurred, and the author added a stirring appeal to the great masses of the people to discountenance violence and outrage, which were the sure precursors of national decay and ruin. This volume was afterwards amalgamated with the one on machinery, and published under the title of *Knowledge is Power*. In 1832, following closely upon the appearance of *Chambers's Edinburgh Journal*, began the issue of the *Penny Magazine* under the auspices of the Useful Knowledge Society. Knight was appointed editor, and he likewise undertook the risk of publication. These were ventures in the right direction. Working-men soon began to look as eagerly for their mental food in the *Penny Magazine* as they did for their daily bread. Nothwithstanding the great initial difficulties which had to be surmounted, the *Magazine* was soon an established success, and by the end of 1832 the sale had reached no less than 200,000 in weekly numbers and monthly parts. This meant in all probability a million readers. Such a result must have been most gratifying to the projectors, for throughout the work there was no sentence that could inflame a vicious appetite, and no paragraph which could minister to prejudices and superstitions hitherto so common. There were no excitements for the lovers of the marvellous—no tattle or abuse for the gratification of a diseased taste for personality, and, above all, no party politics. The writers included Long, De Morgan, Craik, Macfarlane, Pringle the traveller, and John Kitto. The last-named came to occupy important relations towards Knight, for whom he executed a vast amount of good editorial work. Fourteen volumes in all were published of the *Penny Magazine*, before it was discontinued in 1845.

The Society then projected the *Penny Cyclopædia*, its greatest undertaking. The publication began in January, 1833, in weekly numbers and monthly parts. The work was entirely original, and with its supplement was completed in 1846. The total cost for literature and engraving was £42,000. The result to the originator was, unfortunately, a loss of £30,000. Had he not been hampered by the Society this disastrous result might have been averted. The work was under the superintendence of the Society, however, and soon after it began, the Committee determined that it must be enormously enlarged in its scope, and the price of the weekly numbers doubled. The extension of the quantity of the *Cyclopædia* destroyed its commercial value. Had it been a careful compilation, instead of an original work furnished by nearly two hundred contributors, it would have proved a fortune to Knight —instead of which it lost him one. The sale of the first year was double that of the fourth year, and that of the fourth double that of the eighth year. It then found its level, and became steady to the end, with a regular sale of 20,000. In the outset the sale had been 75,000 copies. Charles Knight told the story of this great publication in a volume entitled, *The Struggles of a Book against Excessive Taxation*. His revelations not only showed the difficulties he had to contend with, but demonstrated the amazing impetus which the undertaking must have given directly and indirectly to the printing industry. The following details are full of interest :—

'The *Penny Cyclopædia* and its Supplement were completed in 1846. The two works contain 15,764 pages, and the quantity of paper required to produce a single copy is two reams, each weighing thirty-five pounds. At the period of its completion the entire quantity of paper consumed was fifty thousand reams, the total weight of which amounted to one million seven hundred and fifty thousand pounds. Of this weight, twenty thousand reams, or seven hundred thousand pounds, paid the Excise duty of threepence per pound, amounting to £8,750 ; and the remaining thirty thousand reams paid the reduced duty of three-halfpence per pound (commencing in 1837) upon one million and fifty thousand pounds, amounting to £6,562. The total duty paid up to the completion of the *Cyclopædia* in 1846, was £15,312. Since that period, two thousand reams of paper have been used in reprinting, to correct the inequalities of the stock, making an addition of seventy thousand pounds, excised at £437. But further, the wrappers for the monthly parts have used fifteen hundred reams of paper, taxed at £500, and the milled boards employed in binding the volumes have been also taxed about £300. The total payment to the Excise by the *Penny Cyclopædia* has been £16,500.'

Having thus opened his case, Knight went on to elaborate it as follows:—

'I propose to show—

'1st. That the excessive burthen upon the great work, to which I have devoted seventeen years of toil and anxiety, has been the primary cause that the enterprise has not yet been remunerative.

'2nd. That the continuance of the paper, at the present rate of three-halfpence per pound, prevents me undertaking the publication of a new and improved edition, *upon its first plan of a continuous alphabetical arrangement.*

'1. The positive burthen of £16,500 imposed by the State upon the publication of the book, is far from representing the difficulty and loss which the payment has entailed upon the undertaking.

'It is well known that the amount of a duty upon raw material by no means represents the amount of the charge which it entails upon the manufacturer. Mr. MacCulloch and Mr. Porter rightly state that the price for a ream of one particular sort of printing paper was, in 1831, twenty-four shillings; in 1843, fifteen shillings and sixpence. From 1833 to 1837 the price of a ream of *Penny Cyclopædia* paper was thirty-three shillings; from 1838 to 1846 it was twenty-four shillings. The difference in price was nine shillings per ream; the amount of reduced duty was four shillings and fourpence-halfpenny. The paper-makers and the stationers doubled the tax. Mr. Mill, in his *Principles of Political Economy*, writes: "Whatever renders a larger capital necessary in any trade or business limits the competition in that business; and by giving something like a monopoly to a few dealers, enables them to keep up the price beyond what would afford the ordinary rate of profit."

'But even at the reduced rate it has been satisfactorily shown by my fellow-labourers, the Messrs. Chambers, that the duty enters one-third into the price. If the duty were removed, I could buy a ream of similar paper for seventeen shillings. The tax, preventing competition and giving undue advantage to capitalists, had the effect of making me pay for my paper, from 1833 to 1837, sixteen shillings a ream more than the price of untaxed paper would be, or £16,000 upon twenty thousand reams; and from 1838 to 1846, seven shillings per ream more than I should otherwise have paid, which upon thirty thousand reams amounts to £10,500. *The tax, therefore, operated as a burthen upon my publication to the extent of £26,500*, during its long and difficult progress to completion. The paper since used for reprints, and the paper for wrappers, has been raised in price £2,500 by the same process.

'*The struggles of one book against excessive taxation are, up to this point, to be measured by a burthen of £29,000.*

'But I have not yet done. The tax has been working against the *Penny Cyclopædia* for seventeen years, in the chronic form of interest and compound interest.

'It was not very long before the periodical sale settled into a regular quantity. The work became too extensive for the great bulk of purchasers. For the first few months of the publication the sale was double what it was at the end of the year. The sale of the first year doubled that of the fourth year. The sale of the fourth year doubled that of the eighth year, and then found its level and became steady to the end, reduced from fifty-five thousand at the commencement to twenty thousand at the conclusion. Every publisher of a periodical work knows the accumulation of stock that must inevitably take place with a falling demand. There never was a period after the third year of which I had less than five reams of the *Penny Cyclopædia* in my warehouse; upon which duty had been paid for some portion at the high rate, and for some at the low, averaging £1,500. In 1841 there were in my warehouse twelve hundred reams upon which the high duty, expiring in 1837, had been paid. I consider the accumulating interest in this investment, in actually paid duty, upon dead stock, to have amounted, in the seventeen years during which I have been labouring to sell that stock, to £1,500, and, including the interest upon the extra price charged by the paper manufacturer, to a charge of £3,000.

'And here, then, will the usual conclusion arise, that the publisher has not borne this load of *thirty-two thousand pounds* imposed by the State upon the *Penny Cyclopædia*, but the purchasers of the *Penny Cyclopædia*. My answer is very direct. Had that sum of £32,000 been actually saved to me, I should not have been a pound richer by the publication of the *Penny Cyclopædia*. But with the saving I should not have been to that amount poorer. The outlay was so great, that it could never pay its expenses under a sale of thirty-six thousand copies with the high duty. In the first five years that average number was printed; but the accumulation of stock locked up £10,000. Under the low duty it paid its expenses at thirty thousand copies. The actual average sale during the nine years of that duty was twenty thousand. It would have required that there should be no Paper Duty at all to have paid its expenses on a sale of twenty thousand. Had the duty not been reduced by one-half at the end of 1836, I could not, by any possibility, have carried on the work. As it was, I struggled to the end.

'2. The reduced Paper Duty, as I have undertaken to show, prevents me making the best use of the valuable copyright which remains to me, now that the accumulated stock is in great part exhausted.

'I was advised to propose a subscription for an entirely new edition. The highest personage in the realm accorded me her support, and so did her admirable Consort, who is doing for Science and Industry what is worth far more than any money value. Some of the most eminent in the walks of intellect also came forward to aid me. Of the support of the members of the Legislature which taxed me during fourteen years, I have not much to boast. I have given up the design. Upon a sale that would have merely returned my new outlay, the Paper Duty would have burthened the work to the extent of £3,000. Its abandonment would have lightened my task to the extent of making the work yield me as high a profit from three thousand subscribers as from four thousand subscribers with the duty continued. With this encouragement I should have gone on.

'There is a steady demand for the existing edition of the *Penny Cyclopædia*, to the extent of two hundred and fifty sets annually. The Paper Duty prevents me meeting this demand with any moderate commercial profit. The technical explanation is not difficult to be understood. If I print two hundred and fifty copies only, I use five hundred reams of paper, of which the duty is 4/6 each, and the necessary increase of manufacturer's price 2/6, making a charge, arising out of the duty, of 7/- per ream, or £175 upon two hundred and fifty copies. But in printing only two hundred and fifty copies I have to pay for the press-work as high as 15/- per ream, whereas if I printed five hundred, I should only pay 10/-. As the number of a book first printed increases, the cost of press-work or machine-work diminishes; and for this reason the tax upon a raw material of a book or paper, increasing the risk of printing a large impression, compels a smaller impression at a higher cost. But if there were no Paper Duty I should print five hundred copies, by which I should save £350 in the price of paper, and £250 in the price of press-work, making a saving of £600. This outlay of £600 is imposed upon me absolutely by the existence of the Paper Duty; and that fact will possibly compel me to give up reprinting a book which has done more for the achievement of sound knowledge and general education in these kingdoms than any work ever produced in any country. That £600 saved would afford me an income which would allow me to invest capital in such a reprint. Printing only two hundred and fifty copies at the present price of paper, a set of this book would cost me £1,000. My net profit upon that outlay would not be ten per cent.

'And with all this danger and difficulty—with "this lion in my path"—I am not yet beaten. I have my valuable copyright of the *Penny Cyclopædia* remaining to me; and I have passed many an anxious hour in seeing how I can best turn it to account. I am about to publish a series of separate cyclopædias, with large improvements, and I begin with a *Cyclopædia of British Geography*, and a *Cyclopædia of Arts and Industry*. Let me show the exact track which "the lion in my path" drives me to seek; and then some of those legislators who find that a fashionable novel, sold at a guinea and a half, pays about fourpence Paper Duty, and thence conclude that it is the lightest of taxes, and by all means should be preserved—especially as books, as they hold, are not necessaries of life—some of those who

"Hate not learning worse than toad or asp,"

may know what it is to maintain a tax upon knowledge, struggling to preserve its high rank and its useful extension amidst the widest competition of cheapness.

'Upon these four volumes, estimated to contain about three thousand pages, I shall expend £1,500 upon new editorial labour. I shall further expend about £1,000 upon new plates and maps. The printer's charge for setting up the types will be £800, and the cost of stereotyping will be £500. Add for advertising, £200, and I have thus to expend £4,000 as first outlay, whether I sell five hundred copies or five thousand. At the present cost of paper, three thousand copies (the least number I could print with advantage) will amount to £1,500; the press-work will cost £500; total, £6,000. The three thousand copies, produced upon this scale, will exactly cover my outlay, without a shilling profit. But let us see how the account would stand with the price of paper reduced one-third by the abolition of the duty. My course would then be to print four thousand copies, and not stereotype, which process is chiefly employed to save the outlay of capital in taxed paper. The first outlay is, therefore, £3,500; the paper for four thousand copies, at the lower untaxed price, would cost me £1,333; the press-work £600 (reduced per ream on account of the larger number). I produce, therefore, four thousand copies for £5,433, instead of three thousand copies for £6,000. I expend less by £567, and I have one thousand copies left to sell for my profit. I could sell four thousand copies, under these circumstances, more easily than three thousand as I now stand, for I could afford to advertise more freely, and to offer higher inducements to retailers. This is something different from a fourpenny tax upon a fashionable novel.'

The *Gallery of Portraits*, which Knight next published under the superintendence of the Society, was also next to the *Cyclopædia* in its costliness of production. The task of selecting subjects occupied the Committee from the beginning of 1832 to the Midsummer of 1834, and British and foreign statesmen, warriors, divines, men of science and letters, and artists were all assigned their due place of honour in the work. The first monthly number, published at half-a-crown, and containing three portraits with biographies, appeared in May, 1832. Arthur H. Hallam wrote a number of biographies for the work, and De Quincey contributed a fine memoir of Milton. Charles Knight was an early opponent of the newspaper stamp, as well as of the Paper Duty, and had much to do with securing their repeal. The 13th of August, 1836, was a day of rejoicing for him, and for the press generally, for on that day two Acts of Parliament received the Royal Assent, which materially influenced all the commercial arrangements for rendering knowledge, political or literary, more accessible to the bulk of the people. The first of these reduced the duties on first-class paper from threepence per pound to three-halfpence, so that the former tax of three-halfpence upon second-class paper should apply to paper of all descriptions. The second reduced the stamp on newspapers from fourpence to a penny. In his work on *Post Office Reform*, Rowland Hill observes: 'When the expediency of entirely abolishing the newspaper stamp and allowing newspapers to pass through the Post Office for a penny each was under consideration, it was proposed by Mr. Charles Knight, the publisher, that the postage on newspapers might be collected by selling stamped wrappers at a penny each. Availing myself of this excellent suggestion, I proposed the following arrangement,—let the stamped covers and sheets of paper be supplied to the public from the Stamp Office or Post Office, as may be most convenient, and sold at such a price as to include the postage. Letters so stamped might be put into the letter-box as at present.' It would not be far wrong to say that Knight's suggestion led to the adoption of the penny postage stamp.

Early in 1836 Knight issued the first part of the *Pictorial Bible*. The idea of the work was derived from Germany. John Kitto was editor, and he also furnished notes upon such subjects as had come under his observation during his travels in the East. Fine wood-engravings were given, embracing the scriptural designs of great painters, landscape scenes, eastern costumes, the remains of ancient architecture, and botanical and zoological specimens. The work occupied two years and a half in its publication, and notwithstanding the costliness of the engravings it proved profitable. After its completion came *Palestine*, a new work undertaken by Dr. Kitto. This was succeeded by *The Thousand and One Nights*, or the *Arabian Nights' Entertainments*, a new translation from authentic Arabic originals, by Edward Lane, with admirable illustrations by William Harvey. The *Pictorial History of England*—a work of still greater magnitude—was begun in 1840. It extended to eight volumes, and occupied seven years in a regular monthly course of publication. Charles MacFarlane undertook the larger department of civil and military history, and G. Lillie Craik wrote the history of religion, literature, and commerce. Assistance was rendered by other writers in various departments. Half the whole work was occupied with the reign of George the Third only, and this disproportion proved fatal to its success. Still, with its continuations down to the present day, the work holds its own, and has never been superseded by any other. *London*, another serial which was begun in 1841 and completed in 1844, included among its contributors Craik, Planché, Fairholt, Saunders, Dodd, and Weir. The story of the great Metropolis is told with wonderful interest, past and present scenes in its history being realised with great skill. It is to Charles Knight we owe that graphic title of 'The Silent Highway' as applied to the Thames. The reign of the watermen is traced from the time of John Norman, first Mayor of London, who was rowed to Westminster instead of riding, to the days when even the watermen had become a portion of the antiquities of London—the days of the penny steamboat. Then we get sketches of the Metropolis itself, from Hyde Park in the west to Rag Fair in the extreme east.

In view of the present enormous development of the newspaper and periodical press, it is interesting to note that on Saturday, May 4th, 1844—exactly half a century ago,—the number of weekly periodical works issued in London was about sixty. The monthly issue of periodical literature was unequalled by any similar commercial operation in Europe, there being 227 monthly works sent out on the last day of May, 1844, from Paternoster Row, in addition to 38 works published quarterly. The number of newspapers published in the United Kingdom was 447, and of these, 79 were London newspapers. These figures seemed surprising at the time, but they are small indeed compared with present figures. The total number of periodicals and newspapers in the United Kingdom in 1890 was upwards of 3,000, and the newspapers published in London alone numbered 646. The circulation of these counts by millions.

Knight's *Pictorial Shakespeare* was a work in which the projector took a special interest. It was in eight volumes. The publication began in 1839, and went on for two years. Knight himself wrote the biography of the immortal poet, of whom he was an ardent student and worshipper. Indeed, Miss Alice A. Clowes, Knight's granddaughter, in her sketch of the publisher, states that the various editions of Shakespeare which he edited 'were amongst the pleasantest labours of his life.' She adds these personal details concerning Charles Knight: 'The enthusiasm he felt for everything relating to the poet's genius and career never left him, and to his latest day he loved to quote a line here and there from the writings he knew so well. As children, my brothers and sisters and I listened with perhaps more awe than appreciation, to the quotations, which some chance reference in our idle talk would call forth from the lips of our keen-eyed and sharp-eared grandfather. He very seldom joined in ordinary conversation. When all around him were prattling, as people with the best intentions will prattle, he would sit with his head rather bent down, as if lost in thought; but, if any remark beyond the commonplace were uttered, be it by man, woman, or child, the head would be raised and the eye brighten at once, and words of wisdom would be spoken. It was always a trial to him to put up with assumption and ignorance of any kind, and as children we were rather afraid of expressing our youthful opinion in his hearing, which was, no doubt, very good for us.'

Altogether, Knight published eight different editions of Shakespeare. The first of these was followed by a new undertaking called the *Store of Knowledge for all Readers*. It consisted of a series of original treatises by various authors, dealing with such diversified subjects as Taxation, the Post Office, Europe, the House, the Mineral Kingdom, Schools, Commercial Intercourse with China, etc. At a banquet given at the Albion Tavern in recognition of Knight's services to literature, with special reference to the *Penny Cyclopædia*, Lord Brougham took the chair. In proposing the health of the guest, his lordship ' dwelt on the various services which, in connection with the Useful Knowledge Society, he had been enabled to render towards the advancement of society in moral as well as intellectual knowledge; pointed out especially the great service he did to the State in writing and publishing his two little works, *The Rights of Industry* and *The Results of Machinery*—two publications which, at a time of great public excitement, were eminently conducive to allaying the reckless spirit which, in 1830, was leading multitudes to destroy property and break up machines. He also pointed out what Mr. Knight had done in editing and illustrating Shakespeare; in the projection and carrying on of the *Penny Magazine*, and the completion of the *Penny Cyclopædia*.'

In publishing an account of this gathering, the *Athenæum* added, as equally significant of the change which was coming over the spirit of the age, that the Queen had commanded that copies of Mr. Knight's forthcoming publications, entitled *Knight's Weekly Volume*, should be supplied to the libraries established at all the Royal palaces. The volumes began with a biography of *William Caxton, the First English Printer*, by Charles Knight himself. The projector was desirous of seeing the principle of the Book Club established in the Provinces, and in this desire he was cordially seconded by Charles Dickens. It is curious that one of the first successful efforts to establish a Cheap Book Club was made by Robert Burns. Knight received signal assistance in connection with his Weekly Volumes from Harriet Martineau. In 1845 he began the issue of *Knight's Penny Magazine*, a vehicle of light but good literature, which was followed in 1846 by a second series. The work was fairly successful for the brief period it ran, but there seemed no hope of its progressing, so it was given up. In the last-named year, the Society for the Diffusion of Useful Knowledge announced the suspension of its operations. In doing this, the Committee first alluded to the heavy loss sustained on the incomplete *Biographical Dictionary*, and then added: 'The Society's work is done, for its greatest object is achieved—fully, fairly, and permanently. The public is supplied with *cheap* and *good* literature to an extent which the most sanguine friend of human improvement could not, in 1826, have hoped to have witnessed in twenty years.' But although good literature was now abundant, bad literature was almost equally prevalent, in the shape of blood and thunder romances, which appealed to the passions of the young and the ignorant. Yet there was hope for the future for literature of the higher class, if only the Paper Duty could be removed. Charles Knight remarks on this head: 'My conviction that the cheap press would purify itself was realised in another decade. I had given a name to the wholesome literature for the people, "The Fountain." The noxious I had called "The Sewer." But I contended, as I had ever done, that the Paper Duty was an insurmountable barrier to the diffusion of publications that should combine the qualities of literary excellence and extreme cheapness. I maintained that to thrust out the noxious publications, the supply of the higher class must be abundant. The quality of the writing must be of the best, for to write well for the people is the rarest of literary qualifications; lastly, the price must as nearly as possible approach to the cost of the mischievous production. Whatever interferes with the circulation of the higher periodicals by increasing their price—whatever tends to render a false economy necessary, by lowering their payment for the best literary labour—interferes with one of the most important instruments of National Education, using the term in its highest sense. Such were the injurious consequences of the Paper Duty. That long disputed question has now been settled. The total repeal of this impost took place after my commercial career was in a great degree closed.'

Charles Knight was a determined opponent of the prize system in literature. Originally started with the object of encouraging talent, the system has wofully deteriorated of recent years. Even thirty years ago Knight wrote: 'The prize system has become one of the notable expedients of publishing quackery. The word prize is altogether a delusion. It tempts scores of uneducated young persons to enter upon a competition for a reward for literary labours which seems to them magnificent. They are wholly ignorant of the nature of the literary market, in which the real prizes are ready to be earned by those who possess the requisite qualifications. Instead of being an encouragement to struggling genius, it holds out a temptation to mediocrity to travel out of its proper road to honour.'

For some years Knight was engaged in disseminating a number of pictorial works in the neighbourhood of the great manufacturing towns and other populous districts, by the class of book-hawkers known as canvassers. Four of these books, forming seven volumes in folio, were of a quite superior order, and were entitled respectively, *Pictorial Museum of Animated Nature*, *Pictorial Sunday Book*, *Old England*, and the *Pictorial Gallery of Arts*. The working-man's family which could boast of the possession of these volumes was in a very fortunate position. After Knight disposed of them to a firm of canvassing publishers proper they continued to have a large sale. In 1847 Knight commenced editing and publishing, in monthly parts, his *Half Hours with the Best Authors*. Each extract was preceded by a biographical sketch of the author, and the compiler states that the work furnished him with a really delightful occupation for fifty-two weeks. The *Half Hours* still deservedly maintain their popularity, and Knight would be well entitled to lasting remembrance were it but for this one work alone. Yet it is but one claim out of a hundred that he has upon posterity. In 1849 was completed *The Land We Live in*, an important preparation for writing the history of England. The scope of this work was very wide, for it embraced the courts and offices of government, legislation and the administration of justice; the halls of science, art, and letters; the seats of education; the emporiums of commerce and manufactures; the triumphs of steam and of the locomotive; the havens of maritime power; the material improvements of the day viewed in connection with the moral; the manners and social characteristics of the people; and many other features. During that year of political turmoil, 1848, Knight set up a weekly journal, *The Voice of the People*, whose object was to combat the ideas of the Chartists, which were then considered to be dangerous and revolutionary. But the paper was too moderate to make any impression in times of great excitement, and, as it was too honest to be abusive, its career soon came to a close. In 1849, and again in 1853, London suffered severely from the cholera scourge. At the latter date Knight was publisher to the General Board of Health, of which the Commissioners were Lord Shaftesbury, Edwin Chadwick, and Dr. Southwood Smith. Finding that the directions given by public bodies and individuals for family guidance under a visitation of cholera were too technical and elaborate to be useful to persons of imperfect education, Knight drew up an address, homely and practical, adapted for all ranks. His *Plain Advice* was printed as a broadside, and was purchased and distributed throughout the country by the Local Boards of Health. The circulation of this sheet was upwards of one hundred thousand, a fact which demonstrates the possibility of communicating with the public at large on sanitary matters, through the combination of local activity with central regulation.

The movement in 1847 for the purchase of Shakespeare's House at Stratford had a warm supporter in Charles Knight. He took a prominent part in raising the necessary subscriptions, and when a performance was given at Covent Garden Theatre to make up the deficiency which was still found to exist he was requested by the Committee to write a Prologue, to be spoken by Mr. Phelps. When the house had been purchased, Charles Dickens organised a series of amateur performances at the Haymarket, in aid of the fund for the endowment of a perpetual curatorship of Shakespeare's House. Payne Collier, Charles Knight, and Peter Cunningham were directors of the general arrangements, and Dickens himself was stage manager. *The Merry Wives of Windsor* was performed on the 15th of May, with a cast which included Messrs. Mark Lemon, Charles Romer, Charles Dickens, John Leech, John Forster, Frank Stone, G. H. Lewes, Dudley Costello, Frederick Dickens, Henry Cole, George Cruikshank, Augustus Dickens, Augustus Egg, and F. Eaton ; and Mrs. Cowden Clarke, and Misses Fortescue, Kenworthy, Romer, and Robins. Performances were given in the provinces as well as in London. Difficulties arose as to the appointment of a curator at Stratford, so Dickens and his friends bought an annuity with the proceeds of their labours for Sheridan Knowles, the well-known dramatic author. From this time forward Dickens and Knight had many pleasant relations together, and both were members of the Amateur Company of the Guild of Literature and Art, matured at Sir Edward Bulwer Lytton's seat of Knebworth in November, 1850, when there was an amateur performance of *Every Man in his Humour*, under the management of Dickens. Various town and country performances were afterwards given, and with the proceeds the Guild erected a number of houses for literary men on Bulwer Lytton's estate, near Stevenage.

The first Great Exhibition in 1851 was hailed by Charles Knight as a welcome advance in the free intercourse of peoples, and in 1855 he acted as a juror at the Paris Universal Exhibition. Among the Reports on this Exhibition laid before Parliament was one written by Knight, on 'Letter Press and Copper-plate Printing.' When Parliament met in 1855 there was a general impression that the penny duty stamp would be entirely abolished, except for the purpose of transmitting a newspaper by post. The Chancellor of the Exchequer, Sir George Cornewall Lewis, requested Charles Knight to inform him what was the greatest circulation of each number of the *Penny Magazine* at any time. In giving him this information Knight referred him to a little work he had just published on *The Old Printer and the Modern Press*, in which he had taken a rapid view of the circulation and character of penny periodicals at the beginning of 1854. Of four of these a million sheets were then sold weekly. In his letter to the Chancellor of the Exchequer the author said: 'The change in the character of Penny Periodicals during the last five or six years, from the lowest ribaldry and positive indecency to a certain propriety— and of which frivolity is the chief blemish—is an assurance to me that the cheapening of newspapers by the removal of the stamp will not let in that flood of sedition and blasphemy which some appear to dread. The character of the mass of readers is improved. In my little book I have opposed the removal of the stamp, chiefly on the ground that a quantity of local papers would start up that would be devoted to mere parish politics and sectarian squabbles, instead of being national in their objects; and that would huddle together the worst of criminal trials and police cases, without attempting to suggest any sound principles of politics, or furnish any useful information. To provide a corrective to this, I have devised the plan detailed in the circular which I left with you. I sent out an intelligent traveller into the Midland districts last week, confidentially to explain this plan to active printers in towns that had no local paper; and his report shows that the principle will be eagerly adopted.'

The plan which he had devised was founded upon his old newspaper experience, during which, for several years, three-fourths of the local papers of Berkshire and Buckinghamshire were printed at the *Express* Office at Windsor and one-fourth at a branch office at Aylesbury. In connection with a highly respectable printing firm he began the publication of the *Town and Country Newspaper* immediately upon the repeal of the Stamp Duty in 1855. The complex and expensive organisation required for supplying a few impressions for certain districts prevented the plan from becoming a success at that time, but it has since been largely adopted, and hundreds of provincial newspapers are now partly printed in London, or else receive columns of stereotyped matter from London. In 1855 there were 350 populous towns in Great Britain without a local paper of any kind. This condition of things was remedied within a few years after the repeal of the Stamp Duty. There were many timorous persons, however, who thought that the influence of the newspaper press was inimical to good and quiet government. Arnold of Rugby was not one of these, for long before this period he wrote to the Archbishop of Dublin: 'I think that a newspaper alone can help to cure the evil which newspapers have done and are doing.'

Turning to the publication of useful and interesting books, we find that the number of works published under the names of collections, libraries, series, etc., increased enormously from 1835 to 1863. The compiler of the *English Catalogue*, issued in the latter year, adduced these remarkable facts on the subject: 'Nearly all the leading publishers appear to have engaged, during this period of twenty-eight years, in a species of publication in which Constable led the way. We have four Library Series by Bentley, one of Standard Novels; cheap editions of celebrated publications, by Blackwood. We have eleven Libraries and Series issued by Bohn—Antiquarian; British Classics; Cheap Series; Classical Library; Ecclesiastical Library; English Gentleman's Library, Extra Volumes (not ladies' reading); Historical Library; Illustrated Library; Philological and Philosophical Library; Scientific Library; and Standard Library. It cannot be doubted that many of Mr. Bohn's volumes, which may be counted by hundreds, have brought books of authority, whose scarcity or high price precluded their general circulation, within the reach of the great body of readers. William and Robert Chambers, with whose useful labours during more than thirty years the world is well acquainted, have their Educational Series, their Library for Young People, and their People's Editions. Chapman & Hall have their Standard Editions of Popular Authors, in which we find the works of W. H. Ainsworth, Mrs. Gaskell, Miss Mulock, Thackeray, and Trollope. Murray's Family Library of eighty separate books is still in demand—his Home and Colonial Library, his Railway Reading, and his British Classics, of later date, hold their place amongst the books that have not a mere ephemeral popularity. Knight takes his place as a publisher of The Library of Entertaining Knowledge; of Classics; of Journey Books; of the Library for the Times; of Weekly and Monthly Volumes. Longmans have *Lardner's Cabinet Cyclopædia* of 132 volumes, now issued at a reduced rate, as the collections of many other publishers have been reduced, to meet the pressure of new competition. They have the more modern series of the Traveller's Library, comprising about 150 books. The Parlour Library, chiefly of novels, good, bad, and indifferent, comprises about 300 separate books. The Religious Tract Society has an extensive series of volumes, not professedly religious, in which it is very difficult to see what is the difference between their adopted children and the best of their secular competitors. The same may be said of the general publications of the Christian Knowledge Society. Routledge has collections and libraries almost bewildering from their extent,—American Poets, Books for the Country, British Poets, Cheap Series of 269 works, Railway Library of 327 works,—amongst which we find Bulwer's novels, purchased at what was deemed an extravagant price for the right of reprinting, but the value of which concession was better estimated by the publisher than by his critics. Routledge gives us another series of Standard Novels; and, by way of a "half-pennyworth of bread to this intolerable deal of sack," we have the Useful Library. Smith, Elder, & Company have their Shilling Series of Standard Works of Fiction. I conclude this enumeration with Weale's Rudimentary Series, which comprises 144 works, chiefly on scientific subjects.'

Since 1863 the book trade of the United Kingdom has advanced by still more rapid strides. Taking the issue of books in series and single books, there were three times as many books published in 1853 as there had been in 1828. The annual production in the period 1877-87 averaged 4,000 volumes; of new editions, 1,400. The number of new books issued in 1887 was 4,410; the new editions, 1,276. In 1892 the issue exceeded 6,000. The number of copies issued of these works by all the publishing houses is reckoned by tens of millions annually. Indeed, some idea of the total gigantic sale may be gathered from the fact that in 1885 one London publisher alone reported that he printed, in round numbers, 6,000,000 books annually, of which 4,000,000 were bound, being at the rate of about 14,000 books per day. Weekly and monthly periodical literature has advanced by equally rapid strides. At the end of 1831 there were issued 177 monthly publications; in 1833 there were 236; in 1853, 362; and in 1888, 1,500. The number at the present time exceeds 2,000, and the annual sale reaches millions of copies. The sale of newspapers in the United Kingdom has increased at a still more astounding rate, and a year's issue from the whole of the newspaper press would amount to thousands of millions. Charles Knight was one of the worthy pioneers of the vast industries represented by the book, periodical, and newspaper trades.

The two most important works of Knight's later years were the *English Cyclopædia* and the *Popular History of England.* With regard to the former work, Knight says: 'The new *Cyclopædia* was arranged in four divisions:—Geography, Natural History, Biography, Arts and Sciences. The first two of these divisions were proceeding at the same time, and were each completed in two years and a half. What a store of new materials had been gathering together for the use of the geographer and the naturalist that required to be set forth in the remodelled *Cyclopædia.*' These two divisions were succeeded by that of Biography. If no other additions had been required than the introduction of names of living persons, the new literary labour would have been of no small amount—sufficient, indeed, to form a separate book, not so large but essentially as complete as the *Biographie des Contemporains.* This Biographical division, in six volumes, was completed in 1858. The division of Arts and Sciences included a great number of miscellaneous subjects, not capable of being introduced into the more precise arrangement of the three previous departments. It was completed in eight volumes in 1861. In my introduction to the eighth volume I said: "It has been produced last in the series, that nothing of new invention and discovery in Science—nothing of progressive improvement in the Arts—might be omitted."'

The second important work, the *Popular History of England,* extended to twelve volumes. Its publication began in 1855, and it was completed in 1862. The origin and nature of this undertaking have been explained by Knight in this interesting passage :—

'In 1854 I was instigated by an article in *The Times* seriously to contemplate the task of writing a general history of England. Lord John Russell had delivered an address at Bristol on the study of history, and the leading journal took up the subject of the noble speaker's complaint "that we have no other history of England than Hume's"—that "when a young man of eighteen asks for a history of England, there is no resource but to give him Hume." I had published *The Pictorial History of England* some years before—in many respects a valuable history, but one whose limits had gone far beyond what, as its projector, I had originally contemplated. I altogether rejected the idea of making an abridgment of that history. Many materials for a *History of the People* had been collected by me without any immediate object of publication. The remarks of *The Times* led me to depart from my original design of writing a Domestic History of England apart from its Public History. Upon a more extended plan I would endeavour to trace through our long-continued annals the essential connection between our political history and our social. To accomplish this, I would not keep the People in the background, as in many histories, and I would call my work *The Popular History of England*. For more than a year I was gradually preparing for my task, and was ready to begin the printing at the end of 1855. It was to be published in monthly parts. My publishers desiring that the first part should contain an introduction setting forth the objects of a new history of England, I was induced to explain my motives for undertaking it, with a sincerity which perhaps may be deemed imprudent. It may be as imprudent for the historian as for the statesman to make any general profession of principles at the outset of his career. The succession of events in either case might modify his past convictions. But I have no reason to depart in letter or spirit from what I wrote: "The People, if I understand the term rightly, means the Commons of these realms, and not any distinct class or section of the population. Ninety years ago, Goldsmith called the 'middle order of mankind' the 'People,' and those below them the 'Rabble.' We have outlived all this. A century of thought and action has widened and deepened the foundations of the State. This People, then, want to find, in the history of their country, something more than a series of annals, either of policy or war. In connection with a faithful narrative of public affairs, they want to learn their own history —how they have grown out of slavery, out of feudal wrong, out of regal despotism,—into constitutional liberty,—and the position of the greatest estate of the realm." In the summer of 1858 I had completed four volumes of my history, reaching the period of the Revolution of 1688. In the postscript to the fourth volume I endeavoured to illustrate the principle, so well defined by my friend, Mr. Samuel Lucas, in a lecture on Social Progress, that the history of every nation "has been in the main sequential"—that each of its phases has been "the consequence of some prior phase, and the natural prelude to that which succeeded it." I pointed out that the early history of the Anglican Church was to be traced in all the subsequent elements of our ecclesiastical condition; that upon the Roman and Saxon civilisation were founded many of the principles of government which still preserved their vitality; that the Norman despotism was absorbed by the Anglo-Saxon freedom; and that the recognition of the equal rights of all men before the Law was the only mode by which feudality could maintain itself. "From the despotism of Richard the Second to the abdication of James the Second, every act of national resistance was accomplished by the union of classes, and was founded upon some principle of legal right for which there was legal precedent. Out of the traditional and almost instinctive assertion of the popular privileges have come new developments of particular reforms, each adapted to its own age, but all springing out of that historical experience which we recognise as Constitutional."'

The preparation of his *Popular History* occupied Knight unremittingly for a seventh part of his working life. With the exception of three chapters on the Fine Arts, the work was wholly written by himself. In its composition, he endeavoured to set forth the inestimable advantages of liberty; to look with a tolerant judgment even upon those who had sought to govern securely by governing absolutely; to trace with calmness the efforts of those who had imperilled the national independence by foreign assault or domestic treason, but never to forget that a just love of country was consistent with historical truth; and to carry forward, as far as within the power of one who had watched joyfully and hopefully the great changes of a generation, that spirit of improvement, which had been more extensively and permanently called forth in the times of which his concluding volume treated than in the whole previous period from the Revolution of 1688. In breaking a lance in defence of his *History*, Knight observed that 'to trace the course of long and fierce struggles between the Crown and the Barons; of grievances producing rebellion; of conflicting claims of royal houses; of political factions engrafted on theological sects; and of factions again fermenting—this is not necessarily to minister to a democratic spirit, as those would infer who choose to mistake the true intent and meaning of the word *Popular* as applied to a History of England.'

In 1864, Knight completed his autobiographical work entitled, *Passages of a Working Life during Half a Century*. It was divided into three epochs, and opened with a Prelude of Early Reminiscences. The last words of this record run as follows: 'To my Wife; to her who has been the best friend, the adviser, the sympathiser, the consoler, during half a century of my working life, I inscribe this record, with a grateful heart to the Giver of all Good.' In the course of this biographical sketch, I have quoted several passages from Knight's autobiographical work; and I now reproduce a final extract from it, which may be taken as the author's apologia, in going down the hill of life:—

'A political economist, who professes to speak the opinion of "the middle class" of this country, says that "the life of a man who leaves no property, or family provision, of his own acquiring, at his death, is felt to have been a failure." I do not accept the doctrine as a true expression of the genera feeling. There are thousands of the commercial class and the professional class who have not been inordinately anxious to gather together "muckhills" of riches, to be spread abroad when their accumulators are gone. Nevertheless, these have not been like the "wicked and unprofitable servant," who buried the one talent which his Master entrusted to him. Few of them, probably, have neglected to make some modest provision against absolute poverty which the system of Life Assurance affords. But, if they have wisely incurred a liberal expenditure of capital upon the education of their children; if they have placed their sons in positions where they may "learn and labour truly to get their own living"; if they have qualified their daughters to discharge sensibly and gracefully, whether as child, wife, or mother, the private and public duties which render the English lady the promoter of all social dignity and enjoyment, they have been amongst the most provident accumulators. They have laid up a profitable fund out of their consumption, by preserving their families, whilst they have lived amongst them, in the highest point of efficacy for future production. This doctrine may not be strictly the *science* of "the wealth of nations," but I believe that it has something to do with "the happiness of the greatest number."

'In many worldly respects my own life has not been "a failure." It was probably a blessing in disguise, that circumstances, over which I had little control, long ago taught me that it was not for me to make a fortune, or to indulge in the ostentation of ample means. I have been content with the "plain living" that the philosophic poet sets above a life "only drest for show." If "high thinking" has not been altogether wanting, I owe this to a love of books, and perhaps not less to the companionship of educated and intelligent friends. I believe that I have made very few enemies. Within my own proper sphere I have had as much social enjoyment as is compatible with the belief that "the chief end of man" is duty and not pleasure. The fiftieth anniversary of my marriage has just passed. Half a century of congenial wedlock is a blessing accorded to few. It brought with it the further blessing of a family united in love; of a home where cheerful faces ever welcomed me. During forty years I had known no great sorrow. I had not been bereft of any one of those who were the joy of my manhood and the comfort of my age. A dark cloud has cast its solemn shadow over my Golden Bridal; but I feel that our griefs, and the consolations which should come with them, are for ourselves, and not for the outer world. Taken as a whole, my life has been a happy one.'

In 1865 Knight wrote and published a volume entitled *Shadows of the Old Booksellers;* in 1868 he made a selection from the great letter-writers under the title of *Half-Hours with the Best Letter-Writers and Autobiographers;* and the same year he prepared, for the last time, the *Companion to the Almanac* for 1869, his concluding contribution to it being a paper on 'Mural Records of Pedestrian Tourists.' He had an excellent memory, and worked rapidly, and it was only towards the last that he was compelled to dictate what he wrote, in consequence of failing sight. His last original work was a novel in one volume, written in 1867, and entitled *Begg'd at Court.* It was founded on historical facts, which his retentive memory had enabled him to store up for future use.

His granddaughter thus writes of Knight and his friends:

I can recall him, in later middle life, or earlier old age, as incessantly working. Nothing was ever allowed to interfere with his daily routine of writing, except his frequent attacks of illness, which would incapacitate him for only a day or two. Never a strong man, he was debarred from the pleasure of much social intercourse, although greatly enjoying the society of a few chosen friends. Amongst these may be mentioned, at various periods of his life, the names of Leigh Hunt, John Moultrie, Winthrop Mackworth Praed, Barry St. Leger, De

Quincey, Macaulay, Lord Brougham, the Coleridges, Archbishop Sumner, John Wilson Croker, Henry Malden, Augustus de Morgan, Professor Wilson, Professor Long, Professor Key, Miss Martineau, E. H. Locker, J. R. Planché, George Lillie Craik, Matthew Davenport Hill, Sir Rowland Hill, Thackeray —but with him the acquaintance was only slight,—Charles Dickens, Douglas Jerrold, George Cruikshank, etc., etc. A strong attachment existed between Charles Knight and Douglas Jerrold. At a dinner-party at which they were both present, the conversation had turned upon epitaphs. Douglas Jerrold, on rising to take leave, said, shaking hands with Charles Knight: "We have given epitaphs for each one here; I will now give one to you—Good-(K)night!" On the day of the great humorist's death, Charles Knight walked up and down in front of the house until the blinds were drawn down.'

The published letters of Dickens, Jerrold, Moultrie, Croker, De Quincey, De Morgan, Shirley Brooks, and other friends, show the high esteem with which Knight was regarded by his contemporaries. Happy was it for the busy old man that he could work almost to the end. When for a brief closing period he was unable to do this, he would take a keen delight in listening to a simple old English ballad: ''There would come to the aged face, bent down, with the eyes half closed, and the long silvery hair thrown back from the high and wide forehead, a look once more of enjoyment and of interest.'

There still remain a few personal details to note in connection with Knight's life and character. Although he was fond of change—especially in regard to his residences—he retained to the last a vivid interest in Windsor, as the place of his birth and his early home. When he first left Windsor, he lived in Pall Mall; from thence he went to the once countrified suburb of Brompton; subsequently he dwelt for a time at Highgate and St. John's Wood respectively; next we find him at Hampstead; then between 1860 and 1871 he chiefly resided at Ventnor, in the Isle of Wight, to which charming

K

place he went for his daughter's health; and lastly, in 1871, he removed to Addlestone, in Surrey, where he remained until his death. He rarely went abroad—one or two visits to Paris; one or two visits to Germany, once in company with Professor Long, and on another occasion with his daughter and her future husband, Mr. Clowes; one to Ireland with Douglas Jerrold; a short tour, with two of his daughters, through a portion of France; one or two visits to Scotland; and various expeditions through England—these completed the list of his travels.

In his closing years he took delight in recounting his experiences and friendships in the past; and in reading, or having read to him, novels by Jane Austen and Sir Walter Scott. He was also deeply impressed by the sermons of Robertson of Brighton. Sometimes he would converse with his relatives on the subjects he had long deeply loved, learning and literature, but by-and-by conversation, and the busy memories it evoked, became too much for him, and he would ask to be taken from the room. He gradually and peacefully passed out of life, dying at Addlestone, on the 9th of March, 1873, a few days before completing his eighty-second year. He was buried at Windsor, in his father's grave. Six years later his wife was laid to rest beside him. She belonged to the family of the Eliotts of Stobs, in Roxburghshire, one of whom, Lord Heathfield, was the defender of Gibraltar. One of his lordship's nieces married William Vinicombe, a London architect, and son of a country gentleman in Devonshire; and it was their daughter Sally who married Charles Knight. She appears to have been a lady of a sweet and noble nature, unselfish to a remarkable degree, and endowed with strong common-sense, a high spirit, and a singular power of endurance and hopefulness. When eighty-seven years of age, her eyes were not dim, neither was her form bowed or withered. She could not have a more beautiful tribute than that 'she never gave up a sinking cause or an erring person.'

I have already referred to many of the works written or edited by Charles Knight, and may now add that the volumes of which he was the author numbered no fewer than thirty-seven. The separate works edited or conducted by Knight amounted to sixty. One of these, known as the series of *Monthly* and afterwards of *Weekly Volumes*, consisted of one hundred and eighty-six volumes, while many of the other works ranged from three up to twelve volumes. In the columns of *Punch*, Tom Taylor justly celebrated the veteran worker after his death as one of the truest soldiers of Captain Pen, and one who had borne the flag of 'Peace, goodwill to men,' foremost and farthest of the sacred band of literary workers. A copy of the bust of Knight, executed by Durham in 1865, was presented by his daughters to the National Portrait Gallery. But one wonders why the nation which he so long served did not honour his memory more, or more generously recognise his great services while he was yet alive. When such honours as that of knighthood are lavishly distributed on the vaguest and most insufficient grounds, it does seem strange that one who battled so courageously against ignorance, and on behalf of a pure and free press, for upwards of half a century, should not have received some worthy mark of the nation's gratitude. However, he will have his reward from posterity. Good and cheap literature has been sown broadcast, and knowledge is free, and for these beneficent reforms we are indebted in no inconsiderable degree to the lifelong labours of Charles Knight.

SIR GEORGE BURNS.

SIR GEORGE BURNS.

The shipping industry of Great Britain is one of the great commercial marvels of the world. Its rise, development, and present position would afford material for one of the most interesting chapters in the history of national progress. The influence of our merchant navy is reflex and manifold. Our ships provide employment for hundreds of thousands of workmen long before they are ready to join that majestic fleet which navigates every sea and ocean of the world. The building of the ship is a gigantic industry of itself, and when each vessel is completed and launched upon its career, it yearly adds to the aggregate of that trade between England and the nations which has now assumed such enormous proportions. The value of the shipping industry may be gauged from one fact alone: the amount of British commerce which passes through the Mediterranean every year is worth over £130,000,000, and the annual amount of British commerce which passes within sight of Gibraltar is worth no less than £250,000,000. Add to this our trade with America and other parts, and some conception may be formed of the extent and ramifications of this vast industry.

Sir George Burns was one of the typical merchant princes of Great Britain. Before dealing with his career, however, and his connection with the famous Cunard line of steamships, it will be interesting to glance at the history of the ship before it reached its present stage of perfection. Great indeed have been the changes since the coracles and canoes of the ancients first ventured to navigate unknown seas. The stately galleys of the Romans were followed by the Viking war-ships. The Norsemen built vessels between fifty and a hundred feet in length, and King Alfred introduced galleys pulled by forty and sixty oars. From the days of Canute to Henry VII. some progress was made in shipbuilding, but the greatest advances were undoubtedly those made under the first Tudor king and his successor. Henry VIII. encouraged shipbuilding both for war and commerce, and constructed the *Great Harry*, a really formidable vessel for that time. In 1511 the *Great Michael* was constructed in Scotland. It was 240 feet in length, and is said to have cost about £20,000 Scots. The *Santa Maria*, in which Columbus made his first voyage to the New World, was a vessel of 90 feet keel and 29 feet wide. The ships of the great navigators—Gama, Frobisher, Magellan, Drake, Anson, etc.—were a great improvement on those which went before, and ships have since been specially constructed for Geographical and Polar Explorations.

In the sixteenth century the main principles of wood construction in shipbuilding were already clearly established, and subsequent developments in size, down at least to the beginning of iron shipbuilding, were mainly characterised by such modifications in individual parts or in structural arrangements as made such developments possible. A writer of authority, Mr. David Pollock, author of *Modern Shipbuilding and the Men Engaged in It*, thus briefly traces the history of shipbuilding during the past three centuries: 'Scarcely any advance in the size of ships was made during the reign of Elizabeth, notwithstanding that this was pre-eminently the period of daring navigation. Much was done by her successor to develop both the royal navy and the mercantile marine. He appointed commissions of inquiry into naval affairs, granted a new charter to the East India Company, and endeavoured to raise the standard of knowledge and practice amongst shipbuilders by granting a charter in 1612 to the Shipwrights'

Company, and endowing it with jurisdiction over all shipbuilders in the kingdom. The first president of this body was Phineas Pett, master-shipwright of Woolwich Dockyard. To this eminent shipwright, and to his son Peter and Sir Anthony Deane, naval architecture owed much during the seventeenth century. This period of progress, however, was followed by a century of almost utter stagnation in respect of the application of science to shipbuilding. Skill and thoroughness in ship-carpentry as a craft were indeed not wanting; but there was nothing like adequate application of scientific principles to the evolution and improvement of naval architecture. The best scientific talent during this period, and well on into the nineteenth century, was to be found in other countries than England —France, Spain, Sweden, and Denmark; while the British ships produced—particularly ships of war, but also merchant ships— were, as regards speed, size, and sea-behaviour, far surpassed by the ships of the countries named. "System" had become so stereotyped that glaring imperfections—such as the lack of both longitudinal and transverse strength—were permitted and perpetuated. At length came a shipbuilder who had courage to break away from established practice, and introduce improved methods of construction. This was Sir Robert Seppings, who began as an apprentice shipwright in the dockyards, and rose to the position of surveyor of the navy, which he held till 1832. To counteract the effect of "hogging"—*i.e.*, the dropping of the ends of the ship relatively to the middle—he associated with the transverse "ribs" or frames an inner framework of ties or "riders" arranged diagonally. A more important modification still was the introduction of "fillings" between the frames up to some distance above the bilges. These fillings, occupying as they did the whole space between the ribs, were of great value, both as safeguards in the event of damage to the outside planking and as affording immense assistance to the resistance offered by the lower parts of the ship hogging. A third important change was in the mode of attaching the deck-beams to the frames at the sides of the ship. This bold shipwright suggested, and ultimately effected, the reduction of the long "beak-heads" and lofty square sterns which had for centuries characterised British war-ships. With Seppings's improvements the way was made thoroughly clear for increase in the size and power of wood ships, and the results were exemplified in those towering three-deckers, long the pride and glory of the navy, and in the staunch and elegant merchantmen known on every sea.

'At the present day, however, wood shipbuilding in Great Britain has so fallen into desuetude as to have become mainly a matter of historic interest. It is a thing entirely of the past in the royal dockyards, and is of the smallest importance in British mercantile shipyards, though at a few minor ports a little wood shipbuilding is still carried on. In Canada and the United States, on the other hand, the great bulk of new shipping still consists of wood. Wood is even being employed in the construction of steamships of considerable size, and of sailing ships of dimensions never before attempted in America.

'While wood has thus largely been supplanted by iron and steel in the construction of ships, no such sweeping change has taken place in the means for their propulsion. Steamships have undoubtedly made a wonderful transformation, but spread of sail and "unbought wind" are still potent factors in the speeding of ships across the ocean. Indeed, within recent years the size of sailing ships and the extent of their rig have enormously increased.'

To show the proportions which a five-masted sailing vessel may attain, it appears that the *Marie Rickmers*—built by Messrs. Russell & Co., of Port Glasgow, in 1891-2 for Messrs. Rickmers & Co. of Bremen—has no less than 56,500 square feet of sail area; 21,300 lineal feet, or upwards of four miles, of steel wire in the form of shrouds, stays, etc.; and 31,000 lineal feet, or nearly six miles, of running cordage. The combined height of the masts is 960 feet, and the combined length of the spars, by which the spread of sail is suspended, no less than 2,000 lineal feet. To assist sailing vessels in a prolonged calm, auxiliary steam-engines have been added—the *Marie Rickmers*, for example, being fitted with triple expansion engines of about 600 indicated horse-power.

With regard to steam vessels, the Spaniards assert that as far back as 1543 one Blasco de Gary attempted to propel a vessel by steam in the harbour of Barcelona. In 1707 Denis Papin employed a steam-engine to drive a model boat, fitted with paddle-wheels, on the river Fulda; and in 1736 Jonathan Hulls patented in England a form of paddle-steamer resembling in many essential features vessels still in use. It was only during the last quarter of the eighteenth century, however, that real progress began to be made in steam navigation. The Marquis de Jouffroy in France, James Rumsey and John Fitch in America, and Patrick Miller and William Symington in Great Britain, seem to have been simultaneously at work on the steamboat problem. In October, 1788, upon a lake on Mr. Miller's estate in Dumfriesshire, Symington propelled by steam a small craft twenty-five feet long through the waters of the lake, in the presence of Robert Burns, Nasmyth the painter, and others. Many other trials had been made both in England and America without material result, when in 1801-2 Symington completed for Lord Dundas a steam vessel intended for towing purposes on the Forth and Clyde Canal. It was the first practically successful steamboat ever built, and was named the *Charlotte Dundas*. The engine was of Watt's double-acting type, turning a crank on the shaft of the paddle-wheel, which was situated at the stern. An excellent experiment was made with it in March, 1802, but for some cause or other the vessel was eventually broken up and Symington became disheartened. Robert Fulton was next prominent in this matter. With the aid of Chancellor Livingston, he constructed in the United States a vessel called the *Clermont*, 133 feet long and 18 feet broad. It was fitted with a steam-engine which he had ordered from Boulton & Watt, and it made its first trip between New York and Albany, a distance of 142 miles, in thirty-two hours. The *Clermont* was the first steamboat continuously and profitably employed in useful service, and to Fulton is consequently awarded the distinction of having been 'the first to make steam navigation an everyday commercial success.'

The English and American Governments were approached in vain on the subject of steam navigation, by Henry Bell of Helensburgh, on the Clyde. At length, on his own initiative, he had constructed at Port Glasgow, the *Comet*, a vessel 42 feet long and 11 broad, fitted with an engine of three horse-power. She plied on the Clyde at the rate of five miles per hour, afterwards extended by enlargements to six, when the *Elizabeth* and other steamers were in successful action. The Clyde took the lead in the building of steamships, and the first steamer to ply on the Thames, the *Marjory*, was constructed there. She was launched from the yard of William Penny, of Dumbarton. David Napier, the well-known marine engineer, of Glasgow, was the next to give a considerable impetus to steamship-building. In 1818 he established regular steam service between Glasgow and Belfast, and in the following year the first line of steamers between Glasgow and Liverpool. The Thames steamers began to ply between London and Margate in 1815-16; and in 1817 James Watt crossed over to the Scheldt in a steamer named the *Caledonia*, afterwards ascending the Rhine to Coblentz.

The first steamboat which crossed the Atlantic was the *Savannah*. On May, 25th, 1819, she sailed from Savannah, and arrived in Liverpool on the 20th of June—thus occupying twenty-five clear days. She relied, however, on her sailing powers almost equally with steam. She was a vessel 100 feet long and about 300 tons burden, and was a nine days' wonder until she was shipwrecked off Long Island. In 1825 the *Enterprise*—a vessel 122 feet long and of about 470 tons burden—made a passage from London to Calcutta in 113 days, ten of which were accounted for by stoppages. 'The successful inauguration of Transatlantic steaming,' says Mr. Pollock, 'is due to the *Great Western*, built for the Great Western Steamship Company, by I. K. Brunel, whose bold genius controlled the affairs of the company, and gave to the maritime world several of its most notable steamships. She was 212 feet long, 35 feet 4 inches beam, 23 feet 2 inches depth of hold, and registered 1,340 tons. Her engines, on the side-lever principle, were made by Messrs. Maudslay, Sons, & Field, of London, and were of 440 horse-power.

'On Sunday, April 8th, 1838, the *Great Western* started from Bristol on her voyage across the Atlantic, her completion and despatch being hastened on account of the fact that, four days before, a vessel named the *Sirius* (taken from the service between London and Cork) had been despatched on the same voyage. The *Sirius* was smaller and less powerful than the *Great Western*, and both vessels arrived at New York on the same day, Monday, April 23—the *Sirius* in the morning, and the *Great Western* in the afternoon,—the passage thus taking eighteen days and fourteen days respectively. Their arrival was hailed with immense acclamation by a vast concourse of spectators; the event represented a triumph in steam navigation—regarding the possibility of which much popular unbelief and some scientific doubt had been expressed—and virtually reduced the distance between the Old World and the New by about one-half.'

Other pioneer steamers followed, but, as in the case of the *Great Western*, with indifferent success commercially. Then came the great Cunard line, and it is here that I take up the biography of Sir George Burns.

Burns came of an old and long-lived family in the west of Scotland, whose name was originally Burn. His grandfather, John Burn, remembered seeing the soldiers crowd past his father's house with their wounded after the Battle of Sheriff Muir, in the Jacobite rising of 1715. He was a native of Stirling, and a man of piety and learning, with some repute in letters. He married in 1741, at St. Ninians, Janet Young, and they had one child, born in 1744. This child afterwards became Dr. Burns, of the Barony Church, and the father of George Burns. Young John Burns grew up into an earnest and godly man. He entered the ministry of the Kirk of Scotland, and in 1773 was appointed to the full charge of the Barony Church, Glasgow, of which he had for some time acted as assistant minister. In 1775 he was successfully working Sunday-schools at Calton, in Glasgow, and it is believed that these were the first Sunday-schools instituted in Scotland. During the same year Dr. Burns married Elizabeth Stevenson, daughter of John Stevenson, of the family now represented by Stevenson Hamilton of Fairholm and Braidwood. They had seven sons and two daughters, the youngest of the family being George, the future shipowner.

George Burns was born on Dec. 10th, 1795, in a part of Glasgow known as the 'Holy Land,' so called from the number of ministers who congregated in the locality. Mr. Edwin Hodder, in his Memoir of Burns, observes that he grew up to be a bright, happy, thoughtless boy. Burns himself has stated that his first school was a private one, under a tutor named Angus, who enjoyed the highest repute as a teacher of grammar in preparation for a full classical education. He was next sent to the Grammar School of Glasgow, now called the High School, an ancient seat of education. Here he made fair progress, but out of school he was a mischievous lad, full of fun, and always ready for play or sport. His period of tuition came to an end in 1812, when he was seventeen years of age. During George's early home life there were many changes in the Burns family. Four children had died; John, the eldest—afterwards Dr. John Burns, F.R.S., the first Professor of Surgery in Glasgow University,—had married and left the paternal roof; Elizabeth was also married, and Allan was away either travelling or lecturing on anatomy, and preparing the books which were to bring him fame. The two remaining children, James and George, were at home. All made much of the youngest son, who was bright, energetic, and business-like. There was pleasant hospitality in the Burns domicile, and much discussion of current events by ministerial brethren and others, so that George picked up a good deal of miscellaneous information in an entertaining fashion. Dr. Burns was very cosmopolitan in his clerical friendships, and would often take his son to the Episcopalian Church on a Sunday evening, having no evening service of his own. In this way George Burns had the opportunity of listening to such men as Charles Simeon of Cambridge, and Henry Venn, Secretary of the Church Missionary Society.

The business of life for young Burns began in 1812, when he entered the office of the New Lanark Cotton Spinning Company as a clerk. The superior under whom he served was Mr. John Wright, of whom Burns wrote seventy-two years after he passed under his charge, 'He was truly a father, both in promoting my temporal and spiritual well-being.' The young clerk's recreations were in chemistry and science, and he studied during a regular course of lectures under Dr. Thomas Thomson, Professor of Chemistry in the University of Glasgow. This love for science never left him, and later in life he keenly enjoyed Faraday's lectures at the Royal Institution. George Burns early acquired deep religious convictions, but he was always an enemy of cant. When he was treasurer of the 'Penny-a-Week North-West District Society,' in aid of the British and Foreign Bible Society, he collected in pennies upwards of £400 a year. Whatever he put his hand to he worked at industriously. In 1813 he experienced a great sorrow by the death of his brother Allan, whom he had happily helped to a stronger faith in religion before he passed away. George Burns fell under the magic spell of that celebrated divine Dr. Chalmers in 1815; and 'soon there sprang up between the great preacher and the young man of business a close intimacy, and a love strong as death.' Chalmers set on foot a comprehensive system of

Sabbath evening schools, to counteract in some degree the deplorable ignorance he had discovered among the young people of the wynds and alleys. The teachers were allowed a free hand as regards ways and methods; and George Burns was one of the first to enrol himself in the earnest band of workers. He next became active in the service of the Glasgow Auxiliary to the Moravian Missions, and became acquainted with James Montgomery, the poet, who first stirred Chalmers's interest in the Moravians.

In the year 1818 Burns became engaged to Jeanie Cleland, the young and accomplished daughter of Dr. Cleland, in whose house George had long been a welcome guest. They were in thorough sympathy and accord in their tastes, pursuits, dispositions, and religious ideas. The letters which passed between them show the high aspirations by which both were animated. After that strange but impressive genius, Edward Irving, became assistant to Dr. Chalmers at St. John's Church, Glasgow, Burns saw a good deal of him; and from his interesting reminiscences of Irving I extract these passages: 'Irving had a singular facility in finding his way to easy conversation with the working people in Dr. Chalmers's parish. On one occasion he told me it fell to his lot to visit a shoemaker, who turned out to be of a sceptical turn of mind. The shoemaker showed no inclination to admit any conversation, but continued hammering doggedly at his last. Irving paid no attention to this, but began to speak to him of the work in which he was engaged, and asked him if he had heard of an invention which had lately come out in London for connecting, in an improved manner, the double soles of shoes. The shoemaker put down his last, and fell into eager talk upon the subject. Irving had accomplished his purpose, but was too wise to push at that time the real object he had in view. However, he returned again and again to the man, who welcomed him gladly, and was at length eager to speak with him upon religious subjects.

'Irving was physically a powerful man, and in the days when

the road to Blackheath was infested with highwaymen, he was walking alone, in the darkening of the evening, to London, when two men who were lurking about seemed inclined to join him. Irving at once penetrated their purpose of doing him some mischief, and, determining to make his presence felt amongst them, he opened up a conversation by saying, "I see we are all going the same way—to London, I suppose; let us shake hands and walk together." One of the men responded, but he found that his hand was in that of one who held him like the grip of a vice; and seeing that Irving was evidently not to be trifled with, the two men, after a little while, slunk off quietly behind.

'I have no letters from Irving, but we met frequently at Chalmers's and elsewhere. A favourite theme of conversation with Irving when talking to me, especially during his early days in Glasgow, was of the Spirit of God working among men more by the agency of the heart than of the head. Before he went to London, Irving said to Mr. Chalmers, that when he should enter his church in Regent Street he was determined to open up a career for himself. This he certainly did, but great differences of opinion exist with regard to its value.'

Irving and George Burns were present together in St. John's Church on the 9th of November, 1823, when Dr. Chalmers preached his farewell sermon before taking the vacant Chair of Moral Philosophy in the University of St. Andrews. The day was a memorable one. 'An enormous concourse of people was packed in the church, but no one seemed to feel inconvenienced, so deeply impressed were they with the grandeur and solemnity of the utterances of the great preacher, as, with soul aflame and in a white heat of spiritual fervour, he spoke from that pathetic text, "If I forget thee, O Jerusalem, let my right hand forget her cunning."' The loss of Chalmers from the old scenes in Glasgow was naturally a painful one to George Burns, who had worked under him as under a noble and gifted father—as indeed he was to him in the higher life of the Spirit.

Returning to the business career of George Burns, in 1816 he left the New Lanark Company and entered the house of Andrew Grant & Co., in order to learn the mysteries of the cotton trade. His stay here was brief, however, as in 1818 he entered into partnership with his brother James, as general merchants. Both brothers were men of sterling commercial integrity, and would rather lose an advantage than take it, if it seemed in the least degree injurious to the interests of others. Their liberality of spirit resulted in prosperity for themselves. Honesty was not only a policy but a principle with them. George did all the travelling for the new firm. This was not a light matter, seeing that for years the mail-coach journey to London alone occupied some sixty hours. But he systematically visited the outlying cities in England and Ireland: indeed, in 1818-20 he visited every outport in Ireland, and was well rewarded for his labour. Finding that the grain consignment branch of the business was very hazardous, he did not cultivate it; but in Belfast he obtained the support of the whole town, and its consignment of produce fell entirely into the hands of J. & G. Burns. On no account would George Burns work or travel on Sunday: he said he found it good for him to 'rest on the seventh day according to the commandment.' On the 10th of June, 1822, Burns was married to Jeanie Cleland. The union in their case was really one of hearts. 'The two were one in everything—and henceforth, for over fifty-five years, every joy and sorrow of life, every hope and aspiration, they were to share together.' They at once began to take an active interest in many religious societies. 'Mrs. Burns, who from her childhood had been conspicuous for her philanthropy and benevolence, was a woman of powerful intellect, combined with unusual energy, and threw into everything she undertook a cheerful vigour of manner which exercised a moving influence among her fellow-workers.'

A radical change in the business course of George Burns's life began in 1824. The whole of the Glasgow and Liverpool shipping trade was in the hands of three companies. One of these, the Liverpool firm of Messrs. Matthie & Theakstone, had as agents in Glasgow Messrs. John & Alexander Kidd. The brothers Kidd having died, it became necessary for Matthie & Theakstone to appoint fresh agents in Glasgow; and after a time they gave the agency to Messrs. Burns on very liberal terms—namely, 6½ per cent. commission on all freights, payments to be guaranteed by the agents. This formed a new departure in the life of George Burns: henceforth all his energies were thrown into the shipping business, while his brother James continued to manage the produce business until his death. The produce business was carried on under the style of 'J. & G. Burns,' and the shipping business under that of 'G. & J. Burns'—separate premises being used. Not long after this change, George Burns became a partner in Matthie's Liverpool business; and he took a further important step by embarking in steam navigation between the Clyde and Belfast, which proved to be the cradle of the coasting steam trade of the British Isles. Improvements effected at various times in the Clyde transformed it at last into a great navigable highway.

When steam began to make considerable headway, the agency of the Glasgow and Belfast line of trading steamers became a very important connection for any firm. Great efforts were made by others to obtain it, but Burns was confirmed in his agency, and he occupied so strong a position that he was even able to prevent the steamers from sailing on Sundays, when that proposal was pressed forward. In a short time, we are told, the whole machinery of the trade was in working order, and goods and passengers were being conveyed in large and swift vessels between the Clyde and Belfast. Burns's next step was to purchase, with the aid of Matthie, twelve smacks belonging to the Martins of Liverpool, and to dispose of them with the view of beginning entirely anew with improved steam vessels. This being accomplished, a new co-partnery was entered into, the style being 'Matthie & Martin' for Liverpool, and 'G. & J. Burns & J. Martin' for Glasgow. On the 13th of March, 1829, the first vessel of the new Glasgow company, called the *Glasgow*, steamed down the Clyde; and she was followed in the ensuing month by the *Ailsa Craig*, and in the succeeding year by the *Liverpool*.

A most interesting glimpse of George Burns's character is furnished in this passage from Mr. Hodder's biography:—
'George arranged the sailing day of the first vessel, the *Glasgow*, to be Friday—despite the sailors' superstition with regard to that day; although his object was not to fight a superstition, but to establish a principle, namely, the avoidance, as far as possible, of sailing on Sunday. When Hugh Matthie heard of this arrangement, he wrote back at once to say that it would never do, as the whole of the canal traffic from Stafford and elsewhere arrived in Liverpool on Saturday. "It would be far better," he said, "to sail on Saturday; and, if you think it necessary," he added, sarcastically, "provide chaplains." At that time he was always in the way of saying to Mr. Martin when letters came in the morning, "What will 'King George' have to say to-day?"

'He was dumbfounded when he heard what "King George" had to say in reply. It was a frankly worded letter, saying that " he thought very well of the suggestion about providing chaplains, and that he and his brother would pay the entire expense of the experiment." The letter arrived in the usual course. Mr. Matthie was sitting in his private room on one side of the table, and Martin on the other. He read the letter and threw it across to Martin, saying, "The fellow takes me up in earnest." Mr. Martin replied, "Did I not say you had better not try that game on with Burns?"

'At once the novel idea was carried into effect, and a chaplain was appointed for each of the steamers. Captain Hepburn, in command of the second vessel with a chaplain on board, was jeered by the people on the Broomielaw, as he sailed away, the would-be wits bantering him on "sailing in a steam chapel," and so forth. But the ridicule soon died away, while the boon and the blessing remained. The institution of chaplains continued until the year 1843, when the Free Church started off from the Established Church of Scotland, which made such a draft upon licentiates for the ministry, that operations had to be suspended; but a succession of missionaries was employed to visit the seamen on shore in Glasgow, and part of the duties formerly performed by the chaplains was thus carried on. A mission-room was specially built for this object on premises belonging to Messrs. Burns, near the Broomielaw—where Dr. Love's chapel originally stood,—and on Sunday evenings the services of the highest class of ministers in Glasgow were enlisted, amongst them being the late Dr. Norman Macleod, of the Barony Church, and Dr. Eadie, of the United Presbyterian body. On week-days the room was used for various social purposes, and from time to time entertaining lectures were given.'

The Glasgow company was soon doing a splendid trade, with its excellent steamers, captains, and general business arrangements. It had only one powerful opponent, the Manchester company, and this was so left behind in the competition that it capitulated, and was absorbed by the Glasgow company, which soon had the entire Liverpool and Glasgow trade in its own hands, except for a small steamer called the *Enterprise*. David MacIver was the Liverpool agent for the *Enterprise*, and he was so disturbed by the energy displayed by the Burns firm that he went to Glasgow, determined to float a regular fleet, in order to break up the monopoly. On arriving at Glasgow, much to his dismay he found that G. & J. Burns had already added the *Enterprise* itself to their list of vessels. He was so exasperated that he used all his efforts to establish a new company, and this he did with the aid of a wealthy cotton broker named James Donaldson. The City of Glasgow Steam Packet Com pany began its opposition with Thomson and McConnell as its Glasgow agents, and MacIver as its agent in Liverpool. A vessel called the *City of Glasgow* was bought and employed in the trade; but MacIver 'did not confine himself to Liverpool; he vowed that he would, if possible, drive the Burnses off the seas; and he was constantly on the vessels, backwards and forwards, urging on extra coals, extra pressure, extra speed.' New vessels were put on the Liverpool line, and not on that only, but also on the Ayr line, which the Burnses were working entirely on their own account. But the opposition, though formidable, did not succeed. George Burns was a man of strong individuality, and the event proved that it was stronger than MacIver's individuality. Moreover, he was also wise and generous, so he made a proposal to his defeated antagonists to this effect—'Let us amalgamate and make one common purse by dividing a certain proportion of the revenue derived from the general trade. You shall have two-fifths, and we will have three-fifths and the control of the concern.' The terms were accepted, and from that time forward the most cordial relations subsisted between MacIver and Burns. When the sum of £4,000 was handed over to the City of Glasgow Company at the end of the first year, MacIver said to George Burns, 'It is very good of you to pay it to us. I'm quite certain we should never have paid it to you.' Opposition was further encountered and overcome in the Irish trade, and subsequently Burns opened up the West Highland trade, the Dundee and London trade, and the trade between Liverpool and Malaga and other ports.

All through the stress of business, Burns found his rest and consolation at home. Here he was not without his anxieties, however, for out of seven children born to him, three only survived the period of infancy. As his father was now advanced in age, George took the principal part in finding for him a suitable assistant. One was at length secured in the person of a Mr. (afterwards Dr.) J. Black, a private tutor, but a licentiate of the Church of Scotland. He was a very able man, and something of a wit. After living with Dr. Burns as assistant for nearly twelve years, someone said to Mr. Black, 'You'll be wearying for Dr. Burns's death?' to which he replied, 'Not at all; I'm only wearying for his *living?*' After the Disruption, he was asked whether he was going out with the ' Frees.' His reply was, 'Na, na! I've been far too long in getting *in.*' George Burns's brother, Dr. John Burns, wrote a number of religious works, one of which still retains its place in theological literature, namely, *The Principles of Christian Philosophy; containing the Doctrines, Duties, Admonitions, and Consolations of the Christian Religion.* To this work George Burns gave his hearty adhesion. In the year 1832 Mrs. Burns presented her husband with twin sons. One of them died soon after its birth, but the other, James Cleland Burns, survived his father. Although George Burns was untrammelled in religious matters, he had a great liking for the Liturgy of the Church of England, and he ultimately attached himself to St. Jude's Episcopal Church in Glasgow. In 1838 the Rev. Robert Montgomery was appointed minister of this church. 'Satan Montgomery' is chiefly remembered as a poet because of Macaulay's furious onslaught upon him, but there must have been something in his preaching when so level-headed a man as Sir Archibald Alison described him as ' the greatest preacher of modern times.' Montgomery was a constant visitor at Rose Bank, Burns's beautiful place on the Clyde, and he made Mrs. Burns the almoner of certain funds which he collected for the poor. In 1843 Montgomery's dazzling career at Glasgow came to an end, the rest of his life being spent in London, where he continued to attract crowds of listeners at Percy Chapel.

Burns lost his venerable father on the 26th of February, 1839. He was in his ninety-sixth year, and was the 'Father of the Church of Scotland.' When ninety years of age he remained at a debate on the Catholic Relief Bill until after midnight to record his vote. For a period of sixty-nine years he had exercised the ministerial function of the Barony parish, the largest in Scotland. 'He served a cure for a longer period than had fallen to the lot of any Presbyterian or Episcopalian clergyman in Glasgow since the Reformation in 1560, and there had been no Roman Catholic bishops or archbishops since the renovation of the See in 1129 who had held office for such a length of time. His popularity, which increased through a long life, was that which arises from a faithful discharge of duty; and when he was laid to rest, full of years and honour, men and women of all ranks in life and of all shades of religious belief gathered round his grave to pay their tribute of affection and respect. Dr. Thomas Brown, the minister of John's Church, preached the funeral sermon from the appropriate words, "Mark the perfect man and behold the upright, for the end of that man is peace."'

Another death soon followed—that of Burns's father-in-law, Dr. Cleland. He was one of the best-known citizens of Glasgow, whose history and condition he had at his fingers' ends. Dr. Cleland was the first to draw public attention to the value of regular mortuary tables. Twice he prepared a census of Glasgow, and its bills of mortality were prepared by him for fourteen years, while he took an active part in furthering all the public improvements of the city. When he retired from public life in 1834, a building called 'The Cleland Testimonial' was erected in his honour. He was a great statistician, and was President of the Glasgow Statistical Society, and Fellow of various other statistical and antiquarian societies at home and abroad.

The founding of the Cunard Company was the next, and perhaps the greatest, event in George Burns's life. It is astonishing how even the vaticinations of scientific men are sometimes amazingly and ludicrously falsified. Dr. Lardner, in the course of a lecture delivered at Liverpool in 1835, said, 'As to the project which is announced in the newspapers of making the voyage directly from New York to Liverpool, it is,

I have no hesitation in saying, perfectly chimerical, and they may as well talk of making a voyage from New York or Liverpool to the moon!' So, when iron ships were first mooted, critics exclaimed, 'What nonsense it is, as if anybody ever knew iron to float!' and the chief naval architect of one of the dockyards said to Mr. Scott Russell, 'Don't talk to me about iron ships; its contrary to nature!' Yet, as we have seen, the feasibility of steam navigation to the Unites States was fully tested in 1838 by the performance of the *Sirius* and the *Great Western*. But even when this had been demonstrated, Dr. Lardner raised objections against the safety, regularity, and profit of an ocean steam traffic; but all these objections, likewise, were completely overcome.

As soon as the value of steam vessels had been practically established, the English Government were desirous of utilising the new method for the conveyance of the mails to Canada and the United States. Sir Edward Parry, Comptroller of Steam Machinery and the Packet Service under the Admiralty, gave George Burns an early intimation of the fact. Not long afterwards the Lords Commissioners of the Admiralty issued circulars broadcast, soliciting tenders for a mail service between England and America. Burns considered the question, but did not see his way to venture upon so vast an undertaking. The way was destined soon to be made plain to him, however, through Mr. Samuel Cunard, a citizen of Halifax, Nova Scotia. Cunard came of a Quaker family, which emigrated from Wales to America early in the seventeenth century, and subsequently settled at Halifax. Samuel Cunard was born in that city in 1788. After some years spent in a merchant's office, he became partner in a Boston shipping firm, in which capacity he displayed great energy in opening up trade with the West Indies and the South Sea whale fishery. Then, in 1815, he undertook the conveyance of mails between Boston, Newfoundland, and Bermuda; and the work was so satisfactorily executed that he was awarded the thanks of the British Government. When steam navigation was shown to be feasible, Cunard conceived the idea for a line of steamers which should do for the ocean what railways did for the land. On obtaining possession of one of the Admiralty circulars in 1839, he perceived that his opportunity had come. But he lacked capital. He broached his scheme to the merchants of Halifax, but they were too timid to join him. Consequently he proceeded to London, where he obtained a letter of introduction to Robert Napier, the famous Clyde shipbuilder and engineer, who had constructed several steamers for the East India Company, of which company Cunard was agent in Halifax.

Journeying north Cunard found Robert Napier, and explained his scheme to him. Napier introduced him to Mr. Donaldson, representative of the City of Glasgow Steam Packet Company, who, like Napier himself, was a friend of George Burns. Donaldson saw Burns, and the latter discussed the scheme with Cunard and David MacIver. At first MacIver was dead against the scheme, but after another interview with Cunard, and on the understanding that they were to get friends to join them, if possible, Burns and MacIver began to move in the matter. At length, entirely through the instrumentality of Burns, the requisite capital of £270,000 was subscribed, and a tender was made to the Admiralty for the conveyance of Her Majesty's mails once a fortnight between Liverpool, Halifax, and Boston. This tender was accepted over one made by the owners of the *Great Western* steamship, and a contract was concluded for a period of seven years between the Government and the newly formed company. The contract was taken in the names of, and was signed by, Samuel Cunard, George Burns, and David MacIver, names henceforth indissolubly associated with the Cunard line.

This contract with the British Government contained an important clause providing that the steamers used by the contractors should be of such construction as to be available, on demand, for transporting soldiers or military stores, not only to the colonies in North America, but to any part of the world. The actual receipts of the Cunard firm during the seven years the first contract lasted amounted to £3,295 per voyage. Although this was a large sum, the conditions were very onerous; indeed, after having had considerable experience, Messrs. Burns said they would take less money if certain restrictions were removed. Accordingly a new contract was made for £70,000 a year, and the ships were to carry no naval officer on board. The firm of Cunard, Burns, & MacIver spared no expense in securing the finest vessels for the the ocean mail traffic. One of the partners, Cunard, established himself in London, Burns conducted affairs in Glasgow, and MacIver superintended the practical working of the steamers at Liverpool. Mr. W. S. Lindsay, in his *History of Merchant Shipping and Ancient Commerce*, observes : ' If ever the world's benefactors are estimated at their real worth, the names of Samuel Cunard, George Burns, and David MacIver will rank among those who, by their gallant enterprise, have made the world richer by giving an unprecedented stimulus to commerce, and who have rendered inestimable service to the people of every country. For it was not merely in establishing the first line of Atlantic mail steamers that they deserved credit, but in the framing of the rules for the management of their fleet which has led to such magnificent results. Appreciating the great responsibility there was upon them, they made their plans yield at every point to secure one grand result—safety. They might, without laying themselves open to any complaint, have reduced the cost of their service, by minimising the labour employed, and they might also have engaged a cheaper kind of labour than that which they have always used. But from the first, to their honour be it said, they sacrificed everything to safety. Precious human lives were entrusted to their keeping, and, whatever else had to give way, they were inflexible on this point. Safety first, profit second, was their practical motto ;

and as good wine needs no bush, the public soon found out the high character of the firm, and from its establishment to the present time this great character has been maintained.'

The construction of the earliest vessels, and the reception of the pioneer steamer, the *Britannia*, in America, have thus been described by Mr. Hodder : 'The first four steamships provided by the Cunard Company, or, as it was then formally entitled, "The British and North American Royal Mail Steam Packet Company," were the *Britannia, Acadia, Caledonia*, and *Columbia*—the nomenclature of all the Cunard ships ending in "ia." These four ships were wooden paddle-wheel vessels, built respectively on the Clyde, in 1840, by R. Duncan, J. Wood, C. Wood, and R. Steel, and supplied with common side-lever engines by Robert Napier. The *Britannia*, which was the pioneer vessel of the fleet, measured 207 feet long by 34 feet 4 inches broad by 22 feet 6 inches deep, with a tonnage burden of 1,154, and an indicated horse-power of 740. Her cargo capacity was 225 tons, and she was fitted for the accommodation of 115 cabin passengers, but no steerage. The horse-power and passenger and cargo accommodation of the other three ships were identical with those of the *Britannia*, while their dimensions and tonnage only varied very slightly from hers. Their average speed was 8½ knots per hour, on a coal consumption of 38 tons per day.

'On Friday, the 4th of July, 1840—the "Celebration Day" of American Independence,—the *Britannia*, punctual to the very minute of the advertised time, left her moorings on the Mersey, amidst the cheering of immense crowds, acknowledged by Mr. Samuel Cunard, who himself went out with the first mail American steamer. It was calculated that the *Britannia* would reach Boston in fourteen days and a half, but she entered the harbour four hours before the time, having made the voyage in fourteen days and eight hours, at that time considered a rapid passage. The arrival of the first mail steamer in America created even greater enthusiasm than her departure from the English side. It was testified not only by an unprecedented ovation in bunting and cheering, but the citizens of Boston celebrated the occasion by giving a magnificent public banquet, at which their enthusiasm found vent in speeches of the most complimentary nature. During the first twenty-four hours of his stay at Boston, it was recorded in the local papers with justifiable pride, that Mr. Samuel Cunard received no less than 1,873 invitations to dinner.

'One incident in connection with the return voyage of the *Britannia* gave proof that these expressions of goodwill were not of an evanescent character. The winter of 1840-41 having set in very early with great severity, the *Britannia* was frozen up in Boston Harbour, and there was no little fear that she would be imprisoned in the ice for many months. Thereupon the good Bostonians, at their own expense, and with the willing work of thousands of volunteers, cut a channel of more than seven miles in length to get the steamer into clear water.'

Thus was established steam postal communication between America and Great Britain, while the foundation was laid by the Cunard Company for a success which is unparalleled in the annals of shipping. In January, 1842—or eighteen months only after her initial voyage,—Charles Dickens made his first passage to America in the *Britannia*. Characteristically describing the scene in the Mersey before the vessel's departure, he wrote: 'Every gallant ship was riding slowly up and down, and every little boat was splashing noisily in the water; and knots of people stood upon the wharf, gazing with a kind of "dread delight" on the far-famed fast American steamer; and one party of men were "taking in milk," or, in other words, getting the cow on board, and another were filling the ice-houses to the very throat with fresh provisions—with butcher's meat and garden-stuff, pale sucking-pigs, calves' heads in scores, beef, veal, and pork, and poultry out of all proportion; and others were coiling ropes and busy with oakum yarns, and others were lowering heavy packages into the hold; and the purser's head was barely visible as it loomed in a state of exquisite perplexity from the midst of a vast pile of passengers' luggage; and there seemed to be nothing going on anywhere or uppermost in the mind of anybody, but preparations for this mighty voyage.'

Among personal friends whom George Burns made in the 'forties' were Sir Edward Parry; Canon Melvill, 'the golden-mouthed' preacher; Mr. Thomas Crofton Croker of the Admiralty, the well-known Irish antiquary, and Mr. S. C. Hall. While Burns was compelled by business matters to reside in London during the greater part of 1843, he was severely tried by family affliction. His nephew Allan, whom he loved almost as a son, passed away; he also lost a child of his own, and his wife lay seriously ill in the North. It was at this juncture that Lord Sandon, afterwards known as the philanthropic Earl of Harrowby, wrote to him as follows: 'I sincerely sympathise with you in the various afflictions with which you have been visited, during your protracted stay in London. I hope you may have the strength to bear them with as much resignation as you displayed patience and cheerfulness under the protracted annoyances to which the prosecution of your affair with the public offices has exposed you.' The Chancellor of the Exchequer decided against Burns in the matter of the St. Lawrence Service—the conveyance of the Canadian mails by coach-contract between Halifax and Picton; but he made such representations to the Government as to the loss sustained by the Cunard Company in performing its general service, that a new arrangement was concluded by which the Company secured an addition of £10,000 a year to its existing contract.

It is stated that George Burns was a very contemplative man, fond of silent meditation, and he took a keen delight in the writings of a French author who would certainly be unknown to most Englishmen immersed in business—Blaise Pascal. Indeed, for the works of Pascal he entertained a love beyond that which he felt for any other human productions. He never took part in the public discussion of social and religious questions, but like his friend Sir Andrew Agnew he felt a keen interest in the observance of the Sabbath, and it was in connection with this subject that he made, at Exeter Hall, his first and only speech on a public platform. Sir William Hooker, Director of the Kew Gardens, was another friend of Burns's, and the latter facilitated the passage of his botanical specimens to the United States. The letters between Burns and his wife were very tender. After thirty years he found himself loving his 'old Jeanie' more deeply than ever, and to see her own affection for others made him have a more affectionate heart himself towards all around him. Both ripened and mellowed in Christian character as the years rolled on.

When there was great distress in the Highlands of Scotland in 1847, Burns placed some of his Western Highland steamers at the service of the Government. In the summer of the same year the Grand Duke Constantine made the tour of the Highlands, when a beautifully-appointed vessel was placed at his disposal by the great shipowner. Burns was on the Continent at this time. The following passage relating to his return, and the Queen's visit to Scotland, appears in his diary :—

'When at Boulogne, on my homeward journey, I read in the newspapers that the Queen had determined to journey on the same route that the Grand Duke Constantine had taken in his tour in the Highlands. I immediately hastened homewards, and called on Captain Hamilton at the Admiralty, when he asked me to take charge of the voyaging and pilotage. I readily assented, hurried back to Scotland, and rigged out the smaller passenger boat from the Crinan Canal in the best way I could, taking out of my own drawing-room, in Glasgow, a large mirror to place in the saloon. When the Queen arrived in the Clyde, in the royal yacht *Victoria and Albert*, she was accompanied by H.M.S. *Scourge*, in command of my old friend Captain Caffin, and went up to Dumbarton

Rock to inspect it and the garrison. While she was there, I went on board the yacht to confer with Lord Adolphus Fitz-Clarence, who was in command. In the evening we proceeded to Rothesay, which was on the occasion illuminated, and lay off there, the Queen being on board. The day following, the Queen went to visit the Duke of Argyll at Inveraray, where everything was, of course, in high preparation for her. I remained at Ardrishaig waiting her return, to conduct her through the Canal, the *Victoria and Albert* and the *Scourge* being sent round to join her at the other end. The canal-boats were at that time tracked by horses through the Canal, and I clothed the boys who ran the horses in scarlet. We went through the Canal in the track-boat already mentioned. There my brother joined me, and subsequently my son, James Cleland, and I did all that was necessary for the occasion. I went through the Highlands with Her Majesty. The Highland Service then received the popular name of "The Royal Route" —a name it has ever since retained.'

Her Majesty thus refers to the same incident, in her *Leaves from a Note Book in the Highlands:* 'We and our people drove through the little village (Lochgilphead) to the Crinan Canal, where we entered a most magnificently decorated barge, drawn by three horses, ridden by postillions in scarlet. We glided along very smoothly, and the views of the hills— the range of Cruachan—were very fine indeed.'

Matters domestic and commercial occupied Burns in 1849. His only surviving daughter, Margaret, was married to Mr. Charles Reddie, an Edinburgh advocate, son of the Town Clerk of Glasgow. In business affairs a new enterprise was opened up. The mail service to Ireland had long been inefficiently conducted, although it cost the Goverment about £6,000 per annum. Messrs. Burns were already sending goods and passengers between the Clyde and Belfast in larger and swifter ships than those employed in the mail service, and with remarkable punctuality. But in 1849 an influential company organised opposition vessels on the Ardrossan route, which was a much shorter sea passage than that by Greenock. The company had the support of the Glasgow and South-Western Railway, and of Lord Eglinton, owner of the harbour and lord of the manor of Ardrossan. They exerted all their influence to divert the mails to their Ardrossan route. It was regarded as a settled thing in their favour, when George Burns—foreseeing the advantages to be derived from the mails —offered to carry them free of all charge between Greenock and Belfast, and also to put on extra and faster vessels, which should sail from each port every evening in the week except Sunday. When Colonel Maberley, Secretary to the Post Office, was told of this offer, he exclaimed, 'Burns, you are a fool!' but when he investigated the matter he found that Burns was not such a fool as he seemed. The Postmaster-General (Lord Clanricarde) accepted the offer of Messrs. Burns, and the mails were carried by them free of expense for thirty-three years. At first there was a considerable loss on the contract, but when travellers began to appreciate the excellence of the service, the loss was converted into a gain. The competition between the Ardrossan Company and the Messrs. Burns was so keen that for their mutual protection a system of fares, freights, and sailings was agreed to which continued in force until 1882, when the Ardrossan steamers were purchased by Messrs. Burns. The Glasgow and South-Western Railway Company had previously to this made a determined effort to obtain an Act for incorporating their vessels with the railway, and thus to secure the mails; but Burns successfully opposed this. He was not afraid of private competition, he said, but in principle he was against the incorporation of railroads and steamboats, which would put an end to all private trading.

In 1850 Burns sustained a terrible shock, and one from which he did not recover for years. The *Orion*, one of the Liverpool steamers belonging to the firm, struck on a sunken rock off Portpatrick, and went down almost immediately.

Among the passengers lost were Burns's brother, Dr. John Burns, and Miss Morris, a niece of his wife. Great was the grief of George Burns when news of this harrowing disaster reached him at Glasgow. The brothers had ever been specially devoted to each other, though there was a gap of twenty years in their ages. This blow was still fresh when Burns was called upon to mourn the loss of his beloved sister Elizabeth, Mrs. MacBrayne. Very soon after this there was another shipping disaster. One of the Burns steamers, the *Plover*, was getting up steam in Glasgow Harbour, when the boiler burst and the engineer was killed, great damage being done to the vessel. Only just before the disaster, George Burns's son John was in the engine-room. Feeling at this time that the burden of business was somewhat too great for him, Burns curtailed his responsibilities by giving up the 'Royal Route,' or Western Highland service. For some years the whole of the West Highland trade had been solely in the hands of Messrs. Burns. After they relinquished it, the whole of the fleet became the property of Messrs. David & Alexander Hutcheson and Mr. David MacBrayne, a nephew of Mr. Burns. In their hands the trade has ever since remained, but although they have made many improvements, and added to the service such magnificent vessels as the *Iona* and the *Columba*, the *Clansman* and the *Claymore*, in its main features the service remains what it was in Burns's time.

The family of Dr. John Burns became extinct in 1853, when its last surviving member, Colonel John Burns, of the 2nd Royals, died at the Cape from fatigue and exposure during the Kaffir War. By a strange coincidence, it appears that the place where he was struck down in Kaffraria was Burns's Hill—a mission station founded from Glasgow, and named after Dr. Burns of the Barony. Before the year 1853 closed, another heavy bereavement was sustained by George Burns. His only and much-loved daughter died in her thirtieth year, leaving behind her three infants, a boy and two girls. She seems to have been possessed of a noble and self-sacrificing spirit, and she laid the seeds of her own death by nursing one of her children who had been stricken with gastric fever. Burns was indeed heavily visited, but while his frequent parting with loved ones was a terrible wrench, he was able to exclaim, ' Blessed are the dead which die in the Lord.'

It was not to be supposed that such successful undertakings as the Cunard line would be suffered to go on their course without opposition. First among its antagonists came the Great Western Company, which sought to divert the bulk of the Atlantic traffic by building larger steamers than those owned by the Cunard Company. We have seen that the first-named company had achieved successful Transatlantic voyages with the *Great Western*, but at a later period the Company met with serious reverses. The ill-fated *President*, launched in 1839, made a few voyages to the United States, but in April, 1841, on the return voyage from America, she was lost, and was never more heard of. The Great Western Company then built their immense iron steamer, the *Great Britain*, which far eclipsed anything hitherto attempted. She measured 321 feet long and 51 feet broad, and was of 2,984 tons burden. She was hailed as a maritime wonder, and the Queen and the Prince Consort visited her while she lay in the Thames. The *Great Britain* set out on her first voyage to the United States in December, 1843, but she was stranded in Dundrum Bay, off the Irish coast, and could not be floated till the following spring. Then she was told off on the Australian service, and became the favourite vessel of the line. Ultimately, the Great Western Company abandoned its competition with the Cunard line for the American traffic. But the British and American Steam Navigation Company now stepped forward, and obtained a Parliamentary Committee on the subject of the conveyance of the mails between England and the United States. The result, however, was a report stating that the contract with Messrs. Cunard, Burns, & MacIver was more advantageous than any other that could be made, and that the service had been most efficiently performed. In 1847 the Americans themselves established a line of steamships, to run from New York to Southampton. They were anxious to retain their maritime commerce in their own hands, but their first ship, the *Washington*, started from New York for Southampton on the same day that the *Britannia*, the first Cunard ship, started from Liverpool for New York, and the first race ever run between American and British steamers was won by the *Britannia* by two full days.

Meanwhile the Cunard Company added to its line the *Cambria* and *Hibernia*, each of 500 horse-power and of 1,422 tons, and at a later period the *America*, *Niagara*, *Europa*, and *Canada*, each of about 1,820 tons and 680 horse-power, with an average speed of 10¼ knots per hour. In 1850 the British Government concluded arrangements with the Cunard Company for the conveyance of the mails between Halifax, New York, and Bermuda in small vessels, with constant regularity and despatch; and in the following year another contract was entered into for a monthly conveyance of the mails between Bermuda and St. Thomas, with the view of connecting the West Indies with the United States and the North American Provinces. In 1850 the Cunard Company added two more large steamers to their fleet, the *Asia* and the *Africa*, each of 2,227 tons burden and 750 horse-power. Then came a greater ship still, the *Arabia*, a vessel 285 feet long and of 2,400 tons burden. The *Arabia* was largely used during the Crimean War. In the year 1852 the Cunard Company determined to substitute iron for wood in the construction of their vessels, and from this time forward all the additions to the Cunard fleet consisted of iron steamers. The *Andes*, the *Alps*, the *Jura*, and the *Etna* came in quick succession, all constructed on the iron principle, and their success was undoubted. After a time it was found advisable to abandon paddles as the propelling power, and rely simply on the screw.

The most formidable opposition which the Cunard Company ever encountered was from the Collins line of steamers. This line was founded by Mr. E. K. Collins, of New York, and other American citizens, with the avowed object of driving the Cunard ships off the Atlantic. They made two serious mistakes, however, at the outset. First, they asked from the American Government a monopoly of the business; and, secondly, they complained that the rival line was sustained to a very great extent by the British Government, the fact being that the Cunard Company had no subsidy whatever, but was simply paid freightage for carrying the mail-bags. The Collins Company obtained a subsidy, though not without the unanimous protest of sixty-three distinct American shipping houses of the highest reputation. Four splendid vessels were built—the *Arctic*, *Baltic*, *Atlantic*, and *Pacific*, being the finest ships built of wood then afloat. With a subsidy of about £178,000 per annum, the Collins line began to run, under the binding condition of a greatly increased rate of speed. The Cunard Company likewise put forth its best efforts, and the contest was watched with keen interest on both sides of the Atlantic for a period of twelve months. The result was that although the Cunarders lost in point of speed, they steadily gained favour as regards safety and general excellence of accommodation.

The Americans rejoiced over their temporary success, and it was not begrudged them in England; but it led to the Cunard Company making arrangements for a fleet of steamers which should distance all competitors in speed and in every other requirement. When the competition fever was at its height, Charles MacIver wrote to Samuel Cunard as follows:— 'The Collins Company will be pretty much in the situation of finding that breaking our windows with sovereigns, though very fine fun, is too costly to keep up.' Unfortunately this prediction was fulfilled in a manner that no one would have wished. Although for four years the Collins line encountered no serious accident, in 1854 a series of terrible disasters began. The *Arctic* went down in the autumn of that year with fearful loss of life, the wife, son, and daughter of Mr. Collins being among those who perished. Before the following year closed the *Pacific* left Liverpool, and was never heard of again. Capital was subscribed to repair the losses, but before the vessels could be replaced the new Cunarders were at work, defying all competition—their average speed eclipsing the Collins and all other lines. By the year 1858 the ruinous course pursued by the Collins Company was fully demonstrated. The losses were shown to be immense; attempts at revival failed; and American merchants and ship-owners renewed their protest against monopoly and official subsidies. Ultimately the Collins line totally collapsed, and the American Government declined to subsidise any company which might seek to take its place.

The Cunard Company built six new iron screw steamships in 1853, and established branch lines between Liverpool and the principal ports in the Mediterranean, Adriatic, Levant, Bosphorus, and Black Sea; and also between Liverpool and Havre. At the same time a Select Committee of the House of Commons, appointed to inquire into the matter of contract packets, reported that the Cunard service had been performed with great regularity, speed, and certainty—the average length of passage, Liverpool to New York, being 12 days, 1 hour, 14 minutes.

George Burns having amassed a large fortune, and having also seen the magnificent Cunard fleet brought to a high state of perfection, retired from business in 1858. To him was largely due the credit for that admirable system of administration which has governed the Cunard line down to the present day. It was his resolve, moreover, that each ship added to the fleet should be better, if possible, than its predecessor; yet he would never accept new theories or inventions until they had stood the test of practical experience. The singular immunity from accident which the line has enjoyed is attributable to that strict observance of the Company's regulations which has always been enjoined and enforced. As to the care taken to ensure efficient and well-managed vessels, a writer in *The Naval and Military Magazine* observed: 'Their solicitude begins at the keel of each vessel, and continues throughout the whole course of construction. The progress of the work is closely scrutinised by the Company's general and engineer superintendents; and, in addition, a foreman carpenter and rivet inspector are constantly employed in the building yard for the sole purpose of detecting defective material or workmanship and having it rectified. Before every voyage a thorough examination of ship and crew is made by the general and marine superintendents and other officials. The men are mustered, and exercised in boat drill, fire drill, and pump drill, heed being taken that every man knows his proper position, so as to avoid panic or confusion in the event of a sudden emergency. An inspection is then made of the store-rooms, the rockets and other signals are critically examined, and the doors of the water-tight compartments are shut and tested; and each day while the ship is at sea the men stationed at the water-tight doors are mustered, and every water-tight door in the ship is closed, the chief officer and chief engineer reporting to the captain at 1 p.m. the condition of the doors in their respective departments. Knowing how much depends upon the acuteness of vision possessed by the officers and look-out men, the greatest care is taken to guard against weak sight or colour-blindness in every person connected with the sailing department. An exhaustive code of instructions has been compiled for the use of captains, officers, engineers, and every man on board, plainly stating their individual duties, and laying down distinct rules for their guidance under all circumstances. Lastly, with the view of diminishing the chances of collision, the Company's Atlantic steamers take specified courses, according to the seasons of the year. Indeed, all the means which human forethought can devise, and long experience teach, are enlisted to secure the safety of lives and property.'

With regard to the shares in the Cunard Company, Mr. Hodder states that the original shareholders were by degrees bought out by the founders, until the whole concern became vested exclusively in the three families of Cunard, Burns, and MacIver, each holding one-third of the property. Sir Samuel Cunard—who had been honoured by a baronetcy—died in 1865, and his shares passed to his son, Sir Edward Cunard. The latter died in 1869, and the Cunard interest devolved upon his brother, Mr. William Cunard, who from that time continued to represent the Company in London. David MacIver died in 1845; his share passed to his brother Charles, and in due course to the sons of the latter, but they have since retired from the Cunard Company. When George Burns retired in 1858, his holding was divided between his two sons, John and James Cleland Burns. The Company was registered under the Limited Liability Acts in 1878, and transformed into a joint-stock company, with a capital of £2,000,000, of which £1,200,000 was issued and taken by the families of Cunard, Burns, and MacIver. No shares were offered to the public until 1880, when the growing needs of the Transatlantic trade demanded additional steamships. The required capital was at once subscribed and the directorate reconstituted with Mr. John Burns as chairman of the Board. On many occasions subsequent to the Crimean War the Cunard steamers were requisitioned by the Government for the transport of troops and stores.

Some years ago an article appeared in *Good Words* giving Mr. John Burns's views on the Cunard line—the character of the vessels, the number of passengers carried, the vast quantities of provisions required, etc. These details, and others furnished by Mr. Hodder, are extremely interesting. I consequently reproduce the following remarkable facts: 'The pioneer vessel of the Cunard line, the *Britannia*, built in 1839, took for her outward journey from Liverpool 600 tons of coals, and burned 44 tons a day, while her steam pressure was 9 lbs. and her speed a little over 8 knots per hour. Contrast that with the *Etruria*, built in 1885. Her average speed is 18 knots an hour, which is equal to nearly 21 statute miles, or somewhat greater than the average speed of the ordinary train service on any railway in the world. Her engines indicate 14,000 horse-power, and are supplied with steam from 9 double-ended boilers, each with 8 furnaces, or a total of 72 furnaces. The total consumption of coal is 300 tons per day, or 12 tons per hour, and if the whole of the fires were raked together and formed into one large fire there would be 42 tons of coal, or a mass 20 feet long, 20 feet broad, and rather more than 4 feet high, burning fiercely. Her crew consists of 287 hands, all told.

'The victualling department is under the charge of the chief steward, who is responsible not only for the good order of the servants and the cleanliness of the saloons and cabins and baths, but for providing the passengers with a good and liberal table.

'For a single passage to America the *Etruria*, with 547 cabin passengers and a crew of 287 persons on board, carries the following quantities of provisions: 12,550 lbs. fresh beef, 760 lbs. corned beef, 5,320 lbs. mutton, 850 lbs. lamb, 350 lbs. veal, 350 lbs. pork, 2,000 lbs. fresh fish, 600 fowls, 300 chickens, 100 ducks, 50 geese, 80 turkeys, 200 brace grouse, 15 tons potatoes, 30 hampers of vegetables, 220 quarts ice-cream, 1,000 quarts of milk, and 11,500 eggs (or at the rate of one egg per minute from the time the ship sails from Liverpool until her arrival in New York). The quantities of wines, spirits, beer, etc., put on board for consumption on the round voyage comprise 1,100 bottles of champagne, 850 bottles claret, 6,000 bottles ale, 2,500 bottles porter, 4,500 bottles mineral waters, 650 bottles various spirits. Crockery is broken very extensively, being at the rate of 900 plates, 280 cups, 438 saucers, 1,213 tumblers, 200 wine-glasses, 27 decanters, and 63 water-bottles in a single voyage.

'As regards the consumption on board the whole fleet for *one year* the figures seem almost fabulous; 4,656 sheep, 1,800 lambs, 2,474 oxen are consumed—an array of flocks and herds surpassing in extent the possessions of many a pastoral patriarch of ancient times—besides 24,075 fowls, 4,230 ducks, 2,200 turkeys, 2,200 geese, 53 tons of ham, 20 tons bacon, 15 tons cheese, and 831,603 eggs.

'Other articles are in extensive demand, and in the course of a year there are consumed: one ton and a half of mustard, one ton and three-quarters of pepper, 7,216 bottles pickles, 8,000 tins sardines, 30 tons salt cod and ling, 4,192 four-lb. jars of jam, 15 tons marmalade, 22 tons raisins, currants, and figs, 18 tons split peas, 15 tons pearl barley, 17 tons rice, 34 tons oatmeal, 460 tons flour, 23 tons biscuits, 33 tons salt, 48,902 loaves of bread 8 lbs. each.

'The Cunard passengers annually drink and smoke to the following extent:—8,030 bottles and 17,613 half-bottles champagne, 13,941 bottles and 7,310 half-bottles claret, 9,200 bottles other wines, 489,344 bottles ale and porter, 174,921 bottles mineral waters, 34,400 bottles spirits, 34,360 lbs. tobacco, 63,340 cigars, and 56,875 cigarettes.

'The heaviest item in the annual consumption of the Company is of course coal, of which 356,764 tons are burnt—nearly equal to 1,000 tons for every day in the year. This quantity of coal, if built as a wall four feet high and one foot thick, would reach from Land's End to John O'Groats' house.

'With regard to the aggregate employment of labour by the Cunard Company, it includes 34 captains, 146 officers, 628 engineers, boiler-makers, and carpenters, 665 seamen, 916 firemen, 900 stewards, 62 stewardesses, 42 women to keep the upholstery and linen in order, with 1,100 men of a shore gang, or about 4,506 people to run the ships, which traverse yearly a distance equal to five times that between the earth and the moon! Since the time when George Burns became connected with shipping, the large fleet over which he presided, and his firm owned, has represented from first to last no less a sum than upwards of seven millions sterling.'

The course of ocean traffic during the forty years 1850-90 may be still further traced at this juncture. In 1850 the Inman line of steamers was inaugurated by the iron steamship, the *City of Glasgow*, which left Liverpool for Philadelphia on December 17, and made a satisfactory voyage. Ever since that time the powerful and splendidly-equipped vessels of the Inman line have continued to plough the Atlantic. At first the route was between Liverpool and Philadelphia, but in 1857 New York was constituted the Company's principal port. Mr. Inman always insisted on the finest engineering skill and the most recent improvements. The line sustained one great disaster, when the *City of Boston*, which left Halifax, Nova Scotia, for Liverpool in 1870, was lost, and never heard of afterwards. Other losses, secondary to this, were also sustained. The North German Lloyd line, which began in 1858, the National line, originated by the National Steam Navigation Company in 1863, and the Anchor line, projected by a Scotch firm in 1865, were also successful. Then there were the Allan, Dominion, and American lines. The Guion line, which began in 1866, has among its vessels the *Arizona* and the *Alaska*—the greyhound of the Atlantic; and these ships have made remarkably swift passages across the ocean, accomplishing the distance between Queenstown and New York in less than seven days. The latest great Atlantic line which has been established is that of Ismay, Imrie, & Co., styled the White Star line. The steamers of this line are equal to any which cross the Atlantic. The *Britannic* and *Germanic*, built for the White Star fleet by Messrs. Harland & Wolff, of Belfast, in 1874, were a considerable advance on anything then existing. The *City of Berlin*, of the Inman line followed, and was for a time the largest vessel afloat next to the *Great Eastern*. In 1888-9 four larger and more powerful vessels still were launched. They were twin-screw steamers, and inaugurated a new epoch in Atlantic navigation. They were named respectively the *City of New York*, the *City of Paris*, the *Majestic*, and the *Teutonic*. These were followed by splendid twin-vessels owned by German and French firms, viz., the *Normannia*, *Augusta Victoria*, and *Fürst Bismarck* of the Hamburg-America line, and *La Touraine* of the Compagnie Transatlantique. The longest and swiftest of the above vessels is the *Teutonic*, which is 582 feet long. Its trial speed was 21 knots an hour, and it made the passage across the Atlantic in 5 days, 16 hours, and 30 minutes. But the Cunard Company is still effectively coping with its rivals in every respect, while the line has been singularly free from disasters.

Some surprising figures are given in connection with the steam fleet which began its course in 1824, when the firm of G. & J. Burns was established, and which includes the steamships of the Cunard service since its origin in 1840. It appears that in 1890 the fleet included the following vessels: On the Glasgow and Belfast, Londonderry and Larne route, 48 ; Glasgow and Liverpool, 35 ; Glasgow and the Highlands, 15 ; Glasgow and the Firth of Clyde, 11 ; American steamers, 59 ; Mediterranean and Havre line, 19 ; steam yachts owned by Sir John Burns, 3 ; total number of vessels, 190. The tonnage was no less than 240,526 tons, and the horse-power 252,850. On the 4th of July, 1890, the Jubilee of the Cunard Company was celebrated.

The construction of vessels and the science of engineering were completely revolutionised during the career of George Burns. In perfecting the former he was ever ready to take advantage of the latter. As one of the writers of the series of sketches on *Fortunes made in Business* remarks: 'In regard to all the combinations which go to the creation of a successful line of steamships, the Cunard line is able to claim the possession of these perhaps in the most complete degree. Over forty years' incessant service, without the loss of a single ship, a single passenger, or a single letter, is a stronger claim to public confidence than can be set up by any other line whatsoever. Added to this there are these further facts: the Cunard fleet has been the largest engaged in the Atlantic trade; it sent out the first mail steamers that were despatched from this country to the United States; and whatever improvements have been made in the science of shipbuilding that could increase the comfort and safety of their passengers, or give additional facilities of any kind, have been taken advantage of. Thus we have realised for us all the conditions that constitute a steamship company of the first rank. The men who have built up this gigantic undertaking have, while making fortunes for themselves, done much on behalf of the world's commercial progress, and their names will remain for all time indelibly inscribed in the records of England's maritime history.'

Shipping interests, from their great importance to the community, and from their vast ramifications, have naturally claimed a large share of the attention of the legislature. Interesting details in connection with the progress made in engineering and in shipbuilding were published in the *Quarterly Review* in 1863 and 1876. In reviewing the changes which have occurred, Mr. Hodder says: 'For the last half-century and more there has scarcely been a Session of Parliament without legislation on Merchant Shipping; numberless committees and commissions have been appointed to consider schemes for the improvement of our mercantile marine, and measures innumerable have been passed, having for their object the safety, welfare, and progress of British ships and seamen. The result has been that lighthouses have been multiplied and improved; sound-signals have been established; harbours have been constructed, deepened, and made accessible; charts have been perfected; the classification of ships has been revised; tonnage measurement has been reformed; an excellent system of ship registry has been established;

masters, mates, and engineers have been required to pass examinations, and can be cashiered if drunken or incompetent; offices are set up where seamen are engaged and discharged, where they receive their wages, and where their characters are recorded; savings banks and money orders are provided for them; they have summary means of recovering wages; special provision is made concerning their food, medicine, lodging. Lifeboats and rocket apparatus for saving life from shipwreck are established round the coasts; every wreck is made the subject of an investigation more or less stringent; shipwrecked property is protected from plunder; international rules have been made for preventing collision; an international code of general signals has been established, as well as an international system of signals of distress, and the old law of merchant shipping has been once and again codified. Above all, burdens and restrictions of all kinds, general and local, have been removed, so that ship and sailor are now absolutely free from all burdens, except such regulations and such taxes as are needed for their own welfare.'

George Burns gave practical aid in securing many of these measures, but while he fostered legislation he never shirked individual responsibility. He 'laid it down as a business principle that his highest interest lay in the safety of every enterprise—that the loss of ship, cargo, passengers, or crew, would be his loss; and therefore, while trusting in Providence for protection, he looked with an anxious eye to everything which could conduce to the safety of his ship—to her build, her equipment, her loading, her manning, and her navigation.' His sheet-anchor was his own honest, upright character. He could be thoroughly relied upon in every matter, whether great or small, and he made conscience his king in business, as in his life.

On retiring from the firm, Burns enjoyed his well-earned leisure at Wemyss Bay, where he had built himself a handsome and commodious residence. Wemyss House occupies a commanding position, and affords picturesque and expansive views over the Firth of Clyde. At the back of the house, the owner cut terrace after terrace in the solid rock, all of which were beautified by vegetation. The highest terrace, which is 112 feet above the level of the lawn surrounding the house, has a fine range of plant and fruit houses, the largest of which is devoted to a superb specimen of the New Zealand fern-palm. The *Gardeners' Chronicle*, in describing the gardens of Wemyss House and of Castle Wemyss (the residence of John Burns), remarked that 'the working out of so much picturesque beauty from bare, barren crags in so limited an area, has been no mean feat of landscape-gardening skill, and the result seems like a realisation of the Babylonian Gardens of Nebuchadnezzar.' Castle Wemyss, a handsomer structure by far than Wemyss House, is built upon a rock at the extreme edge of the promontory, where the river Clyde widens into the Firth of Clyde. The views from this point are magnificent.

For thirty years George Burns lived in retirement after quitting the active business of life, and through all that period he devoted himself to charitable and philanthropic enterprises. His benevolence was judicious and widely diffused, not concentrated on one or two important objects. Besides gifts to individuals, he liked to assist poor and struggling churches and to build new ones; he furthered the spread of Protestantism on the Continent; he liberally supported Sunday-schools, as well as the humanitarian projects of his friend Lord Shaftesbury for the unfortunate and the destitute in London; and, assisted by his wife, he distributed good and useful literature in his own district. Sailors had his special sympathy, and he not only did what he could for the men of his own fleet, but seized every opportunity of advancing the moral and spiritual conditon of seamen generally, warmly collaborating in the efforts of Admirals Parry and Hope, the Rev. C. B. Gribble, and others. In the Irish Island Society—founded in 1818 by Mrs. Pendleton, of Dublin, for promoting the scriptural education and religious instruction of Irish Roman Catholics in their own language—he took a keen interest. Education in Scotland, and the welfare of the crowded population of Glasgow, enlisted his sympathies; but the parochial school system received its death-blow owing to the immigration of the Irish.

The Pilgrim Mission, founded by Father Spittler near Basle, received Burns's warm support. Young men of the artisan class were gathered together, 'with the object of training them as Christian missionaries, and then sending them forth to gain their livelihood by the work of their hands and at the same time to preach the Gospel.' As a result of the Mission efforts, numbers of young men were sent out as evangelists to Palestine, Egypt, Nubia, Central Africa, etc., as well as to Austria, Germany, and Switzerland. Houses were erected in the vicinity of the old church of St. Chrischona, and a printing-press, a bookbinding establishment, and other useful adjuncts were set on foot. There was affiliated to the institution a Home of Rescue for men of all ages and conditions who had gone astray, but who were willing by strict discipline, constant manual labour, and total abstinence to return to a better life. All the teachers and students of the institution worked without salary, being content with food and raiment. Burns was President of the Glasgow Branch of the Church Missionary Society, and always received and entertained the deputations from the parent Society, besides assisting its operations with liberal donations. He further took a deep interest in the Jews, and supported all the societies established for their material and spiritual welfare. Miss Whately's Cairo schools found in him a friend, 'but there was nothing in the East which absorbed him more than the education of the children of Mohammedans, Druses, Maronites, and Greeks in the hill country of Lebanon.' Mrs. Burns also took up the cause of these schools with enthusiasm, and through her influence a society was formed in the Lebanon with the object of doing good work amongst the hill population. In 1870, at the request of Mr. Burns, Principal Lumsden of the Free Church, and Dr. Alexander Duff, the Indian missionary and reformer, went out to the Lebanon to examine the schools, and found them in a satisfactory state of efficiency. The schools were in consequence taken up by the Foreign Mission Body of the Free Church of Scotland, by whom they are still carried on.

Among other institutions which had Burns's hearty support were—the Royal Infirmary of Glasgow, of which Dr. John Burns was the first house-surgeon; the Magdalen Society; the Glasgow Branch of the London City Mission; the Cottage Home for Infirm Children; and the House of Shelter for Women. The establishment of the *Cumberland* training-ship —which was largely due to his son John—interested him deeply. This vessel did a wonderful work in reforming the street Arabs of Glasgow, and in fitting them for a useful and honourable life. Burns was fond of reading—religious and secular, but chiefly the former. When in his ninety-third year he plunged into Lansdell's *Central Asia*, having just finished Professor Drummond's *Natural Law in the Spiritual World*, concerning which he wrote: 'The consequence of his Biogenesis chapter is so decisive in favour of evangelical teaching on the subject of conversion, that it is impossible it could be palatable to the carnal mind.' But, he by no means accepted all the conclusions of the author of this popular treatise. Burns was, however, catholic-spirited in religious matters, and for sixty years never turned away from taking the Communion in any Church whatever.

This extract from his biography reveals something of the personal character of George Burns:—

'Mr. Burns was always a lover of dogs. One that was a great favourite was lost, and his master mourned for him. Every search was made, but without effect, and one evening, when he was at last obliged to give it up as hopeless, he talked much about his old and faithful friend. It was a trouble to him, for he loved the dog, and in the simplicity of his faith he believed that every shadow of a trouble might be brought before the Heavenly Father in prayer. And so in the family worship that night he prayed "to Him who preserveth man and beast, and without whose knowledge not a sparrow falls to the ground," and reverently asked that "wherever his old friend and companion went, it might please God to find for him a home where he would be kindly treated."

> '"He prayeth well who loveth well
> Both man and bird and beast;
> He prayeth best who loveth best
> All things both great and small;
> For the dear Lord who loveth us,
> He made and loveth all."

'Like all really good men, Mr. Burns was a lover of humour and bright innocent merriment in any and every form. He saw no piety in dulness, there was always fun of some sort or other going on where he was; everybody who had a really good story to tell would take it to him, certain that he would not only see and enjoy the point of it at once, but would "cap" it with another. Everything that made life glad and bright and beautiful, song of bird, scent of flower, love of friends, pursuit of ideals, merry jest, and "happy thought," quip, crank, subtilty, oddity, even nonsense itself, were enjoyed in their proper time and place.'

'The Gaiter Club' was a society formed in Glasgow by a band of men who made walking tours in Scotland, and held annual dinners to celebrate their peregrinations. John Burns was president of the club, J. Cleland Burns, secretary, and Dr. Macleod, chaplain. The members included George Burns —who was long the only honorary member,—Sir Daniel Macnee the artist, and President of the Royal Scottish Academy, Laurence Oliphant, Anthony Trollope, Sir William Thomson, Professor Ramsay, Lord Kinnaird, John MacGregor ('Rob Roy'), Admiral Sir James Hope, and others. Norman MacLeod was the life and soul of the party on many occasions, for he was always brimming over with humour. In March, 1863, Lord Palmerston was on a visit to Glasgow as Lord Rector of the University, and he was elected an honorary member of the club. There was a rule 'That at "Gaiters" there shall be no upright speaking,' but it was resolved to waive the rule on this special occasion. John Burns, as President, proposed Lord Palmerston, and Norman Macleod in seconding said 'he was sure that the highest lady in the land would wish all honour to be paid to Lord Palmerston, but he did not know what the Sovereign would say to a subject receiving both the Garter and the Gaiter.' Instead of availing himself of the privilege of speaking on his feet, Lord Palmerston buried half his body under the table and made this genial and humorous response: 'Gentlemen, I am very proud and flattered to be associated with such a distinguished body. I am informed, though gaiters have an intimate connection with legs, that no gaiterman is allowed to speak upon his legs. He may speak about his legs, but not upon his legs. Now, as we in these days never show our legs, inasmuch as trousers would conceal even the gaiter if we wore it, you will excuse me if I am very short in my thanks. I can only assure you that whether I wear long gaiters or short gaiters, my memory of your kindness will be long, and not short.'

'Apropos of the visit of Lord Palmerston to Scotland,' observes Mr. Hodder, 'it may be mentioned that Mr. John Burns gave him a sail down the Clyde in the Royal Mail Steamship *Wolf*, and on going past one of the shipbuilding yards he pointed out to the Premier a blockade-runner then being constructed. Palmerston looked at the vessel with great interest, but, putting his sleeves across his eyes, he said slyly, "I don't see her." What most affected the Premier upon this voyage was the *Wolf* carrying the flag of the Lord Warden of the Cinque Ports at the main, the flag having been woven on purpose from a sketch obtained from the Admiralty to do him honour, as he then held that office. When the *Wolf* arrived at the tail of the Bank (off Greenock) H.M.S. *Lion* and the other war-ships saluted the flag with nineteen guns, to which it was entitled; yards were manned, and all honour paid to the chief of the State. The flag now hangs in the hall at Castle Wemyss, as a memento of a great man and a great occasion.'

Among the intimate friends of George Burns was Captain Trotter, a gentleman who was once very prominent in the religious world. He was an ex-Life Guardsman, and married a daughter of the first Baron Ravensworth. As a young man he was fond of skating, dancing, and the amusements of fashionable society. In 1839, he went over to Paris to rescue his sister, Lady Bethune, from a religious circle which she had joined with Methodistic fervour; but instead of doing this, he remained, to be completely changed himself by the ministrations of Mr. Lovatt, chaplain of the English Church in the Rue Marbœuf. When he did ultimately return to England, preparations were in progress for a grand ball to be given in his house at Dyrham Park, Barnet, but instead of the ball a meeting was held for the advancement of home missionary work. From this time forward Captain Trotter took a profound interest in religious institutions, and he also effected much good personally, having a most persuasive manner. He organised the Army Prayer Union and the Paris City Mission. Among other eminent men whom he personally influenced was the great lawyer, Lord Lyndhurst, who was three times Lord Chancellor. This brilliant and powerful thinker drew up a Confession of Faith, which he submitted to Captain Trotter; and there is a touching anecdote of his old age, in which the great judge and statesman is represented as studying the Church Prayer Book with his little granddaughter of seven or eight years of age. Other friends of Burns's were the Rev. John East of Bath, the Rev. W. H. Havergal of St. Nicholas, Worcester, the Rev. Charles Gribble, a manly and unconventional clergyman, and the Earl of Roden, a staunch Protestant of the old Orange School.

The English Episcopalians in Scotland desiring to have a bishop of their own, legal opinion was taken on the point, which was in their favour. Accordingly Bishop Beckles, formerly Bishop of Sierra Leone, accepted the appointment, which he held for a definite period. Since that lapsed, however, the Episcopalians have dispensed with a bishop of their own, and confirmations have been taken by such men as Dr. J. C. Ryle, Bishop of Liverpool. Burns had followed this movement with interest, and it may also be stated that he engaged from time to time many eminent men in the English Church to officiate at Wemyss Bay. Each minister who supplied had a nicely furnished parsonage, and he was sure of a warm welcome at Wemyss House and Wemyss Castle. The first who officiated was the Rev. Thomas Tate, grandson of the hymnologist. Dr. John Bardsley, the present Bishop of Sodor and and Man, and Dean Close, of Carlisle, were highly appreciated. Then there were Hugh MacNeile, Dean of Ripon, the Rev. Fielding Ould, an Irishman of great eloquence, Dr. Gobat, Bishop of Jerusalem, Canon Thorold, afterwards Bishop of Rochester, Archdeacon Taylor, Rev. W. Champneys, afterwards Dean of Lichfield, Dr. Lefroy, Dean of Norwich, the Rev. Dr. Flavell Cooke, and Archdeacon Whately.

The friend with whom Burns was perhaps in closest sympathy was the philanthropic Lord Shaftesbury. It was in the year 1850, at Roseneath, the Duke of Argyll's place on the Clyde, that he first met him. We are told that their hearts opened to each other at once. 'Each found that in speaking to the other, it was as though he thought aloud. Both were sound Evangelicals, backbone Protestants, haters of Popery, lovers of the Jews, and students of Scripture; both in their respective spheres were engaged in numberless works of philanthropy; both were mild Conservatives; both were, above and beyond everything else, possessed of that vital Christianity which puts the love of God in Christ Jesus in the forefront of all things.' In 1871 Lord Shaftesbury paid his first long visit to Wemyss Bay. He was always highly appreciated in Scotland, and it was on this occasion that his first public honour was conferred upon him—the freedom of the town of Nairn. That of Glasgow immediately followed. Lord Shaftesbury and his family, Lord Lawrence, Sir Harry Parkes, the Hon. Arthur Kinnaird, and other friends were entertained by Mr. and Mrs. Burns.

The distinguished company afterwards left Wemyss Bay in the *Camel* for Inveraray, and returned the same way with the Marquis and Marchioness of Lorne, the Duke of Argyll, and Earl Percy on board. George Burns thus related an incident which occurred on the way to Inveraray: 'On this voyage Lord Shaftesbury and Lawrence were like schoolboys. After luncheon, on the Loch going up to Inveraray, Lord Shaftesbury suddenly rose, and, in an eloquent speech, proposed his own health; but taking the character and life of Lord Lawrence as his own, he said, "Some people call me the 'Saviour of India,' others the 'Conqueror of the Punjaub,' but by whatever name I go, I am a very great man," and so on, telling many interesting stories of Lawrence. As soon as he sat down, Lord Lawrence rose and said that he, too, wished to propose his own health. He began by saying that he was the greatest philanthropist of the day, and had been picking up little boys and girls out of the gutters all his life; and so on he went through the life of Shaftesbury, making a most humorous speech which, coming from the grave Lord Lawrence, astonished everyone present.'

Lord Shaftesbury and George Burns came to have a strong affection for each other, and for fourteen years in succession the earnest-minded nobleman and his family visited Wemyss Bay for several months in each year, Lord Shaftesbury never failing to find much-needed rest and repose. He called his friend Burns Abraham, and his wife Sarah. Many touching letters passed between them during Lord Shaftesbury's sorrowful time of domestic trial in 1873. When so many gaps had been made in his own home, his lordship visited that second home at Wemyss Bay, where all that affection could suggest was done to assuage his sorrow. In John Burns's yacht *The Ferret* he made many pleasant cruises in search of health. On one occasion Lord Shaftesbury said, 'I can never thank God enough for the dear Burns family; I believe that, humanly speaking, my visits to them have added ten years to my life.' And again he wrote, 'I long for Wemyss Bay as a schoolboy longs for his holidays.' In August-September, 1884, he paid his last visit to his 'old Scotch home,' and in his diary was this brief but tender entry: 'Sept. 18th. Sat a long time with Abraham at Hebron.' The two friends never met again in this world, for Lord Shaftesbury died in the following year.

In the year 1865 Burns's old partner, Sir Samuel Cunard, died. He was a very devout man, and expired happily and peacefully. During his last illness, he frequently referred to the old times of forty years before, and spoke of the Burns family in the strongest terms of affection. Another link with the past was broken in 1871, when James Burns, the brother and partner in business of George Burns, died at the age of eighty-two. This great merchant had used his enormous wealth nobly and wisely in the furtherance of benevolent and religious objects. On the 10th June, 1872, Mr. and Mrs. Burns celebrated their golden wedding. They were in Paris at the time, but received congratulations from relatives and friends. The year did not close, however, without another severe trial in the loss of Mrs. James Cleland Burns, who died, leaving a husband and five daughters to mourn her untimely end. Five years more passed, and then, in June, 1877, came George Burns's heaviest sorrow. His wife, who had been his loving and understanding companion for fifty-five years, passed away in the fulness of years. Her end was solemnly beautiful in its tender and suitable farewells to each individual survivor. When her spirit had fled, and the blinds of the house were drawn down, her stricken husband said, 'Nay, draw them up again; she is not dead, she has entered into fuller, even eternal life.' The deceased was carried by her own people through the garden where she had her last walk, and laid in peace in a chamber behind the little church she loved so well—prepared, like Abraham's cave in Machpelah, by the kindness of friends, who worked night and day. Sympathetic letters came to Mr. Burns from all quarters, and from all classes. In memory of his wife, Mr. Burns raised a handsome church at Wemyss Bay, in place of the previous temporary structure.

The few closing years of Burns's life witnessed the passing over to the majority of many old friends—Dean Close, Colonel Gardner, Sir Duncan MacGregor, and Admiral Sir James Crawford Caffin among the number. All this time Burns's own strength and freshness were remarkable. A surprising instance of his vigour is given in connection with the General Election of 1886, when he was in his ninety-first year. He journeyed from Wemyss Bay to Glasgow and back the same day—a distance of over sixty miles—in order to record his vote in favour of the Unionist candidate for his district. He was recognised at the polling-booth by the Liberal candidate, Dr. (now Sir Charles) Cameron, who shook hands with him, saying magnanimously, 'Long may you live, Mr. Burns, to come and vote against me.' Further, he was not only present at the laying of the memorial stone of the new Barony Church, Glasgow, in June, 1887, but delighted the spectators by delivering a racy and entertaining speech.

The members of his family cheered the final days of Burns's life, while the patriarch himself also added to the store of happiness by his bright and genial reminiscences. He was a capital talker and story-teller, and very fond of a witty anecdote. Burns never took a prominent part in politics, and, indeed, he did not carefully study political questions, being much more deeply concerned in those which were religious. But among his reminiscences is this passage, in which he notes some of the great public movements contemporaneous with his own earlier years, and gives his views on the Constitution: 'In my early days I did not take much interest in political affairs, but in later years I have been ranked amongst the Conservatives, although I have never occupied any very prominent position amongst them. I may describe myself as being satisfied that the constitution of our country is well balanced, and gives an example of great liberty combined with efficient, moderate control. For instance, I value highly the House of Peers, as a balancing weight against what I fear is, at the present time, a too democratic tendency in the House of Commons. I am not willing to surrender the term "Liberal" entirely to the opposite party, because I have had liberal tendencies all my life. I think, however, that our too rapid progress should be controlled by checks, and that the Upper Chamber furnishes wise and salutary restraints. My confidence was shaken in Peel, but it recovered as I observed his action with regard to the Corn Laws. I lamented the way in which the Reform Bill was carried, by threats such as those used by Lord Grey, who proposed to create an extra number of peers. I also regretted, in 1829, that what was called Catholic Emancipation was unavoidably yielded.

On the 23rd of May, 1889, the Marquis of Salisbury wrote to George Burns as follows: 'I have the pleasure of informing you that Her Majesty has been pleased to direct that a Baronetcy of the United Kingdom should be conferred on you on the occasion of her birthday, in recognition of the great benefits which your enterprise and administrative power have preserved to the commerce of the country.' His biographer says 'he was greatly overcome, and no wonder. Suddenly, when lying in bed, almost alone, and ninety-four years of age—the oldest recipient of such an honour in the world's history,—he realises that Her Gracious Majesty, the head of our social system, has recognised his life-work and has conferred upon him a high honour. The old man bowed his snowy head in his hands, and thanked the King of Kings and Lord of Lords, blessing Him for putting it into the hearts of others to give him this honour, praying that he might use it aright, and when it should descend to his beloved son that he might sustain it unsullied, and through all the future of his life walk humbly with God.' Telegrams and letters of congratulation soon came pouring in, and the press warmly complimented the new baronet on his well-earned honour.

The sunset of Burns's life was calm and peaceful. As late as the spring of 1890 he loved to sit in the gardens and watch the annual renewal of the great miracle of vegetation, or on the upper lawns to see the shipping entering or leaving the Clyde. He had everything that, as Shakespeare says, 'should accompany old age, as honour, love, obedience, troops of friends.' His biographer feelingly refers to 'his perfect acquiescence in God's will, as he lay calmly in the shadow of the wings of the Almighty, and the intensity of his compassionate sympathy with suffering. Wounded and bruised affections, blighted capacities, broken and defeated hopes, desolation, solitariness, silence, sorrow, anguish, and sin—all things that caused or consummated the "death of life"—touched him keenly. At the same time he had the most intense interest in the young, and all the avenues of his heart were open to them. Everything bright and beautiful, joyous and glad, seemed in him to have the charm of dewy freshness. All the world was a mirror revealing the image of God; all its gladsome sounds—song of birds, plash of ocean, words of friends—echoes of His voice. His spiritual sympathy with God caused him to see men and things in the intense light of the Divine love, and his whole being was filled with charity, patience, forbearance, and good.

Although in great pain, Burns was well enough to be wheeled in his chair along the Bay on the 28th of May, but as he returned he quietly said, 'I shall never see the Bay again.' A few days more of suffering in his own room, and silent communion with his Maker, and the end came for the fine old patriarch on the 2nd of June, 1890. Three days later his mortal remains were laid to rest beside those of his wife in the rock-hewn cave.

Many loving and honourable tributes were paid to his memory, and in his case these can be said to have been deserved, for he was a model son, husband, father, citizen, and Christian. His services to the nation which he so deeply loved were great and enduring, and his example will doubtless serve to inspire his descendants and his fellow-countrymen to worthy and beneficent deeds through many generations.

SIR JOSIAH MASON.

SIR JOSIAH MASON.

'THE pen is mightier than the sword,' Lord Lytton makes one of his characters exclaim in *Richelieu ;* and as we lavish honours on the heroes of the battlefield, we should surely not be backward in paying tribute to the heroes of industry. The pen has certainly been a greater instrument of civilisation than the sword, and its maker as well as its wielder is deserving of recognition. And when, with the industrious manufacturer is combined the eminent philanthropist, as in Josiah Mason's case, no apology is needed for sketching his career, as an example and an incentive to others. Mason, Gillott, and Mitchell practically revolutionised one of the staple trades of the Midlands, and gave it an immense impetus whose effects are still being felt.

Before relating the story of Mason's life and labours, it will be of interest briefly to trace the history of the pen before his time. The desire to express thoughts and ideas by means of written characters is almost coeval with the race. The Egyptians, Greeks, Romans, and other ancient nations wrote upon papyrus or parchment with a reed pen ; and when they used tablets of wood or stone covered with wax, they wrote with a pointed stylus of bronze, bone, or other material. It is stated that reed pens are still the only kind used by the natives of Persia and some neighbouring countries, the metal pen being unsuited to their style of writing. Reed pens are cut almost in the same way as quills. Quills were used for caligraphic purposes as early as the seventh century ; and reed pens were also still employed in Europe at that time, having been then in use for upwards of a thousand years. To a limited extent, metal pens must have been in use among the Romans, for in the Naples Museum there is a bronze pen, nibbed like a modern steel pen, which was found at Pompeii. Silver pens were also occasionally made in the Middle Ages; but more as curiosities, it is thought, than as articles in general use, and the same may be said of all metallic pens of more recent date, until we come to the nineteenth century. For twelve centuries before the present, quills were universally employed in Western Europe, and it was not until about the year 1840 that steel pens began to be substituted for them in British schools. Even in the latter half of the nineteenth century there have been authors and statesmen who have remained faithful to the quill, and have never used any other instrument for writing.

There are traces of the metallic pen, however, in France, Italy, and England, as far back as the fourteenth century, but it was never made of steel. In the records of the prosecution of Robert d'Artois, in 1329, a bronze pen plays a conspicuous part in the forgeries for which the accused was tried. In one of the earliest printed books at Padua, it is stated that the work was 'fashioned and by diligence finished for the service of God, not with ink of quill *nor with brazen reed*, but with a certain invention of printing or reproducing by John Fust, citizen of Mayence, and Peter Schœffer, of Gernsheim, Dec. 17th, 1465 A.D.'

Careful researches into the history of metallic pen-making have been made by Mr. Samuel Timmins, a well-known Warwickshire antiquary. In a contribution to the *Birmingham Weekly Post* some years ago he wrote: 'While steel pens, as an advancing article of manufacture, do not date further back than about 1825, there is no doubt that they were made in Birmingham for special private use as early as 1790. There is no reason why a piece of metal or steel should not have been made in the form of a quill pen long before; but no example of a very early date seems to be known.

'The example I am going to mention is beyond all doubt of the date assigned, so long ago as 1717. The pen forms part of a very remarkable little volume in the magnificent library of Mr. William Bragge, C.E., of Sheffield. It is attached (like a pencil, through loops in an ordinary memorandum book) to an old Dutch volume, dated 1717. The silver pencil unscrews in two places—one to produce a lump of solid plumbago, mounted like a crayon, and the other showing a metallic pen, either silver or plated steel, polished, and with the peculiarity of having the slit all up to nearly the top of the pen; evidently a very early example of pen-making before steel was found flexible enough to write well. The exact date of this early pen is given beyond doubt by the title page of the book, of which the subjoined is a translation from the Dutch original—"Newly-invented Merchant's Office Almanack and Memorandum Book, for the year of our Lord MDCCXVII. (New Style.) Containing the List of Horse, Cattle, and Leather Markets for the Year, and the Daily Changes of the Moon. By John Albertz van Dam, Amsterdam. By the Heirs of Albert Magnus, at the House of Cornelius Danckerts, New Dyke, at the Sign of the Atlas. With Privilege." Mr. Nyhoff, the librarian at the Hague, stated to Mr. Bragge that this rare almanack was supplied officially to the members of the States General. As no other volume with a pencil of plumbago and steel pen seems to be known, and as the pen, pencil, and volume are beyond all doubt coeval, the manufacture of at least one steel pen must be carried back as far as the year 1717.'

That French steel pens were early in use is shown by a letter in Roger North's *Autobiography*. Writing to his sister under date March 8, 1700-1, North says: 'You will hardly tell by what you see that I write with a steel pen. It is a device come out of France, of which the original was very good, and wrote

O

very well; but this is but a copy, ill made. When they get the knack of making them exactly, I do not doubt but the Government of the Goose Quill is near an end, for none that can have these will use others.' French metallic pens are also amusingly alluded to in a volume entitled *A Journey to Paris in the Year 1695*, by Dr. Martin Lister. After touching upon the various kinds of pens, the author adds: 'A Quill soon spoils; Steel is undoubtedly the best, and if you choose China Ink, the most lasting of all Inks, it never rusts the Pen, but rather preserves it, like a kind of Varnish, which dries upon it, though you take no care in wiping it.' In Sainte-Beuve's *History of Port Royal* there is likewise a reference to metallic pens. 'One owes to Port Royal,' remarks the author, 'the use of pens of metal, which have saved the pupils much time, and have spared them many small miseries.' In 1691 La Fontaine prayed the Reverend Mother for a few copper pens, if she still made them. Pope, in one of his minor poems, refers to steel and golden pens made by one Bertrand. Johann J. Janssen, writer to the Mayoralty of Aix-la-Chapelle, claimed in 1748 to be the inventor of the steel pen. 'Just at the meeting of the Congress,' says Janssen, in his *Historical Chronicle of Aix-la-Chapelle*, 'I may without boasting claim the honour of having invented new pens. It is perhaps not an accident that God should have inspired me at the present time with the idea of making steel pens, for all the envoys here assembled have bought the first that have been made, therewith, as may be hoped, to sign a treaty of peace, which, with God's blessing, shall be as permanent as the hard steel with which it is written. Of these pens, as I have invented them, no man hath before seen or heard. If kept clean and free from rust and ink, they will continue fit for use for many years. Indeed a man may write twenty sheets of paper with one, and the last line would be written as well as the first. They are now sent into every corner of the world as a rare thing—to Spain, France, and England. Others will no doubt make imitations of my pens, but I am the man who first invented and made them. I have sold a great number of them at home and abroad, at one shilling each, and I dispose of them as quickly as I can make them.'

From information gleaned by technical writers on the subject, we learn that the earliest English metallic pens of which there is definite knowledge were some made in 1780 by Mr. Harrison, split-ring maker, Birmingham, for the eminent Unitarian divine Dr. Priestley. They were made of sheet steel, formed into a tube and filed into shape, the joining of the metal making the slit. Brass pens were likewise made in England before the end of last century, and one of these was sold in the Strawberry Hill collection of art objects and curiosities in 1842. Various plans were tried early in the nineteenth century to produce pens more durable than ordinary quills. There were quills pointed with metal, and pens constructed of horn and tortoiseshell with small pieces of diamond and other hard gems embedded in them by pressure. Sometimes gold was attached to the points, but of course such pens were costly, and out of reach of the general public. Barrel pens of steel were made by Mr. Wise in London in 1803, but these also were too high in price.' The first English patent for the manufacture of steel pens was granted to Bryan Donkin in 1808; and the first patent in America was granted in 1810 to Peregrine Williamson of Baltimore for the manufacture of metallic pens. Sheldon of Sedgley made steel pens of the barrel type in 1815, and sold them at eighteen shillings per dozen. Five years later the number of manufacturers had increased. To James Perry must be awarded the credit of bringing steel pens into general use. In 1819 he began pen-making at Manchester, using for the purpose the best Sheffield steel, made from Swedish charcoal coal. Perry was the first to overcome the rigidity previously complained of in steel pens, by introducing apertures below the shoulder and point of the pen—thus transferring the elasticity of the implement to a position below instead of above the shoulder. About 1824 Perry removed to Red Lion Square, London, where he continued the manufacture of pens under his patents, which included the invention above cited. The Perryian pens were pressed into the market with great energy, and they were soon known and used throughout the country, before the leading Birmingham pen-makers, Mitchell, Gillott, and Mason effected a new departure in the trade by the use of machinery in the production of pens.

At this point I shall take up the biographical sketch of my subject. As Mr. J. T. Bunce has shown in his excellent *Memoir* of Mason, he was in all respects a self-made man, having no advantages of birth, connections, education, or means. 'So far as regarded the probability of wealth or of personal eminence, no life could have begun in a manner less promising. He started, indeed, not so much upon the lowest round of the ladder, as at the very foot of it, with little chance, as it seemed, of getting so high as the first round. He was not even a mechanic by any formal training, for he was taught no trade, served no apprenticeship, was inducted into no "art" or "mystery" of handicraft. How this happened is not very clear; but his own recollection was distinct that it was so, and that he stood a good chance of going through life as a labourer in the ordinary sense, or of earning a precarious livelihood by turning his hand to those odd jobs which fall to the lot of one who, according to the common saying, is jack of all trades and master of none. From this shiftless kind of life Josiah Mason was preserved by his natural resolution, ingenuity, and industry, and by an innate conviction that, somehow or other, he must do something in the world, both for himself and for others.'

The ancestry of Josiah Mason has not been taken further back than three generations. His paternal grandfather was a working bombazine weaver at Kidderminster, with a turn for mechanics and music, and also for dealing with machinery of a simple character. He was named Josiah, and he had an only son, also named Josiah, who married Elizabeth Griffiths, the daughter of a respectable workman at Dudley. Josiah the second moved to Kidderminster, where he attained a position of trust in a carpet manufactory. He had four children, three sons and a daughter. The second son was Josiah Mason the third, and the one destined to make the family known to future generations. He was born on the 23rd of February, 1795, in a little house in Mill Street, Kidderminster. The street is now called Josiah Mason Street, to commemorate a benefaction by Sir Josiah to the dispensary of the town. Mason survived his sister and both his brothers. So far from being ashamed of his humble origin at Kidderminster, he had it duly set forth in the trust deeds of Mason College; and he directed that both in regard to this institution and his orphanage, preference should be given to children belonging to Kidderminster, his earliest home, and to those of Birmingham, which was his home in later years.

Young Mason went to a dame's school, held in a cottage next door to his father's house. The tuition was of course cheap and inefficient. Nor was it of any long duration, for at eight years of age he began the business of life by selling cakes in the streets. His cakes and rolls were so much appreciated that purchasers sometimes gave the industrious lad an extra penny. Owing to his perseverance he was soon able to enter upon a more ambitious field. Purchasing a donkey, which he named Admiral Rodney, he became a dealer in fruit and vegetables, which he sold from door to door. His mother gave him practical help, while his father sagely recommended him never to let anybody know how much money he had got in his pockets. Desiring at length a more settled occupation, Josiah took to shoemaking at home, where he could help to nurse his elder brother, who was a confirmed invalid. He began by simply mending shoes, but passed from a cobbler into a shoemaker proper. Quality was what he aimed at, and he was rather too conscientious to make it pay. He would buy the best leather and put into it the best work, so that in later years he would say with a twinkle, 'I found I couldn't make it pay, and must become bankrupt, so I gave it up.' Distressed by his defective education he taught himself writing, and obtained casual employment by writing letters for those who were unable to conduct their own correspondence. In a short time he was able to buy a few books, and where he could not buy he borrowed. His reading was of the severer kind—history, science, theology,—and it is said to be doubtful whether he ever read any work of fiction in his life. First at the Unitarian Sunday-school, and later at that of the Wesleyans, he was able to supplement his hardly-acquired knowledge by valuable lessons.

About the year 1812 Mrs. Mason opened a little shop for the sale of groceries. Josiah was her right-hand man, and when to the shop was ultimately added a bakehouse, used for the cooking of Sunday dinners, he superintended it. But he still hankered after a settled trade, and assumed in turns the *rôle* of a carpenter, a blacksmith, and a house-painter, making progress in all, but being satisfied with none. Then, in 1814, when he was nineteen years old, he found employment in Mr. Broom's carpet-works, at Tinker's Hill. For two years he laboured here, thoroughly mastering the business, and doing his work so well that his employer showed it to others as a pattern and a stimulus. But carpet-weaving was monotonous and led to nothing, while the utmost remuneration he could secure at it was a pound per week. Consequently he wanted more scope, and craved for a wider field. The 'hardware village' of Birmingham had already come into note, and thither Josiah Mason turned his steps. There was plenty of employment, and new industries were constantly being introduced, or old ones developed. In his twenty-second year he paid a visit to Birmingham to see what it was like. This proved the turning point in his career, and he never went back to live in Kidderminster. He found in Birmingham all that he wanted. It was a free town, full of enterprising citizens, and offering abundant opportunities for young men of business ability and perseverance. Work was not concentrated in the hands of a few wealthy men, but there were numbers of small masters who shared in the various trades rapidly springing up. When young Mason entered Birmingham he found it 'a town fast rising in population, wealth, and influence'; there was 'an industry varied beyond computation, and embracing every kind of metal work, from the great engines made at Soho to the steel trinkets forged and filed and polished in some garret in a bye-street'; and there were 'an army of workers, energetic, ingenious, and inventive in the highest degree, capable of independent exertion, and at the same time susceptible of adapting themselves to the complex organisation of large factories. It was precisely the place to suit Mason, who was possessed of courage, industry, and activity, and who was qualified to develop an organising faculty which, later in life, exerted an important influence upon his own fortunes and upon the trade of the town.' Mason always spoke of it as a providential circumstance that his steps were directed towards Birmingham. Settling down there in 1816, he married on the 18th of August in the following year his cousin Annie Griffiths. Their union, which was one of unclouded happiness and perfect confidence, lasted for more than fifty-two years. When Mrs. Mason died, on the 24th of February, 1870, the surviving husband, though grief-stricken, could look back on a far longer span of blissful married life than most men.

    Mason's first occupation in Birmingham was in looking after a gilt toy business, in which his uncle Griffiths was the chief, and subsequently sole proprietor. The gilt toy trade included the production of common jewellery, gilt rings, buckles, chains, fancy buttons, clasps, and personal ornaments of all kinds. Through the fault of his original partner Griffiths had nearly lost all the money he had invested in the business; but Mason worked with such a will for a period of nearly seven years, that he recovered his uncle's money, paid off all the debts of the concern, increased its value as a business, and largely increased the profits. When all this had been done, his uncle behaved with base ingratitude. He had led Mason to believe he would be taken in as a partner, and now, when he had turned a worthless business into a prosperous one, it was sold over his head, and the fruits of his skill and industry were denied to him. When Mason learnt the facts, he exclaimed, 'I will never re-enter the place; I have done with it at once and for ever.' With the Griffiths family he would have no further business transactions whatever, and all through life he felt keenly the injustice of the treatment to which he had been subjected.

For a short time he was thrown upon his own resources, but in 1822 he was introduced by a mutual friend named Heeley —a member of the Wesleyan body—to Mr. Harrison, a split-ring maker, in Lancaster Street. Harrison was soon satisfied of Mason's capacity and his willingness to work, and he engaged him at the first interview. As Harrison was leaving the house in Lancaster Street for a cottage which he had built for himself, Mason went to live at the former. The house had workshops behind it, and a pleasant garden beyond. This site, with about an acre of ground besides, was afterwards occupied by Mason's steel-pen manufactory, in one portion of which the old split-ring business continued to be carried on. For a period of twelve months Mason drew no settled salary from the business, merely taking what he wanted for himself and wife to live upon. Then he spoke to Harrison, who said he was willing to sell the business, and retire altogether if his assistant could find anyone to help him with the money. Mason tried, but failed, and then his master behaved most generously to him, practically making him a present of the business. 'Give me,' he said, '£500 for the stock and the business, and pay me that amount out of the profits as you make them.' Mr. Bunce thus remarks upon the circumstance, and upon the relations between the two men:

'The value of the bargain may be inferred from the facts that the first £100 was paid in August, 1823, and the last £100 in May, 1824. To the close of his life Sir Josiah Mason kept, as a precious relic of his old friend and master, the little octavo memorandum-book—thumbed and blurred, and "dog-eared" by the use of years, but always treasured by its owner, and shown by him with honest pride to his friends—in which these payments were entered, together with other records of ordinary trading transactions: purchases of metal, sales of goods, payments of wages, deposits with the bank, investments of savings. On the last leaf of the book were Mr. Harrison's entries of receipts for £500, the purchase-money: the only accounts which ever existed between the two.

'Nothing could have been simpler than this transaction; nothing more honourable to both parties to it. The old manufacturer, who had made what he desired—a modest competence—and who wished to be free in his declining years to enjoy it, recognised in the probity, industry, and intelligence of the younger man the qualities requisite to the successful conduct of a business in which, while retiring from it, he still felt a natural interest, and which he desired to see conducted on the same principles as those which had governed his own conduct of it. The confidence thus displayed by Mr. Harrison was justified by his associate so entirely that a close and tender friendship, lasting throughout the remainder of Mr. Harrison's life, sprang up between the two.'

Though he had given up the business, Harrison continued to be a frequent visitor to the factory in Lancaster Street, and the feeling of affectionate veneration in which Mason held him was so strong, even in old age, that he never tired of speaking of his many estimable qualities — his kindliness, honesty, and capacity, and he traced to him his own success in business life. Before Harrison's time, split-rings were laboriously made in small numbers by filing and bending, but he adapted the stamping press to their manufacture, and was the inventor of the flat ring now commonly used for bunches of keys. Harrison was a great friend of Dr. Priestley, who could never understand how split-rings were made, so on one occasion the manufacturer took him to Lancaster Street and showed him the operation of the stamp, which made the ring at a single blow. Upon this the Doctor threw up his hands, and exclaimed, 'With all my philosophy, I could not have dreamt of such a thing.' It was owing to Dr. Priestley's complaining that he could not obtain satisfactory pens wherewith to write that Harrison made him the first steel pens produced in Birmingham.

Master of a business which promised to secure him a competency, Mason now looked forward to the future with confidence and hope. He had a deeply religious nature, and never failed to attribute his various openings in life to the intervention of a Higher Power. He was, unfortunately, not blessed with children, and his business probably occupied more of his thought in consequence, for he was not a man to put up with a life of inactivity. In three years he had prospered so greatly that he bought the buildings in Lancaster Street, and also took in new premises. The split-ring trade expanded rapidly owing to his improvements. Hoop rings had up to this time been finished by hand, the bevelling being done slowly, and at considerable cost. Mason felt that they could be done much more quickly and cheaply, and accordingly devised a bevelling machine, by which he gained £1,000 in a single year. The actual machine which he constructed in 1825 still continued in use after his death.

Mason next took up the work by which he amassed his enormous wealth, and by which he will be known to posterity, viz., the improvement and manufacture of steel pens. Following upon Donkin's English pen patent already referred to, came one in 1809 by Frederick Bartholomew Folsch and William Howard for a pen 'made of glass, enamel, of any sort of stone or metal'; and in May of the same year Folsch took out another patent in his own name only, for a pen 'which may be made of any sort of metal,' and with a socket in the holder to contain ink. The next patent was one granted nine years later to Charles Watt, to protect an invention for coating quill pens with gold. Nine or ten years more elapsed, and then George Poulton obtained a patent for a reservoir tube to hold ink, the pen to be made of steel. Then, in April, 1830, Perry took out a patent for making pens by a new method, from hard, thin, elastic metal, and a 'length of slitted or cleft space' scarcely exceeding that of quill pens. In 1832 Perry made other improvements, securing greater flexibility. But the greatest improvement in pen manufacture was the adoption of the screw hand-press for the cutting out of pens, thus enabling the manufacturer to supply them cheaply and in quantities. At first the method of slitting pens by machinery was kept a profound secret. To John Mitchell, a Sheffield cutler, who removed to Birmingham in 1822, belongs the credit of first making pens by machinery. His step-son, Gillott, also began to use machinery for pen-making in 1829, at which time likewise Mason began to use the press for the same purpose, though both of them worked unknown to each other. But it was afterwards demonstrated, and fully admitted by Mason, that Mitchell had the prior claim to the invention of making steel pens by machinery. Mason made barrel pens in 1828, and 'slip' pens for Perry in 1829. Gillott took out a patent in 1831 for his method of making pens by machinery.

In the hands of the three leading pen-makers mentioned above, the steel-pen industry became in the course of twenty years one of the most important in Birmingham. Though a simple-looking instrument, the pen has to go through some sixteen different processes before it is finished ready for use. A technical authority thus describes the method of manufacture:

'The steel of which the pens are made comes from Sheffield, and is in sheets 6 feet long and 1 foot 5 inches wide. It is first cut into strips of convenient width; next it is annealed and rolled to the requisite thickness, when it is found to have trebled its original length and to have acquired a bright surface from the action of the rollers. The "blanks," or first shape of the pen, are now cut out by means of a press; next comes the operation of *marking* or stamping the name on the pen, then *piercing;* but before they can be formed into the shape of a pen they require to be softened by *annealing*. They are freed from dust and grease, placed in round pots, which are again enclosed in larger ones, are covered with charcoal-dust, put into a muffle or iron box, heated to a dull red, and then allowed to cool. The pens are next *raised* or formed into the required shape by a blow from a screw-press fitted with a punch and a die. Then they are *hardened*. This is done by arranging them in thin layers in covered iron pans of a round shape, which are heated to a bright redness in a muffle. The contents of the pans are next emptied into a bucket, immersed in a tank of oil, and transferred to a perforated cylinder, which, being quickly rotated, drains off the oil. The pens are still greasy and as brittle as glass, and in order to cleanse them they are again placed in perforated buckets and plunged into a tank of boiling soda-water. They are next tempered, or softened, by enclosure in an iron cylinder which is kept revolving over a charcoal fire until the requisite degree of softness is attained. The pens have been blackened by this operation; they are next *scoured* by being dipped into a tub of diluted sulphuric acid, and then put into iron barrels containing water and material made from broken and finely-ground annealing pots. The barrels are kept revolving for five, or sometimes eight hours; then the pens are subjected to a second process of scouring in barrels filled with dry material of the same kind; and then to a third process, in which dry sawdust is the scouring or cleaning agent. The pens have now acquired a bright, silver tone, and the points have been rounded. They have then to be ground between the pierced portion and the point; this is done on a small revolving solid wheel or "bob" made of wood, covered with leather, and coated with emery-powder. Next comes the operation of *slitting*, which is cleverly accomplished by a cutting-press; but, the edges of the slit being sharp, the pens are again polished in revolving barrels. They are now coloured and varnished; the colouring is done in a copper or iron cylinder over a coke fire; if to be lacquered they are placed in a solution of shellac. Afterwards the spirit is drained off, the pens are placed in wire cylinders, and kept revolving until the lacquer is dry. Next the pens are spread on iron trays and put into an oven, the heat of which spreads the lacquer evenly over the surface. Girls now look over the pens, throw aside the faulty ones, and the good ones are packed into boxes ready for sale.'

In 1849 there were twelve pen factories in Birmingham, employing about 2,000 men, women, and girls, the weekly output of pens being stated at 65,000 gross. In 1866 the following returns of the trade were made by the manufacturers:— Number of makers, 12; men employed, 360; women and girls, 2,050; horse-power, 330; number of pens produced weekly, 98,000 gross; quantity of steel used weekly, 9½ to 10 tons; prices of 'slip' pens, from 1½d. to 1s. per gross, and of barrel pens, 7d. to 12s. per gross. About 2,000 additional hands, chiefly women, were employed in making pen-holders, paper-boxes, and other accessories of the trade. The conditions of work and rates of pay were thus described in a volume on the industries of Birmingham: 'The condition of the work-people employed in metallic pen-making is very satisfactory, in consequence of the large and lofty rooms in which the work is usually done, and the generous care which the principal manufacturers display for the welfare and improvement of the persons they employ. The wages of girls vary from 5s. to 12s. per week, some of the younger earning only 2s. 6d. to

3s. 6d., while some few of the older and more skilful workwomen earn as much as 15s. or 20s. per week. The men earn from 18s. to 20s.; the boys 4s. 6d. to 8s., or if skilful, 8s. to 16s.; and the skilled adult males (chiefly tool-makers) from 30s. to 80s., and some even 90s. to 100s. per week. The hours of labour are usually from 52 to 57 hours per week, all beyond those hours being reckoned as "over-time," and the Saturday half-holiday is nearly universal in the pen factories.'

The *Handbook of Birmingham*, edited by Mr. Timmins, and published in 1886, gives the following account by Mr. Maurice Pollack of the trade as it existed at that date: 'There has been little improvement since 1865. Muffles heated by gas, on the plan of Dr. Siemens, have been introduced for tempering and colouring, and ordinary gas is also used in connection with these processes; but these improvements are only used by one or two firms, and more as a matter of convenience than as a means of making pens of a better quality or lower price. Many patents have been taken out since 1865, for new styles of pens; the most successful have been those which deal with the points; these have been turned up or turned down, thickened or planished, all for the purpose of producing smooth points to glide freely over the paper even with a rough surface.

'The fashion in paper and ink materially influences the style of pens. The J pens (so-called because that letter was embossed upon one of the first and best-known broad points) have been extensively used, and have influenced handwriting, especially that of ladies.

'Caligraphy as an art has fallen off in this country, and this has influenced pen manufacture. The most delicately made pens are manufactured for foreign use. There are, perhaps, not so many pen works now as there were in 1865, but the productive power has vastly increased. The present weekly average of pens manufactured is about 160,000 gross, requiring from 16 to 18 tons of steel, of which only eight tons appear in the article, the rest being loss or waste. Pen steel is still produced in Sheffield, the best being made from Swedish iron. The number of girls and women employed is from 3,200 to 3,600, whilst the number of men employed as tool-makers, rollers, engineers, stokers, etc., hardly exceeds 500. The increase in make since 1865, of quite 60 per cent., is mainly due to the export trade. No new pen manufactories have been established since 1865, except in the United States, where there are now four pen works, but of these only one is of importance. In France there are now only three pen manufactories, and the production is less than it was three years ago. In Germany there is only one, and its make, though improved in quality, is very inconsiderable in comparison with the large consumption of steel pens in Germany. An attempt has been made to establish works in Russia, where the duty on steel pens is high, but after existing one or two years the manufactory was burnt down, and no attempt has been made to rebuild it. The Customs duty on steel pens, with the exception of Russia or the United States, where it is sixpence per gross, is very moderate, and prevents the importation of low or middle-class pens. The price obtained for steel pens depends more upon the reputation of the maker or of the mark than upon their intrinsic value—hence the difficulty of giving an average value of each gross of pens produced.'

Josiah Mason stated that from the time of his introduction to James Perry, in 1829, he became a steel-pen maker. An improvement which he had made in a Perry pen, and of which a sample was sent to the maker in London, brought Perry down to Birmingham in great haste. He at once began to employ Mason, and Perry & Co. were his only customers for many years. From their first interview until the year 1873 Mason was the sole and only maker of the Persian and the steel B pens sold under Perry's name. At first the trade was small, but in 1831 pens to the value of £1,421 were made by Mason for Perry. Then, as the greater demand resulted in reduced prices and a larger production, increased machinery and an increasing number of work-people became necessary, until at length Mason became the largest pen-maker in the world, and employed by far the largest number of hands in the trade. For a long time one part of the process of pen-making was kept a profound secret. This was the method of slitting pens by means of the press, instead of by the old and uncertain methods of cracking. Mason himself, with his own hands, made the dies and punches required for the slitting, and the presses in which these were fixed were worked by two or three women in a separate room, to which none but the actual workers and their master were admitted. Gillott was so struck by the quality of Mason's pens that he proposed they should go into partnership, saying, ' Let us join, and not another man shall make a pen besides us.' Mason preferred to stand by himself, however, though he and Gillott had many business transactions together. Mason's own name appeared on great numbers of pens which he made for Somerville & Co. and Perry & Co. For a time he received valuable assistance in the production of pens from Isaac Smith, who revealed much mechanical ingenuity, and afterwards from W. F. Batho, who remained with Mason until he resumed the personal management of his pen-works after the opening of the Erdington Orphanage. The increase of trade induced Mason to extend his works, and he constantly added to them until he laid the foundation for producing 40,000 gross of pens weekly, although this quantity was not reached when he sold his works in 1875 to the trustees of Perry & Co., Limited. At that time the output exceeded 32,000 weekly, and the works embraced, in addition to the industry of pen-making, the manufacture of pen-holder sticks, pen-holder tips, paper-binders, and numerous minor articles. At the close of 1873 a series of steel pens of the most perfect finish, each pen being stamped ' Sir Josiah Mason,' began to be produced and these pens are sold at the present day. When Mason gave up business, nearly 1,000 work-people, four-fifths of whom were women, were employed in his works. About sixty tons of pens were constantly in movement through the works. As nearly a million and a half of pens may go to a single ton, some idea may be formed of the magnitude of an establishment capable of dealing with sixty times this number.

Mason's connection with the electro-plating trade was also of considerable importance, and now demands attention. The ancients knew how to gild metals, and to plate silver upon copper. In England, likewise, gilding was used in the Middle Ages, and in 1403 an Act was passed to prevent persons from selling gilt articles as the genuine metal. A Sheffield mechanic named Bolsover invented in 1742 the method of plating which was commonly in use before the application of electro-plating. Bolsover discovered the art of laying silver upon copper, and his discovery was improved upon by Joseph Hancock, one of the Sheffield cutlers, who used it to imitate the finest and most richly embossed plate. Birmingham soon took up the manufacture of plated goods, James Watt's partner, Matthew Boulton, establishing his well-known factory at Soho. Sir Edward Thomason followed in 1796, and from this time the trade rapidly increased. Volta's great discovery of chemical electricity in 1799 was developed by various English and European chemists between that date and 1805; and in 1807 Sir Humphry Davy made a decided advance in the science of electro-metallurgy. In 1831 Faraday achieved still further triumphs, and three years later he made the important discovery that 'when a voltaic current was passed through different salts in solution or in a state of fusion, the amount of salt decomposed by the current was in direct proportion to the quantity of electricity; and that the quantities of substances dissolved and set free in electrolysis were in definite proportions by weight, and that those proportions were identical with the ordinary chemical equivalents of the substances, and thus established the important law of definite electro-chemical action.'

Experiments by Professor Daniell, Mr. De la Rue, and Dr. Golding Bird followed; and then, in 1839, came an avalanche of discoveries by M. Jacobi of St. Petersburg and Mr. Jordan and Mr. Spencer in England, each of whom claimed to have invented the method of electro-deposition. In 1842 a similar claim was made on behalf of Mr. J. S. Woolrich of Birmingham —the inventor of the electro-magnetic method,—who 'succeeded in gilding an article by voltaic precipitation from the ammoniacal solution of gold, before the published experiments of Mr. Jordan and Mr. Spencer appeared.' The credit for the earliest commercial use of the electrotype process is due to Mr. George Richards Elkington and his cousin, Mr. Henry Elkington, who were engaged in 1838 in coating military and other ornaments with gold and silver by simply immersing them in solutions of those metals, particularly a boiling one of carbonate of potash containing dissolved gold. In conjunction with Mr. O. W. Barratt, they patented a process in 1838 for coating articles of copper and brass with zinc, by means of an electric current, generated by a piece of zinc attached to the articles by a wire, and immersed with them in a boiling and neutral solution of chloride of zinc. Dr. George Gore states in his *Art of Electro-Metallurgy* that this was the first patent in which a separate metal was employed for electro-plating purposes. But the grand discovery of electro-metallurgy was eventually made in 1840 by Mr. John Wright, a surgeon of Birmingham. By an ingenious experiment, Mr. Wright obtained what had never been acquired before, namely, a thick deposit of firm and white silver by electrolytic action. He submitted his results to Messrs. Elkington, who embodied the discovery in a patent. Mr. Wright received a royalty of one shilling for every ounce of silver deposited, but after his death an annuity was paid to his widow instead of the royalty.

Two years after the discovery of Mr. Wright's process, Mr.

Woolrich patented an invention which—as Mr. Bunce remarks in an interesting passage—'was destined to effect a great advance in the mode of producing the electrical current required for the depositing process. Amongst the most brilliant discoveries of Faraday was that of magneto-electricity. He found that, when the pole of a magnet is made to approach towards and recede from the core of a coil of insulated copper wire, alternating shocks are induced in the coil. These alternating shocks may be made to act in the same direction; they can then do the same kind of work that is accomplished by a galvanic battery. The idea of applying the currents so developed to the purposes of electro-metallurgy was formed by Mr. Woolrich, who, in 1842, patented a machine—a dynamo, in fact—for producing them in such a way as to be applicable to electro-deposition. The patent was originally worked by Mr. Thomas Prime, of Northwood Street, Birmingham, where Faraday saw the machine in operation. Dr. Percy mentions this interesting fact in his volume on the *Metallurgy of Iron and Steel*. In 1845, he says, "I conducted Mr. and Mrs. Faraday over Mr. Prime's works, where, for the first time, that great philosopher saw his discovery of the magneto-electric current applied to the electro-deposition of silver. I shall never forget the sparkling delight which he manifested on seeing this result of his purely scientific labours rendered subservient to a beautiful art and to the advantage of others." The superior constancy of the current obtained by the magneto-electric machine over that furnished by the battery soon became manifest; and, though Woolrich's form of the dynamo has long since passed out of the practical into the historical stage, the method embodied in his invention is now in almost universal use as a source of electricity for coating metals. The first dynamo made by him for use by Mr. Prime has been presented by the son of the first user, the present head of the firm, to the Corporation of Birmingham, and is now preserved in their Museum at Aston Hall.'

A further improvement of great importance was due to another Birmingham discoverer, Mr. M. Milward, of Elkingtons' establishment. In 1847 Milward and a person named Lyons took out a patent for producing bright deposited silver by 'adding compounds of sulphur or carbon,' bisulphide of carbon being preferred, to the cyanide of silver solution. This process has been constantly and extensively employed ever since. Dr. Gore states that since the year 1847 the chief improvements which have been made in electro-metallurgy 'have been the gradual extension of the process for multiplying printing surfaces, in stereotyping, etc., and in the production of works of art, etc., of increased size, in copper, until deposits several tons in weight have been attained; the extensive use of nickel as a coating upon harness furniture; the protection of articles of cast-iron from rusting by a coating of copper; the substitution of magneto-electric machines and thermo-electric piles for voltaic batteries; the purification of crude copper in the process of copper-smelting, and the economical production of coppered iron rollers for calico printing by means of magneto-electric deposition.'

An interesting and condensed description of the process of electro-plating is given by a scientific writer in the latest edition of *Chambers's Encyclopædia*. He observes that the 'art of coating the baser metals with silver by the galvanic current is theoretically of great simplicity, but requires in the successful application of it very considerable experience and skill. Articles that are electro-plated are generally made of brass, bronze, copper, or nickel-silver. The best electro-plated goods are of nickel-silver. When Britannia-metal, iron, zinc, or lead are electro-plated, they must be first electro-coppered, as silver does not adhere to the bare surface of these metals. Great care is taken in cleaning the articles previous to electro-plating, for any surface impurity would spoil the success of the operation. They are first boiled in caustic potash to remove any adhering grease; they are then immersed in dilute nitric acid to dissolve any rust or oxide that may be formed on the surface; and they are lastly scoured with fine sand. Before being put into the silvering bath, they are washed with nitrate of mercury, which leaves a thin film of mercury on them, and this acts as a cement between the article and the silver. The bath where the electro-plating takes place is a large trough of earthenware or other non-conducting substance. It contains a weak solution of cyanide of silver in cyanide of potassium (water, 100 parts; cyanide of potassium, 10 parts; cyanide of silver, 1 part). A plate of silver forms the + electrode, and the articles to be plated, hung by pieces of wire to a metal rod lying across the trough, constitute the − electrode. When the plate is connected with the copper or + pole of a one or more celled galvanic battery, according to the strength required, or subjected to the magneto-electric current, and the rod is joined with the zinc or − pole, chemical decomposition immediately ensues in the bath, the silver of the cyanide begins to deposit itself on the suspended objects, and the cyanogen, liberated at the plate, dissolves it, re-forming the cyanide of silver. According, then, as the solution is weakened by the loss of the metal going to form the electro-coating, it is strengthened by the cyanide of silver formed at the plate. The thickness of the plate depends on the time of its immersion. The electric current thus acts as the carrier of the metal of the plate to the objects immersed. In this way silver becomes perfectly plastic in our hands. We can by this means, without mechanical exertion or the craft of the workman, convert a piece of silver of any shape, however irregular, into a uniform plate, which covers, but in no way defaces, objects of the most complicated and delicate forms. When the plated objects are taken from the bath, they appear dull and white; the dulness is first removed by a small circular brush of brass wire driven by a lathe, and the final polish is given by burnishing. The process of electro-gilding is almost identical with that of electro-plating. Success in either is attained by proper attention to the strength of the battery, the strength of the solution, the temperature, and the size of the + electrode.'

The process of 'finishing' plated articles is a careful and elaborate one. Mr. Ryland, in a paper contributed to a work on *Midland Hardwares*, describes the methods of burnishing, and then contrasts the old with the new process of silver-plating as follows:—'Under the old process all ornamental work was produced by the die-sinker, and, as a consequence, every portion of the die had to be so arranged that the work would 'leave' it. The foliage, if attempted, was clumsy, the stems and leaves, being massed together, were heavy and shapeless, and the human form was never attempted. Now, by the aid of modelling, casting, and electro-depositing, the most delicate forms are capable of being applied by the manufacturer, and the human figure stands out pre-eminently as a great addition to the plater's art. The graceful forms of animals, birds, and insects are seized upon by the modeller, and made subservient to his productions. The old method of proceeding was by first plating the copper, and then, by means of various manipulations, producing an article which was finished, all but burnishing, when it left the hands of the workman. Electro-plating has reversed all this, and that which was formerly the first is now the last operation, for it is necessary that the article should be finished and nicely polished before it receives its coat of silver. Owing to the new mode of plating, there is no occasion to protect the edges of the work by the silver thread soldered on, all the edges being filled and polished.

'Soft solder is almost banished, silver solder has taken its place in putting on the mountings, and these mountings are all filled with brass instead of lead or tin. This mode of work renders the article more durable, and, if well plated, it will last in domestic use for twenty years; and then, if the silver be worn off, the goods can be re-plated, which was impossible under the old process. A well-made and well-plated article, manufactured by the electro process, is a far better production than those made by the old method of plating. On the other hand, a poor electro article is far inferior to the worst class of work manufactured under the old system.'

The Birmingham and Sheffield platers resisted the introduction of the new process, but Messrs. Elkington persevered, and ultimately overcame all obstacles. The metal used in electro-plating is that which is variously known as German silver, nickel-silver, albata, etc., and it was chosen on account of its near approach in colour to silver. The best quality, and that most difficult to work, is an alloy of 40 parts of copper 20 parts of spelter, and 20 parts of nickel. It is very hard and white, and is that used by all manufacturers. It is much more expensive than the ductile copper which was previously used, and the difficulty of working it led at first to a serious loss in some departments. But, by the division of labour and the employment of machinery, many difficulties were overcome, and a good workman can now do better than under the old process. The report of the jury on exhibits at the Great Exhibition of 1851 stated that Elkington & Mason were the first who introduced into England the application of the electro process to gilding and silvering.

In the development of the electro-plating industry Josiah Mason bore a conspicuous part. On the invitation of Mr. G. R. Elkington he entered into partnership with the firm in 1842, the Elkingtons feeling that they needed the support and assistance of a man of undoubted business capacity and position in their new enterprise—one who could bring in both brains and capital. The supporters of the old processes predicted Mason's ruin, but his own faith in the recent scientific discoveries was strong, and he felt that the new process of plating must inevitably supplant the old, slow, and costly system of hand-plating. Yet, at one time, there was actual danger lest the patent should run out without yielding valuable results to its possessors. The firm therefore resolved to demonstrate the value of the process by the manufacture of plated wares, and it was now that Mason's practical business abilities, and his capacity for organisation, proved of the highest service. Mr. Elkington had been hampered by apparently insuperable difficulties, and it was largely owing to Mason's efforts that these were overcome, and one of the staple industries of Birmingham was saved to the city.

Mason's biographer observes that his energies were 'directed to the work of making the new trade pay. Being embarked in it, he undertook it with characteristic energy, and with a power of concentrated labour which few men could have equalled. It was necessary to provide suitable buildings for a manufactory; and the great establishment now existing in Newhall Street, Birmingham, was resolved upon.

'This was Mr. Mason's own design. He laid out the plans of the workshops and the showroom, which were built largely after his own arrangement. These works were intended for the production of articles of taste, and of those domestic articles to which ornament could be applied. But, with his partner, Mason saw clearly that for a considerable time the business must largely depend upon productions of a humbler description, in common use, capable of being supplied in any quantity equal to the demand, and of being sold at a comparatively cheap rate. This led to the extension of a manufactory in Brearley Street, Birmingham, previously used for the production of electro-plated spoons and forks. Here, with ample space and abundant means, every appliance of mechanical skill was provided for the preliminary processes, and the electro-deposition was carried out upon a scale which proved to the hand-platers that in the new method, backed by capital and energy, and directed by a spirit of courage and enterprise, they had not so much encountered a rival, as they had found a master, and ultimately a destroyer.

'The new firm did not, however, stop here. Their views extended with the growth of their business, and with the progress of their goods in public favour. While Birmingham formed the headquarters of the trade, and while visitors were attracted to Newhall Street from all parts of England, the Continent, and America, it was thought desirable to go boldly into the great markets, and consequently extensive showrooms and warehouses were opened in London and elsewhere. After these years of labour and outlay, Elkington & Mason reaped a rich reward for their skill and enterprise. The Great Exhibition of 1851 gave them the means of demonstrating their triumph; and from that date to the present day—holding their ground by successive advances—they have stood at the head of the electro-plating trade throughout the world: foremost in quality and design, in enterprise, in the magnitude of their operations, and in the reputation they have achieved.'

While Mason devoted himself to the practical part of the concern, he also took a deep interest in the artistic developments of the trade, and he saw with delight that many of the articles produced became, if not 'a thing of beauty and a joy for ever,' at least objects really beautiful to look upon, as well as distinguished for their durability. Mason's first partnership was with George Richards Elkington and Henry Elkington. This lasted from 1842 to 1852, when Henry Elkington retired, and the partnership between the others was renewed. It was finally dissolved in 1857, and Mason did not join the newly-constituted and still existing firm of Elkington & Co. Many anecdotes are related of Mason's readiness to consider suggestions, and his honourable business methods generally. One of these relates to Herr Krupp, the founder of the famous steel works at Essen. Krupp had invented machinery for rolling the metal 'blanks' from which spoons and forks are made—the object being to lengthen the blanks by rolling, in the manner in which a piece of steel is thinned down, and at the same time to impart greater density to the metal. He offered the invention to Elkingtons, but Mason thought the price too large, and offered £10,000. At the same time he advised the inventor to sell his patent elsewhere for a greater sum if he could, promising to abide by his offer of £10,000 if he could not. Krupp could not obtain a larger amount, and came back and accepted Mason's offer. The German inventor was so impressed by Mason that he subsequently more than once invited him to become his partner, but Mason declined because he was fully absorbed by his occupations in Birmingham.

The manufacture of indiarubber rings was another trade which Mason indirectly assisted in developing; but a greater undertaking than this was the copper industry which Elkington & Mason established at Pembrey, near Llanelly, in South Wales. Alexander Parkes, an able chemist employed by the firm, took out a patent for smelting copper ores, and purifying the copper by means of phosphorus. Elkingtons acquired the patent, and then prospected for a suitable place where they could set up works for smelting the Cornish ore. Elkington & Mason first went to Swansea, but they found it too smoky, and at length they pitched upon a spot on the Burry River, not far from Llanelly. Here extensive works were laid out, and operations begun, Parkes, the inventor, taking the scientific, and Mason the general management. In the course of a short time the village of Pembrey sprang up, and the proprietors of the copper-works displayed a genuine interest in the physical, moral, and intellectual welfare of the workmen. Cottages were built, with a small garden allotment to each; collieries were opened to supply coal; schools were erected for 350 children; and provision was made for religious instruction. The industry and the little colony generally still remain in a flourishing condition. Mason had great difficulty in persuading the children to attend the schools, although the educational facilities were excellent in every way. Having tried various plans, he at length took down with him from Birmingham, on his visits to Pembrey, supplies of useful articles such as hats, bonnets, shoes, and articles of clothing, which he distributed as rewards to the children who attended the schools. It was not long before the hitherto empty schools were half-full, and ultimately they became wholly so. Small fees and a judicious system of rewards were afterwards introduced, and the schools prospered.

In addition to the profits derived from his various undertakings, Mason made large additions to his wealth by the successful purchase and sale of land and building sites, and by investments in commercial and miscellaneous companies. Wealth is like a snowball, and it is astonishing how it increases when it is rolled along, after once the nucleus has been obtained. It was so in Mason's case. But he was not only a money-getter; he was a money-spender on a great scale, and in a noble way. Some misjudged his character because he was strict and business-like in his dealings, taking exactly what was due to him, as he gave to others with equal exactitude what was due to them. But all through the accumulation of his gains he had a settled purpose, which was to do something for the helpless and the friendless, those who were left stranded in the race of life. And he was resolved to do this in his lifetime so that he could to a certain extent act as his own steward and almoner, and thus secure the right use of his benefactions.

His first benevolent enterprise was a small institution begun at Erdington—the suburb of Birmingham which he always favoured—in 1858. It combined an almshouse for aged women and an orphanage for girls. How he came to do this was because he had seen the evil effects of his own indiscriminate charity. He had been imposed on again and again, and he determined to do good in such a manner that imposture should be rendered impossible. Not satisfied with his first experiment, however, he desired to have an orphanage on a much larger scale, with something of a public character, and under public management. He therefore sought out Dr. Miller, who was then Rector of St. Martin's, the chief parish in Birmingham. They were unknown to each other, and as Mason unfolded his plan, Dr. Miller gave him little encouragement, as he feared the requisite number of people could not be found to support a great scheme. But at length the Doctor said: 'Well, what about a donation to start it with—£20 or £50 is not much in this case.' Mason's reply fairly electrified the Divine: 'Plenty of such sums would tell up, Doctor; I would give £100,000 to start it!' Dr. Miller felt as though he could embrace his visitor. A meeting of clergymen, ministers, and others was convened at St. Martin's Rectory to discuss the scheme. The offer of £100,000 amazed those present. After about a dozen meetings, however, an insuperable difficulty arose. Mason belonged to no religious order or denomination, but he wanted the children to be taught the Holy Scriptures as Timothy was taught. Many of the clerical sympathisers held out vigorously for the Catechism, and so the project fell through. The donor felt that he could not found the institution solely upon a Church basis.

Thrown upon his own resources, Mason determined to carry out his plan for an orphanage alone. He selected a suitable site at Erdington, obtained plans and designs, and began the work of construction in 1865. The position was conspicuous, and as the building first, and then its lofty towers, gradually loomed up on the horizon, people questioned each other as to its object. The donor went quietly on, constructing the strong, durable, and magnificent building, and at the same time preparing the trust-deed of his foundation. The trust-deed was a very important matter, for in order to satisfy the requirements of the Mortmain Act it had to be enrolled twelve months during the life of the founder, or otherwise it could not take effect. Other arrangements had also to be made in view of the possibility of the founder's death in the interim. All difficulties were overcome, however, and on the 31st of July, 1869, Mason was able to enjoy the deep and unalloyed pleasure of personally opening his splendid institution, by presiding over the first meeting of the trustees. The buildings forming the Almshouses and Orphanage at Erdington were valued at £60,000, while the princely endowment was estimated at no less than £200,000. This great charity on the part of a simple Birmingham manufacturer entitled him to rank with such philanthropists as George Peabody, and it has been noted as a coincidence that these two men were born in the same month of the same year. Mason's noble work was wholly his own, both in conception and execution, down to the smallest detail. Without asking or receiving help of any kind, he gave to trustees, 'and through them to the public, a set of almhouses for twenty-six women, an orphanage for three hundred children, finished in building and arrangement, with plans of management laid down carefully throughout and perfected, both charities in full working order and actually at work; and to crown all, with an endowment in land, so well-chosen as to promise rapid growth in value with each successive year, and so ample as to shut out for ever the need of an appeal for other help.'

With regard to the inmates of the Orphanage, it was provided that the number of boys should never exceed one-half the number of girls for the time being inmates therein. There was only one qualification for admission—namely, that every child should be of or under the age of nine years, and the legitimate child of poor parents, both of whom were dead. There was no restriction as to locality, condition, country, or religious persuasion. Boys might remain in the Orphanage until they were fourteen, and girls until they were eighteen years of age. A good sound education was provided for—and everything was perfectly free, lodging, clothing, maintenance, and training. The girls were to be brought up to all household and domestic duties. The religious instruction imparted was to be completely unsectarian. Seven trustees were appointed by the founder to act with him during his lifetime, and after his death seven others were added, appointed by the Town Council of Birmingham. The trustees were to be laymen and Protestants, and were to hold their appointments for life, except for certain disabling conditions specified. The education given in the Orphanage is so thorough that not long after its foundation, at the Government examinations the boys passed cent. per cent., and the girls and infants more than 97 per cent. in the general standards. The Almshouses for Aged Women are admirably conducted, and connected with this portion of the charity is a home for servants who have been sent out from the Orphanage, and who may be temporarily disabled, or may need a place of residence while seeking new situations.

The third, and in some respects the greatest, of Sir Josiah Mason's benefactions was the famous Science College, erected and founded for the purpose of systematic higher education. There were many admirable educational institutions in Birmingham, but there was no place for the higher instruction of students who found the existing means inadequate, and were consequently obliged to rely upon private tuition, or to resort to the universities or provincial colleges. He therefore resolved to offer to the community the free gift of a great teaching institution, carefully arranged, thoroughly equipped for its work, and well endowed, to bear the name of the Mason Science College. On the 12th of December, 1870, the foundation-deed was formally executed. When the twelve months required by the Statute of Mortmain had expired, Dr. J. G. Blake and Mr. G. J. Johnson were legally constituted the first trustees of the College, and as such held in trust the various properties conveyed to them by the founder for the purposes of the College. The College was erected in Edmund Street, Birmingham. It formed one side of a square, the others being occupied by the Town Hall, the Council House, the Corporation Art Gallery, and the Free Libraries—worthy institutions for a free city. There were six trustees of the building, four being appointed in addition to Messrs. Blake and Johnson, already named.

The plans having been approved and the works begun, the

donor laid the foundation-stone on the 25th of February, 1875, that being the eightieth anniversary of his birthday. In consequence of the extremely inclement weather, the outdoor proceedings were brief, and an adjournment was made to the Queen's Hotel. Here were assembled representatives of the Corporation, the Magistracy, and of the institutions connected with education, literature, science, and art. Mr. John Bright specially attended to show his interest in the event, and his sympathy with the aims of the founder; but the Mayor of Birmingham, Mr. Joseph Chamberlain, was absent through severe domestic affliction. The Deputy-Mayor read an address of congratulation and thanks to Sir Josiah Mason for his magnificent gift, and the hope was expressed that he might live to witness the completion of a work which would be imperishally associated with his name. Mason's reply, which was read for him on account of his advanced age, was a document of profound autobiographic interest. No apology is therefore needed for reproducing the text of it, which ran as follows:—

'I have to thank you most sincerely for your presence here to-day, to witness the laying of the foundation-stone of my Scientific College, and I have to thank you also for the kind address which has just been read, and for its full and generous recognition of my labours. It is, indeed, a matter of deep satisfaction to me that at my advanced age I am still in possession of sufficient health and strength to allow me to take this personal share in commencing the work I have so much at heart; it fills my mind with gratitude to the Giver of all Good, and if it should please Him to allow me to see the completion of the building which we have just begun, I shall be content to depart, with the confident belief that others, rightly appreciating my design, will carry out the scheme of the College in the spirit in which I have been permitted to begin it. This work, gentlemen, has been long in my mind, for I have always felt the importance of providing enlarged means of scientific instruction, on the scale required by the necessities of this town and district, and upon terms which render it easily available by persons of all classes, even the very humblest. The experience of my own life has long since satisfied me on this point.

'When I was a young man—it is so long ago that while still living in this generation I can recall the memories of a time long past—there were no means of scientific teaching open to the artisan classes of our manufacturing towns; and those who, like myself, would gladly have benefited by them were compelled to plod their weary way, under disadvantages and difficulties of which our young men of the present day can form no adequate idea. Schools at that time were few and poor; there were no institutions of popular teaching, no evening classes to which youths might go after their day's work was ended. Whatever I learned I had to teach myself in the intervals of laborious and precarious occupations, first at Kidderminster, my birthplace, and later in Birmingham, the home of my adoption, and the place where sixty years of my life have been spent. At Kidderminster, as a youth, I worked at a variety of trades—baking, shopkeeping, carpet-weaving, and others. When I came to Birmingham, in my twentieth year, I was first connected with one of the then staple trades of the town, the gilt toy making, and it was not until after ten years of hard work and heavy disappointment, that I found the position that Providence had destined for me.

'At thirty years of age, with twenty pounds of savings as my whole fortune, I was brought into association with one of the most honourable, industrious, and ingenious of men, Mr. Samuel Harrison, the inventor of split-rings, whom I served for a time, and to whose business, on his retirement, I succeeded. Mr. Harrison was no common man; he was a friend of Dr. Priestley, whom he assisted in many of his philosophical experiments, and for whom, I may mention, as a matter of interesting local history, he made the first steel pens that ever were made in Birmingham. To me he was a dear and good friend, whose memory I have never ceased to cherish with continual affection. To the business I received from him I afterwards added the trade of steel pen making, which I have now followed for more than forty-seven years, first as the maker of the well-known Perryian pens, and later in my own name, until I have developed the works into the largest pen factory in the world—though I ought to say that the building in which they are now conducted no longer belongs to me, but has been conveyed to the Trustees of the College, as part of their endowment, so that I am now the tenant of my own foundation. This business and that of the split-ring making were my sole occupations until 1840, when accident brought me in close relations with my late valued friend and partner, Mr. G. R. Elkington, who was then applying the great discovery of electro-deposition, and through my association with him in this undertaking I may claim a share in the creation of a form of scientific industry which has so largely enriched the town of Birmingham, and increased its fame throughout the world. To this we afterwards added the establishment of copper-works in South Wales. Since the death of my friend Mr. Elkington, I have restricted myself to my original work as a penmaker and a split-ring maker, with an occasional deviation into other employments in which science has been brought to the aid of industry.

'I mention these facts to show you how the means with which God has blessed me have been acquired, and to show also how natural it is that I should devote some portion of those means to assist in promoting scientific teaching, to advance the varied forms of scientific industry, with which, throughout my Birmingham life, I have been so closely connected. But before I could take in hand the foundation of this College I had another work to do. I had always had a great desire to do some deed of love for the poor and helpless, and therefore my first care was to make provision for the aged and the orphans. This I was enabled to do by founding the Orphanage and Almshouses at Erdington; and this being done, I was at liberty to turn my attention to the project of the College. There were many difficulties to be overcome. Willingness to give money will do much, but it will not do everything. The site, for example, was a great hindrance; many places were thought of and put aside; others were sought for, and could not be obtained. These delays, however, did not really do any harm to the scheme; indeed, they afforded time for the proper consideration of the plan of the College, and the preparation of a deed of foundation of a nature to give full effect to my wishes. For this I must acknowledge my great obligations to my friend and adviser, Mr. G. J. Johnson, and to other gentlemen, some of whom are included in the number of my trustees. At last, all difficulties being overcome, and the plans for the College being settled, we are assembled to witness the commencement of the building which I have undertaken to erect as the future home of the foundation, and before long I hope to see the first body of students collected within its walls.

'The scheme of the College, as most of you know, is a large one, and I have sought to make it as liberal as possible in the character and extent of the teaching, the system of management, and the mode and the terms of admission. Whatever is necessary for the improvement of scientific industry, and for the cultivation of art, especially as applied to manufactures, the trustees will be able to teach; they may also, by a provision subsequent to the original deed, afford facilities for medical instruction; and, as has been mentioned in the address read by the Deputy-Mayor, they are authorised, and indeed enjoined, to revise the scheme of instruction from time to time, so as to adapt it to the requirements of the district in future years, as well as at the present time. It is not my desire to set up an institution in rivalry of any other now existing, but to provide the means of carrying further and completing the teaching now given in other scientific institutions, and in the evening classes now so numerous in the town and its neighbourhood, and especially in connection with the Midland Institute, which has already conferred so much benefit upon large numbers of students, and which I am glad to see represented here to-day.

'My wish is, in short, to give all classes in Birmingham, in Kidderminster, and in the district generally, the means of carrying on, in the capital of the Midland district, their scientific studies as completely and thoroughly as they can be prosecuted in the great science schools of this country and the Continent ; for I am persuaded that in this way alone—by the acquirement of sound, extensive, and practical scientific knowledge—can England hope to maintain her position as the manufacturing centre of the world. I have great, and I believe well-founded, hope for the future of this foundation. I look forward to its class rooms and lecture halls being filled with a succession of earnest and intelligent students, willing not only to learn all that can be taught, but in their turn to communicate their knowledge to others, and to apply it to useful purposes for the benefit of the community. It is in this expectation that I have done my part, thankful to God that He has given me the means and the will to do it ; hoping that from this place many original and beneficial discoveries may proceed ; trusting that I, who have never been blessed with children of my own, may yet, in these students, leave behind me an intelligent, earnest, industrious, and truth-loving and truth-seeking progeny for generations to come.'

On the 1st of October, 1880, the College was opened. The proceedings of the day began with a meeting in the Town Hall, presided over by Mr. Richard Chamberlain, Mayor of Birmingham, and attended by representatives of the Corporations of Birmingham and Kidderminster, and of the leading scientific and literary institutions of Birmingham, and the Universities of Oxford, Cambridge, and London, the Victoria University, and by the Trustees and Professors of the College. An enthusiastic greeting was accorded to the venerable

Founder, who was fortunately able to be present. A choir, selected from the Birmingham Choral Festival Society, sang Mendelssohn's hymn 'Let our theme of praise ascending.' Then Professor Huxley delivered the opening address, remarking at the close of it that there were many present who could look back to the time when the anticipations of the building or dedication of a College such as that they had now seen launched would have been looked upon as a piece of chimerical absurdity, and when there was not, in the whole of the three kingdoms, accessible to the inhabitants, high or low, such teaching as would now be available to every inhabitant of Birmingham, rich or poor, in 'Mason's Scientific College.' Speeches were afterwards delivered at a luncheon by Mr. G. J. Johnson (the President), Professors Huxley, Max Müller, Greenwood, and Roscoe, Mr. R. W. Dale, and Dr. Tilden, Professor of Chemistry in the new College. At a conversazione held at the College in the evening, the ceremony of transferring the building to the Trustees took place. The Founder, standing on a dais in the Physics Laboratory, and holding in his hand the key of the College, said, 'This key of the College is now mine, and I can say that the College is mine; but in a moment I shall be able to say so no longer, for I now present it, and with it the College, to my old friend Mr. Johnson, on behalf of my trustees, to be held by them in trust for the benefit of generations to come.'

The total value of this great gift—buildings and endowment—was about £200,000. The buildings of the College are four stories in height and extend in their greatest depth to about 300 feet. The style is Gothic of the thirteenth century. The accommodation includes five lecture rooms, commodious laboratories, three museums, a handsome library containing 20,000 volumes, class rooms and offices, a common room for students, and separate retiring and reading rooms for women students. Originally, the deed of foundation provided for scientific instruction only, with the addition of the English,

French, and German languages; but by later deeds the Founder authorised the Trustees to provide instruction in all branches of science—including medicine and surgery—in art, languages, and literature, and all subjects required for degrees in arts or science. One restriction only was imposed on the Trustees: they were to permit no lectures, teaching, or examinations on theological questions or political subjects of a party nature. The number of trustees was fixed at eleven, six of whom were nominated by the Founder, while the remaining five were elected by the Town Council of Birmingham after his death. The institution made rapid progress. During its first year there were 85 students, but in 1888-9 there were no fewer than 415 students in the day classes, and 309 other students in the evening classes, making a total of 724. The usefulness of the College had thus exceeded the most sanguine expectations.

The Town Council of Birmingham desired to erect a statue of Mason, to be placed in the Corporation Art Gallery, but as none of the designs pleased the philanthropist the project fell through, much to his satisfaction, as he had most reluctantly consented to the proffered honour. However, as the result of a private subscription, Mason's portrait, painted by Mr. H. T. Munns, was formally presented to the Town Council in 1872, and placed in the Art Gallery. In the same year, the Queen conferred upon him the honour of knighthood, and, in consequence of Mason's advanced age and the state of his health, her Majesty specially directed that the usual ceremony and presentation at Court should be dispensed with.

As far back as 1841 Sir Josiah Mason had suffered from a gastric affection, complicated by heart disease, for which he tried many remedies, French and English, and finally found considerable relief under the water cure at Malvern. Twice he made a continental tour, on the first occasion in quest of health. During his long career in Birmingham, Mason had various residences, his final home being Norwood House, Erdington, a fine mansion which he built on the main road from Birmingham to Sutton Coldfield. Here he took delight in grape-growing. It is noteworthy, as showing the self-abnegation of the man, that the very house he lived in belonged to the Orphanage, and he paid rent for it as an ordinary tenant; his manufactory also, while he remained in business, was the property of the Mason College Trustees, and he paid the fair ordinary rent for it. He thus literally gave up everything for others. In the noble picture gallery at Norwood House there was a Viennese self-acting organ, an expensive instrument. In accordance with his last wishes, this organ was removed to Mason College, and placed in the Examination Hall. His last public appearance was at the opening of the College; but, although seriously failing in health, he received the Trustees and Professors of the College at dinner on his eighty-sixth birthday, February 23rd, 1881. He took cold in the month of April following, and a slight accident which occurred to him caused him to take to his bed, from which he never rose again. He passed away quietly and painlessly on the 16th of June, 1881, and on the 25th he was laid to rest in a mortuary chapel erected by him in the Orphanage grounds to receive the remains of his wife, who had pre-deceased him by eleven years. A statue by Mr. F. J. Williamson was publicly erected in his honour, being placed in the square of the Mason Science College.

In indicating Josiah Mason's personal characteristics his biographer lays stress upon his resolution and tenacity of purpose, his kindly humour, his tenderness towards children, his business aptitude, his benevolence, his practical intuition, his faith in himself, his power of detachment and faculty of continuity, his skill in organisation, his simplicity and yet conscious mastery, his dislike to notoriety, his homely and regular habits of life, and his firm belief in an over-ruling God. There is no doubt that such men as Mason have had much to do with making England what she is, and in maintaining her position in the world.

THE WEDGWOODS.

THE WEDGWOODS.

The potter's art is the most ancient in the world, for even in the most primitive and rudimentary ages serviceable pottery was a necessity to the human race. But between the rude vessels of the savage—which consisted of almost shapeless masses of clay hardened by the sun—and the beautiful products of Wedgwood, with designs by Flaxman, there was as much difference as between the veriest daub which ever shocked the artistic sense on the walls of the Royal Academy and the 'Transfiguration' of Raphael.

Excellence of manufacture, however, especially as regards porcelain, goes back for thousands of years. We owe to the Chinese the manufacture of porcelain, and, alike as regards antiquity and skill in the use of the raw materials, they easily stand first. During the terra-cotta vase period of the Greeks the Chinese were manufacturing porcelain. They claim to have been making pottery nearly 2,700 years before Christ, and it has been established beyond question that porcelain was made in China under the Han dynasty between 206 and 87 B.C. Ever since that time the industry has been pursued with more or less success. Early in the eighteenth century there was one town alone which boasted of 3,000 porcelain furnaces, but the place was ruined by the Tai-ping insurrection. Animals of all kinds, mythical and actual, serve as decorations for Chinese ware. The old blue ware which the Delft manufacturers subsequently copied is the most sought after, and it seems that the workers possess the secret of causing the cracks in the glaze to be large or minute at will. The porcelain industry was known in

Japan a few years before Christ, and in the eighth century a corporation of porcelain manufacturers was established. The Japanese, however, are more celebrated for their pottery, and their Satsuma ware—which is of a pale yellow colour, and richly painted and lavishly gilt—is highly esteemed. Japanese potters are very clever in imitating woods of various kinds, basket-work, etc. Banko ware—which consists of small teapots and other unglazed earthen vessels—is another product much appreciated. Kaga ware is known for its rich gilding and ornamentation. Soft porcelain and pottery have been made in Persia since the twelfth century, the art having been imported from China; but there is also an original ware peculiar to the country, together with enamelled tiles, which exhibit brilliant metallic lustres on a fine white enamelled glaze.

Coming westward, we find that the Egyptians come first with a credible pottery record. It is stated that vases of baked earthenware were in use at the earliest period of Egyptian civilisation, and glazed tiles are preserved which belong to the epoch of Rameses III., not long after the exodus of the Israelites from Egypt. 'That the Egyptians attained considerable skill as potters,' remarks a writer on this subject, Mr. James Paton, 'is attested by the lustrous red ware they made for holding perfumes, wine, honey, and other delicacies; but their most remarkable pottery was their so-called porcelain made of a fine sand or frit covered with a thick siliceous glaze, blue, green, white, purple, or yellow in colour. The blue colour—which is that principally employed—was produced by an oxide of copper which yielded tints of unrivalled beauty and delicacy. This famous porcelain was made as early as the eighteenth dynasty (about 1600 B.C.), and continued to be produced till the period of the Greek and Roman rule. It was fashioned into vases, sepulchral figures of deities, scarabæi, beasts, etc.; and it must have attained a great reputation, for remains of it are found in most of the ancient countries which had commerce with Egypt.' The Assyrians and Babylonians likewise produced pottery at a very early period; and they used terra-cotta for historical and legal purposes, making cylinders, tablets, etc., of it, on which were impressed cuneiform writings dealing with such events as the Creation, the Flood, etc. There are scarcely any remains of ancient Hebrew pottery, but a considerable quantity of Phœnician pottery has been excavated in Cyprus.

The Greeks, however, were the greatest makers of pottery in the ancient world. They claimed the invention of the potter's wheel, and almost every city attained distinction in the art. 'The Greek vases which remain to this day, principally recovered from tombs in Greece, and in the lands to which its commerce extended, show that within a few centuries the art rose from the rude condition like that shown in prehistoric pottery till it reached a perfection and variety of form, and a grace and dignity of decoration, not since attained by the efforts of any people.' Many exquisite figures and groups have also been discovered in Greece and the East of Europe during the past quarter of a century. The black Etruscan ware which was in vogue from 500 to 300 B.C. gave rise to the Araline and so-called Samian ware of Rome. This Samian ware was of a bright red colour throughout, but it was covered by a lustrous siliceous glaze. Brilliant enamelled pottery was made in the island of Rhodes early in the fourteenth century, and the Moors likewise began to produce thus early their famous Hispano-Moresque enamelled faience. The Majolica ware of the Italians is another well-known species. Enamelled faience was made in France in the sixteenth century, and in 1555 the celebrated Bernard Palissy discovered independently an enamelled glaze, which he applied to rustic dishes, embellished with exquisitely moulded figures, in high relief, of fishes, reptiles, fruits, etc. Of the famous Henri Deux decorative ware only 65 pieces are known to be in existence, and whenever any of these pieces are for sale they fetch fabulous prices. The celebrated enamelled faience of Holland, known as Delft ware, dates from the seventeenth century only. Several German cities became known for their stoneware vessels. With regard to the New World, the ancient Mexicans and Peruvians made a good deal of decorated black and yellow pottery from a very early period. Porcelain began to be made in Europe about the year 1580, by Francis de Medici II., Grand Duke of Tuscany. Paris and Rouen took up the art nearly a century later. In 1760 the establishment at Sèvres became national property, and has remained so ever since. The fame of Sèvres rests on its beautifully glazed and coloured soft porcelain, but hard porcelain has also been made there since 1764. The Germans were the first among European makers to discover the secret of making hard, or kaolinic, porcelain, and the original credit is due to the alchemist Böttger, who in 1709 was in the service of Frederic Augustus II. of Saxony.

The porcelain made in Great Britain is chiefly of the soft description. Works were established at Chelsea, Bow, and Derby about the middle of last century, and the industry was founded at Worcester in 1751. William Cookworthy began to make hard porcelain at Plymouth in 1768, but after three years the works were transferred to Richard Champion, who continued the manufacture at Bristol until 1781. Cookworthy discovered at Carclaze, in Cornwall, the finest china-clay to be found in Great Britain, and his discovery was fraught with important consequences for the home manufacture of porcelain and fine pottery. The commoner potter's clay, or pipe-clay, is largely obtained from Poole, in Dorsetshire. The purest potter's clay, known as china-clay, or kaolin, is formed by the decomposition of granitic rocks, and consists of the hydrated silicate of alumina, with small proportions or traces of one or more of lime, potash, soda, and magnesia. Pottery has three divisions: namely, earthenware, of which there are four kinds, plain, lustred, glazed, and enamelled; stoneware; and porcelain. Staffordshire porcelain was made at Longton Hall in 1752, but it was not until towards the close of the eighteenth century that the celebrated artistic ware of Minton & Co. and of Josiah Spode—the predecessor of Copeland & Co.—was produced. Pennington manufactured porcelain at Liverpool from 1760 to 1780, and valuable porcelain was made not long after this at Leeds, Yarmouth, Worcester, Derby, Lowestoft, Burslem, Coalport, Nantgarw, Swansea, and other places. Parian or statuary porcelain was introduced by Copeland and Minton about 1848. But of all those who have developed the art of fine pottery in England, no maker is entitled to more lasting remembrance than Josiah Wedgwood, the principal subject of this biographical sketch. Before his time the brothers Elers had made fine red ware in imitation of that of Japan, at Bradwell; and their secrets were penetrated by one Samuel Astbury, who feigned idiocy in a most remarkable manner. Astbury was in fact a man of genius, who improved upon the productions of the Messrs. Elers, and Miss Meteyard, the biographer of Wedgwood, states that it was Astbury who was the real precursor of Josiah Wedgwood.

Wedgwood, who has been described as the creator of British pottery as an art, was born at Burslem, Staffordshire, on the 12th of July, 1730. Before sketching his career, it may be well to say something of his ancestry. It appears that 'the surname of Wedgwood half fills the parish registers of Burslem through the seventeenth and eighteenth centuries.' Among other common names which have been associated with potters are those of Cartwright, Bagnall, Tilewright, and Mayer. The Mayers claim a descent of great antiquity. Among the early Wedgwoods—originally Weggewodes—was one John, who resided at Dunwood, near Leek, towards the close of the fifteenth century. His grandson became lord of the manor of Horton, near Leek, by purchase, and he was made high collector of the subsidy of 1563. The high collector's grandson, John Wedgwood, married a gentlewoman of property named Margaret Ford, and died in 1658, at the age of 87. A kinsman of John, Gilbert Wedgwood, married an heiress, Margaret Burslem, in 1612. It was through this Gilbert that the

Wedgwoods who were potters came. One of these, Thomas Wedgwood, the grandfather of Josiah, was regarded as a man of substance in Burslem. His son Thomas was a well-known manufacturer of moulded white ware, to which he afterwards added his father's business in mottled and black ware. Wedgwood married Mary Stringer, a Quakeress, by whom he had a family of thirteen children. Their last child, Josiah, was born, as we have seen, in 1730.

Up to the time of the publication of authoritative memoirs of the Wedgwood family, erroneous notions prevailed as to Josiah's upbringing and the alleged poverty of his family. Miss Meteyard thus deals with these points: 'It is said that Wedgwood's mother was a small and delicately organised woman, of unusual quickness, sensibility, and kindness of heart. Though her husband occupied his seat in the parish church, and her children were baptized at its font, she seems to have strictly enforced, though without austerity, the gravity and moral discipline of the sect amongst which she had been bred. Her children were taught to value sobriety and industry, to observe merit in others, and to see that all their hopes of advancement in this life depended upon the daily exercise of self-restraint, integrity, and the due cultivation of those natural gifts with which Nature has endowed the individual. The manhood of Josiah Wedgwood betrays an early influence of this superior kind, as well as others of a tender character. It has been hitherto assumed that he was born in a mean hovel, surrounded by the rudest associations, and whilst yet a child consigned to the coarsest drudgery. The facts, as we thus find, were essentially different. His father, as we have seen, was a man in easy, if not in affluent circumstances. His relatives, Aaron Wedgwood and Dr. Thomas Wedgwood, junior, were persons of position in their native place. The latter was a man of the nicest skill in his art, and for those days extremely well educated. His handwriting is that of a gentleman. John and Thomas Wedgwood, the sons of Aaron, who commenced business in 1740, and in eighteen to twenty years from that date had acquired a fortune and built the handsomest house in Burslem, were, when Josiah Wedgwood was a child, active and intelligent young men, busy in improving their staple, and as keenly alive to the commercial needs, as to the intense spirit of industry then taking growth throughout the country. A few years later, when they had erected their conspicuous dwelling, and earned comparative leisure, their hospitable hearth became a gathering-place for men of keen and active intelligence. Here Brindley, Thomas Gilbert, the Duke of Bridgewater's agent, John and Hugh Henshall, father and son, met to discuss the various plans then afloat, for constructing and improving roads and flint walls, and the first surveys for canal navigation. Other of Josiah Wedgwood's relations held an equally influential position in their native place; and as to a simplicity of habits and manners, such prevailed everywhere. It is also certain, that the worthy and substantial class from which Wedgwood sprang were, generally speaking, as well educated as the greater portion of the gentry.'

There is no reason to doubt that not only was the home in which Wedgwood was reared one of plenty, but one in which family affection was strongly manifested. Josiah was sent to the Dame school in Burslem, but the serious aspects of life were brought home to him very early, for at nine years of age he lost his father. For a long time he was sent to a school at Newcastle-under-Lyme, kept by a man of superior education named Blunt. Here he met many of his future friends, with whom he was generally popular. The journey from Burslem to Newcastle and back—about seven miles—was made on foot by Wedgwood and his fellow-pupils, alike in winter as in summer. Josiah was distinguished for his sagacity, his warm and generous temper, and his uncommon vivacity and humour. We learn also that he was a favourite at home; with his little sisters especially—'Like other children, they kept birds, rabbits, and similar pets; and it is handed down, that some shelves in one of his father's working sheds were turned into a sort of museum, being decorated with fossil shells and other curiosities, which the men who attended the coal-laden pack-horses from Sneyd and Norton Green brought from the mines there. It is a remarkable fact in connection with this tradition, that many of Wedgwood's best forms were derived from natural objects; particularly from shells. In middle life he studied fossils scientifically; he bought a collection of shells, and attended sales where specimens of more than common beauty were likely to be seen. He encouraged this objective taste in his own children. It is told that on one occasion when a boy about twelve, some labourers whilst digging in a field near Newcastle came, as often happened, upon various fragments of pseudo-Samian ware, of which a fragment reached his hands. He was so delighted with its colour, glaze, and impressed ornaments, that he carried it home, and carefully preserved it on his mother's dresser shelves. At an earlier date, he took pleasure in contrasting the colours of her patchwork; thus proving how soon came into use the powers of hsi artistic eye for colour, and his classic taste for form.'

By his father's will, Josiah Wedgwood was to receive £20 on attaining twenty years of age. But this event was as yet a long way ahead. When eleven years old he was put to the family business of a potter, as a thrower. He thus began, as he afterwards said, 'at the lowest round of the ladder.' His skill in throwing or forming the vessel upon the potter's wheel soon singled him out as one of the best workmen in the neighbourhood. This skill he always retained, so that after the lapse of forty years he could still give a practical example to his throwers, and by merely poising a newly-thrown vessel in his left hand he could tell at a glance its beauties or defects. If it failed even minutely in its geometrical proportions, he would break it up with the stick which he always carried, remarking as he did so, 'This won't do for Josiah Wedgwood.'

When Wedgwood was in his twelfth year there was a virulent outbreak of small-pox in Burslem, and Josiah suffered grievously from the disease. He had it in the malignant form, and, although he recovered, among the after-effects was a permanent injury to the knee. At the age of fourteen, Josiah was bound apprentice to his eldest brother Thomas—his father's successor—for a period of five years, 'to learn his art, mistery, occupation, or imployment of Throwing and Handling.' The indenture was signed by himself, his mother, and brother Thomas, as the three parties to the deed, and attested by Samuel Astbury and Abner Wedgwood, the two paternal uncles of the young apprentice. The deed contained a stringent clause against contracting the prevalent vices of the day—card-playing, drinking, uncleanness, etc. This interesting historical document is now to be seen in the museum of the Hanley Mechanics' Institution, together with other relics relating to Wedgwood.

At the Churchyard Works, Burslem, young Wedgwood was soon taking an active part. He devoted himself to the important branch of the industry pursued by the throwers, which consisted in producing tea and coffee cups, basins, ordinary jugs, globular teapots, circular tureens, and other articles. But the pain and stiffness in his right knee returned, and as he could procure no relief, he was obliged to abandon the thrower's bench altogether at the age of sixteen, and to sit whilst at work with his leg extended before him upon a stool. For twenty-two years he bore his infirmity patiently, suffering much pain, and being frequently laid aside from work; and at last he had the limb amputated, in order to be able to pursue his avocations. His biographer remarks that 'this necessity to leave the thrower's bench, and turn his attention to other branches of his trade, led to the most important consequences. Had he remained stationary there during the larger portion of his apprenticeship, he would not have obtained that grasp of details, and that practical knowledge, which gave him subsequently such a mastery in his art. With the skill already

R

acquired in throwing, joined to a perfection of vision which ensured to him at a glance the accuracy or inaccuracy of geometrical proportions, he was master of enough in this direction, of which the limits may be said to be stationary; and he was left free not only to pursue discoveries in the channels where they were likely to be made, but to turn his attention towards the improvement of minor points of detail. This may be said to have been the turning point in his great career; the true beginning, environed as it seemed at the moment with the sad shadows of physical disability and disappointed hopes. The remainder of his apprenticeship, from his sixteenth to his nineteenth year, embraced that critical passage from youth to early manhood, when the mental and moral characteristics so strongly indicate themselves. And in this case they were of the highest kind: no tavern-hunting, no brawling, no vice of other kinds, but a steady attention to the duties before him, and a determinate self-culture.'

During his apprenticeship, Wedgwood lost his mother, to whom he was deeply attached, and who had done much to stimulate the nobler elements of his character. She was laid to rest near her husband, in the graveyard adjoining the works. When Josiah's apprenticeship expired, he made overtures to his brother to be taken into partnership, suggesting various methods for increasing their trade. But Thomas Wedgwood was afraid to open up new fields of effort, and declined the offer, so that Josiah was thrown upon his own resources. In 1752, however, he entered into partnership with John Harrison, at Stoke. Harrison knew nothing of pottery, but he supplied the capital necessary to work a business which belonged to a potter named Thomas Alders. Alders was no great master of his art, so it was agreed to take young Wedgwood as partner. The wares made at Cliff Bank Pottery, Stoke, were for the most part mottled, cloudy, and tortoiseshell, glazed with lead ore or salt, and shining black ware of good quality. Tea-services, jugs, and other articles were also manufactured in 'blue scratched ware.' This ware had an ordinary white body, and was scratched with a sharp nail by women. Wedgwood not only extended the business, but produced articles of a superior class, which found a ready sale in Birmingham, Manchester, and elsewhere. But Harrison and Alders manifested such greed and cupidity that Wedgwood brought the partnership to a speedy end.

He soon found a more worthy partner in Thomas Wheildon, who like himself had both skill and taste in the potter's art. He was upright in character, and a conscientious seeker after perfection in his work. He was likewise very cautious in his experiments, for Shaw, in his *History of the Staffordshire Potteries*, states that 'to prevent his productions being imitated in quality or shape, he always buried the broken articles.' Wheildon's works were at Little Fenton. Although Wedgwood was not twenty-three years of age when he entered into this parnership, his fame was already considerable. One of his agreements with Wheildon was to the effect that he should practice for their joint benefit such secret processes as genius and experimental industry had made his; but this without any necessity of revealing to others what they were. The first grand result of his laborious experiments was a new kind of green ware, exquisitely moulded, in perfect imitation of such natural objects as leaves and fruits. But the glazing was its greatest distinction. The secret of the green glaze which was prevalent during the latest period of Roman pottery in England, and also during the Middle Ages, had been lost. 'The green ware which up to this date had been manufactured by the Wedgwoods, Wheildon, and others, seems to have been simply coloured in the body with oxide of copper, and then washed over with a thin mixture of lead, flint, and water. But Wedgwood's great improvement was in the glaze itself. Unlike the ordinary flint glaze, it was composed of several substances which, after being fritted together, received a due proportion of calcined copper. The formula of this glaze, which has been preserved to us in an old receipt-book once belonging to Guy Green of Liverpool, shows clearly the vast amount of young Wedgwood's ability; and that he was keenly alive to the increasing efforts which were then being made in the various porcelain works both here and on the Continent to bring all the finer class of glazes as near as possible to the perfection of those in use by the Oriental potters.'

Wedgwood's green consisted of these parts vitrified—flint glass, 6; red lead, 2; and white enamel, 4; with calcined copper, $\frac{1}{12}$. This constituted a blue-green, and required a good deal of yellow ground with it to make it a grass-green. The new firm made in improved form pickle-dishes, plates for confections and preserves, dessert services, and even teacups and saucers—all in the beautiful green ware. Tea, coffee, and chocolate pots were introduced in great variety and elegance of shape, and tea-ware and candlesticks were improved in glaze and form. One choice speciality in small wares was an elegant little oval snuff-box. Wedgwood now visited Birmingham occasionally to transact business with the wholesale houses.

While vigorously and enthusiastically pursuing his labours, Wedgwood had the misfortune to injure his affected leg. Inflammation set in, and to reduce it purgatives and bleeding were resorted to, which greatly reduced the patient himself, and compelled him to keep his room for months. His mind, however, was soon as active as ever, and this is how he utilised his enforced leisure: 'He had always been fond of reading, and had indulged in it so far as his hitherto busy life had permitted. But this taste now grew by what it fed on, till it became a passion. He saw clearly that this was a golden time, though a brief one, in which he might supplement the narrow limits of his early education by new acquisitions. He saw clearly the great philosophic fact—and one of which he made such valuable use in after years, in relation to his great art—that the sources of truth and knowledge are limitless. With his usual sagacity and humility of spirit, he began this self-culture on "the lowest round of the ladder." He improved his constructive knowledge of his native tongue, as also of arithmetic. He read such histories of his country as were then extant; made himself well acquainted with its social and industrial features, and its commercial and political relations to other countries. Much as all this was, there was a point still beyond, towards which his high capacity tended. He had a passion for chemical analysis and philosophical speculation, so far as such speculation was founded in Nature. He bought and borrowed books, some of which, on chemistry, he copied with his own hand, and he thus enlarged his insight into these two great branches of knowledge; and so ardent became his desire to still further widen the limits of what he knew, as to lead him to say often, as health returned, that the height of his ambition was to obtain a moderate competence which should enable him to devote the rest of his days to pursuits connected with literature and science.'

The partnership of Wedgwood with Wheildon expired in 1759, and it was not renewed. The former now left Stoke and returned to Burslem, where he entered into business for himself. He had gained great experience, and considerably extended his artistic ideas. He engaged his second cousin, Thomas Wedgwood, as a journeyman for a period of five years, and this step was the beginning of a lifelong and honourable business connection between the two relatives. Wedgwood first occupied the old pot-works at the Churchyard, but subsequently moved to the Ivy House and its adjacent works. It is rather amusing, but the rival biographers of Wedgwood, Miss Meteyard and Mr. Llewellynn Jewitt, reproduce very different pictures of this Ivy House, and the signatures they likewise reproduce from the apprenticeship indenture of Josiah Wedgwood are considerably different in character. This only shows that anachronisms may creep into very excellent works. The Ivy House and pot-works, which were situate in the very centre of the village of Burslem, belonged to Thomas and John Wedgwood of the 'Big House,' to whom Josiah became tenant, covenanting by written agreement to pay for the whole premises the yearly rent of £10. Mr. Jewitt notes that this rent might be good when Burslem was but a village, and when its pot-works were scattered about the almost waste lands; but at the present day, for similar premises, it would have to be multiplied at least ten-fold before a tenant could have possession. The Ivy House, with its kilns and workshops, would have formed in the eyes of posterity one of the most interesting memorials of Josiah Wedgwood—but the whole place was swept away in 1834 to make room for new public buildings.

Wedgwood's capital being limited, he could not contemplate any immediate expansion of trade; indeed, for a time he made most of his own models, prepared his mixtures, superintended the firing processes, and was his own clerk and warehouseman. But his name was known, and his work was growing in repute. On one occasion he managed successfully to replace, for an aristocratic family near Burslem, an eighteen-inch dish which belonged to a dinner-service of Oriental Delft, and which had been broken. The copy was absolutely perfect, and commissions for various kinds of ware followed. Wedgwood gradually added to his productions the manufacture of white stoneware, of which tiles for fireplaces formed a portion. On these, natural objects were worked in relief. After about a year he began sensibly to increase his business, and, as his health also was now re-established, things were brighter with him. He had yet, however, to advance the results of his art by moderate stages, for 'he saw distinctly that the time had not yet arrived for the development of his manufacture on a large scale.' He added cottages and working sheds to his works, and increased the number of his workmen, assigning to each a certain branch of labour. Miss Meteyard remarks that it was 'still the ordinary custom for the journeymen potters to pass from one kind of labour to another, just as impulse or convenience prompted, and this without reference to either the necessities of the moment or their master's interest. Wedgwood had long observed the evils of this system—the idle, slovenly, and irregular habits it begat in the workmen, and the loss of time and waste of efficiency in regard to productive results. Whilst his brother's apprentice, and still very young, he had, as we have seen, tried to modify somewhat this old system of things; and now that he was thoroughly his own master he resolved that, so far as he was concerned, it should no longer exist. At first he met with much sullen opposition, often amounting to an insubordination that necessitated immediate dismissal; but by firmness, patience, and great kindness he succeeded, in a comparatively short time, in bringing his manufactory into efficient order. His men found that it was much better to obey than to oppose; and that the regulations that they had at first clamoured against facilitated their labour to a surprising degree.'

There was something truly noble about Wedgwood's devotion to his art, and his conscientious efforts to bring it to perfection. We are told that every essential of body, glaze, form, and ornament was alike the object of his care. His patience was severely tried, and his repeated failures were most disheartening. Yet he pulled down one kiln after another in order to correct some defect, or effect some necessary improvement. His pecuniary loss was great, and the ware itself was often destroyed before he could obtain the necessary degree of excellence; at times he would be baffled by his chemical combinations, while, notwithstanding the greatest pains, experiments in body and glaze would prove abortive; but through all, his energy and indomitable spirit sustained him, until at length success crowned the work. He had to improve or invent almost every tool, instrument, or apparatus, and he personally instructed his men at the bench, himself making the designs for the articles which they produced.

While all this was going forward, he also took an interest

in the people of Burslem generally. When a new school was proposed for the poorer children of the town, Josiah Wedgwood subscribed £10, and his brother, Thomas Wedgwood, of the Overhouse, contributed a similar amount. Such a sum was considerable to one still struggling on the threshold of his career. Eventually, instead of an additional school to the Free School already in existence being erected, a Town Hall was built, which formed the centre for what soon became a flourishing market. Wedgwood was very anxious for the mental and moral improvement of the working-classes of the district. When John and Charles Wesley first visited Burslem they were struck by the vice and brutality which prevailed, but after these good men had paid several visits there was a marked change for the better in the spirit and habits of the population. The main roads in the district round Burslem were a disgrace to civilisation, and as the result of the efforts of Wedgwood and others, in the Session of 1763 an Act was obtained to improve a portion of the chief road to Liverpool and the Salt-Wyches of Cheshire. Carts and waggons were soon engaged in carrying pottery-ware to the north, and in bringing back shop-goods, flints, and clay to Burslem and the Potteries. But land and water carriage were so expensive as to be almost prohibitive, in addition to which there were such evils to contend with as slowness of transit, and risk from floods, breakage, and the notorious dishonesty of many of those employed in the conveyance of goods. To James Brindley, who was a constant visitor at the Wedgwoods, the great facilities subsequently afforded by canal navigation for traffic throughout the Midlands were largely due.

At the end of 1761 Wedgwood had brought his cream-ware to a high degree of perfection. His chief pieces, such as compotiers, tureens, sauce-boats, and salt-cellars, were chiefly modelled from natural objects such as shells, leaves, and the husks and seed-valves of plants. In shops and noted collections, and wherever he had opportunity, he sought out such specimens of Oriental and Dresden ware as might furnish him with new ideas.

But so far he only employed the softest and most subdued colours in enamelling. A cup and saucer preserved in the Museum of Practical Geology show the simple means by which he produced his best effects. 'They are painted with autumnal leaves, and edged with red lines; and he is ever thus recurring to Nature, and making her simplicity subservient to the highest effects. Such a new art, as it were, graceful, simple, and beautiful, because its forms were geometrically perfect, found for its specimens, though as yet comparatively few in number, ready purchasers. They seem to have been sent to London, and there consigned to the hands of the export merchant.' An important discovery, made by Mr. John Sadler, a master printer of Liverpool, proved of great utility in the decoration of Wedgwood's cream-ware. This discovery was the application to glazed earthenware of impressions taken upon paper from engraved copperplates; the ware, after printing, being passed through the muffle, or enamelling oven, to fix the colours. With the exception of the Staffordshire Potteries, Liverpool was the only considerable centre at this period for the manufacture of earthenware. The fame of Wedgwood's improvements had spread thither, and one of the most eminent potters, Mr. Chaffers, saw that the pottery trade of Liverpool was doomed unless it could advance in a like direction. After many futile efforts, and a journey into Cornwall, Chaffers at length discovered a material which enabled him to produce a beautiful ware, that in many instances rivalled Oriental china in its shell-like thinness, its compact solidity of body, its smoothness of glaze, and the deep richness of its brilliant colours.

Wedgwood made frequent business journeys to Liverpool, and on one of these occasions he sustained injury to his disordered knee while on the road. On reaching his hotel in Dale Street, Liverpool, he took to his bed, and Mr. Matthew Turner, an eminent surgeon living close by, was sent for. Turner not only brought his patient physical relief, but manifested a strong interest in him personally. Dr. Turner was a man of unusual attainments, and possessing amongst other things a knowledge of chemistry, he supplied Wedgwood with several receipts for varnishes and other appliances of great service in his manufacture. On one occasion the doctor was accompanied by a friend, one Thomas Bentley, a Liverpool merchant, and a man of exceptional ability. As the result of an almost accidental visit, Bentley became Wedgwood's greatest friend for life, as well as his partner. From the moment of their meeting in the Liverpool inn, 'these men were more than brothers. Friendship is hardly the word for the zeal, kindliness, truth, unselfishness, inflexible justice, with which one served the other. It was a memorable meeting, a memorable friendship, both for themselves, their country, and the arts they loved.' Bentley was a native of Derbyshire, and was born in the same year as Wedgwood. He was well educated, and became a man of culture. In 1757 he assisted in founding the Warrington Academy, among whose earliest tutors were three famous men—Dr. Taylor of Norwich, Dr. Aikin (father of Mrs. Barbauld), and Dr. Priestley of Birmingham. At Bentley's house Wedgwood met these and other well-known men. Dr. Priestley was already acquainted with the Rev. William Willet of Warrington, who had married Wedgwood's youngest sister Catherine. Mr. Willet is said to have been among the first to inspire Priestley with a love for philosophical investigations. Bentley and Priestley likewise highly esteemed each other, but their opinions on religious topics widely differed. Bentley's theology was not to be confined within the narrow limits of Priestley's dogmatic views; though their discussions, which were often continued till far into the night, 'were carried on with the utmost unanimity, and never disturbed the tenor of their friendship. There can be no doubt that this largeness of view, this ingenuous spirit of inquiry, this perception of an underlying current of truth in most things, this absence of one-sidedness and dogmatic rule, lay at the very root of the friendship thus newly formed between Wedgwood and Bentley, and led, by a natural inductive process, to all the more masterly of the artistic achievements which resulted therefrom. Bold and uncompromising in their opinions, these matchless friends, for such they were, could yet see the threads of truth in the beliefs of other men, and thus lived in perfect charity amongst them. And thus it was also in their secular art: they sought far and wide for those conceptions of ideal grace which they ultimately embodied in their works, and the result was in all higher instances, a perfection such as those only can rival, who, like them, are bound by neither period, style, nor conventional rules, but are willing to catch up the expressions of ideal truth and grace from a range as wide as Nature.'

Wedgwood began his correspondence with Bentley in May, 1762, on his return to Burslem, and from this date their friendship ripens. As time passes on, 'not a joy or a sorrow, a hope or a fear, a difficulty or a success, but the one imparts it to the other, with a manly frankness worthy of such men.' A few glimpses of Wedgwood's political sentiments are obtained at this time. After reading and admiring Thomson's poem on *Liberty*, he exclaimed—' Happy would it be for this Island were his three virtues, the foundation of British liberty—Independent Life, Integrity in Office, and a passion for the Common Weal—more strictly adhered to among us.' He asks Bentley's advice as to purchasing Rousseau's *Émile*, which was just then making a great stir, having been banned by the Pope. Next we find him writing from London a graphic account of the debate on the unpopular Cider Tax Bill, which led to Lord Bute's downfall.

On the 25th of January, 1764, Josiah Wedgwood, being then in his thirty-fourth year, married his distant cousin, Sarah Wedgwood, the daughter, and eventually sole heiress, of Mr. Richard Wedgwood, of Smallwood, in Cheshire. The wedding took place at the fine old parish church of Astbury. The bride is said to have eventually brought Wedgwood a fortune of £20,000—a very large amount in those days: but the bridegroom was himself already a man of position, and enjoyed the distinction of being Potter to her Majesty the Queen. His biographers again differ as to the house to which he brought his young wife. Mr. Jewitt says it was to Ivy House, and Miss Meteyard affirms that it was the Bell House, known also as the Brick House. The latter appears to have been correct. The Brick House and the adjacent works stood on what now forms part of the site of the Wedgwood Institute—which is but fitting, as it was the scene of many of the most momentous events in Wedgwood's career. Miss Meteyard observes on this point:—

'Here it was, as he confides to Bentley, months after marriage, he and his wife were still "married lovers." Here in the leisure hours of evening he reads to her the last new Review, containing maybe some paper written by his friend Bentley: here he teaches her the curious cipher or shorthand in which he preserves the precious and self-discovered secret of his art, consults her invariably sound judgment, as he finds it to be, in matters of form, ornament, and combined results, and here dismisses to the lumber-room the spinning wheel which has accompanied her from Spen Green, for he is soon aware that more intellectual vocations befit her. Here her first three children are born; the eldest a daughter, whose noble destiny is to become the mother of an eminently gifted man. Here he celebrates the festival attendant on the cutting of the first sod of the Trent and Mersey Canal. Here he buries his second-born son Richard: and suffers the amputation of his long-diseased limb with a fortitude and courage inherent in the highest natures. Here he welcomes the great Erasmus Darwin, and confers with him on many topics of philosophic interest. Here he receives his dear friend Bentley with generous hospitality; and here unfolds to him, whilst the smoke of the homely pipe curls upwards, all his plans and projects; and here he receives the quaintest and worthiest though most prosaic of clerks, Peter Swift. In short, Josiah Wedgwood unravels, like all of us, much of the mingled web of Fate; its hopes and joys, its pains and sorrows! There are courtlier scenes to paint—visits from those of genius, rank, wealth, and beauty—days dedicated to science and to art, evenings to social communion and the sweetest music, when Tassie's sulphur casts from antique gems, Sir William Hamilton's loans of drawings and pottery, Hackwood's designs, Mrs. Landre's models, Flaxman's or Webber's latest works from Rome, are scattered on the tables, and his daughters play or sing the last sonata of Haydn, or the last song by Dr. Arne; but even such yield in vivid interest to the history of these more homely days of love, aspiration, and friendship. The Wedgwood Institute could have no more fitting site than the ground hallowed by associations so eminently characteristic of the great artist and generous Englishman it is raised to commemorate and honour.'

When Wedgwood threw his energies into his business again, he turned his attention to the engine-lathe, which he considerably improved. There was a good deal of discussion as to the developments in the use of the lathe. It seems certain that one Baddeley made great improvements in it, and that a turner named Greatbach suggested certain concentric movements which added greatly to its value; but Wedgwood further improved this useful implement, and to him also is undoubtedly due the discovery of the method of fluting slightly hardened bodies. Plumier's work on *L'Art de Tourner* had afforded him many valuable suggestions, but its illustrations had to be so altered and adapted to another and a wholly different art, as ultimately to bear upon them the impress of original inventions. Improved lathes were brought from Paris to London, and it is said that Wedgwood paid the possessor the sum of five guineas, in order to be present whilst one of them was put through its various working capabilities. One thing is certain—he left no stone unturned to advance his mechanical knowledge in this respect. The first application of his engine-lathe was to 'red china' tea and coffee pots, of which large numbers were consigned to his brother in London for export.

All during this time the great scheme of inland navigation was closely occupying Wedgwood's thoughts. The idea eventually attained fruition in the great work of James Brindley, the Grand Trunk Canal. The struggle was long and fierce, however, before an Act of Parliament could be obtained authorising the scheme. When this important step had been gained, the honour of cutting the first sod was accorded to Wedgwood, its most prominent, most energetic, and most liberal promoter. The ceremony was performed with all due formalities on the 26th of July, 1766, the first sod being cut on the declivity of Brownhills, the event being celebrated at Burslem with great rejoicings in the evening. A private manuscript furnishes many interesting details respecting Wedgwood's connection with the Grand Trunk Canal. It is related that when he once fairly took up the matter, 'business, family, everything, gave place to this important subject, for many months in the year 1765. Drawing around him the few that then thought with him on the subject, or were inclined to take an active part, they concerted on the means of gaining friends, and overcoming opposition. At this time the principle itself of the utility of canal navigation was disputed, and if any advantages were admitted, they did not appear to a very powerful class of the people as of sufficient importance to counterbalance the injuries they apprehended to themselves. Here was a great deal of intellectual ground to be cleared, and the contest was not for this or that modification, but whether the thing itself should exist at all. In this struggle Mr. Wedgwood was certainly the foremost and most active person, and for three months, during the progress of the Bill in Parliament, was nearly as much lost to his private connections as though he had been in China. The canal in question was called the Grand Trunk because it was foreseen that many lesser ones would break out of it, as has since happened. It is upwards of ninety miles in length, joining the Trent about a mile below Cavendish Bridge, in Derbyshire, and terminating in the Duke of Bridgewater's Canal, at Preston Brook, in Cheshire. The internal passage through the hill at Harecastle is an object of great curiosity, being a mile and three-quarters in length, and crossing many veins of coal, which are got at a small expense, being thus laid dry, and the canal is greatly benefited by the supply of water. Mr. Brindley began this work on both sides at the same time, and his workmen met in the middle. The contrivances of this great man, by which he executed stupendous works in a short time that seem to have required ages, have been properly noticed in the account of his life in the *Biographia Britannica*, the materials for which were furnished by Mr. Wedgwood, who lived in habits of intimacy and friendship with him, and ever revered his memory. Mr. Wedgwood was the first treasurer of the canal, and an active member of the committee for making and carrying it on for more than twenty years.

'The Grand Trunk Canal was finished by Mr. Henshall, brother-in-law to Brindley, in May, 1777, and it was immediately productive of the greatest benefit to the neighbourhood. Trade increased, freight of goods was lowered to about the rate of thirteen shillings per ton, where fifty shillings had before been paid, the despatch and receipt of goods was more rapid and more certain, and the whole district assumed a vitality which has gone on regularly increasing to the present day.

'If for no other reason, the part he took in the carrying out to a successful issue the scheme of canal communication, to which undoubtedly the Staffordshire potteries owe their prosperous increase, would fully entitle Josiah Wedgwood to the thanks of his country, and to be ranked amongst the foremost benefactors of mankind.'

It appears that one of Wedgwood's earliest friends and patrons was Sir William Meredith, Bart., M.P. for Liverpool.

The master potter was often at Sir William's seat at Henbury, near Macclesfield, and this influential patron was indefatigable in securing the loan of gems, prints, and rare specimens of antique and other pottery for his friend, and sometimes he sent him as a gift prints representing vases and antique sculpture. When Wedgwood was unable to go over to Henbury he would send as his representative his brother Thomas, who discussed with Sir William commercial and artistic topics, and met under his friendly roof such patrons as Sir Henry Chairs and Lord Foley. It was for Sir William Meredith that Wedgwood completed the finest dinner-service that had as yet been sent out from the Potteries. He also executed commissions for the famous politician, Sir George Savile, and others.

In 1765 Wedgwood began a series of experiments for a white body and glaze, which promised very well. His wife—who not long before had presented him with his first child, a daughter named Susannah—was his chief helpmate in this and other matters. She had learnt to write her husband's secret characters for his ware. He had resolved not to make this new ware at Burslem, and was already looking out for an agreeable and convenient situation elsewhere. In one of his letters to Sir William Meredith, Wedgwood showed that he was unable to rise beyond the prevalent Protectionist ideas of the time. There was a project for establishing new pot-works in South Carolina, and he was alarmed lest this should lead to the spread of the manufacture elsewhere, with consequent loss to the English potteries. He could little dream that within a hundred years from the date of his complaint to Sir William, the English export trade in earthenware with America would be multiplied a thousandfold, and that it still counts among our best foreign markets, and one to which the manufacturing firm he founded still contributes.

The Royal patronage was early extended to Wedgwood, but it is interesting to know that it was the potter who was applied to, and not he who applied for the Royal favour. Queen

Charlotte required a beautiful tea-service in cream-ware, some specimens of which she had seen in the houses of the nobility, and as Wedgwood was the only person competent to execute the work satisfactorily, he received and accepted an invitation to undertake it. The complete set of tea things was duly made, with a gold ground and raised flowers in green. He followed this up by making a number of beautiful vases for Her Majesty, and on the occasion of the first Royal accouchement succeeding this patronage, he presented the Queen with a finely-executed caudle-service. Ware for the young Princess followed, and the interest which George III. and his Queen took in Wedgwood's productions made them still more widely and favourably known in influential circles. The Duke of Marlborough, Lord Gower, Lord Spencer, and others visited the pottery works, and suggested that Wedgwood should have a London warehouse—an idea which had already occurred to the potter himself. The Duke of Bridgewater gave an order for the completest table-service of cream colour that Wedgwood could make, and he followed this up with many acts of kindness as well as patronage. 'From all we gather from the Wedgwood correspondence,' says Miss Meteyard, 'Francis Egerton, Duke of Bridgewater, seems to have been a kind man and a true friend—a little wayward and eccentric in some things, but with an instinctive perception of truth and genius in others that led necessarily to his keen enjoyment of the society of two such men as Brindley and the great potter. What an illustrious trio it was, as they thus supped and smoked their pipes together in the old timbered hall at Worsley, or the more palatial building at Trentham—their chief talk about Inland Navigation, with now and then a little diversion on the subject of cream-colour ware or Roman antiquities, which only made the subject of the grand scheme still more weighty when it was renewed.'

When the Queen's patronage became fully known, commissions for cream-coloured services poured in upon Wedgwood, among his new patrons being Lady Broughton, the Duke of Grafton, Sir Charles Coote, General Honeywood, etc. In November, 1765, Mr. and Mrs. Wedgwood visited London. Amongst those who hospitably entertained them was Griffiths, editor of the *Monthly Review*, 'who feasted his friends and starved his authors.' Wedgwood transacted business at Court with Miss Chetwynd on behalf of the Queen, and we find him visiting the houses of many of the nobility, and at the Duke of Bedford's taking patterns from an elegant set of French china valued at £1,500. He also spent an agreeable time at Blenheim House. In the midst of this he did not forget his friends, and he did whatever he could to give publicity to the works of Dr. Priestley, at a time when the writings of that distinguished man were very unpopular in certain quarters. He further took the deepest interest in his many relatives, and followed carefully and affectionately the course of a young nephew named Byerley, who had at first caused him some concern. Wedgwood's family affections were very strong.

Among Wedgwood's intimate friends was Erasmus Darwin, the celebrated physician, botanist, and philosopher. Darwin's house in Lichfield was the intellectual centre of the Midland districts; and it was in many senses a hospital as well, for its owner was ever ready to minister to the comfort and the needs of the suffering. Wedgwood probably became acquainted with him about 1756, and in ten years from this time these two remarkable men were on intimate terms of friendship. 'There can be no doubt,' remarks Wedgwood's biographer, 'that almost from its commencement the friendship of Mr. Wedgwood and Dr. Darwin partook of a strongly intellectual character. It was not mere meeting and feasting, but a mental attrition of great value to their respective characters; for though different they were yet alike. Both were men of great native genius, both had a taste for philosophical speculation and mechanical invention, and both were generous men. The Doctor had stronger passions, some acerbity of temper, and a satirical vein that often wounded the truest of his friends; but Mr. Wedgwood appears to have received these little rubs and tokens of asperity as a giant would a blow from a child's hand. He laughed and thought no more about them; though others were not so philosophic. On more than one occasion Dr. Darwin had the felicity of saving Mrs. Wedgwood's life, a service which no one could so truly estimate as he who had found in her the most judicious and tender of wives. On the other hand, Mr. Wedgwood had no profounder admirer of his beautiful art than Erasmus Darwin. This is not only testified by direct eulogium, but by indirect evidence. In the pages of the *Botanic Garden* are many descriptions which are clearly drawn not so much from classical sources as from Mr. Wedgwood's interpretation in cameo of the antique gems—as in the passages descriptive of Cupid snatching the lightning from Jupiter, Venus rising from the sea supported by Tritons, the Nereid on the Sea-horse, and the marriage of Cupid and Psyche. Of course the gems themselves were, if in the cabinets of our nobility, accessible to a man of Dr. Darwin's fame and position; but his life was one of incessant professional occupation, and it is thus more likely that his descriptions were drawn from his friend's exquisite interpretation of the originals. Darwin, like Wedgwood, owed as much to industry as to genius. He had sprung from a lettered and intellectual race, as his father, "Robert Darwyn, Esq., of Elston, near Newark," was one amongst the early members of the celebrated Spalding Club; and he supplemented these advantages of genius and birth by a laborious culture which ended only with his life.'

Darwin and Wedgwood were destined to be, the one the paternal and the other the maternal grandfather of one of the greatest men of the nineteenth century, the illustrious Charles Darwin.

In one of Erasmus Darwin's entertaining letters to Wedgwood, he mentioned a French Count named De Lauraguais, who had been to Birmingham and offered the secret of making the finest old china by a process as cheap as that for making the most ordinary pottery. The Count declared that the secret had cost him £16,000, but he was willing to sell it for £2,000. Darwin distrusted the Count's alleged passion for science, but thought there might be something in the secret. The Count had already taken out an English patent for his discovery, and it was afterwards demonstrated that one of the chief ingredients in this new porcelain was similar to that which Wedgwood was in search of for the purpose of fabricating a fine white terra-cotta body.

Wedgwood sought out the company of artists who could help him in his work, and among other distinguished men with whom he became acquainted was Roubiliac the sculptor. Roubiliac died before he could be of personal service to him, however, but his widow presented the potter with a book of her husband's sketches. This has been unfortunately lost, as were sketches by Flaxman, Webber, and Hackwood, but Roubiliac's designs proved serviceable to Wedgwood, and some of his articles of cream-ware, as well as later black Egyptian and crystalline ware, were designed or ornamented wholly or in part from the sculptor's sketches.

When on his visits to London, Wedgwood was several times sent for to Buckingham Palace. The King would want tiles or something new in milk-pans for the dairy at Frogmore, or the Queen wished to see the latest patterns in cream-ware. Wedgwood was handsomely dressed on these occasions: his sword—bought at the Sign of the Flaming Sword in Great Newport Street—was of the best make, his waistcoat was resplendent with lace, and the barber profited by both his chin and wig. He looked remarkably well, although time and thought had not yet illumined his strongly marked face with all that mingled expression of benevolence, refinement, goodness, and meditation, which sit enshrined on Sir Joshua's noble portrait of this great Englishman. Here is an extract from Miss

Meteyard's Memoir touching this period:—'A most charming anecdote has come down to our day in relation to one of these visits at Court. Mr. Wedgwood was summoned to the Palace, and, on arriving at the appointed hour on a sunny spring or summer's morning, was ushered into the royal presence. The Queen stood with her ladies beneath an unshaded window, and here it was that Mr. Wedgwood advancing, made his obeisance, and, displaying the ware he had brought, answered the royal questions. But as her Majesty thus stood examining some exquisite specimen of the art, which years of ceaseless toil and unrepined obscurity had brought to this perfection, the sun's power increased, and its rays, falling on her face, caused her obvious annoyance. The possible etiquette was to have mentioned the matter to one of the unobservant ladies in attendance, who in turn would have summoned a page or a royal footman. But Mr. Wedgwood thought only of removing the intruding glare, and that speedily. He simply walked straight to the window, and pulled down the blind. The Queen, aware in an instant of the relief and its cause, looked up from the object she was regarding, and, inclining her head, smiled her thanks. "Ladies," she said, addressing her attendants, "Mr. Wedgwood s, you see, already an accomplished courtier." It was courtesy, however, learnt in the school of nature—the offspring of a manly and generous respect for woman—and he would have shown as much to a peasant as to the Queen, who was his foremost patron.'

In the spring of 1766 Wedgwood's eldest son John was born, and it was about the same time that the great potter took his cousin, Thomas Wedgwood, into partnership. Thomas had not the original gifts of Josiah, but he was a skilful potter, and had gained valuable experience in the porcelain works of Worcester. Until the partnership was dissolved by death in 1788, Thomas Wedgwood was at the head of the useful works both at Burslem and afterwards at Etruria, 'and within this period the ware of this department reached its highest perfection.' Wedgwood, who regarded his cousin Thomas with the affection of a brother, built him a house at Etruria, 'and seconded in every possible way the well-being of this able, yet gentle and unambitious man.' The business at Burslem had increased so much that Josiah Wedgwood was desirous of purchasing an estate in the immediate neighbourhood, and after a good deal of difficulty he secured the Ridge House estate—which was one of considerable extent, and admirably adapted to his purposes—for the sum of £3,000. The estate lay on the banks of the intended canal, and within two miles both of Burslem and Newcastle. Having obtained it he then began to plan out the future Etruria. On the recommendation of his friend Bentley, he engaged at this time as clerk, one Peter Swift, who was quite a character, and his wife and children settled down at Burslem, and Swift began what proved to be lifelong services to his master, who enjoyed to the last his undiminished affection and veneration. Mr. Bentley was now doing a large export trade, in which pottery had become the leading item, and Wedgwood, with his usual liberality, voluntarily gave him the most advantageous terms.

Meantime, Wedgwood was pursuing his unwearied researches and experiments, both to better the character of the materials in which he worked and the artistic nature of his productions. He purchased a copy of Count de Caylus's great work on *Antiquities*, and derived considerable assistance therefrom, although partial reproductions from this source were more abundant than direct ones. Antique gems, lamps, and borderings were pressed into service as models. Seeing great prospects ahead, he urged Bentley to join him as partner—an idea which he had long indulged, and although the former at first declined from honourable motives, and pleaded ignorance of the industry, Wedgwood at length conquered his scruples. A great sorrow which befel Wedgwood by the sad and mysterious drowning of his brother John in the Thames, off Westminster Bridge, was made the subject of a final appeal to Bentley which the latter could not resist, and from this time forth they were one in sympathy and action in all their noble undertakings. The firm of Wedgwood & Bentley witnessed a still larger expansion of business than before, and continued to acquire a wider fame.

Hearing that there was a fine porcelain clay to be obtained in South Carolina, Wedgwood went to great labour and expense in verifying the fact, and was not only successful in obtaining clay from that State, but also from Florida. He further completed his own crowning discovery as a philosophic chemist, viz., that of the use of the *terra ponderosa*, the *spath fusible* of the French chemists, or the carbonate of baryta, and ultimately its sulphate, in the body of the pottery. The result soon achieved was an artistic perfection hitherto supposed impossible. Wedgwood had no guide in his researches, and 'the great merit therefore undoubtedly belongs to him of introducing, through the discovery of chemical affinities existing in nature, but previously unknown, a new porcelaneous substance of exquisite adaptability and beauty. Of the successive stages of his analyses and experiments we necessarily know nothing, as the results were written in cipher, and confided to none but his wife, to Darwin, or to Bentley.' But from a portion of Plumier's treatise Wedgwood seems to have derived valuable assistance in relation to the turning of columner forms in their three variations of plain, fluted, and twisted. He then devoted his attention once more to perfecting his engine-lathes, picking up ideas at the famous works of Boulton & Watt, at Soho, Birmingham. Indeed, had it not been that that ingenious man, Matthew Boulton, was occupied closely with the steam-engine, Wedgwood might have found him a formidable rival in his mechanical possesses, though he lacked the strong artistic sense of Wedgwood. Advised by Bentley, and assisted by his own workmen, Wedgwood—by the spring of 1768—'had brought his improvements of the engine-lathe, considering them as referable to the potter's art, to a considerable degree of perfection. Combining these under one effective generalisation, he employed a skilful hand to prepare some new lathes for the furnishing of the ornamental works then fast progressing at Etruria.' Dr. Darwin also constructed for him at this time the model of a windmill, which was intended to grind colours. Wedgwood approved its principle, but as the buildings at Etruria were absorbing his attention, nothing further was done in the matter of the windmill until 1779, when Watt and Edgworth assisted in perfecting it, and it was set up in the new works. In course of time, however, the giant steam superseded other forces in the domain of the industrial arts. In August, 1768, Wedgwood succeeded in another object he had long had in view, when he opened a London warehouse for his goods, for which purpose he secured commodious premises in a house at the corner of St. Martin's Lane and Newport Street.

During the spring of 1768 Wedgwood began to suffer excruciating pain in his leg. All that medical skill could do in alleviating it was tried but without avail, and the sufferer resolved to have the limb amputated. As we learn from Miss Meteyard, his fortitude under this operation was remarkable :—

'As there was no relieving the pain without imperilling the patient's life, another surgeon was called in, with probably Dr. Darwin in consultation, and amputation of the limb was agreed to ; indeed suggested by Wedgwood himself, who had long looked forward to this necessity with philosophic cheerfulness. His leg was like a dead branch on a vigorous tree, an incumbrance and a hindrance in every way ; and even apart from this illness, which hastened the crisis, he had mentally resolved to have it removed prior to opening the works at Etruria. A master-potter is incessantly ascending and descending ladders and stairs to his various shops and rooms ; and if Wedgwood had felt pain, difficulty, and fatigue in doing this in old-fashioned buildings of no altitude, such as those of the "Brick House Works," how much more was he likely to suffer in traversing the ascents and descents of a vast manufactory. He knew full well that a true master's eye is everywhere, and must be everywhere if justice is to be done to his commands; and even into this question of physical suffering and danger, his calculations had entered, so that he might give force to the genius which prompted him, and the duties which lay before him. It is an extraordinary instance of moral courage and decision of character, in connection with a power to gather in and make subservient every effect necessary to a given end. The amputation took place on May 28th, 1768, two surgeons and Bentley, as is evident, being with him at the time. He would not be assisted, or have the operation hidden from his view; but seated in his chair, bore the unavoidable pain without a shrink or a groan. This power of endurance is the more remarkable, as there existed at that date none of our modern chemical agents for producing a temporary state of coma, and, consequently, an oblivion of physical suffering; and, what was more, operative surgery was still carried on with much of the barbarism of the Middle Ages.'

In announcing the event to the London house, Wedgwood's clerk, Peter Swift, was laconic enough to please even the Duke of Wellington. The information was thus conveyed, in the middle of an invoice-note: 'Mr. Wedgwood has this day had his leg taken of (*sic*), and is as well as can be expected after such an execution.' Writing again a few days later to the London agent, the prosaic, but faithful, Peter said: 'I have now the pleasure to acquaint you that Mr. Wedgwood continues in a good way, his Leg was opened on Thursday for the first time, and both the Surgeons said it could not possibly be better, and he has every good Symptom, so that we have the greatest hopes of a perfect cure. Poor Master Dicky, after being violently sized (*sic*) with a Complaint in his Bowels for some time past, expired on Thursday morning, and was Inter'd Last Evening. Indeed, I think Mrs. Wedgwood has had severe tryals of late, but the great hopes of Mr. Wedgwood's perfect recovery seems to keep her Spirits up in a tollerable degree.' Mrs. Wedgwood's devotion was greater than even Peter was aware of. Although she had just lost her infant son Richard, and was weary with her vigils and full of grief that he was taken from her, she crushed down the burden of her sorrow. 'She dressed her husband's wound, administered his medicines, wrote his letters, warded off from him every possible business care, was his right hand in everything, and through her serene cheerfulness greatly hastened his recovery.' Bentley also proved himself an 'incomparable friend' during this time of trial. So great was the esteem in which Wedgwood was held, that in London the Dukes of Bedford and Marlborough, Lord Bessborough, the Russian Ambassador, Sir George Savile, the Hon. Mrs. Chetwynd, and many others sent for daily news of his condition, while the Duke of Bridgewater despatched a daily messenger from Trentham on the same errand.

Before the close of the year 1768 Wedgwood lost his aged mother. She had spent her closing years at the Bank House, Newcastle, with her daughter Katherine Willet. Mrs. Willet was Wedgwood's favourite sister. She had been his companion in childhood, and her union with the Rev. William Willet had been very beneficial from the intellectual point of view. Brother and sister, therefore, found much to interest them beyond the ordinary level of human thought. After the London warehouse in Newport Street had been opened, she generally travelled with the Wedgwoods to the Metropolis, and was deeply interested in the numerous attractions which London offered. When Wedgwood's children were ill, they would be sent to Aunt Willet at Newcastle to be nursed. Wedgwood had a deep attachment to his children—dearly as he loved his work, it could not shut them out. 'It is interesting to catch glimpses of the tender father shining through the graver aspect of the concise, determined, and austere man of business. The heavy duties of the day over, the occasionally long vigils of the night in chemical experiments, modelling, or letter-writing not begun, he rides away to see these little babes. How dearly he loves them! How, throughout his life, he loves his children! How in years to come we shall see him taking pride in the handsome presence and polished manners of his son Josiah, and in the great intellectual gifts of his son Tom; indeed, in all his children, for he had no favourites; and yet for the little maid "Sukey," his firstborn, there is a something not expressed in words, and yet apparent to us, that she was gathered up in the innermost folds of his deep affections. As after-life showed, there was something very much akin in their respective natures, though gentleness and consideration for others were perhaps intensified in their feminine expression.'

Nor did Wedgwood neglect any who were connected with him by the ties of blood. He provided a post in his works for Joseph Wedgwood, a young man descended from one of the elder branches of the family; and again and again we find him providing for his nephew, young Byerley, who seemed to be an unconscionable time in sowing his wild oats. However, his kindness was rewarded in this case, for, after some final bitter experiences in America, Byerley returned, to become a dutiful son to his mother, who had a business in Newcastle, and to repay his uncle by long and faithful service.

From the year 1768 onward Wedgwood's cream-ware was in great request. It was universally admired, and was exported to almost every part of the globe. The designs upon the ware were mostly engraved by Sadler of Liverpool and his partner Guy Green. They were generally of a pastoral character, and were copied from a variety of sources. But, excellent as were the engravings, Wedgwood's originality of taste led him to incur great expense in commissioning entirely new designs. Amongst those who early worked for Wedgwood was Stothard, afterwards the R.A. Beautiful antique forms were also pressed into requisition, principally derived from the work of the Count de Caylus. In addition to the popular cream-ware, a vast demand sprang up for ornamental vases. The names given to these vases—the 'Bedford,' the 'Oxford,' the 'Pope's,' etc.—signified that they were modelled after specimens in the cabinets of those whose names were thus specified. Lord Cathcart, who was now an admirer and a patron of Wedgwood, was a friend of Mr., afterwards Sir William Hamilton, our representative at Naples. Sir William had purchased the famous Porcinari collection of ancient vases, and at great expense he had prepared a description of the treasures, with reproductions, in four folio volumes. It was a splendid undertaking, and as proofs of the plates were struck off, Sir William distributed a few amongst his friends. Lord Cathcart was among the recipients, and he entrusted some of his proofs to Wedgwood. The potter was inspired with new ideas, and made a resolve that he would rival the masterpieces of Etruscan and Grecian ceramic art. He also began at the same time his elaborate experiments for bronzing his vases. Boulton, too, proposed to decorate works in earthenware with metal ornaments. Although he thus stepped out of his own province into that of Wedgwood, the latter indulged only feelings of generous rivalry, and there was no diminution of friendship between the chiefs of Soho and Etruria. Yet 'it might have been different, had not Watt appeared and turned anew Boulton's peculiar talent for metallurgic art into its legitimate channel.'

In November, 1769, Wedgwood took out his first and only patent. It was one for 'the purpose of ornamenting Earthern and Porcelaine Ware with an Encaustic Gold Bronze, together with a peculiar Species of Encaustic Painting in various Colours, in imitation of the Antient Etruscan and Roman Earthenware.' Competitors soon arose in the manufacture of bronze and Etruscan vases, the cleverest of whom was a potter named Palmer, of Hanley. 'His imitations of the Etruscan vases never reached the excellence of those of Mr. Wedgwood, but they were passable in the market, and led, as we shall subsequently see, to the overthrow of the patent, not through the verdict of a Court of Law—though there is reason to think that had the matter been brought to trial, the adjudication would have been in favour of Palmer—but by the generous relinquishment of the patentee. As soon as he saw the whole bearing of the question, and that Palmer's imitations, even though inferior to his own, and suspiciously indicative of processes surreptitiously obtained, evinced the ability and industry of an experienced potter, he resolved to throw up the patent, very wisely considering that he could hold his own; and, still more rightly judging that he, least of all men, who had such true opinions respecting art and its tendencies relative to civilisation, should not attempt to curtail its advance by an impossible monopoly, and stultify, as it were, the growing influences of recovered antiquity. To his lasting honour, he ceased to contend as soon as his strong understanding pointed out to him that contention was unworthy.'

The first pair of bronze antique vases finished by Wedgwood were presented to Miss Tarleton, daughter of one of the Members for Liverpool. In the public interests, Wedgwood was anxious to obtain Mr. Tarleton's interest with the Liverpool Corporation in behalf of that public scheme, the Runcorn aqueduct. The vases sent to Miss Tarleton were of the largest size, finished with satyrs' heads. Such vases sold at 18s. a pair, but they would now fetch £8 or £10. In June, 1768, the Etruscan Works at Etruria were opened, and Bentley's residence there was completed. Wedgwood engaged in London a perfect master of pottery in the antique style named John Voyez. He was sent down into Staffordshire, and a residence found for him. He was inclined to be a sot, however, but he did excellent work under the master's eye. At length he got into prison for some crime or other, and on coming out he soon proved to be a vindictive wretch, who betrayed his master. While receiving the pay of Wedgwood he worked for his rival Palmer, and even set up for himself, using the knowledge he had gained in the factories of Etruria.

Wedgwood was liberal-minded in his business course, and

he entrusted some of his best work to female hands. Mrs. Landre modelled subjects for him, but he also employed, in 1769, a greater artist still—John Bacon the sculptor. His chief enameller was David Rhodes, who was Wedgwood's right hand in this department until the death of Rhodes in 1777. The ornamental vases produced at Burslem and Etruria are divided by Wedgwood's biographers into seven leading sections. These were: the cream-colour and its variations, as those with blue necks, and ornaments variously gilt; the black basaltes; the terra-cotta pebble and marbled bodies; the bronze antique; the encaustic Etruscan and Grecian; and the jasper. But there were variations again in the separate sections themselves. The last class produced was the jasper, which was first manufactured in 1775. This form was exquisitely and delicately finished.

The first day of labour at the new Etruria Works was a memorable one in the annals of the Potteries. It was on the 13th June, 1769, that the works were inaugurated, Wedgwood himself throwing the first productions. There were present his wife and two children, Mr. Bentley, Mr. Wedgwood of Spen Green, Mr. and Mrs. Willet from Newcastle, and other relatives and friends, together with a large body of workmen. The company being assembled in the throwing-room, Wedgwood threw off his hat and coat, put on a workman's apron, and began the labours of the day. Says Mr. Jewitt: 'Here sat the great Josiah Wedgwood—great in fame, great in reputation, great in worldly goods, but greater far in mind and intellect, and in nobleness of character—at the potter's bench, his bare arms encircling the ball of pliant clay, while his busy fingers and practised eye formed it into classic shape; and there stood his partner, Thomas Bentley, at the potter's wheel, which he turned with a care suited to the auspicious occasion and to the requirements of his great chief. Standing by, no doubt, and watching with pleasurable anxiety the progress of the work, were Mrs. Wedgwood and many friends; while on the board in front of the "father of potters" would be ranged the urns as he produced them. The vases thus formed, of Etruscan shape, went through all the subsequent processes of baking, etc., and were ultimately painted in the purest Etruscan style, with figures, and each piece bore this appropriate inscription :—" June XIII. MDCCLXIX. one of the first day's productions at Etruria, in Staffordshire, by Wedgwood and Bentley. Artes Etruriæ renascuntur." Three of these vases, the historical interest attaching to which it is impossible to overrate, are in the possession of Mr. Francis Wedgwood, of Barlaston.'

The body of the vases was hard, of a slightly bluish tinge, with the surface, like the original Etruscan, black. On this the figures and inscriptions were painted in red. The vases were about ten inches in height, and each one bore a group—differing from the others—of Hercules and his companions in the Garden of the Hesperides. On the opposite side was the inscription given above, and around the lid and upper portion were characteristic and elegant borders. A few months after the ceremony just described, Bentley removed to London, and established himself at Chelsea. Near to his house in Little Cheyne Row the firm established workshops, where some of the orders which now poured in for every variety of ornamental ware were completed. Before the ensuing winter set in, Wedgwood and his family moved to Etruria. They occupied for a time Bentley's house, but left it in 1770 for Etruria Hall, Wedgwood's new and elegant residence. Just before the removal to Burslem a third surviving child, Josiah, was born to the Wedgwoods.

The demand for ornamental ware increased so enormously that, in a letter to Bentley, Wedgwood assured his partner he could sell £50 or £100 worth a day if he had them. There was a like demand for cream-ware services, even Quaker families becoming customers for them. Lord Bessborough rendered Wedgwood essential service, not only by permitting him to have casts taken from a fine cabinet of gems, which were afterwards sold to the Duke of Marlborough, but by introducing the vases amongst the Irish nobility, who became enthusiastic patrons. Another artistic and personal friendship sprang up with Sir Watkin Williams Wynn, and a large proportion of Wedgwood's list of intaglios was derived from Sir Watkin's gems. Nor were these solitary instances of friendly patronage. On some occasions there was no getting to the door of the warehouse in London for the line of coaches, and no getting into the rooms for the crowd of ladies and gentlemen who were vase-hunting. The firm were threatened with piratical goods, which somewhat discomposed Bentley, but Wedgwood thus philosophically reassured him: 'We are far enough before our rivals, and whenever we apprehend they are treading too near our heels, we can at least manage them better than Lord Bute can manage the merchants, to compare great things with small.' We now see the firm of Wedgwood & Bentley employed over a vast variety of productions, including bas-reliefs, encaustic bronzes, statuettes of Mars, Venus, etc., small groups and single figures, vases in black basaltes, crystalline terra-cotta wares, Etruscan painted vases, lamps and other light-bearing ornaments, an incredible variety of flower-pots, bough-pots, and root-pots, articles studied from antique gems, Roman figures, Egyptian lions, sphinxes, Tritons, tripods, and other ornaments.

A dangerous disease of the eyes attacked Wedgwood towards the close of 1769. The affection seems to have been epidemic, and several persons died from it. Doctors were consulted: the active potter, who was always miserable when laid aside, was forbidden to use his eyes at all by artificial light. Referring to this and to his lameness, he plaintively wrote: 'I am learning to acquiesce, whatever may be the issue, as I would wish to do, in every unavoidable evil. I am often practising to *see* with my *fingers*, and I think I should make a tolerable proficient in that science for one who begins so late in life; but shall make a wretched walker in the dark with a single leg.' He became somewhat hypochondriacal, taking gloomy views of the future, and dreading the worst. But in the course of a few weeks, his eyesight began to improve under proper treatment, and life generally took on a brighter hue. He began to seek for superior enamel painters at Worcester, Liverpool, Derby, Birmingham Bow, and Lambeth, and many were engaged. Wedgwood's partner Bentley settled down handsomely at Chelsea, bought a carriage and pair, and kept up a useful but not extravagant hospitality. Soon after this settlement, Bentley, who was a widower, married Mary Stamford, daughter of the well-known smith and engineer of that name, of Derby. She was about twenty-five years of age, and was comely, cheerful, and vivacious. She took an interest in her husband's work, and was skilful in cutting out vases and other forms on paper. On the 15th of December, 1770, dating from Chelsea, Bentley thus wrote to his Liverpool partner Boardman: 'Last Monday Mr. Wedgwood and I had a long audience of their Majesties at the Queen's palace, to present some *bas-reliefs* Her Majesty had ordered; and to show some new improvements, with which they were well pleased. They expressed in the most obliging and condescending manner their attention to our manufacture, and entered very freely into conversation on the further improvement of it, and on many other subjects. The King is well acquainted with business, and with the characters of the principal manufacturers, merchants, and artists; and seems to have the success of all our manufactures much at heart, and to understand the importance of them. The Queen has more sensibility, true politeness, engaging affability, and sweetness of temper, than any great lady I ever had the honour of speaking to.' Miss Meteyard adds: 'As time wore on, Mr. Bentley's popularity grew. His handsome person and polished manners were irresistible to otherwise haughty duchesses and ladies; and whilst he poised a vase, or showed bas-relief or cameo, and related the antique stories its designs sought to express, the ladies listened, smiled, bowed, and, what was

T

more to the purpose, bought. An aristocrat by nature, he was the most courtly of chapmen. "Be so good," writes Mr. Wedgwood soon after Mr. Bentley's settlement in Newport Street, "to let us know what is going forward in the Great World. How many Lords and Dukes visit your rooms, praise your beauties, thin your shelves, and fill your purses? and if you will take the trouble to acquaint us with the daily ravages in your stores, we will endeavour to replenish them." By degrees the popularity attracted to itself something worthier than the fashion of the hour; and by the close of 1772 Mr. Bentley reckoned among his friends, "Athenian Stuart," Dr. Solander, Mr. Banks (afterwards Sir Joseph), and others whose names live in the scientific and literary history of their time.'

The works at Etruria were likewise constantly visited by the great, many of whom were taken over by Wedgwood's able and accomplished friend Earl Gower, who frequently received the potter in turn at Trentham Hall. When the workrooms were completed at Chelsea, Wedgwood drafted off from Etruria thither some of his best assistants, including a clever painter, Mrs. Wilcox, Hutchins, a printer, and Cooper, an excellent flower painter. Then, as the great demand for enamelled table-services and vases still increased, other hands were obtained amongst the London fan, coach, and fresco painters. In 1770 Wedgwood learnt that cheap Etruscan painted vases were in the market, which, as far as possible, were copied from Sir William Hamilton's great work. The bodies were made in Staffordshire and the painting effected in London. The pirates were Palmer of Hanley, his wife, and Palmer's partner Neale, their London shop being in Shoe Lane. An injunction was served upon them, and a trial seemed inevitable, though Wedgwood saw clearly that a jury might be impressed by Palmer's plea that his vases were copied from the prints in Sir William Hamilton's work, and not from those made by the patentee. Palmer was a very unscrupulous fellow, and the manufacturers almost to a man were in favour of Wedgwood's right in his patent, which had been infringed ; but rather than have all the harassing and expensive proceedings of a public trial, Wedgwood agreed to refer the matter to arbitration. The result was that both parties agreed to share in the patent, and to divide its cost between them, as well as the law charges. But originality and superiority always tell in the long run, and when Palmer was left at liberty to make Etruscan vases at will, their manifest inferiority both of form and design soon brought them to their true level in the market. Yet, when Palmer found that he could do little with the vases, he had the audacity next to pirate Wedgwood's seals and intaglios, making what harvest he could, and he reaped for a time considerable profit.

In April, 1771, Wedgwood's fourth and last son was born. He was named Thomas, after his paternal grandfather, uncle, and cousins; and he was the fifth Thomas Wedgwood in a direct line. From his earlier years he was a delicate child, and had within him the seeds of organic disease, which ultimately made life a weary burden to him. 'But when we first catch a glimpse of him,' remarks Miss Meteyard, 'he was a merry little fellow, full of drollery and fun, and the life of the household.' There were no indications then, that, before he was twenty, he would be poring into the deepest secrets of nature, particularly those relative to space, light, and heat; be the hardest of students, or, conjointly with his father's chemist, Alexander Chisholm, be rendering the laboratory at Etruria a place on which, for scientific reasons, the savans of our own day would cast back their gaze, to penetrate, if possible, into some of the early mysteries of the photographic art effected there. But, from the first, Dr. Darwin thought highly of the boy's mental powers; and happily Josiah Wedgwood had passed away before bodily disease had rendered all but useless his son's extraordinary mental powers, or unnerved the assiduous hand which had served him as devotedly in matters relative to art, as in chemical experiments.'

Wedgwood received from the Empress Catherine of Russia

a commission of extraordinary magnitude. He was directed to make a very large service of Queen's ware for her Majesty's use, and to 'paint in black enamel upon each piece a different view of the palaces, seats of the nobility, and other remarkable places in this kingdom. Upon every piece there was also to be painted the image of a green toad or frog. He was very unwilling to disfigure the service with this reptile, but was told it was not to be dispensed with, because the ware was intended for the use of a palace that bore its name. The idea of such a service was well worthy the mind of a sovereign, but the undertaking seemed a great one for the powers of an individual manufacturer. The number of views necessary, to avoid a repetition of the same subjects, was about twelve hundred, and a great proportion of them were original sketches. He spent three years in making the collection and painting the views upon the pieces of this service, with all the correctness of design and drawing that is necessary to a good picture. The Empress, we have been told, was entirely satisfied with the execution of this work; and no doubt it conveyed to her mind a pretty just sentiment of our national splendour, ingenuity, and character.'

When this magnificent Russian service was completed in 1774, there was a great desire for it to be exhibited in London. Wedgwood demurred for a time, but at length consented, and when it was at length on view it caused quite a sensation. Mrs. Delaney, writing to Mrs. Port, says: 'I am just returned from viewing the Wedgwood ware that is to be sent to the Empress of Russia. It consists, I believe, of as many pieces as there are days in the year, if not hours. They are displayed at a house in Greek Street, Soho, called Portland House. There are three rooms below, and two above, filled with it, laid out on tables; everything that can be wanted to serve a dinner. The ground, the common ware, pale brimstone, the drawings in purple, the borders a wreath of leaves, the middle of each piece a particular view of all the remarkable places in the King's dominions, neatly executed. I suppose it will come to a princely price: it is well for the manufacturer, which I am glad of, as his ingenuity and industry deserve encouragement.'

The price which the Empress paid for the service is stated to have been £3,000, but even that afforded the makers 'no adequate remuneration for the incessant anxiety and immense labour involved in its production. But it served as a splendid advertisement to the whole continent of Europe, and spread Wedgwood & Bentley's fame to the most distant foreign Courts. Catherine was fond of using these services at her State dinners; and as she outwardly at least attached herself to the English policy, favoured Englishmen, and dealt in a liberal spirit with all that concerned the commerce of our country, there can be no doubt that in the abstract this generous spirit, which looked more to great worth than great gain, was richly and amply rewarded.' The Empress showed the service with great pride to Lord Malmesbury, when he visited the Grenouillière Palace in 1779. It was used in the splendid entertainments which Catherine gave from time to time in the palace of Tzarsko-selo, and she preferred it to royal gifts of Berlin and Dresden porcelain. It has been remarked that the great service was in every sense a national work, and its fame was not only national but European.

In 1771 Wedgwood opened showrooms at Dublin and Bath. The Irish business was at first very promising, being stimulated by such patrons as the Duke of Leinster, Lords Charlemont and Bessborough, etc.; but social troubles, combined with the pecuniary embarrassments of the resident gentry, prevented a large trade from being developed. The business at Bath also suffered from 'bad seasons and the caprices of the fashionable world.' By the year 1774 the whole of the new works at Etruria had been finished; and they formed a noble pile of buildings, with the canal skirting the whole, and the green upland on which Etruria Hall stood rising beyond. In arrangement, the Etruria manufactories formed then, as now, two distinct groups, the 'useful' and the 'ornamental,' with separate ovens, yards, workshops, and rooms of every character. 'The showroom, when finished, was an important place. Here were displayed, from time to time, to the chief aristocracy of all countries, as they passed through or paid visits into Staffordshire, the finest masterpieces of the potter's art. The enamellers at the works in Chelsea, as afterwards in Greek Street, vied with each other in the several processes of their art, and the results were often returned to Etruria to decorate this room. With these in contrast were the labours of the gem setters of London, Birmingham, and Uttoxeter; enshrining as rings, buckles, brooches, earrings, or seals, cameo work after the finest models; and here were to be seen the noblest vases and the most exquisite bas-reliefs. Princes and potent dukes, lords and ladies, might well linger in this room, and tell Wedgwood, as they did, that neither Dresden nor Sèvres had anything to show which bore comparison with his ornamental ware, either in beauty of form or chastity of design. But the room in which was laid the foundations of these masterpieces has a still greater degree of interest for all real lovers of Wedgwood's art. In the modelling-room the moulds were made or the modelling done from designs in clay or wax, supplied by Bacon, Flaxman, Tassie, Webber, Hoskins, Coward, Mrs. Landre, Theodore Parker, and various other English and Italian artists. Here Hackwood, the exquisite modeller of small things, passed the chief hours of his long service; and we catch glimpses of Webber, Tebo, Boot, and Massey. If Flaxman ever worked at Etruria for a brief season, this was the place of his labours; and Wedgwood himself passed whole days here amidst his modellers. From hence came the Sleeping Boy, the statuettes in the fine white biscuit body, the life-like busts of the heroes of the old and modern world, the bas-reliefs which reflected the glories of antique art, and the vase, which, as a masterly reproduction of a great original, spread Wedgwood's fame far wider than any other of his multitudinous labours.'

The death of the great Brindley in September, 1772, affected Wedgwood deeply, and he poured out his feelings in a letter to Bentley. After referring to his deceased friend's personal character, and virtues, he went on to observe that 'what the public has lost can only be conceived by those who best knew his character and talents—talents to which this age and country are indebted for works that will be the most lasting monuments to his fame, and show to future ages how much good may be done by one single genius, when happily employed upon works beneficial to mankind. Mr. Brindley had an excellent constitution, but his mind—too ardently intent upon the execution of the works it had planned—wore down, at the age of fifty-five, a body which originally promised to have lasted a century, and might give him the pleasing expectation of living to see those great works completed for which millions yet unborn will revere and bless his memory.'

The loss of Wedgwood's brother, Thomas Wedgwood of the Overhouse, in February, 1773, brought much trouble and anxiety upon Josiah. Though on friendly terms always, the brothers had not been deeply attached; but Josiah loyally did all that was possible for the survivors. Thomas Wedgwood had been married twice, and by both wives had children; and he, unfortunately, left his affairs in a very unsettled state. The widow was a harsh and selfish woman, and her cruelty had done much to drive her step-son into evil courses. She ultimately lost her reason, but the son was reclaimed to an honourable life by the good influence of Josiah Wedgwood, who established him in his father's works, and assisted him with loans of money.

In April, 1774, the firm of Wedgwood & Bentley opened

new showrooms in Greek Street, Soho, and thither Mr. and Mrs. Bentley removed their household from Chelsea. Bentley and his enamellers were soon indefatigably at work, and on a grand scale. The number of hands was largely augmented, for the demand for household enamelled ware especially was increasing. Bentley supplemented his partner's labours with untiring zeal, searching around him everywhere for artists, books, and prints. He went to Boydell, Major, Cadell, and Hooper; employed Pye the engraver; while Mr. Pennant of Lichfield, as well as some others, sent him presents of prints. The Russian service was being pushed forward at this time, and Bentley had the honour of receiving a visit from the Queen and her Royal brother, who were most anxious to view it.

A change came over the fashionable taste for Queen's or cream ware, the fickle public asking for something whiter. Wedgwood was disinclined to yield to this caprice, but he improved his ordinary biscuit body, and began experiments for one still finer. The virtues of the *terra ponderosa*, or carbonate of baryta, had already been proved, and a further discovery was now made, viz., that the sulphate of baryta, or cawk, was a valuable ingredient in the new body. In fact, it began largely to take the place of the *terra ponderosa*. It was to be found on Middleton Moor, but the utmost circumspection had to be used in obtaining it, the cawk having to be disguised by pounding. In 1775 Flaxman began to model for Wedgwood, and the famous sculptor's first bill of charges, amounting to £12 18s. 9d., included *basso-relievos* of Melpomene, Sappho, Apollo, Hercules, etc., as well as a pair of vases, one with a Satyr and the other with a Triton handle. But Wedgwood was catholic in his tastes, and besides mythological subjects, produced a head of Shakespeare, medals of the Popes, and the heads of the English kings. His beautiful wares in jasper also began to be produced at this time. The first edition of Wedgwood & Bentley's Catalogue was published in 1773.

It was a little insignificant-looking pamphlet of sixty pages. Various editions followed, the sixth, issued in 1787, being a remarkably full and handsome work. It was translated into French, German, Dutch, and Italian. These catalogues formed a kind of history of the art pursued by Wedgwood. During the time of his connection with the firm, Flaxman produced a long and varied list of noble antique designs and models. Before Flaxman's time, Wedgwood had employed, among others already specified, an able artist named Tassie, who subsequently acquired a great vogue for his imitated gems and medallion portraits; but there was no rival who could come up to Wedgwood's best work in any class of manufacture. By and by an enormous trade came to be done by Boulton, Wedgwood, and other manufacturers in such articles as cabinets and other pieces of furniture decorated with cameos, knife and fork cases, cane and bamboo wares, gold bronzes, inkstands, crucibles, retorts, evaporating baths, etc., etc.

Wedgwood was strongly opposed to the American War, which he regarded as fratricidal. He sympathised with the colonists; and from his trading relations with America he was likewise able to see the sacrifice which the mother-country was making in this senseless struggle. Just before the strife began Great Britain exported to North America nearly the whole of the surplus products of her industry; and between 1704 and 1774 the American trade had grown from £500,000 a year to £6,500,000. Wedgwood's view that it was 'a wicked and preposterous war with our brethren and best friends' was endorsed by many before the Americans achieved their independence.

The war in America drove Wedgwood's nephew, Thomas Byerley, to England again. He was warmly welcomed, and soon showed that his character was more stable than formerly. Wedgwood took him into his employment as traveller, and with the wares of Etruria he penetrated into every nook and corner of Great Britain. About this time John Wedgwood, son of Richard Wedgwood of Spen Green, was stricken down and died; and a few years later Richard Wedgwood himself—Josiah's last brother—also passed away. Of other domestic incidents, we may mention that three daughters, being his last children, were born to Josiah as follows: Catherine in 1774, Sarah in 1776, and Mary Ann in 1778. Wedgwood grieved sorely over the death of his learned brother-in-law, the Rev. William Willet, the Unitarian minister at Newcastle, in 1778. But in November, 1780, he was called upon to bear a still severer loss, and one that for a time seemed to overwhelm him. Bentley, his friend and partner—and between whom and himself there had existed an affection resembling that of David and Jonathan —died at his residence at Turnham Green. He had long been ailing, but the end came suddenly at last. Wedgwood raised a tablet to his memory in Chiswick Church. The inscription was furnished by their mutual friend, 'Athenian' Stuart, and the monument, with medallion of Bentley, was the work of Scheemaekers, the artist who executed the monument to Shakespeare in Westminster Abbey. Stuart's inscription runs thus: 'Thomas Bentley, born at Scrapton in Derbyshire, Jan. 1st, 1730. He married Hannah Oates, of Sheffield, in the year 1754: Mary Stamford, of Derby, in the year 1772, who survived to mourn her loss. He died Nov. 26th, 1780. Blessed with an elevated and comprehensive understanding; informed in variety of science; he possessed a warm and brilliant imagination, a pure and elegant taste; his extensive abilities, guided by the most expansive philanthropy, were employed in forming and executing plans for the public good. He thought with the freedom of a philosopher: he acted with the integrity of a virtuous citizen.' Judging from the testimony of his contemporaries, this estimate of Bentley appears to have been in no wise exaggerated.

After the death of Bentley, Wedgwood engaged the services of Alexander Chisholm, an able man, as secretary and chemical assistant; and some time afterwards Henry Webber, a modeller of uncommon ability, recommended by Sir William Chambers and Sir Joshua Reynolds, became the head of the ornamental department at Etruria. These and other changes gave Wedgwood more freedom, and saved him from a good deal of drudgery. In Chisholm the great potter found a kindred spirit, as well as a faithful friend and servant. Wedgwood invented a thermometer for measuring heat; and in May, 1782, his paper on 'The Pyrometer, or Heat-measuring Instrument' was read before the Royal Society. Some other experiments followed, in which he anticipated portions of the glacial theory; and in consideration of his valuable researches Wedgwood was elected a Fellow of the Royal Society in 1783.

The condition of the rural districts of England in 1783 was lamentable. The American struggle had crippled us, trade was paralysed, and a bad harvest aggravated the situation. Riots took place in the Potteries amongst other places, and it was only owing to the energy and presence of mind displayed by Wedgwood that the works at Etruria were not sacked by the mob. When tranquillity had been restored, Wedgwood wrote and published a pamphlet entitled 'An Address to the Young Inhabitants of the Pottery,' in which he showed the folly of looking to such outbreaks for a redress of social wrongs. The writer admitted that provisions were dear, and recommended the opening of the ports to foreign food supplies, thus supporting the principle of free trade. He also showed that there had been still worse times in the past, and pointed out that riots were the most foolish and expensive way of redressing grievances. The operation and the effects of economical laws could not be destroyed by violently breaking them. Wedgwood then made this stirring appeal, as he drew a picture of the past: 'Let me now beg of you who are approaching to manhood, and who by your future behaviour must stamp the character of the potters of the rising generation; let me entreat you, as you value your own reputation and happiness, and the welfare of your country, never to harbour a thought of following the fatal example which has been set you by men who have so greatly mistaken their own and your real interests; but when you labour under any real grievances make your case known in a peaceable manner to some magistrate near you, or to your employers, who are best acquainted with your situation, and I have not a doubt of your meeting in this way with speedy and effectual redress, which it would be impossible for you to procure for yourselves by the measures you have lately seen pursued, or any illegal ones whatever. Before I take my leave I would request you to ask your parents for a description of the country we inhabit when they first knew it; and they will tell you, that the inhabitants bore all the signs of poverty to a much greater degree than they do now. Their houses were miserable huts; the lands poorly cultivated, and yielded little of value for the food of man or beast; and these disadvantages, with roads almost impassable, might be said to have cut off our part of the country from the rest of the world, besides not rendering it very comfortable to ourselves. Compare this picture, which I know to be a true one, with the present state of the same country. The workmen earning nearly double their former wages—their houses mostly new and comfortable, and the lands, roads, and every other circumstance bearing evident marks of the most pleasing and rapid improvements. From whence and from what cause has this happy change taken place? You will be beforehand with me in acknowledging a truth too evident to be denied by anyone. Industry has been the parent of this happy change—a well-directed and long continued series of industrious exertions, both in masters and servants, has so changed for the better the face of our country—its buildings, lands, roads, and notwithstanding the present unfavourable appearances, I must say the manner and deportment of its inhabitants too—as to attract the notice and admiration of countries which had scarcely heard of us before; and how far these improvements may still be carried by the same laudable means which have brought us thus far, has been one of the most pleasing contemplations of my life. How mortifying then is it to have this fair prospect endangered by one rash act ! . . But I place my hopes, with some degree of confidence, in the rising generation, being persuaded that they will, by their better conduct, make atonement for this unhappy, this unwise slip of their fathers.'

Wedgwood further issued 'An Address to the Workmen in the Pottery on the Subject of Entering into the Service of Foreign Manufacturers.' In consequence of the great increase of the English trade in earthenware, certain German and French masters sent over spies to this country with a view to discover all the processes of manufacture, as also to bribe workmen to emigrate. Trenchantly dealing with the false representations, Wedgwood pointed out the fallacy of the bribes held out to his workmen, and the miseries and misfortunes of those who had already been tempted to leave their native country, and who were only too anxious to return. Acts of Parliament had been passed in this reign to prevent the emigration of workmen, and subsequently still more stringent efforts were made to stop the enticement of artisans from their employment in England for the purpose of mastering the methods of their respective trades. Such an interference with freedom on the part of workmen, however, was not justifiable, seeing that masters were at liberty to carry their trades out of the kingdom if they wished. Wedgwood's foreign trade rose greatly, notwithstanding the labour troubles, and after the signing of the Commercial Treaty with France in 1786, it increased still more enormously. He found his markets as far apart as North America, the West Indies, Amsterdam, Cadiz, St. Petersburg, Moscow, Leipsic, Genoa, Naples, Berlin, Turin, Lisbon, Bayreuth, etc.

Flaxman executed for Wedgwood beautiful cameo medallions of Mrs. Siddons, Sir Joshua Reynolds, and Dr. Johnson, and many other works, including his celebrated set of chessmen. All these were very popular, at home and abroad. Jasper ornamental ware began to be extensively made in 1786, and Wedgwood also invented a jasper dip, or wash, as a substitute for colouring in the mass, or for a body wholly jasper. Further, the jasper ornamental wares, such as tea things, were polished within in the manner in which agate and other stones were polished. Among the fine jasper vases executed at the period of their perfection were the bridal vase and those with bas-reliefs of Apollo and the Muses and the Dancing Houris. There were also ornamental vases in great variety. Wedgwood also showed his originality in personal ornaments.

The prohibition of ware to France and the duty on exports led Wedgwood to agitate earnestly for free trade, and it was owing to his untiring energy that a General Chamber of Manufacturers was established. He gave evidence before a Committee of Privy Council on the hindrances to English trade, and had several interviews with Pitt. He was also thrown into relations with the leaders of the Opposition, and Fox sent him designs from Lady Diana Beauclerk. Pitt, urged by Wedgwood and others, proposed wise and liberal measures with a view of giving Ireland commercial freedom, but the jealousy and opposition of traders and others in the House of Commons compelled him to abandon them. The Commercial Treaty with France, however, concluded in 1786, abolished most of the protective duties between France and England. It is pleasant to find that Wedgwood was not only engaged in the struggle for commercial freedom, but that from July, 1787, till the close of his life he was more or less active in the cause of the Abolition of Slavery. He was one of the Society's committee, and contributed largely to its funds. In 1790 this indefatigable man contributed his last paper to the Transactions of the Royal Society, on a new mineral substance which had been sent from New South Wales. He also formed from some clay despatched from the same colony a medallion showing the figure of Hope addressing Peace, Labour, and Plenty, which he sent out to the colonists for the purpose of encouraging the arts. Suffering at this time greatly from ill-health, he was ably assisted in the works at Etruria by his sons Josiah and Thomas.

Wedgwood was the liberal patron and friend of arts other than his own. His portrait and that of his wife were painted by Sir Joshua Reynolds, and he gave commissions to Wright of Derby for his well-known paintings, 'The Maid of Corinth,' a 'Moonlight Scene with the Lady in Comus,' 'Penelope unravelling the Web,' and the fine portrait of Sir Richard Arkwright, which now hangs in the Manchester Royal Exchange.

The reproduction of the celebrated Barberini Vase is one of the greatest triumphs associated with the name of Wedgwood. 'The Barberini Vase was discovered between the years 1623 and 1644, during the pontificate of Urban VIII. (Barberini), beneath a mound of earth called Monte del Grano, about three miles from Rome, on the road to the ancient Tusculum. It was enclosed in a sarcophagus of excellent workmanship, and this in a sepulchral chamber. An inscription on the sarcophagus, which was otherwise covered with fine basreliefs, showed it to have been dedicated to the memory of the Emperor Alexander Severus and his mother, Julia Mammæa, both of whom were killed in the year 235 during a revolt in Germany. The vase, in height ten inches, was deposited in the library of the Barberini family, and the sarcophagus in the museum of the capital. The material of which the former was composed was by Montfauçon and others conjectured to be a precious stone, but Mr. Wedgwood's examination proved it to be formed of glass, the ground being a dark blue, so nearly approaching black as to appear of that colour except when held in a strong light. The white bas-reliefs are of glass or paste; the material having been fused on in a mass, and then cut out by the skill and patience of the gem engraver into the designs required. The subjects of these bas-reliefs, as also the age and place of production of the vase, are points so wholly unknown as to be still open to conjecture and criticism. With respect to the first, every critic has differed. The Italians and French first entered upon the discussion, and the introduction of the vase into England was a signal for the critics here. Mr. Charles Greville, who published some very fine engravings by Bartolozzi of the vase, considered the bas-reliefs typified the death and resurrection of Adonis. Darwin, who consulted Warburton's *Divine Legation* and many other works, thought the bas-reliefs bore reference to the Eleusinian mysteries, and this, with some trifling difference, was the view adopted by Wedgwood in his pamphlet on the vase. Another critic, Dr. King, in entire ignorance of the arts of antiquity and their best periods, conjectured that these designs bore reference to the birth and acts of the Emperor Alexander Severus, whilst a far more learned and enlightened critic of our own day considers that one of the groups represents Peleus approaching Thetis. These critical differences might be repeated to a wearisome extent. It is, on the whole, perhaps safest to conclude that the subjects of the bas-reliefs are simply a heathen and poetised allegory on the trials of human life and its close. Such vases, as in the case of the Greek encaustic vases prepared for the Olympian games, may have been designed with a view to a general purpose, rather than a particular one. Of the vase itself, if it does belong to the best period of Grecian art, that prior to the age of Alexander, it may have former a portion of those innumerable spoils which we learn from Livy, Plutarch, and other writers were poured into Rome, as proofs of subjugation and conquest. But it is questionable if the Greeks excelled as much in the art of the verrier as in that of the potter; whilst the Alexandrians, at a date when Rome was in its glory, supplied the most matchless specimens in glass and paste the world had yet seen. Wedgwood discovered that the Portland Vase had been broken previously and repaired, as also that the bas-relief head which forms the bottom had belonged originally to some other vase or fragment of antiquity, and that it had been ground down and then inserted by processes far inferior to those used by the original artist. A mould of the vase was made by Peckler the gem engraver, whilst it was in the possession of the Barberini family, and from this, on its first arrival in England, a certain number of copies were taken in plaster of Paris by Tassie, who afterwards destroyed the mould.'

The Barberini, or, as it is sometimes called, the Portland Vase, was brought to England by Sir William Hamilton, and sold to the Duchess of Portland. Her Grace acquired it by the most secret negotiations, and at the sale of her museum it was purchased by her son. The Duke lent the vase to Wedgwood for the purposes of reproduction, and although the potter encountered unusual difficulties in his task, he ultimately triumphed. Webber was the moulder, under Wedgwood's direction. One of the finest copies of the vase was made in 1791, and conveyed to London. After being shown to the Queen, it was placed for some days in the rooms of the Society of Antiquaries, and whilst there its entire similitude to the original was certified by Sir Joshua Reynolds. It was afterwards removed to Greek Street, where it was viewed by hundreds of aristocratic connoisseurs, and then it was taken abroad, and exhibited before several crowned heads and many collectors. Subscribers were few, however, and owing to the difficulties attending the various processes and their great cost, it appears that not more than about fifty copies were made in Wedgwood's lifetime. Copies of the vase by Wedgwood are in the British Museum and the museums of Dresden and Rome, and there are twelve known copies in the possession of private persons in England.

In 1788 Wedgwood lost his partner and cousin, Thomas Wedgwood; and in less than two years afterwards he himself retired from the more active part in the business. Between

January, 1790, and June, 1793, the firm consisted of Josiah Wedgwood, Sons, and Byerley. The eldest and youngest sons, John and Thomas, then retired, and the firm next consisted of Josiah Wedgwood, senior, Josiah Wedgwood, junior, and Thomas Byerley. The firm of Wedgwood & Sons has passed through other changes since that time, but it still continues to carry on the works; and it may be mentioned as an interesting fact that in 1854 an Etruria jubilee photograph was taken of nine workmen, whose average time of serving the firm was fifty-four and a half years. The manufacture of majolica was added to the other productions of Etruria in 1860, and a large and artistic business in this department is still carried on.

After his practical retirement from business, Josiah Wedgwood spent portions of the spring, summer, and autumn at Weymouth, Buxton, Blackpool, or the Lakes, where he would be joined occasionally by Dr. Darwin. When at home his favourite hobby was his garden. He lived on terms of great cordiality with his neighbours, and opened a bowling-green for their use. The hospitality of Etruria Hall was proverbial, and dinner would be daily laid for unexpected as for expected guests. English and foreign visitors loved to examine the choice works of art—vases, bas-reliefs, cameos, medallions, etc.—to listen to the newest music, or to read the newest books. Scarcely a day passed but the service of the table was changed, an endless variety of exquisite ware being constantly produced. On books, prints, and models Wedgwood spent immense sums, the love for collecting books especially growing upon him towards the last. He was a most generous supporter of noble and philanthropic causes. English societies of all kinds received from him liberal contributions. His benevolence was likewise cosmopolitan, and he contributed to the relief of the emigrant French clergy and laity, while in 1792 he and his sons subscribed £250 towards the succour of the people of Poland. He was a kind friend to his workmen, and to the poor of the Potteries. He supported Parliamentary Reform, as the true remedy for many social and political evils. So highly esteemed was he in his personal character, that Dr. Darwin declared he never knew an instance of a man raising himself to such opulence and distinction who excited so little envy. Yet the more he gave the more he seemed to have, for he was able to bequeath to his widow, his sons, and his relatives half a million of money. His courage was indomitable, his energy untiring, while all were impressed by his simple modesty and his frank and unaffected demeanour. To a clear intellect he united high moral qualities, which gave an unmistakable elevation to his character.

Wedgwood was seized with alarming symptoms of illness in December, 1794. Besides suffering from great debility, and from pain and fever, a mortification set in in the mouth. Dr. Darwin and two other physicians and a surgeon sedulously attended him, but he passed away on Saturday, January 3rd, 1795, in the sixty-fifth year of his age. He was buried in the porchway of the old parish church of Stoke-upon-Trent, and twenty years later his devoted wife was laid to rest beside him. Flaxman executed a monument to Wedgwood, which was placed in the chancel of the church. The monument bears this happy inscription: 'Sacred to the memory of Josiah Wedgwood, F.R.S. and F.S.A., of Etruria, in this County, born in August, 1730; died January 3, 1795, who converted a rude and inconsiderable manufacture into an elegant art and an important branch of national commerce. By these services to his country he acquired an ample fortune, which he blamelessly and reasonably enjoyed, and generously dispensed for the reward of merit and the relief of misfortune. His mind was inventive and original, yet perfectly sober and well-regulated; his character was decisive and commanding, without rashness or arrogance; his probity was inflexible, his kindness unwearied; his manners simple and dignified, and the cheerfulness of his temper was the natural reward of the activity of his pure and useful life. He was most loved by those who knew him best, and he has left indelible impressions of affection and veneration on the minds of his family, who have erected this monument to his memory.'

The Wedgwood Memorial Institute was projected at Burslem in 1863, in honour of the man who had done so much for the prosperity of the district. It was raised by public subscription, and dedicated to the uses of a Free Library, a School of Art, and a Museum. The foundation-stone was laid by Mr. Gladstone, who was then Chancellor of the Exchequer in Lord Palmerston's Government, on the 26th of October, 1863. After the ceremony, Mr. Gladstone delivered an Address on Wedgwood, in which he ably, and with much insight, discussed the artistic value of the great potter's manufactures, and showed the noble position which the potter's art occupies among British industries. After some preliminary observations, Mr. Gladstone said: 'We may consider the products of industry with reference to their utility; or to their cheapness; or with regard to their influence upon the conditions of those who produce them; or, lastly, with reference to their beauty; to the degree in which they associate the presentation of forms and colours, agreeable to the cultivated eye, with the attainment of the highest aptitude for those purposes of common life for which they are properly designed. First, as to their utility and convenience, considered alone, we may leave that to the consumer, who will not buy what does not suit him. As to their cheapness, when once security has been taken that an entire society shall not be forced to pay an artificial price to some of its members for their productions, we may safely commit the question to the action of competition among manufacturers, and of what we term the laws of supply and demand. As to the condition of the work-people, experience has shown, especially in the case of the Factory Acts, that we should do wrong in laying down any abstract maxim as an invariable rule. Generally it may be said, that the presumption is in every case against legislative interference: but that upon special grounds, and most of all where children are employed, it may sometimes not only be warranted but required. This, however, though I may again advert to it, is not for to-day our special subject. We come, then, to the last of the heads which I have named; the association of beauty with utility, each of them taken according to its largest sense, in the business of industrial production. And it is in this department, I conceive, that we are to look for the peculiar pre-eminence, I will not scruple to say the peculiar greatness, of Wedgwood. Now do not let us suppose that, when we speak of this association of beauty with convenience, we speak either of a matter which is light and fanciful, or of one which may, like some of those I have named, be left to take care of itself. Beauty is not an accident of things, it pertains to their essence, it pervades the wide range of creation; and wherever it is impaired or banished, we have in this fact the proof of the moral disorder which disturbs the world. Reject, therefore, the false philosophy of those who will ask what does it matter, provided a thing be useful, whether it be beautiful or not: and say in reply that we will take one lesson from Almighty God, Who in His works hath shown us, and in His Word also has told us, that "He hath made everything," not one thing, or another thing, but everything, "beautiful in His time." Among all the devices of creation, there is not one more wonderful, whether it be the movement of the heavenly bodies, or the succession of the seasons and the years, or the adaptation of the world and its phenomena to the conditions of human life, or the structure of the eye, or hand, or any other part of the frame of man,—not one of all these is more wonderful, than the profuseness with which the Mighty Maker has been pleased to shed over the works of His hands an endless and boundless beauty.'

Detailing next the personal claims of Wedgwood, the speaker said: 'His most signal and characteristic merit lay, as I have said, in the firmness and fulness with which he perceived the true law of what is termed Industrial Art, or in other words, of the application of the higher Art to Industry; the law which teaches us to aim first at giving to every object the greatest possible degree of fitness and convenience for its purpose, and next at making it the vehicle of the highest degree of Beauty which, compatibly with that fitness and convenience, it will bear; which does not, I need hardly say, substitute the secondary for the primary end, but which recognises, as part of the business of production, the study to harmonise the two. To have a strong grasp of this principle, and to work it out to its results in the details of a vast and varied manufacture, is praise high enough for any man, at any time, and in any place. But it was higher and more peculiar, as I think, in the case of Wedgwood, than in almost any other case it could be. For that truth of Art, which he saw so clearly, and which lies at the root of excellence, was one of which England, his country, has not usually had a perception at all corresponding in strength and fulness with her other rare endowments. She has long taken a lead among the nations of Europe for the cheapness of her manufactures: not so for their beauty. And if the day shall ever come, when she shall be as eminent in true taste, as she is now in economy of production, my belief is that that result will probably be due to no other single man in so great a degree as to Wedgwood.'

On the practical branch of artistic workmanship, Mr. Gladstone remarked: 'I submit that considering all which England has done in the sphere of pure Beauty on the one side, and in the sphere of cheap and useful manufacture on the other, it not only is needless, but would be irrational, to suppose that she lies under any radical or incurable incapacity for excelling also in that intermediate sphere, where the two join hands and where Wedgwood gained the distinctions which have made him, in the language of Mr. Smiles, the "illustrious" Wedgwood. I do not think that Wedgwood should be regarded as a strange phenomenon no more native to us and ours than a meteoric stone from heaven; as a happy accident, without example, and without return. Rare indeed is the appearance of such men in the history of industry: single perhaps it may have been among ourselves, for whatever the merits of others, such in particular as Mr. Minton, yet I for one should scruple to place any of them in the same class with Wedgwood; no one is like him, no one, it may almost be said, is even second to him;

"Nec viget quicquam simile aut secundum;"

but the line on which he moved is a line, on which every one, engaged in manufacture of whatever branch, may move after him, and like him.

'And, as it is the wisdom of man universally to watch against his besetting errors, and to strengthen himself in his weakest points, so it is the study and following of Wedgwood, and of Wedgwood's principles, which may confidently be recommended to our producers as the specific cure for the specific weakness of the ordinary products of English industry. Of imagination, fancy, taste, of the highest cultivation in all its forms, this great nation has abundance. Of industry, skill, perseverance, mechanical contrivance, it has a yet larger stock, which overtops our narrow fence, and floods the world. The one great want is, to bring these two groups of qualities harmoniously together; and this was the peculiar excellence of Wedgwood; his excellence, peculiar in such a degree, as to give his name a place above every other, so far as I know, in the history of British industry; and remarkable, and entitled to fame, even in the history of the industry of the world.'

The energetic character of Wedgwood, and his determination to achieve success in his undertakings, are thus described: 'Here is a man who, in the well chosen words of his epitaph, "converted a rude and inconsiderable manufacture into an elegant art and an important branch of national commerce." Here is a man, who, beginning as it were from zero, and unaided by the national or the royal gifts which were found necessary to uphold the glories of Sèvres, of Chelsea, and of

Dresden, produced works truer, perhaps, to the inexorable laws of art, than the fine fabrics that proceeded from those establishments, and scarcely less attractive to the public taste of not England only, but the world.

'Here, again, is a man, who found his business cooped up within a narrow valley by the want of even tolerable communications, and who, while he devoted his mind to the lifting up of that business from meanness, ugliness, and weakness, to the highest excellence of material and form, had surplus energy enough to take a leading part in great engineering works like the Grand Trunk Canal from the Mersey to the Trent. These works made the raw material of his industry abundant and cheap, supplied a vent for the manufactured article, and opened for it materially a way to what we may term its conquest of the outer world.

'Lastly, here is a man who found his country dependent upon others for its supplies of all the finer earthenware, but who, by his single strength, reversed the inclination of the scales, and scattered thickly the productions of his factory over all the breadth of the continent of Europe.'

With respect to the personal tribute due to Wedgwood for the artistic beauty and practical usefulness of his productions, Mr. Gladstone said: 'It is plain that, in an enterprise so extended and diversified, there not only may, but must, have been, besides the head, various assistants, perhaps also various workmen, of merit sufficient to claim the honour of separate commemoration. As to the part which belongs to Flaxman, there is little difficulty: notwithstanding the distorting influence of fire, the works of that incomparable designer still in great part speak for themselves. To imitate Homer, Æschylus, or Dante, is scarcely a more arduous task than to imitate the artist by whom they were illustrated. Yet I, for one, cannot accept the doctrine of those who would have us ascribe to Flaxman the whole merit of the character of Wedgwood's productions, considered as works of art. And this for various reasons. First, from what we already learn of his earliest efforts, of the labours of his own hands, which evidently indicate an elevated aim, and a force bearing upwards mere handicraft into the region of true plastic Art: as, again, from that remarkable incident, recorded in the history of the Borough of Stoke, when he himself threw the first specimens of the black Etruscan vases, while Bentley turned the lathe. Secondly, because the very same spirit which presided in the production of the Portland, or Barberini, Vase, or of the finest of the purely ornamental *plaques*, presided also, as the eye still assures us, in the production not only of *déjeûners*, and other articles of luxury, intended for the rich, but even of the cheap and common wares of the firm. The forms of development were varied, but the whole circle of the manufacture was pervaded by a principle one and the same. Thirdly, because it is plain that Wedgwood was not only an active, cheerful, clear-headed, liberal-minded, enterprising man of business,—not only, that is to say, a great manufacturer, but also a great man. He had in him that turn and fashion of true genius, which we may not unfrequently recognise in our Engineers, but which the immediate heads of industry, whether in agriculture, manufactures, or commerce, and whether in this or other countries, have more rarely exhibited. It would be quite unnecessary to dwell on the excellences of such of the works of Wedgwood as belong to the region of Fine Art strictly so-called, and are not, in the common sense, commodities for use. To these all the world does justice. Suffice it to say, in general terms, that they may be considered partly as imitations, partly as reproductions, of Greek art. As imitations, they carry us back to the purest source. As reproductions, they are not limited to the province of their originals, but are conceived in the genuine, free, and soaring spirit of that with which they claim relationship. But it is not in happy imitation, it is not in the successful presentation of works of Fine Art, that, as I conceive, the speciality of Wedgwood really lies. It is in the resuscitation of a principle, of the principle of Greek art: it is the perception and grasp of the unity and comprehensiveness of that principle. That principle, I submit, lies, after all, in a severe and perfect propriety; in the uncompromising adaptation of every material object to its proper end. If that proper end be the presentation of Beauty only, then the production of Beauty is alone regarded; and none but the highest models of it are accepted. If the proper end be the production of a commodity for use and perishable, then a plural aim is before the designer and producer. The object must first and foremost be adapted to its use as closely as possible; it must be of material as durable as possible; and while it must be of the most moderate cost compatible with the essential aims, it must receive all the beauty which can be made conducive to, or concordant with, the use. And because this business of harmonising use and beauty, so easy in the works of nature, is arduous to the frailty of man, it is a business which must be made the object of special and persevering care. To these principles the works of Wedgwood habitually conformed. He did not in his pursuit of Beauty overlook exchangeable value or practical usefulness. The first he could not overlook, for he had to live by his trade; and it was by the profit derived from the extended sale of his humbler productions that he was enabled to bear the risks and charges of his higher works. Commerce did for him what the King of France did for Sèvres, and the Duke of Cumberland for Chelsea; it found him in funds. And I would venture to say, that the lower works of Wedgwood are every whit as much distinguished by the fineness and accuracy of their adaptation to their uses, as his higher ones by their successful exhibition of the finest art.'

The Memorial Institute was duly completed, and opened in 1870. Erected in the place which gave Wedgwood birth, and on the site of his first factory, it has already served to stimulate the intellectual life of the district, and to encourage many a youth stepping forward to fight the battle of life, as Wedgwood fought it manfully and hopefully a century before. The building, in addition to the features already mentioned, has an excellent Laboratory, and a Free Public Lending Library. There was a peculiar fitness in this institution being reared within little more than a stone's throw of the birthplace of the great potter. Stoke and Hanley likewise commemorated their indebtedness to Wedgwood by raising a bronze statue to him near to the church where he is buried. Other memorials also, of a minor character, perpetuate his fame.

Wedgwood was a true leader of industry. Unlike the warrior, who makes a solitude and calls it peace, he raised a hive of workers in a place which before his time was almost desolate. Towns and villages may almost be said to owe their origin to him, and he was practically the creator of a noble and humanising art in England.

THOMAS BRASSEY.

THOMAS BRASSEY.

AMONG the pioneers who have helped to transform the world by the peaceful triumphs of industry, an honourable place must be assigned to Thomas Brassey. He began his active career at the period when George Stephenson achieved his first great railway success, and from that time until his death he was indefatigable in his labours as a contractor at home and abroad. He was one of those men who are bound to elevate any trade or profession they choose, by reason of the serious earnestness with which they pursue it, and the fine integrity of character which shines through all their business relations. His skill and power of organisation were remarkable even in this enterprising age; and there is no doubt that in foreign lands he did much to maintain the prestige of England as a nation not only able in conceiving, but in successfully carrying through, the most gigantic undertakings.

Brassey was born at Buerton, in the parish of Aldford, Cheshire, on Nov. 7th, 1805. His family was an ancient one, and it is stated that his ancestors came over with William the Conqueror. Artemus Ward humorously remarked that his did the same: 'I know they did,' he said, 'because I never knew a man whose didn't.' Many a man has claimed Norman ancestors on quite as shadowy grounds as Artemus's: but, if Norman ancestors be worth anything, Brassey really seems to have been entitled to claim them. For nearly six centuries his predecessors resided at Bulkeley, near Malpas, in Cheshire, where they possessed a small landed property of about four hundred acres.

It still remains in the family, and Brassey was much attached to it. When the old mansion became uninhabitable, he built a large and handsome one upon the site. The Brasseys did not lose their ancient inheritance, like so many other families, during the Wars of the Roses; but after two more centuries of vicissitude they moved to Buerton, certain documents showing that they were already there in 1663. The father of Thomas Brassey, in addition to farming his own land, rented a large farm from the Marquis of Westminster at £850 per annum.

Sir Arthur Helps, who gives these details in his memorial sketch of Brassey, says: 'I am particular in noting these facts about the history of Mr. Brassey's family, because it resembles that of many of those families from which our most distinguished men have sprung—an origin which I conceive is very favourable for a man who is destined to do great things in this world. There is a certain amount of culture and of knowledge in such a family; while at the same time it has run no risk of being enervated by luxury, or of having, if I may venture to use the expression, thought itself out. We cannot be blind to the fact that there are amongst us but few descendants of our most eminent men. It certainly seems as though a family, after long ages, like some slowly developing plant, produces its best flower, and then dies off. And when we see distinguished families still producing remarkable men, I believe that if we could investigate the records of those families, we should find that there had been a frequent accession of new blood— of minds unwearied by mental labour, of bodies not exhausted, or rendered unfruitful by luxury.'

From twelve to sixteen years of age, Brassey was at school at Chester, and then he was articled to a land surveyor and estate agent named Lawton. One of his first pieces of work was to assist Mr. Parsons of Oswestry in making the surveys for Telford's well-known and magnificent highway, the Holyhead Road. Brassey soon became such a general favourite, that his master, Lawton, proposed to take him into partnership.

The offer was accepted, and at the age of twenty-one, Brassey went to reside at Birkenhead as Lawton's partner. The whole of the Birkenhead estate was the property of Mr. Francis Richard Price, of Bryn-y-pys, Overton, Flintshire, for whom Lawton acted as agent. When Lawton died, Brassey became sole agent and representative of Mr. Price, and he did much towards developing the now flourishing town of Birkenhead, which in 1818 consisted of only four houses.

After being at Birkenhead for eight years, Brassey was introduced to George Stephenson—an introduction which changed the whole current of his life. There was a certain stone-quarry at Stourton under Brassey's charge, and Stephenson wanted stone for repairing the Sankey Viaduct on the Liverpool and Manchester Railway. He therefore examined the quarry, being accompanied by Brassey, and he was so struck with the latter that he endeavoured to draw him into the enterprise of railway-making. Acting on the great man's advice, Brassey sent in his first tender, which was for the Dutton Viaduct, near Warrington, on the London and North-Western system. He failed to obtain it, however, his estimate being £5,000 higher than the successful tender. His next tender, in 1834, was for the Penkridge Viaduct, between Stafford and Wolverhampton — including also ten miles of railway on the same line—and this was accepted. A contractor at this time had to do all his own work, for sub-contracts were almost unknown, and he had to show great skill in selecting and directing large bodies of workmen. Stephenson's successor on the Grand Junction Railway, John Locke, was afterwards engaged for the London and Southampton Railway. He invited Brassey to go with him, and the latter contracted for and executed the important works between Basingstoke and Winchester, as well as works on other parts of the line.

When Brassey was thirty-one years of age he settled in London, and entered into an extended scale of business. All who had to do with him soon discovered that he could be thoroughly relied on to complete his contracts in the time and manner specified. Throughout his career, 'his faithfulness, his desire to do his work efficiently, whether at a gain or a loss, together with his resolution to avoid all petty subjects of dispute, naturally made him a most welcome fellow-worker to any person placed in such an arduous position—a position requiring so much watchfulness and supervision as that of engineer-in-chief to a railway. It was an immense comfort to have a man to deal with whom it was not necessary to be looking after in respect of any of the details of the work entrusted to him.'

In December, 1831, Brassey was married to Maria, second daughter of Mr. Joseph Harrison of Birkenhead. Mr. Harrison—who, by the way, was the first resident in the new town of Birkenhead—was a forwarding agent in Liverpool for the great Manchester houses. It is stated that Brassey's first connection with railways was partly due to the advice he received from his wife, who saw that he was capable of greater things than come within the necessarily restricted sphere of an agent or a land surveyor. Mrs. Brassey was also a believer in railways when many scientific men regarded them as impracticable. So, although she foresaw much domestic discomfort from the frequent change of residence necessary to a railway contractor, she would not allow her own feelings to weigh in the matter, but encouraged her husband in his new calling. During the first thirteen years of his career as a contractor, Brassey changed his residence no fewer than eleven times. Three of these temporary homes he was compelled to make in France. Then, again, wherever the family was temporarily located, little could be seen of Brassey himself, whose engagements usually caused him to be absent from nine or half-past nine in the morning until ten o'clock in the evening. The education of the children at this period rested entirely with Mrs. Brassey, and to this and their welfare generally she devoted herself with true motherly affection.

The construction of railways is a work peculiarly adapted to being executed by contract, and the practice consequently speedily increased when once it had been instituted. 'It may be noted,' says Sir Arthur Helps, 'that in carrying out work in foreign countries, great benefit has accrued both to those countries themselves, and to the country in which these projects originated, from the works being confided to contractors who carried hither and thither bands of skilful workmen; and who, indirectly, brought much profit to the mother-country, while gradually they instructed the natives of other countries in skilled labour, and made them more useful citizens than they were before. There are some parts of Europe where the condition of the whole labouring population has been permanently raised by the introduction of British skill and British labour in the execution of a particular work. And this would hardly have been the case, or at any rate would not so soon have been the case, but for the presence of the British contractor and his accompanying army of British workmen—bringing new tools, new modes of working, new methods of payment; and, in short, introducing an element of vigour and prosperity which could not have been so well introduced in any other way.'

When Brassey became thoroughly known as a contractor, and commissions multiplied with him, he let out portions of his work to sub-contractors. But these contracted for the manual labour alone; he furnished the materials and all the plant, and also provided the horses. Finding, however, in France that to provide horses did not pay, he afterwards stipulated that the sub-contractors should find their own horses. Brassey fixed the prices the sub-contractors were to receive, but he always raised them where the contracts proved unprofitable. He would make careful visits of inspection, and one who worked for him stated that such visits would often cost him a thousand pounds. So keen was his memory that as he went along the line he remembered even the navvies, and saluted them by their names. In making sub-contracts he recognised each man's speciality, and acted upon it. The sub-contracts varied from £5,000 to £25,000, and the number of men employed upon them from one to three hundred. Sub-lettings by sub-contractors he did not approve of, but he always favoured the co-operative system, and approved of the 'butty-gang' system—a system whereby certain work was done by ten or thirteen men, who shared equally in the proceeds, something extra being allowed to the head man.

In the year 1841 Brassey began his foreign work. France, which first claimed his services, was not in as good a position for the introduction of railways as Great Britain, where the public roads and canals had been brought to a state of comparative perfection. However, the French desired to have railways at an early stage, and the Government were willing to give guarantees in view of their failure as a purely commercial speculation. The Paris and Rouen Railway was projected, as a line which would bring London and Paris nearer together, and the French Board suggested an amalgamation of interests with the London and Southampton Railway. This was agreed to, and a joint company formed called the Paris and Rouen Railway Company. Locke was appointed engineer to the new line; but the pretensions of French contractors were so greatly in excess of his expectations, that at his suggestion the Board invited English contractors to go over and compete with the French. It was found that Brassey and Mackenzie, however, were the only serious English competitors, and these two contractors agreed to join their forces, and tender conjointly. With only a very trifling exception, they succeeded in securing the execution of the whole of the works. Thus began Brassey's series of undertakings in foreign countries. He fixed his abode in France, and gave up the whole of his time to the new line. The works were begun in 1841, and the line was opened to the public in May, 1843. The undertaking was a very important and onerous one. 'Added to its extent, and the consequent and natural difficulties of organisation and management, it possessed the new feature of being in a foreign country, where railway works were as yet unknown, and where, consequently, it was not easy to secure assistants in the shape of practical agents, foremen, and gangers, or even the necessary labourers, miners, and navvies accustomed to that style of work, and to the means of execution adopted by the contractor. All this considerably enhanced the difficulties, more especially as the whole time for completion was very limited, and necessitated, therefore, great energy, decision, and discernment in organising rapidly a very large staff of *employés* of every description, and the bringing over from England numbers of workmen of all classes—amounting at times to several thousands.' But Brassey was like Napoleon in one thing—he did not believe in the 'impossible.' He had tact and shrewdness, skill in organisation, and a wonderful hold over those whom he employed—so much so, indeed, that master and man were alike loth to part after they had once established relations together. The oversight of everything he took, looking after the quarters of the men, and providing for them medical assistance and hospital accommodation when necessary. No fewer than eleven languages were spoken on the works of this one railway. The undertaking was successfully carried through, and within the specified time. Higher wages for the natives followed the introduction of railway work into France and Belgium. When Brassey constructed the railway from Charleroi to Givet, as the works were light he sent out only a few Englishmen to commence and superintend the construction of the line. One of the sub-contractors, describing the effect of the work upon the natives, said, 'When we went there, a native labourer was paid one shilling and threepence per day; but when we began to pay them two francs and two francs and a half per day, they thought we were angels from Heaven.' As the native workmen were remarkably provident and abstemious, they managed to save a considerable amount even out of those very moderate wages, as they would be counted in England.'

The Rouen and Havre Railway—which was a continuation of the Paris and Rouen line, and completed the communication between Paris and London, *viâ* Southampton—was begun by Messrs. Brassey and Mackenzie in 1843. Mr. Francis Murton stated with regard to this new line: 'The works of the Havre railway were extraordinary in magnitude. The line, leaving the valley of the Seine at Rouen, had to cross several important valleys to attain the plateau or summit level, and then to descend to the level of the port of Havre. This necessitated a large bridge over the Seine, many tunnels, eight or ten in number, several large viaducts of 100 feet in height, and huge cuttings and embankments; moreover, the whole of the work had to be completed in two years. Mr. Brassey took up his residence at Rouen, and laboured at this heavy and important work with unbounded energy. I should say that, never up to that date, had such heavy works been carried out in so short a time. Although many of his people had had two years' experience in France, still, owing to the severe character of the work, there was much difficulty in obtaining the necessary labour, more especially as regards the mining, brickwork, and masonry. The contractors were again obliged to bring over from England hosts of bricklayers, from London or from any place where they could be found; and it may here be mentioned that, of all classes of railway labour, as a rule, the brickmakers and the bricklayers are the worst and most unscrupulous, and great indeed was the trouble and expense they caused. The necessity also of working night as well as day, rendered the supervision very difficult, particularly in the tunnels, and much anxiety was thereby occasioned to the engineers as well as to the contractors. During the progress of the works, a great accident occurred in the second section of the line, in the fall of the Barentin Viaduct—a huge brick construction of 100 feet in height and about one-third of a mile in length, having cost some £50,000; and which had, but a very short time previously, elicited the praise and admiration of the Minister of Public Works, and the other high French officers who visited it. This great downfall occurred a very short time before the proposed opening of the line. It is scarcely necessary here to seek to establish the causes of this failure; very rapid execution in very bad weather, and being built, in accordance with the contract, with mortar made of lime of the country (but with which the other smaller works had been successfully built), were no doubt the principal causes. Mr. Brassey was very greatly upset by this untoward event; but he and his partner, Mr. Mackenzie, met the difficulty most manfully. "The first thing to do," as they said, "is to build it up again," and this they started most strenuously to do; not waiting, as many would have done, whether justly or unjustly, to settle, by litigation or otherwise, upon whom the responsibility and the expense should fall. Not a day was lost by them in the extraordinary efforts they had to make to secure millions of new bricks, and to provide hydraulic lime, which had to be brought from a distance. Suffice it to say that, by their indomitable energy and determination promptly to repair the evil, and, by the skill of their agents, they succeeded in rebuilding this huge structure in less than *six months*. I should mention that, as one inducement to the contractors to open the Havre line a few months before the contract time, a premium of about £10,000 was offered them. This, of course, they stood to lose by this accident. The company, however, in consideration of their marvellous and successful efforts to redeem the loss of time, allowed them the benefit of this sum, but the whole of the remainder of the expense they themselves bore. This is one of the many cases where, in spite of all loss, of all difficulty, that determination never to shrink, upon any pretext, from a contract, fully evinced itself; and therefore, it is a case worthy of note.'

In one portion of his work, Brassey's biographer draws interesting comparisons between the railway labourers of different countries, and their methods of work. An expert on manual labour has stated that the amount of work done by an English 'navvy'—a word corrupted from navigator—exceeds in severity that accomplished by any other class of workman. The power of English navvies in lifting earth during excavations is not nearly equalled by that of the navvies of any other country in the world. Strikes were almost unknown amongst Brassey's workmen. The English navvy abroad was rather troublesome at first, but he soon got into steady and regular grooves. The French navvy, owing partly to the inferiority of his tools, was worth only two francs a day, while the English labourer could earn four francs and a half. But in time, the Frenchman improved, and his value rose largely in consequence. The result was that ultimately the great bulk of the railway work executed in France was done by natives. Plate-laying was for a long time an English speciality, but French workmen came at last to do it extremely well. In mining, the English labourer always maintained his superiority, being hardier and capable of more endurance. The English engineer was also superior to the French, and laboured as though he intended his work to be eternal. Piedmontese workmen were found to be quiet, orderly, and capable, and in cutting rock they could do the work cheaper than English miners. People born in the mountains were stronger than those born in the plains. The Neapolitans, who flocked in shoals to places where railway works were going forward, could only do light work; and as they generally worked in such districts as the Maremma, they could only labour for some six months in the year. Their wages were from one franc to two francs per day. The Germans were not first-class labourers, but the Belgians were very good, though behind the English in many things. They were not so ingenious in their methods.

Sir John Hawkshaw, who had experience of unskilled labour in almost all parts of the world, said on this question: 'I have arrived at the conclusion that its cost is much the same in all. I have had personal experience in South America, in Russia, and in Holland, as well as in my own country; and as consulting engineer to some of the Indian and other foreign railways, I am pretty well acquainted with the value of Hindoo and other labour; and though an English labourer will do a larger amount of work than a Creole or a Hindoo, yet you have to pay them proportionately higher wages. Dutch labourers are, I think, as good as English, or nearly so; and Russian workmen are docile and easily taught, and readily adopt every method shown to them to be better than their own.'

The work of a contractor is not to be measured only by the undertakings brought to a successful completion. Preliminary surveys and laborious calculations are made with respect to schemes which frequently prove abortive; indeed, it is said that Brassey himself unsuccessfully tendered for works to the extent of £150,000,000. This points to a vast amount of investigation which was not only unremunerative but exhausting to the contractor. Brassey seems to have had a genius for seizing upon the essential points of any scheme submitted to him, and he was extremely rapid in his mental arithmetic. And it is a remarkable fact that his conclusions were scarcely ever found to be wrong.

Brassey became so widely known that in 1845 he had on his hands no fewer than thirteen large railway contracts, representing a length of about 800 miles, scattered over various parts of England and Wales, Scotland, and France. This did not leave him time to superintend everything in detail, nor was there any necessity for this, as it was one of his leading characteristics to be able to engage intuitively men competent to carry out all the minutiæ of his plans, and he had many such men in his employment who served him ably. In course of time he became as it were 'the great consulting physician in railway matters, only making his appearance on critical occasions.' But whenever anything went wrong, he was on the spot immediately. His visits were likewise taken advantage of 'as opportunities for the redress of grievances, and for the settlement of all questions of difficulty.'

The great contractor loved his work better than anything. It was his ambition, we are told, to furnish large and continuous employment to his fellow-countrymen, and to the natives of other countries. He determined that this work should occupy all his lifetime, and he could never bear the thought of retiring from business. For the rewards which attended him—and which many men would have hailed with pride and delight—he cared little. When the Emperor of Austria conferred upon him the Cross of the Iron Crown, he remarked that he did not know what good crosses were to him as an Englishman; but as the Emperor had graciously offered it, he accepted the distinction, knowing also that his wife would appreciate the honour, as she took a deep interest in his works and his growing fame. He received two other crosses—those of the Legion of Honour of France and the Chevaliership of Italy, but so little did he regard them that when they were enquired for on one occasion they could not be found. The Emperor of the French invited Brassey to dine at the Tuileries, after conferring upon him the Order of the Legion of Honour; and at this dinner he sat near the Empress, 'with whose grace and manner he was much charmed, and he was especially pleased with her kindness in talking English to him during the greater part of the time.'

Some idea of Brassey's surprising energy and activity may be gathered from this statement of his brother-in-law, Mr. Henry Harrison: 'I have known him come direct from France to Rugby. Having left Havre the night before, he would have been engaged in the office in London the whole day; he would then come down to Rugby by the mail train at twelve o'clock, and it was his common practice to be on the works by six o'clock the next morning. He would frequently walk from Rugby to Nuneaton, a distance of sixteen miles. Having arrived at Nuneaton in the afternoon, he would proceed the same night by road to Tamworth, and the next morning he would be out on the road, so soon, that he had the reputation, among his staff, of being the first man on the works. He used to proceed over the works from Tamworth to Stafford, walking the greater part of the distance ; and he would frequently proceed that same evening to Lancaster, in order to inspect the works then in progress under the contract which he had for the execution of the railway from Lancaster to Carlisle. The journey which I have described from Havre, *viâ* London to Rugby, thence over the Trent to Stafford, and by railway to Lancaster, to inspect the Lancaster and Carlisle line, was a route which he very commonly followed.'

The Great Northern Railway was one of the most formidable undertakings contracted for by Thomas Brassey. There was one special difficulty in connection with it, viz., how to get the line over the fens adjacent to Whittlesea Mere. In connection with this he called into his counsels Mr. Samuel Ballard, the skilful engineer of the Middle Level Drain, part of the Great Bedford Level in the Fens. The depth of the bog to be crossed was twenty-two feet, and its extent about three miles. Mr. Ballard laid layer upon layer of stakes over the surface upon which the soil was gradually piled up, giving the water time to run out. The effect was thus to displace the water, but to leave the solid parts behind, and eventually a solid basis was made. The construction of the bridges in the Fens was another great difficulty, but Mr. Ballard successfully overcame it. Mr. Ballard was struck by Brassey's faculty for economising his time, and bringing his experience and judgment to bear where they were useful. He had a keen eye for discovering any defective point, and a comprehensive way of estimating its various bearings. Easy or trifling things he left to others to deal with, and only fixed his mind on those things which were of primary importance. He would indicate where difficulties might be expected, and predicate the condition of the works six months in advance. The number of men employed on the Great Northern line was from 5,000 to 6,000, yet he directed all their labour without a hitch. When the undertaking was finished, those interested in the line subscribed a sum of about £2,000, and presentation portraits were painted of Mr. and Mrs. Brassey. A large silver-gilt shield, a fine piece of work designed by Mr. H. P. Burt, was likewise presented to the contractor. The shield, which measures a yard in diameter, has in the centre the Brassey arms, surrounded by portraits, enamelled in gold, of twelve of the engineers under whose direction Brassey executed important works. There are also twelve views of the principal undertakings he had carried through up to that period—1851,—and outside them a blue ribbon in enamel, bearing the names of thirty-six of Brassey's agents. This trophy of labour is probably unique of its kind.

Brassey's financial method seems to have been a very simple one. The agent for each contract was made responsible for the amount of money he received, and he was to furnish information to the contractor in London, whenever required, as to his expenditure. This system with many masters would have been liable to abuse; but Mr. Tapp, Brassey's financial secretary, says that as the agents were put upon their honour, and trusted implicitly, they felt a pride in being thus confided in, and really carried on their business as though it were their own. In making the Bilbao railway in Spain monetary difficulties were frequently experienced. The banks were not accustomed to cash cheques for large amounts, so that the cash had to be obtained piecemeal. But Brassey taught the Basques the use of paper money. He and his partners had 10,000 men in their employment, but Brassey's credit was so high in the district that on one occasion, at Chambéry, where no one had been authorised to draw cheques, Brassey's agent was allowed to draw as much as £28,000 on his own cheque. Brassey and his partners sustained a great loss over the Bilbao railway, for owing to the quantity of hard rock which had to be cut, to the very wet climate, and the frequent recurrence of *fête* days, the men were not able to work more than 200 days out of the 313 working days in the year.

Sometimes Brassey was ignorant as to the extent of his own pecuniary resources, and it took a long time to get together an accurate statement of his assets. With respect to the way in which he remunerated his agents, his secretary remarks that 'it was a system of paying sometimes by salaries and sometimes by a percentage on profits. The salaries which Mr. Brassey gave were decidedly not large; but he assigned to his principal agents a percentage upon the profits of the undertaking. In some instances these agents received cheques varying from £3,000 to £16,000. Indeed, several of these gentlemen who served under him succeeded in realising fortunes.' Brassey bore his business losses with singular equanimity. One who knew him well said he never appeared so happy as when he had lost £20,000. At the Westminster Palace Hotel one night, when during a severe panic it was thought he had lost a million of money, he merely said, 'Never mind, we must be content with a little less; that's all.' His cheerful way of regarding misfortune was of the greatest advantage to him, keeping him up when many would have collapsed under their troubles.

Monetary difficulties of a formidable nature, however, fell upon Brassey in the year 1866. And as usual in such cases, they 'came not as single spies but in battalions.' To begin with, there were liabilities in connection with the Victoria Docks to the extent of £600,000; then there were contracts for certain railways in Denmark for which Brassey and Messrs. Peto & Betts were jointly responsible. The latter firm failed and the total Danish liabilities were about £800,000. Next in connection with the construction of the Lemberg and

Czernowitz line, Brassey had received bonds from the Company to the amount of £1,200,000. He was unable to negotiate them, and an effort to place them in a foreign market only yielded £13,000. They then became perfectly unsaleable; yet at this time the contractor was paying from £40,000 to £50,000 a month for wages alone on this line. For the Evesham and Redditch Railway Brassey was entirely paid in shares, and for the Warsaw and Terespol line he was also largely paid in bonds upon which he could not realise, while the Queensland railway involved further heavy liabilities. He had several English contracts running upon which he could get nothing, and there was a heavy loss going on at the Barrow Docks and at Runcorn Bridge, which amounted to £44,000. These were difficulties enough to appal any man, but he pushed forward with the contract for the Lemberg line, and finished the works three or four months before the stipulated time. This not only gained him prestige with the Austrians, but it released large funds hitherto unavailable, as the Anglo-Austrian Bank now found it could do a profitable business by selling the bonds, of which Brassey held upwards of a million.

As the Austro-Prussian War was in progress while the Lemberg line was being constructed, there was great difficulty in conveying the money from Vienna to Lemberg—a distance of 500 miles—in order to pay the men. This daring feat was undertaken by Mr. Victor Ofenheim, afterwards the Chevalier d'Ofenheim, Director-General of the Company, and one of Brassey's advisers on Austrian questions. Sir A. Helps thus relates how the task was achieved: 'The intervening country was occupied by the Austrian and Prussian armies, who were on each side of the line, that is on that part between Cracow and Lemberg; for Mr. Ofenheim had succeeded without much difficulty in getting the money carried on the Northern Carl-Ludwig Railway as far as Cracow. However, he was full of energy, and was determined to get on somehow or other. They said that there was no engine; that they had all been taken off; but he went and found an old engine in a shed. Next he wanted an engine-driver, and he found one, but the man said he would not go, for he had a wife and children; but Mr. Ofenheim said, "If you will come, I will give you so many hundred florins, and if you get killed I will provide for your wife and family." They jumped on to the old engine and got up the steam. They then started and went at the rate of forty or fifty miles an hour, passing between the sentinels of the opposing armies; and Mr. Ofenheim states that they were so surprised that they had not time to shoot him. His only fear was that there might be a rail up somewhere. But he got to Lemberg, and that was the saving point of the line—they distributed the "pay"—otherwise the men would have gone away to their homes, and the line would have been left unfinished through the winter, and they would have had to wait until the next spring before they could have returned again; but that difficulty being overcome, they got the line duly opened. Mr. Ofenheim's conduct on this occasion is a notable instance of the influence Mr. Brassey exercised over those who worked with him, as well as those who worked for him; for Mr. Ofenheim had become a devoted friend, as well as a skilful and daring representative of Mr. Brassey. The Emperor of Austria, with that appreciation shown by monarchs for devoted service—a thing they naturally very much approve of,—was much struck by what he had heard of this daring feat in getting to Lemberg, and sent for Mr. Ofenheim, and asked this pertinent question: "Who is this Mr. Brassey, this English contractor, for whom men are to be found who work with such zeal, and risk their lives?" The answer must have been satisfactory, for the Emperor said Mr. Brassey must be a very powerful man, and sent him the Cross of the Iron Crown.'

Notwithstanding the financial difficulties under which Brassey at times laboured, and which were almost inseparable from the gigantic nature of his undertakings, he yet amassed great wealth. But his profits on transactions were anything but large. His percentage of profit, taken as a whole, was only about three per cent. His expenditure of other people's money was £78,000,000, and upon that outlay he retained £2,500,000. The rest of his enormous fortune came through accumulations. His capital was in constant use—it was never suffered to lie idle. A typical instance of his liberality is given. One of his agents entrusted with an important mission died soon after reaching his destination, while his wife—whom he had left in good health in England—died suddenly almost at the same time. Six orphans were left entirely without provision. Brassey, who had already advanced several thousand pounds on the agent's life policy, immediately relinquished the policy in favour of the children, and headed a subscription list in addition with a handsome sum. He does not seem to have cared for money as money, but only as he could keep using it beneficially, or turning it over and over in business. Although his name did not appear much in connection with public charities, it is estimated that his benefactions during his lifetime amounted to £200,000. Two causes are cited which led to his accumutation of wealth : first, the very moderate nature of his personal expenses ; secondly, the immense extent of his business, which he built up by quick, straightforward dealing. He always went straight to the point, and exhibited great determination and perseverance. In fact, one of his admirers declared that 'if he'd been a parson, he'd have been a bishop ; if a prize-fighter, he would have had the belt.'

The contracts which Brassey carried out between the years 1834 and 1870—either singly or in conjunction with partners— numbered no fewer than 174. Of these, the most extensive lines were the following :—Paris and Rouen Railway, 82 miles ; Orleans and Bordeaux line, 294 miles ; Lancaster and Carlisle Railway, 70 miles ; Caledonian Railway (first contract), 125 miles ; Great Northern Railway, 75 miles ; Mantes and Caen Railway, 113 miles ; Le Mans and Mezidon Railway, 84 miles ;

Grand Trunk Railway, 539 miles; Royal Danish Railway, 75 miles; East Suffolk Railway, 63 miles; Caen and Cherbourg Railway, 94 miles; Leicester and Hitchin Railway, 62 miles; Bilbao and Miranda Railway, 66 miles; Eastern Bengal Railway, 112 miles; Victor Emmanuel Railway, 73 miles; the Maremma, Leghorn, &c., Railway, 138 miles; the Jutland Railway, 270 miles; Mauritius Railway, 64 miles; Meridionale Railway, 160 miles; Queensland Railway, 78 miles; North Schleswig Railway, 70 miles; Central Argentine Railway, 247 miles; Lemberg and Czernowitz Railway, 165 miles; Delhi Railway, 304 miles; Warsaw and Terespol Railway, 128 miles; Chord Line (India), 147 miles, Kronprinz-Rudolfsbahn, 272 miles; and the Suczawa and Jassy Railway, 135 miles. The engineers with whom he was at various times associated included Robert Stephenson, Locke, Gooch, Bidder, Neuman, Cubitt, Hawkshaw, Robertson, Rendel, Brunel, Neale, G. R. Stephenson, Berkley, Tite, Liddell, Vignoles, Whitton, Wylie, Fowler, McClean, Bazalgette, Sinclair, Fitzgibbon, Woods, Harrison, and Galbraith, in addition to many foreign engineers. During Brassey's career there were periods when he and his partners were giving employment to 80,000 persons, upon works involving an expenditure of £17,000,000. This was a prodigious effect for one man to have upon British industry and labour.

Some interesting facts are adduced concerning the Turin and Novara Railway, the length of which was 60 miles. Brassey was thrown a good deal into contact with the celebrated Count Cavour in constructing this line, which was begun in 1853. At first the Piedmontese public would have nothing to do with the shares, but Cavour was determined to have the line, and he persuaded Brassey to share the deficiency with the Government. Then when the subscriptions were covered, the public applied for far more shares than had been originally offered to them. Again Cavour applied to Brassey, saying, 'The public are now crying out that they cannot get a share, and the shares are at a good premium. Will you give up some shares, as I am anxious to whet their appetite for other enterprises by letting them taste a profit on their first speculation?' Brassey consented to give up 2,000 of his shares, although they then stood at more than £2 premium. Brassey mentioned the remarkable fact in connection with this railway, that it was 'completed for about the same money as was spent in obtaining the Bill for the railway from London to York.' It appears, too, that the total charge of the Sardinian Government against Brassey for the concession was only £100! Soon after the railway was in operation, Cavour observed to Brassey, 'I am told that the line *per se* is yielding 14 per cent., and yet there was a time when I could not induce my Piedmontese to take a share!'

Quite a network of railways in Piedmont followed the opening of the line from Turin to Novara. Brassey was concerned in several of them, and frequently received the thanks of Cavour for the way in which he responded to the wishes of the Piedmontese Government. On one occasion, during a grand dinner at Coire, Cavour said: 'Mr. Brassey is one of the most remarkable men I know; clear-headed, cautious, yet very enterprising—and fulfilling his engagements faithfully. We never had a difficulty with him. He would make a splendid Minister of Public Works; and, if report be true, he understands the Finance Department equally well.' In addition to Count Cavour, the Prime Minister, the Marquis D'Azeglio, and the Minister of Public Works, M. Paleocapa, were anxious to promote railway enterprise in Italy. In 1850 a contract was entered into between the Piedmontese Government and Messrs. Brassey, Jackson, and Henfrey, for the construction of the Turin and Susa Railway. The object of this line was to facilitate communication between Italy and France, Susa being situate at the foot of the Mont Cenis Pass. As Mr. Henfrey remarked, 'By the construction of this line railway communication would be complete from the Alps to the Mediterranean, and the first link in the chain of international communication with France and the West of Europe would be forged.' The Victor Emmanuel Railway followed, its course being on the northern side of the Pass of Mont Cenis, along the Valley of the Arc to Chambéry, and thence to the French frontier at Culoz. Into this line came the cutting of the Mont Cenis Tunnel—a gigantic work extending to seven and a half miles. The undertaking would have been impossible but for the adoption of a machine for boring rock, invented by Mr. Thomas Bartlett, Brassey's agent for this line. The railway was begun in 1853 and finished in 1858.

Reviewing the work accomplished by English contractors in Italy, Mr. Henfrey says: 'It will be seen that the railways completed by Mr. Brassey and his partners formed a continuous line from the then French frontier at Culoz, on the Rhone, to the old Austrian frontier at Buffalora, on the Ticino, with the exception only of the pass over the Mont Cenis; and the years during which these contracts were executed comprised that bright period in the history of Italy during which the Kingdom of Sardinia, emerging from comparative obscurity, took its place by the side of the great Powers of Europe.' There is no doubt that British labour and British capital had some share, though an indirect one, in advancing towards a triumphant issue the great movement for the unification of Italy.

Brassey next turned his attention to the American Continent, and, in conjunction with Messrs. Peto & Betts, he took the contract for the Grand Trunk Railway of Canada. Robert Stephenson was consulting engineer to the company, and Alexander Ross the company's engineer for the whole undertaking. This memorable line was begun in 1852 and completed in 1859. It was an important link in the system of American railways, and was not only of immense service to the vast districts of territory surrounding Lakes Erie, Huron, Michigan, and Superior, but also in opening up other large districts of valuable land, and in connecting the Erie and Great Western of Canada Railroads, and other lines of lesser importance. Brassey visited Canada, and was received at the works by his agent, James Hodges, who assisted in the construction of the Grand Trunk Railway until the Prince of Wales had laid the last stone and put in the last rivet. Great attention was paid to Brassey, special cars being attached at the end of the trains for him, so that he might have a better opportunity of viewing the country, and the managers of the various lines invariably accompanied him. The scarcity of labour at first hampered the execution of the Grand Trunk line, notwithstanding the fact that a man who received five shillings per day in England would receive seven shillings and sixpence in Canada. But against this must be set the fact that outdoor work is impossible in Canada for four months in the year, which is more than double the time that English workmen are debarred from labour. To get over the labour difficulty, Brassey suggested that the agents should bring up a large body of French Canadians from Lower Canada. This suggestion was carried out, but although the French Canadians were useful for light work, they had not the physical strength for the heavier kinds of labour. It appears that Brassey's main object in going to Canada was a financial one. The Canadian Government had lent the Grand Trunk Company £3,000,000, on condition that this sum should have priority of interest over all other claims upon the shares. Brassey greatly relieved the company by persuading the Canadian Government to remit the priority of its claims.

Obstacles of a very unusual character had to be encountered in the construction of the Victoria Bridge over the River St. Lawrence. Some reference has been made to this bridge in the article on the Stephensons. It was carried out from the designs of Robert Stephenson and Alexander Ross. From a paper written by James Hodges we may quote the following passage, showing the difficulties experienced in constructing the bridge: 'The site of the bridge is at the lower end of a small lake, called La Prairie Basin, which is situated about one mile above the entrance to the canal, at the west end of Montreal Harbour. At this point the Saint Lawrence is 8,660 feet from shore to shore, or nearly a mile and three-quarters wide. The most serious difficulty in the construction of the Victoria Bridge arose from the accumulation of the ice in the winter months. Ice begins to form in the Saint Lawrence in December. Then ice first appears in quiet places, where the current is least felt. As winter advances " anchor," or ground, ice comes down the stream in vast quantities. This anchor ice appears in rapid currents, and attaches itself to the rocks in the bed of the river in the form of a spongy substance. Immense quantities accumulate in an inconceivably short time, increasing until the mass is several feet thick. A very slight thaw, even that produced by a bright sunshine at noon, disengages this mass, when, rising to the surface, it passes down the river with the current. This species of ice appears to grow only in the vicinity of rapids, or where the water has become aërated by the rapidity of the current. Anchor ice sometimes accumulates at the foot of the rapids in such quantities as to form a bar across the river some miles in extent, keeping the water several feet above the ordinary level. The accumulation of ice continues for several weeks, until the river is quite full. This causes a general rising of the water, until large masses float, and, moving farther down the river, unite with accumulations previously grounded, and thus form another barrier, "packing" in places to a height of twenty or thirty feet. As the winter advances, the lake becomes frozen over. The ice then ceases to come down, and the water in the river gradually subsides till it finds its ordinary winter level, which is some twelve feet above its height in summer. The "ice bridge," or solid field of ice across the river, becomes formed for the winter early in January. By the middle of March the sun becomes very powerful at mid-day, and the warm heavy rains rot the ice. The ice, when it becomes thus weakened, is easily broken up by the winds, particularly at those parts of the lakes where, from the great depth of water, they are not completely frozen over. This ice, coming down over the rapids, chokes up the channels again, and causes a rise of the river, as in early winter. In order to avoid the dangers consequent on these operations of nature, the stone piers of the Victoria Bridge were placed at wide intervals apart, each pier being of the most substantial character, and having a large wedge-shaped cut-water of stone-work, slanting towards the current, and presenting an angle to the advancing ice sufficient to separate and fracture it, as it rises against the piers. The piers of the bridge were, in fact, designed to answer the double purpose of carrying the tubes and of resisting the pressure of the ice. In each of these respects they have fully answered the important objects sought to be attained.'

The agents had difficulties with the Indian chiefs, who owned the best stone-quarries of the district; then numerous strikes arose among the workmen, while the cholera at one time committed dreadful ravages in their ranks; and finally great financial stringency was felt by the Company in 1855, in consequence of the rise in the value of money caused by the Crimean War. Nevertheless, the works were pushed forward with energy. Great assistance was derived in the conveyance and shifting of stone by a steam-traveller designed by one of the sub-contractors, Mr. Chaffey. This machine had a span of sixty feet; it unloaded the waggons, and stacked with the greatest ease large blocks of stone, some of which weighed ten tons; upwards of 70,000 tons of stone were twice moved by this machine, and yet only one man was required upon the traveller, while one other could stack the stone. The following statistics are supplied as to the materials used in constructing the Victoria Bridge, and the number of men, etc., employed: Total length of the tubes, 6,512 feet; weight of iron in the tubes, 9,044 tons; number of rivets in the tubes, 1,540,000; number of spans, 25, one being of 330 feet, and the others from 242 to 247 feet; quantity of masonry in piers and abutments, 2,713,095 cubic feet; quantity of timber in temporary works, 2,280,000 cubic feet; number of men engaged, 3,040; horses, 144; locomotive engines, 4; and, finally, steamboats, 6, and barges, 75, representing together 12,000 tons and 450 horse-power. This magnificent structure remains a lasting monument to British skill, industry, and perseverance.

Of works carried through by Brassey and his partners between the years 1852 and 1865 may be enumerated the Crimean Railway, the Victoria Docks, the Northern Mid-Level Sewer, the East London Railway, and various Danish railways, etc. The construction of the Crimean Railway was a great feat because of the difficulties of organisation and of transport. Field-Marshal Burgoyne stated that it was impossible to overrate the services rendered by the railway, or its effect in shortening the time of the siege and alleviating the fatigues and sufferings of the troops. The Victoria Docks, which were carried out for the firm of Brassey, Peto, & Betts, under the direction of G. P. Bidder, have a water area of over 100 acres, divided by eighty-feet gates into a tidal basin of about 20 acres, and a wet dock of about 80 acres. They have vaults for wines, and warehouses for general merchandise, to the extent of about 20 acres of floor. The Thames Graving Docks, constructed by the same firm, possess a water area of 15 acres, and hydraulic machinery and lifts for docking and under-docking vessels of all capacities. The Northern Mid-Level Sewer, which Brassey made for the Metropolitan Board of Works, was a great undertaking, though only twelve miles in length. It took nearly three years to construct, and it runs from Kensal Green—passing under the Bayswater Road, Oxford Street, and Clerkenwell—to the River Lea. The contractors had to tunnel under houses and streets, and to cross the Metropolitan Railway with a very large tube; and the whole undertaking is regarded as one of the most difficult ever carried through in this country. The East London Railway—running from New Cross through the Thames Tunnel to Wapping—was another of Brassey's difficult enterprises successfully accomplished. The Danish railways, constructed by Brassey, Peto, & Betts, were about 500 miles in extent. They took ten years to complete, as the Government would not allow the contractors to do more than a certain amount of work annually. The work was largely executed by Danish sub-contractors and labourers, who were a steady and superior class of men. Construction was somewhat hindered by the war over Schleswig-Holstein, the sub-contractors being obliged to assist in making military earthworks.

The Australian works of Brassey were executed between 1859 and 1863. Here, again, the railways constructed had a wider influence than any mere value they possessed as a convenience for the resident population. They had much to do with stimulating emigration, and opening up the colonies to settlers from the mother-country. Wilcox and Rhodes, Brassey's agents, went out to Australia in 1859, their mission being to construct three important lines in New South Wales —the Great Southern, the Great Northern, and the Great Western Railways. Although there were no serious engineering difficulties to surmount, the cost of labour was so much higher that a similar length of line to that of the Great Southern Railway could have been laid in England at a reduction of £3,000 or £4,000 per mile. Everything for the Australian railways except the timber came from England. The wages were very high: labourers earned from 7s. to 8s. per day, masons and bricklayers 12s., and carpenters from 10s. to 12s. The cost of living in Queensland was only 8s. or 9s. a week individually; but a good deal of beer-drinking went forward, and that was very expensive. About 2,000 labourers were exported from England and Scotland, their selection and outfit costing the contractors £5 per man, while the Government paid the passage out, some £12 in addition. Altogether, the taking out of the 2,000 men involved an expenditure of £34,000. Mr. Wilcox, who might thus be regarded as a great emigration agent, stated in his evidence on this subject, that it would be a safe venture to send out say 20,000 people a year to the Australian colonies: they could all be readily absorbed.

The Argentine Railway was constructed by Brassey, Wythes, and Wheelwright in 1864. A special interest attaches to this enterprise, for, as Sir Arthur Helps observes, 'it is the first time in the history of railway constructions that railway promoters have been great colonizers.' The Argentine Government gave the railway company one league of land on each side of the railway throughout its entire extent, commencing at a distance of four leagues from the stations of Rosario and Cordova, and one league from each of the towns, San Geronimo and Villa Nueva, subject to the condition of such lands being peopled. The contractors accepted from the company one-half of the above-mentioned lands in part payment of their contract price. The line proved a very easy one to construct, and the railway has been most favourable to emigration. In the Argentine Republic, 'the colonizer may occupy land remote from cities, and therefore cheap, and yet find himself in immediate contact with one of the principal means and appliances of modern civilization.' If the Argentine were only in a settled condition politically, this fine field for emigrants might be more widely utilised and opened up.

The contract made by Brassey for the Moldavian railways illustrates the difficulties which sometimes attend preliminary negotiations. In this case they were of the most protracted character, plan after plan falling through, and at the end of ten years (1858-68) Brassey had only been able to complete 360 out of the 500 miles originally projected. A contract for the remaining 140 miles between Roman and Galatz was concluded with Dr. Strousberg in 1868.

The Indian railways, constructed between 1858 and 1865, formed another interesting and important feature in the labours of Brassey and his partners. To India and its development railway communication was a necessity. In 1858, Brassey, Wythes, and Sir Joseph Paxton agreed to construct the Eastern Bengal Railway, a line 112 miles in length, commencing at Calcutta, and terminating at a village named Kooshtea on the River Ganges. Brunel was the consulting engineer in England, and Purdon the chief engineer in India. This railway proved an unfortunate speculation—being a second similar experience for Brassey. In consequence of the numerous public works set on foot after the suppression of the Indian Mutiny, the utmost difficulty was experienced in getting sufficient labourers for the line, but the railway was persevered with and opened for traffic at the end of the rainy season of 1862. The line was expensive, the cost, including rolling stock, being about £14,000 per mile. In conjunction with Wythes and Henfrey, he next constructed the Delhi Railway, Bidder being the consulting engineer to the Company in England, and Joseph Harrison the chief engineer resident in India. The railway extended from Delhi to Umritsir in the Punjab, a distance of 304 miles. It included some very long viaducts over the Rivers Jumna, Sutlej, and Beeas, in addition to many minor structures, but the works were executed at an inclusive cost of £14,630 per mile. 'All the ironwork and machinery were imported from England, and had to be carried upwards of 1,000 miles from the ports where they were landed. Including rolling stock, these materials weighed nearly 100,000 tons.' Labour was always obtainable for this line, and it was completed within the specified time, the eastern half of the line being opened in 1868 by the Viceroy, Sir John Lawrence.

In May, 1867, Brassey went to Paris with his family. He had a good many business interviews in the French capital, and on the day he was to have left he was taken ill. He would only postpone his departure for a day, however, and then he travelled all night to Cologne. He made trial trips on the engines of the Fell Railway, and Mrs. Thomas Brassey could not help remarking 'the large-hearted way in which he entered into its merits, the anxiety he expressed for its success, and the interest he took in its completion as a great enterprise and an extension of civilization.' His generous wishes here were directly opposed to his pecuniary interests, for with the completion of the tunnel under the mountain the greater would be his loss on the line over the mountain. He returned to England in June, but set out again early in October to attend the proposed opening of the Mont Cenis Railway. He revisited the Fell Railway, the weather being extremely severe and his health bad. Following upon these things came another trial—for the opening of the railway proved a disastrous failure. The French Government had insisted upon having French engines and carriages, and they ignominiously broke down. Brassey was now taken alarmingly ill with bronchitis. He was conveyed with great difficulty to Turin, and his family were telegraphed for. Though suffering from fever, he insisted upon proceeding to Venice, and he was in a critical state when his family arrived there. He rallied, nevertheless, in a remarkable manner, and in November he was able to travel by easy stages to England, safely reaching St. Leonard's.

It was the beginning of the end, however, and in September, 1868, he had a second stroke of paralysis. Though remonstrated with, he would pursue his labours; and, by a strange coincidence, his latest—or one of his very latest undertakings, the Wolverhampton and Walsall Railway was close to the Penkridge Viaduct, the scene of his first railway contract. But death drew on apace. For some time before the end Brassey knew his disease was fatal, but he bore the news with fortitude and resignation, for he had ever been a deeply religious man. The last days of his life were spent at Hastings, where he expired on

December 8th, 1870. His death was mourned far beyond the limits of his own immediate circle.

Lord Brassey, the great contractor's eldest son, supplied Sir Arthur Helps with some interesting reminiscences of his father. The eminent virtues of the latter did not blind the son to his defects, which, in some degree, resulted from those very virtues. Brassey's whole existence was not centred in his own labours; the triumphs of science and engineering elicited his warmest enthusiasm, and in many instances his liberal pecuniary aid to bring them to fruition. He also took an intense delight in nature, and especially in mountain scenery. But whether in country or town, little escaped his keen observation. He had a special appreciation of sculpture, of paintings, and indeed of art in every form. His love of yachting was proverbial, as well as his love of hospitality. His politics tended towards Conservatism, but he appreciated whatever was good and great among all classes of men. His hobby was correspondence, and although he made no pretence to literary skill, he was singularly clear in his statements and facts. He was of a very patient disposition, and indulged the most generous sentiments—so much so that he sometimes failed in reproof where reproof would have been justified. Chivalrous in heart and mind, he had that further characteristic of the true gentleman, a never-failing consideration for the feelings and susceptibilities of others.

In supplementing these recollections, Brassey's biographer refers to his fitness for the work which devolved upon him; his common-sense; his trustfulness; his excellent treatment of, and confidence in, his subordinates; his generosity and unworldliness; his tenderness and mental refinement; his freedom from vanity; and his appreciation of the merits of others. I rejoice in all this, because such men are an honour to human nature; and if I have one objection to Thomas Brassey it is that he left too much money behind him. The accumulation of such a sum as £7,000,000—which he is reputed to have died possessed of

—cannot be defended in such an age of suffering and privation as ours is for hundreds of thousands of the human race. No doubt all this vast wealth was obtained in a blameless manner; but its concentration in one individual cannot be defended on general humanitarian or Christian grounds. Apart from this, however, one cannot but admire the character of Brassey, and feel a national pride in his achievements.

THE FAIRBAIRNS.

THE FAIRBAIRNS.

The Fairbairns are a remarkable family, whose chief representatives did much to advance the material prosperity of England during the first half of the nineteenth century. Their principal centres of operation were Manchester and Leeds; and to William and Peter Fairbairn especially, the science of engineering owes much of its recent extraordinary development and usefulness. Their scientific inventions and improvements rank among the most important of those associated with shipping, firearms, agricultural machinery, etc. Like many other good things—together with some others not so good—the family came from Scotland. Looking at the records of genius and talent as a whole, we must cheerfully recognise that the Scotch people take a high intellectual level. Directly or indirectly they have, since the Union of 1707, done much towards moulding the destinies of this great Empire at home and abroad.

I propose, first, to trace briefly the career of William Fairbairn, the eminent civil engineer. He was born at Kelso, in Roxburghshire, February 19th, 1789, his father, Andrew Fairbairn, being descended from one of those small lairds who farmed their own land. His grandmother, whose maiden name was Anderson, claimed descent from the ancient Border family of Douglas. Andrew Fairbairn had a somewhat chequered career. While residing near a seaport in England he was pressed for the war, and served under Lord Howe at Gibraltar. At the close of the war the fleet was ordered to Spithead, and he was here in August, 1782, when the *Royal George* went down, and assisted in saving the survivors. On receiving his discharge he returned to Scotland, and married a Miss Henderson, daughter of a tradesman in Jedburgh, who was also descended from an old Border family of the name of Oliver, though the Hendersons were now stock-farmers at the northern foot of the Cheviots. A large family quickly gathered round the Fairbairns, and Andrew had some difficulty in maintaining them all, notwithstanding his sober and industrious habits. Sir William Fairbairn states in his *Recollections*—which have been edited and expanded into a biography by Mr. Pole—that he had little education. At the parish school he read selections from the best poets and prose writers, and if to these be added a course of arithmetic as far as Practice and the Rule of Three, they constitute the whole stock of book knowledge up to his tenth year. But he gained a great deal of outdoor experience, and was a proficient in athletic sports. His father was intimate with the Scotts of Sandy Knowe, and though in a humbler position was highly respected by them. He was well acquainted with Sir Walter Scott in his youth, and used often to carry him, when unable to walk from the dislocation of the hip-bone, which made him a cripple for life.

While William Fairbairn's father was a hard worker, his mother appears to have been the same. Indeed she was often remonstrated with over her heavy labours at the spinning-wheel, which were supplementary to her arduous domestic duties. 'For nearly twenty years,' says her son, 'from 1785 to 1804, I believe the whole, or nearly the whole, of the woollen clothes, shirting, sheets, and blankets were spun and manufactured by my mother. In addition to these industrial resources, which always formed a prominent feature in my mother's character, there were her knowledge and skill in the useful arts. She was thoroughly acquainted with dyeing and bleaching; when my father resided in the Highlands of Scotland, she made his coats, waistcoats, and breeches, as well as all the jackets and trousers for her sons. She was also an adept at dressmaking, and used not only to make for herself and daughters, but frequently cut out for the neighbours, and she encouraged the same system of economy in other families as she practised in her own.' Ladies of London dying from *ennui*, please copy—in the spirit at least, as you cannot in the letter. In the autumn of 1799 Andrew Fairbairn and his brother Peter leased from Lord Seaforth a farm called Moy Farm, on the banks of the River Conan, about five miles from Dingwall, Ross-shire. Andrew was to supply the skill and industry required for the management, and was to have one half of the stock and one half of the proceeds. The Kelso home was broken up, and in October Andrew Fairbairn set forth for his northern home with a delicate wife and a family of five children, the youngest only six weeks old. The journey was upwards of two hundred miles through a wild country, and at a most inclement season of the year. It was made in a farm-cart which had some canvas stretched over it. Mrs. Fairbairn was so ill as to require to be lifted in and out of the cart every night and morning.

Young Fairbairn's next two years were spent at Moy Farm. He was only eleven years of age when he first exhibited his strong bias towards mechanics. He has thus related what took place at this period: 'After the first year's residence at Moy, my younger brother Peter, then a child of fifteen months old, required a great deal of nursing, and as that duty devolved upon my eldest sister and myself, I managed, in order to relieve myself of the trouble of carrying him on my back, to make a little waggon with four wheels, and by attaching a piece of old rope, used to drag him in all directions, sometimes to a considerable distance from the farm. The construction of the waggon was, however, a formidable undertaking, as I had no tools but a knife, a gimlet, and an old saw. With these implements, a piece of thin board, and a few small nails, I managed to make a respectable waggon, which, though frequently out of repair, was nevertheless much better than could be expected. The greatest difficulty was the wheels, which I surmounted by cutting sections from the stem of a small alder tree, and with a red-hot iron burnt the holes in the centre to receive the axle. The success which attended this construction led to others of greater importance, which I continued to practice, and which my father encouraged during the whole time we were in the Highlands. In the formation of boats and ships I became an expert artificer, and was at once a "Jack-of-all-trades," having to build, rig, and sail my own vessels. From shipbuilding I proceeded to construct wind- and water-mills, and attained such proficiency that I had sometimes five or six mills in operation at once. They were all made with the knife. The water-spout was composed of the bark of a tree, and the mill-stones were represented by round discs of the same material. It is not for me to offer an opinion as to the influence these exercises had upon my future fortunes; I may leave others to form their own judgment.'

Changes soon came, and for a time Andrew Fairbairn acted as steward to Mackenzie of Allan Grange, and subsequently as farm-steward to Sir William Ingleby of Ingleby Manor, Knaresborough. Meantime, William acquired some further rudiments of an English education at a school at Mullochy; and then he was taken for a time by his Uncle William of Galashiels, who improved his arithmetic and gave him a short course of book-keeping and land-surveying. But in 1803, being then a tall lad of fourteen, he was taken away from school and recalled to Kelso, in order to do something to help his family, who were reduced to great straits before the father's return from Yorkshire. William obtained employment at the New Bridge, which was then being built by Rennie, but when his father was appointed early in 1804 manager of a farm near the Percy Main Colliery, North Shields, he joined him there. It is at this place that his real history begins. He was bound apprentice for seven years to a millwright named Robinson, and was to receive wages beginning with five shillings per week and increasing to twelve shillings. By extra work the young apprentice sometimes doubled his wages and rendered great assistance to his parents, who still had a severe struggle in rearing and educating their children. During the winter evenings, when he did not work overtime, he entered upon a systematic course of study, which included arithmetic, mensuration, history, mathematics, Euclid, and some lighter reading. There was an excellent library at Shields to which he had access. Astronomy and music he likewise devoted some attention to.

In course of time he was promoted from the workshop to take charge of the pumps and steam-engine of Percy Main Colliery, and this gave him an independent position. In this post he remained until he came of age, and his apprenticeship indenture was cancelled. Then he began the serious business of life. He obtained employment as a millwright at Newcastle, and near that city he met with his future wife. She was Dorothy Mar, the youngest daughter of a Morpeth burgess, who had long occupied a farm on the Wansbeck called Mar's Banks. He indulged many day-dreams of fortune and domestic happiness, and it was with some pangs that he took leave of Dorothy in December, 1811, in order to proceed to London. He embarked on board a collier-ship, which passed through a terrible time before it reached the Nore. Fairbairn's early experiences of the Metropolis were anything but cheerful, for during the very first night he slept on shore, a whole family were murdered in the next house to his own. London was frost-bound and provisions were dear, but the brave young fellow at once set forth in quest of work. He and a friend appeared before the Millwrights' Society, but owing to some informality in their qualifications they were rejected by that body, and refused permission to work for Rennie, as Fairbairn had hoped to do. Cold, hunger, and despair ensued for about a month. Among other undertakings, the two friends walked from London to Hertford without food, and reached the latter place with a combined purse amounting to thirteenpence. After they joined the Independent Society of Millwrights things became brighter, and Fairbairn found employment successively at Shadwell, Wandsworth, and Greenwich. His income varied from two to three pounds a week. He came greatly to enjoy London; visited the theatres; heard Major Cartwright and Gale Jones declaim at the Westminster Forum, and spent pleasant Sundays with some relatives in St. Martin's Lane.

In conjunction with a clergyman named Hall, who was also somewhat of a mechanician, Fairbairn constructed a steam plough, but it found favour neither with the Society of Arts nor the Board of Agriculture. Fairbairn, too, at length saw its inutility, and abandoned the machine, which, however, had exhausted all his savings. His next venture, which was entirely on his own account, was more successful. He agreed with a pork-butcher in Tottenham Court Road to make him for £33 a machine for chopping meat for sausages. The machine was constructed, and it worked admirably. He now made a tour in the South and West of England, reaching Bath in April, 1813. Having worked for a short time at Bathgate, he again set out on foot, and visited Bradford in Wilts, Trowbridge, Bristol, Newport, Llandaff, and Cardiff. Then he took passage to Dublin, and in the Irish capital found employment in making nail machinery at the Phœnix Foundry. Returning to England in a few months, he engaged himself at Manchester to Mr. Adam Parkinson, with whom he remained for two years. He saved a little money in view of his marriage, and eventually he and Miss Mar were united at Bedlington, near Newcastle, on June 16th, 1816. They remained a few days in the North, and then journeyed to Macclesfield, subsequently removing to Manchester, where they took a little cottage. In March, 1817, a daughter was born to them, but for a time Mrs. Fairbairn was dangerously ill. By desperate struggles, however, the young couple kept out of debt. He was employed for a time as draughtsman by a Mr. Hewes, but in November, 1817, he retired from his service and began business on his own account. He found a partner in an old shopmate, Mr. James Lillie, and they remained together for fifteen years. Their first contract was for an iron conservatory, over which there was some difficulty on a complaint of infringement of patent, and the early years of the partnership were years of struggle.

The partners hired a small shed at a rent of twelve shillings per week, and having set up a lathe they engaged an Irishman to turn it, feeling that they were now ready to receive orders. We learn from an authoritative source that 'success was slow in coming, and Lillie began to have gloomy forebodings. As a last resource it was resolved to try what could be done by personal solicitation amongst spinners and manufacturers, and Mr. Fairbairn went round and interviewed many of them. This led to the young millwrights being engaged by Messrs. Murray, the cotton-spinners, "to renew with horizontal cross-shafts" the whole of the work by which their mule-spinning machinery was turned. Fairbairn and Lillie were almost frightened at the magnitude of this order; nevertheless they set steadily to work to execute it; and so well were their employers satisfied that Mr. Murray recommended the engineers to the firm of MacConnell & Kennedy, who then had the largest cotton-spinning concern in the country. Messrs. MacConnell & Kennedy were about this time erecting a large new mill, and they intrusted Messrs. Fairbairn & Lillie with the important task of supplying the necessary engineering work, gearing, etc. Improvements of a valuable character were introduced by Mr. Fairbairn, whereby the construction of the driving shafts and their connections was greatly simplified and lightened, giving increased speed and additional security. The firm of Fairbairn & Lillie had now a prosperous career before them; their reputation was made; orders came in faster than they could be executed; and larger premises and more extensive machinery had to be resorted to. Ten years after their start in business, Fairbairn & Lillie were amongst the foremost firms of mechanical engineers in the country. The improvements they effected had a wonderful influence on the development of our textile manufactures. Iron-work of every description came within the scope of Mr. Fairbairn's operations; his fame as a scientific mechanic extended far and near.'

In 1824 Fairbairn accepted a contract to construct two great water-wheels for Buchanan's Catrine Cotton Works, in Ayrshire. These powerful wheels were fifty feet each in diameter, with 120, or collectively 240, horse-power. The work was successfully executed, and the water-wheels started in June, 1827. 'They have never lost a day since that time,' wrote Fairbairn in 1851, 'and they remain, even at the present day, probably the most perfect hydraulic machines of the kind in Europe.' The engineer's next important task was in Switzerland—or rather it was carried on simultaneously with the Ayrshire one. He remodelled a water-mill and erected two water-wheels for Mr. G. Escher of Zurich. Numerous orders now followed in quick succession for new water-wheels in the Vosges, Alsace, and other parts of France. Such was the increase of business, that in 1830 the stock-book of Fairbairn & Lillie showed a balance of nearly £40,000 in their favour, and left them sufficient capital to build a foundry, and increase the works in other departments to the extent of giving employment to upwards of 300 hands. In April, 1830, Fairbairn was formally enrolled as a Member of the Institution of Civil Engineers.

Fairbairn's investigation into the properties of iron boats, and the possibility of applying steam-power for traction on canals, led to important practical results, as well as to the production of his first treatise on engineering matters, entitled *Remarks on Canal Navigation*. The Forth and Clyde Company commissioned him to construct a light passage boat, worked by steam-power, to ply between Glasgow and Edinburgh. He accordingly built the *Lord Dundas*, which was 68 feet long and 4 feet 6 inches deep, drawing sixteen inches of water. She was built of iron plates, about one-sixteenth of an inch thick, and she was fitted with cabins fore and aft. The engine was on the locomotive pattern, having two cylinders, one on each side, and was equal to about ten horse-power. Several trials were made of the vessel, and then for upwards of two years she carried passengers from Port Dundas, Glasgow, to Port Eglinton, Edinburgh. At a low velocity of about five miles an hour she steamed beautifully, but it soon became apparent that nothing could be effected in the shape of high velocities on canals to compete with the new locomotives then in process of development on the Liverpool and Manchester Railway.

Writing to Baron Charles Dupin more than twenty years afterwards with regard to his early experiments in iron vessels, he thus spoke of the *Lord Dundas:* 'Although it did not realise the objects for which it was originally constructed,' namely, the attainment of high velocities, it nevertheless paved the way to a new system of marine construction which has since become general amongst the nations of Europe and America. In the construction of the *Lord Dundas*, which was entrusted to my care, several important ideas presented themselves. First, the superior strength of iron as compared with wood; the distribution of the material in these constructions; and the superiority and lightness which a judicious application of this material afforded. All these circumstances were present to my mind in the construction of the *Lord Dundas*, and by the introduction of T and angle ⌐ iron as frames and ribs I found that the requisite rigidity and strength was attained at a comparatively small expenditure of material. In the construction of iron ships I may mention that our knowledge at the commencement was very imperfect; and I had to watch with the utmost care and attention the position and disposition of the material in order to effect economy in its use, and that with as near an approach as possible to the maximum of strength. In this respect I laboured under great difficulties; and having no data on which we could rely for guidance in these constructions, I felt the want of information, and at a very early period (1834) determined to institute a series of experiments on the strength of malleable-iron of different forms and conditions, in order to effect an improved system of construction, both as regards the strength and a judicious application of the material. These experiments were laid before the Royal Society, and published in the transactions of that body.'

A speculation by Fairbairn and his partner in taking up the Egerton dye-works led to disaster, and other incidents which followed led Fairbairn to believe that they would be better apart, so the partnership was dissolved in 1832. As soon as Fairbairn began business on his sole account he turned his attention to the new branch of engineering manufacture—iron shipbuilding. He constructed an iron steamer called the *Manchester*, with high-pressure engines of forty horse-power. She was tried with great success on the Mersey, and for years she plied between Port Dundas and the towns along the Firth of Forth up to Dundee. The vessel had great strength, buoyancy, and lightness. Encouraged by his efforts, Fairbairn turned his eyes towards London, and bought a plot of land at Millwall, Poplar. Here, with one of his pupils, Andrew Murray—whom he gave a small share in the concern,—he entered into business in 1835. In the course of a single year orders were received for twelve iron vessels for navigating the Ganges, for the East India Company, and four others for different parts of Europe. Of course opposition soon sprang up, and Fairbairn had many anxieties, while he was compelled frequently to travel backwards and forwards from his works in Manchester to those in London. He employed altogether now more than 2,000 hands. Fairbairn alternated shipbuilding with miscellaneous work, for we find him engaged on a drainage scheme for the Soham Mere, in Cambridgeshire, reporting with

J. F. Bateman (who afterwards married his daughter) on the water-power of the River Bann, in county Down, Ireland, and on other matters. He next, in conjunction with Mr. Eaton Hodgkinson, made experiments on hot and cold blast cast-iron for the British Association, and the results were embodied in a paper read before the Manchester Literary and Philosophical Society in 1837. He then invented and introduced the riveting machine, which has been of the greatest utility in engineering manufacture, greatly improving the quality and reducing the price of labour. In perfecting this invention he received valuable aid from his assistant-engineer, Robert Smith, to whom he gave a share in the patent.

From 1839 to 1843 Fairbairn was chiefly engaged in the Turkish dominions, executing various important works for the Sultan. On the completion of his enterprises, Sultan Abdul Medjid conferred upon him an imperial decoration set in diamonds, together with a *firman* constituting him chief fabricator of the machineries required to be cast and fitted up in England for the use of the imperial Turkish factories. Fairbairn made experimental researches into the properties of the iron-ores of Samakoff in Turkey and of the hæmatite ores of Cumberland, with a view of determining the best means for reducing them into the cast and malleable states. He also examined into the relative strength and other properties of cast-iron from the Turkish and other hæmatite ores. A paper on these enquiries was laid before the Institution of Civil Engineers in April, 1844, and Fairbairn was awarded the Telford silver medal for his communication. Further experiments on cast-iron he made shortly afterwards, and he took out a patent for improvements in joining metal plates. He likewise made suggestions to the factory authorities for the diminution and prevention of accidents, and recommended the use of iron in the construction of large buildings. In November, 1847, he gave important evidence before the Iron Structure Commission, and in a subsequent communication made useful suggestions for experiments, and furnished full particulars of the investigation he had made for the Britannia and Conway Tubular Bridges. He next invented the ventilating bucket for water-wheels, constructing a small passage opening upwards out of the bucket, by which, when the water entered, the air could rise and get away, and thus leave the vessel free for the reception of the water.

Among Fairbairn's pupils taken in 1840 was George Birkbeck, son of the celebrated founder of Mechanics' Institutes, and he was a frequent visitor in Fairbairn's house. In September, 1841, the inventor's daughter, Anne, was married to Mr. Bateman. A pathetic story is narrated of Fairbairn's relations with the eccentric artist, B. R. Haydon. In December, 1844, Haydon wrote to his friend as follows: 'You once gave me hopes of an order. Shall I make a proposition? Frank goes up for examination and his degree in a week or ten days at furthest. His fees are £15, and his college bill £41 14s. 11d. = £56 14s. 11d. I have brought him through all his terms but this last, and if this last be not paid up, he is ruined, and will not have his degree. I will paint you a small picture for that amount, or for any portion you will advance me at once. You were kind to Frank, and may feel an interest in getting him through. I never broke my word about a picture in my life. Close at once and you shall have an ornament for your house.' Fairbairn gave an order for a picture of the value of £30. Poor Haydon painted it, and about the middle of June, 1845, called at the house of one of Fairbairn's relatives in London, and left an unfinished sketch in the hall, giving a hasty message. On the 22nd of the same month the unhappy artist shot himself in his studio. The picture, 'Christ before Pilate,' still remains in the possession of the Fairbairn family.

In January, 1846, Fairbairn's father died at the venerable age of eighty-six. Fairbairn felt the visitation keenly, for there was a deep strain of tenderness in his nature; and in writing to his wife he said, 'Although a father myself, I experience the weakness of a child at the bereavement I have sustained.'

Fairbairn rendered valuable aid to Robert Stephenson in the great series of experimental investigations necessary to determine the details and proportions of the Britannia and Conway colossal Tubular Bridges. After the completion of the bridges, he published a work describing their construction, and giving a complete history of their progress, from the conception of the original idea to the conclusion of the elaborate experiments which determined the exact form and mode of construction ultimately adopted. Stephenson's idea was a circular tube, supported by chains; but the bridges, as finally completed, were rectangular structures, without chains, invented and designed by Fairbairn. A patent was taken out for the discovery under the title of 'Improvements in the construction of iron beams for the erection of bridges and other structures.' The improvements consisted in the novel application and use of plates of metal, united by means of rivets and angle-iron, for such or similar purposes, and forming by such combination a hollow iron beam or girder. Full details concerning the Britannia and Conway bridges are given in the article on the Stephensons, but I may append here a passage from Fairbairn respecting the patent: 'The patent for wrought-iron girder bridges was a joint affair between Mr. R. Stephenson and myself. It was in my name as the inventor, but he paid half the expense, and was entitled to one-half the profits, but it ultimately became a dead letter, and was abandoned by Mr. Stephenson. Under the circumstances the question was, Shall I continue to build the bridges? I chose to do so, and I believe I did right, as the principle was quite new, and no one understood the construction so well. I therefore gave designs, and received orders for more than one hundred bridges in the course of a very few years. Up to the present time, 1870, I have built and designed, with the assistance of the Fairbairn Engineering Company, nearly one thousand bridges, some of them of large spans varying from 40 to 300 feet.'

Between 1849 and 1852 Fairbairn was much occupied with

a scheme for a great bridge over the Rhine at Cologne. He gave a great deal of consideration to the work, and went over to Berlin, where he saw much of the famous Baron von Humboldt and of the Chevalier Bunsen. Fairbairn combated the idea of a chain bridge, and submitted a design based on his own principle. This was generally adopted in the construction of the bridge, though the tubular form of girder was rejected for the open lattice one. On August 23rd, 1852, Fairbairn thus wrote to Humboldt: 'From the condescending manner in which I was received by his Majesty, and the unwearied attention you personally bestowed on the objects of my journey, I was taught to believe that at no very distant period I should again have the pleasure of meeting you, and that the projected bridge across the Rhine at Cologne, in which you took so deep an interest, would sooner or later have been carried into effect. I believe this is now likely to be accomplished, not upon the principle I recommended, but some other construction, which doubtless the authorities believe superior to those I had the honour to lay before them. One important consideration was, however, obtained by our united exertions, and that was to condemn an imperfect and abortive construction, and to direct the public mind to the importance of having a structure that was not only capable of supporting the railway, but all the other objects contemplated in the requirements of the public traffic. These objects have now been attained; at least, I am so informed, and that the drawbridges, as well as the hoisting and lowering of the carriages from one level to another, are to be dispensed with. This, you will recollect, is what we contended for, and I consider it fortunate for the country that his Majesty suspended the perpetration of a project that would never have realised the expectations of the Government or the wants of the public.'

The Rhine Bridge, as finally constructed, was begun by two Prussian engineers, Wallbaum and Lohse, in 1855, and finished some years later. Crossing the river in a line with the axis of the Cathedral, it has four spans, each 313 feet wide in the clear. There are two pairs of girders, side by side, one pair carrying a double line of railway, and the other the road traffic. The girders are formed of open lattice-work, instead of plates, as Fairbairn had proposed, but in all other material respects there was little departure from the English engineer's designs.

Fairbairn's scientific standing was now assured, and in June, 1850, he was elected a Fellow of the Royal Society. He was next admitted into that august body which composed the National Institute of France. A vacancy occurred in the middle of the year 1851 among the Corresponding Members of the Academy of Sciences by the death of Sir Marc Isambard Brunel. At the instigation of his friends Generals Poncelet and Morin, Baron Dupin, and M. Arago—who were influential members of the Institute—Fairbairn offered himself as a candidate, and was elected in May, 1852. A third distinction awaited him in 1853, when he was elected, without ballot, into the Athenæum Club, under the rule which permits the Committee to elect every year a certain number of men eminent in science, literature, or art, or who have been distinguished by their public services. Among those elected under this rule in the same year as Fairbairn were Thomas Carlyle, Baron Marochetti, and Sir Francis Grant, P.R.A. During the ensuing fourteen years these further honours were conferred upon Fairbairn: In November, 1855, he was elected Member of the Académie Nationale Agricole, Manufacturière et Commerciale, Paris; in December, 1856, a Corresponding Associate of the Royal Academy of Sciences, Turin; in November, 1860, an Honorary Member of the Prussian 'Verein für Beförderung des Gewerbfleisses,' Berlin; in July, 1861, an Honorary Member of the Royal United Service Institution, London; in November, 1861, a Corresponding Member of the Literary and Philosophical Society of Liverpool; in the same month, an Honorary Associate of the Institution of Naval Architects, London;

in February, 1862, an Honorary Member of the Yorkshire Philosophical Society; in June, 1862, an Honorary Associate of the Society of Arts, Geneva; and in October, 1867, an Honorary Member of the Society of Engineers, London.

During a great portion of his life, Fairbairn was engaged in the manufacture of steam-boilers, greatly improving them as regards design and construction. In 1844, says Mr. Pole, he introduced a particularly valuable change in boiler design. 'He was always an advocate of high-pressure steam, on account of its economical advantage; but its use was limited by a fear of danger in the vessel wherein it was generated. The kind of boiler which had been found by experience to be best adapted for this purpose was that known as the Cornish or Trevithick's boiler. This was of cylindrical form, having a tube running through it in which the fire was placed. This had the disadvantage that the tube must necessarily be of large size, so as to admit sufficient fire, and it was on that account exposed to a severe external crushing strain, which its form was not well calculated to bear. It had also the evil that the water over the top of the tube was only of small depth, and if by accident the water level happened to get low, the top of the tube, being exposed to the most intense action of the fire, was liable to become over-heated, which would lead to danger of explosion. The steam space was also contracted by the necessary height of the water-line. Mr. Fairbairn's improvement consisted in using *two* internal fire-tubes, of smaller size, instead of one large one. These tubes were subject to a much diminished external strain, while at the same time they allowed of an increase of the fire-grate and heating surface; and, what was of more importance, a much greater depth of water could be maintained over them, and the level could, if necessary, be lowered so as to enlarge the steam room.'

This simple but useful design was patented by Fairbairn and an engineer who had aided him named John Hetherington. The boiler was soon widely adopted and became the one in general use in the northern manufacturing districts. Steam-boilers were sometimes so defectively constructed that fatal accidents ensued, and Fairbairn was called in as a scientific expert to explain the cause or causes of the disasters. He attended inquiries of this nature at Bolton, Halifax, Blackburn, Manchester, and other places. He was also invited by Sir Edward Baines, President of the Yorkshire Union of Mechanics' Institutes, to lecture on the subject, and he accordingly delivered two lectures at Leeds 'On the Construction of Boilers' and 'On Boiler Explosions,' and these were repeated in several other manufacturing towns. The lectures were afterwards republished in *Useful Information for Engineers*, and in various foreign scientific periodicals. Then to the Hull meeting of the British Association in 1853 he communicated a paper entitled 'Experimental Researches to determine the Strength of Locomotive Boilers and the Causes which lead to Explosion.' But, not content with theorising, he proceeded to initiate practical reforms by founding the 'Association for the Prevention of Steam-boiler Explosions'—an association which has been of incalculable benefit in saving life and property. Under Fairbairn's guidance it became one of the most valuable mechanical institutions of the country.

The following passage from the memoir of Fairbairn shows the absolute necessity which had arisen for such an organisation :—'The *Mining Journal* of September 9, 1854, recorded the verdict of the coroner's jury on a fearful boiler explosion at Rochdale, which verdict concluded with the following paragraph :—" The jury cannot separate without pressing on the consideration of the owners and users of steam-boilers throughout the kingdom the necessity there is that measures should be taken by them to ensure a thorough and frequent inspection of boilers, so as to prevent, so far as human foresight can, the recurrence of explosions." In giving his evidence on this tragic case (where ten persons were blown to atoms and an immense deal of property was destroyed), Mr. Fairbairn suggested it was possible, and indeed quite practicable, to establish associations in the several districts, the members of which should appoint inspectors to take cognizance of the boilers within their respective precincts, and to report to the association weekly in what state they found them, and the causes which prevented them from being in working order, if the inspectors should consider such to be the case. He did not conceive that it would be any tax on the proprietors of boilers to pay a trifling sum yearly to meet the expense of such an association, for it struck him forcibly that, in addition to preventing those very serious accidents, it would be productive of benefit to the proprietors themselves, and save a great deal of money.'

The *Journal* added :—

'Since the above observations were written, we perceive that Mr. Fairbairn's earnest recommendation has been adopted, and that an association has been formed in the district for the inspection of steam-boilers and the prevention of boiler explosions. We cannot avoid anticipating from it the best results.'

Influential meetings were held in the Manchester Town Hall, and the association was successfully established, with Henry Houldsworth as the first president. The full title of the Society was 'The Manchester Steam-users' Association, for the Prevention of Steam-boiler Explosions, and for the Attainment of Economy in the Application of Steam.' The objects and constitution of the Association were thus defined: 'This Association undertakes the periodical inspection of steam-boilers, and gives a pecuniary guarantee of the integrity and efficiency of its inspections to the amount of £300 on each boiler enrolled, so that in the event of the explosion of an approved boiler, whether that explosion arise from collapse of the furnace tubes, or from rupture of the shell, or failure of any part of the boiler whatever, all damage done thereby, other than by fire, whether to the boiler itself, or to the surrounding property, will be made good to the extent of £300. The

Association also assists its members by taking indicator diagrams when requested, as well as by affording competent engineering advice with regard to the working of boilers and engines, the prevention of smoke, the economy of fuel, and any other points calculated to prove of value to the members of the Association as steam users. Its system of inspection is voluntary and permissive on the part of its members. Its reports are suggestive and recommendatory on the part of its officers. Its benefits are mutually shared by all enrolled. There are no shareholders to whom dividends are paid out of the members' subscriptions, but the funds are devoted solely to promoting the direct objects of the Association. The executive committee are appointed by the general voice of the members of the Association. They receive no remuneration for their services. They employ a considerable amount of steam-power themselves, and are thus interested in everything that affects its use. The object of the guarantee is not so much to ensure the members against pecuniary loss in case of explosion, as to give a pledge of the *bonâ fide* intention of the Association to prevent the occurrence of explosions by efficient supervision and careful periodical boiler inspection.'

In less than twenty years the Association boasted of a membership of 768, with an annual income of £5,236, and of recent years it has prospered with like rapidity, though not to the extent it should have done, considering the terrible risks run with steam-boilers. As soon as he had founded the Boiler Association, Fairbairn proceeded to take up the theoretical side of the subject; and he prevailed upon the Royal Society and the British Association jointly to authorise an enquiry into the principles of boiler construction. There were two branches for investigation, viz., the methods of boiler construction and the steam question. With regard to the first, he associated with him a practical mathematician, Thomas Tate, a young engineer named Unwin being engaged as secretary. The first result was a paper read before the Royal Society in 1858, 'On the Resistance of Tubes to Collapse.' Fairbairn demonstrated by a series of experiments that the strength of the tubes in boilers diminished in an important degree as their length increased. To remedy this, he found that it would be possible effectively to shorten the tubes without shortening the boilers, and he further suggested improvements in the riveting. Fairbairn's experiments on this subject—which were very expensive—led, in his own words, 'to the establishment of the law of collapse from pressure on the external surfaces; and the improvements deduced from this law led to the security of steam-boilers, by doubling or trebling their powers of resistance, and thus were the means of saving many valuable lives from violent death by explosion.' The Royal Society made a grant towards the expenses of the experiments, which were conducted at the engine-shed of the London and North-Western Railway Company at Longsight, Manchester. In 1859 a second paper—this time by Fairbairn and Tate—was laid before the Royal Society. A sequel to the former one, it was entitled 'On the Resistance of Glass Globes and Cylinders to Collapse from Internal Pressure, and on the Tensile and Compressive Strength of various Kinds of Glass.' Like the previous paper, it was published in the *Philosophical Transactions*. The experiments with glass testified that the law of their strength corresponded with that deduced for iron tubes. Another paper by Fairbairn and Tate, read before the Royal Society in 1860, was entitled 'Experimental Researches to determine the Density of Steam at Different Temperatures; and to determine the Law of Expansion of Superheated Steam.' The paper was recognised as of such importance and merit that it was selected by the Society as the Bakerian Lecture for the year, while it was also duly published in the *Philosophical Transactions*. The researches indicated in the paper proved of great practical service.

When the question arose whether legislative measures should be introduced to ensure the safety of boilers, or to prevent or diminish the danger of explosion, Fairbairn entered into the controversy. In France, also, the matter excited much interest, and an eminent mechanical engineer, M. Charles Combes, wrote to Fairbairn for his views on the subject. In answer to the question, 'Is it desirable to fix by law, under penalty of fines, the thickness of plates, etc.?' Fairbairn replied, 'It is not desirable, as there is a great difference in the quality of plates. These points are left to the makers, and the Association make no recommendations.' To the question, 'Do you consider the previous testing necessary?' he answered, 'We consider a hydraulic test necessary up to one-and-a-half times, or in some cases to double the pressure at which the boiler is worked.' To the question, 'Is it desirable to prescribe, under penalty of fines, the combustion of smoke?' he replied, 'Yes, under local acts applied to towns, as the emission of smoke from furnaces may be prevented.' Finally in answer to the query, 'Are there any rules in England respecting the condition of the boiler-house, etc.? he said, 'There is no condition by law, but it is desirable in every case to have boilers in a separate building, distinct from the factory where a number of persons are employed.'

In 1868 the British Association appointed a Committee, consisting of Messrs. Fairbairn, Whitworth, Penn, Hick, Bramwell, Webster, Fletcher, and others, to consider 'how far coroners' inquisitions are satisfactory tribunals for the investigation of boiler explosions, and how these tribunals may be improved.' The Committee reported in the following year to the effect that the inquests were unsatisfactory, and they recommended that coroners should get the assistance of skilled engineers. Meantime Parliament made two attempts to place all steam-boilers under Government inspection. The Committee, as well as the British Association, were opposed to this, and in place of such legislation, Fairbairn obtained in 1870 the appointment of a Select Committee to investigate the question. This Committee sat during two Sessions, and in their report recommended that the responsibility of explosion should remain upon the steam-users, and that the efficiency of coroners' inquiries should be somewhat improved.

Fairbairn took out a patent for boiler improvements in 1870, by which he contrived that boilers should have a resistance equal to 750 lb. pressure per square inch. There were also arrangements by which the examination, cleaning, and repair of boilers might be much facilitated. He took out a further patent in 1873, in conjunction with Thomas Beeley, for improvements in the 1870 form of boiler, which rendered it more especially suitable for steam vessels; and in February, 1874, he forwarded to the Admiralty a design for the adaptation of the new boiler to one of Her Majesty's frigates, the *Daring*. At the instance of Mr. William Hopkins of Cambridge, Fairbairn was engaged for some years in an inquiry as to certain physical properties of the materials of the earth's crust. Mr. Hopkins had contributed papers to the Royal Society on the Phenomena of Precession and Nutation, the Thickness and Constitution of the Earth's Crust, and the Geological Theories of Elevation and Earthquakes; and he was anxious for Fairbairn—as a practical engineer and a man of science—to make experiments for the purpose of determining whether great pressure has any sensible effect on the temperature of fusion of any proposed substance (a metallic substance for instance), or, what would probably be found to be the same thing, on the temperature at which any substance, in a previous state of fusion, would become solid. Mr. Hopkins obtained from the Government an allowance of £250 'for investigations on the effect of pressure on the temperature of fusion of certain substances,' the inquiry to be conducted under the superintendence of a Committee, of which Mr. Joule was to be a member. Elaborate experiments were made and gratifying results obtained, Mr. Hopkins warmly acknowledging his obligations to Fairbairn and Joule, and the former's assistant, William Ward. The results were stated in a lecture given by Mr. Hopkins at the Royal Institution. Among other things resulting from the data obtained, was the inference that the actual thickness of the solid crust of the earth must probably be at least 200 miles, and might be considerably greater.

After Fairbairn had dissolved partnership with Lillie, he devoted himself specially to iron-shipbuilding and the construction of steam-engines. The Canal Street Works at Ancoats, Manchester, were greatly enlarged and improved, and here a brisk business was soon done in steam-engines. Boiler-making was also another important branch of the manufactures carried on. Then, in course of time, Fairbairn became a famous locomotive maker, and more than 600 locomotives were built at his workshops. He was likewise the first designer of the tank-engine, in which the fuel and water are carried on the engine itself, dispensing with the separate tender. His son Thomas joined him as a partner in 1841, and five years later another son, William Andrew, entered the firm, which was now carried on under the name of William Fairbairn & Sons. The business rapidly extended, and became very prosperous. Among extensive works undertaken by the firm were, the iron arrangements for the large landing-stage at St. George's Pier, Liverpool, and the construction of a huge wrought-iron caisson for closing the entrance to one of the docks at Keyham Dockyard, near Plymouth. In 1850 Fairbairn took out a patent for an improved crane for hoisting and lifting purposes, by which heavy articles could be raised to a greater height, while the machine at the same time offered greater strength and security. Six of these large cranes were made for Keyham Dockyard, each crane being calculated to lift 12 tons to a height of 30 feet from the ground, and to sweep a circle 65 feet in diameter. Later, a still larger one was constructed, which lifted 60 tons 60 feet high, with a circle of 106 feet diameter.

When the Small Arms Factory at Enfield was established by the Government in 1852, Fairbairn's aid was invoked. In conjunction with the officials of the Ordnance Department, he laid out the works, arranged the general design of the mechanical provisions, and constructed most of the machinery and iron-work, with the exception of the wood-working machines. Then in 1853 Fairbairn finished the largest work he had undertaken in mill construction, namely, Sir Titus Salt's great woollen works at Saltaire, near Bradford, Yorkshire. Mr. Pole remarks of these works, and of Fairbairn's improvements in such works generally: 'This kind of work was peculiarly his own; it was by it that he first acquired his fame; his practice in it was exceedingly large, and he kept up his interest in it during the whole of his manufacturing career. In addition to the improvements originally introduced by him in the arrangement of the driving machinery, he had continued to add other beneficial changes from time to time; and among others he was the first to take the driving power from the rim of the fly-wheel of the steam-engine, by providing it with teeth working into an adjoining pinion of smaller size, which he considered had much advantage in the directness of the action and the convenience of the mechanical arrangements. But it was not only the machinery of mills that he improved; at a later period he devoted considerable attention to the design and construction of the buildings in which the machinery was placed, more particularly as to their strength and the preservation of them from fire. Many accidents from malconstruction had come under his notice, and he had turned every opportunity of this kind to account in the improvement of his designs. Iron was largely used in these structures, and he made it his business to perfect the experimental knowledge of the strength of the material in its different forms, and of the best modes of applying it to the purposes in question. The Saltaire mill was remarkable not only for its great extent, but for the perfection of its design. It was entirely planned by him, except the architectural features. A description of it, with plates, is given in Mr. Fairbairn's book on the application of cast and wrought iron to building purposes, published in 1854. The mills and dependencies extend over $6\frac{1}{2}$ acres of ground. The main range of buildings, or the mill proper, is 550 feet in length, 50 feet in width, and about 72 feet (six storeys) in height. The loom-shed, one storey high, is nearly 300 feet long by 200 feet wide; and another, the combing shed, is a little smaller. The engines are 1,250 horse-power, and the length of shafting is very nearly 2 miles, weighing upwards of 60 tons, and making from 60 to 250 revolutions per minute. The mills contain within themselves every means of preparing from the raw material the supply of 1,200 power looms, the yield of which is 30,000 yards of alpaca per day, or upwards of 5,000 miles per annum.'

The Manchester works of Fairbairn & Sons were so prosperous from 1848 to 1860 that they not only made good a loss of £100,000 sustained at Millwall, but enabled the partners to amass considerable fortunes besides. During the Siege of Sebastopol, Fairbairn constructed a floating flour-mill and bakery for the troops, adapting for this purpose two iron screw-steamers placed at his disposal by the Government. Fairbairn practically retired from the firm before 1860, and, as his son William also retired in 1859, Thomas became the sole proprietor, and the works were now carried on under the style of Fairbairn & Company. Nevertheless, it was under the father's direction that the firm rebuilt in 1860 two large viaducts on the Manchester and Sheffield Railway, in which iron girders took the place of old timber arches.

The future course of the firm is thus detailed by Fairbairn's biographer: 'About 1864 the business was transferred to a Limited Liability Company, who thenceforth traded under the title of "The Fairbairn Engineering Company." Mr. Fairbairn and his family retained, however, a considerable pecuniary interest in the concern, and Mr. Fairbairn himself still kept an office on the works, and gave much personal attention to them. The firm undertook several large contracts, among which was the construction of some forts for the Government to be erected at Spithead; the roof of the Royal Albert Hall; many large bridges and roofs for railways, etc., etc. But about the time of Sir William's death the tide of a long-continued prosperity seemed to have turned, and in the face of a serious depression in the iron trade, which was obviously coming on, it was considered expedient not to risk further losses, but to wind up the concern. The shops were accordingly dismantled, and the plant was sold.'

The record of the shipbuilding yard at Millwall, which was in existence about twelve years, was one of disaster. The business never proved a paying one, and it absorbed a great amount of capital; yet much good work was executed there. Mr. Pole thinks that if Liverpool had been chosen instead of London for Fairbairn's shipbuilding works they might have proved a success. The original outlay on the Millwall works was heavy, and it was provided entirely by borrowed money, which had to be increased from time to time, thus hanging like a dead weight on the concern. The firm built for the Admiralty the frigate *Megæra*, 2,000 tons, with engines of 600 horse-power, and they also constructed large engines for several other frigates. For the East India Company they likewise constructed, as we have seen, twelve iron vessels, and for the Peninsular and Oriental Company the *Pottinger*, 1,700 tons. Vessels were constructed for the mercantile marine service; eight steamers were built for the Baltic and four for the Black Sea, etc.; and iron steam yachts were built for the Emperor of Russia and the King of Denmark. Fairbairn took out two patents for improvements in marine steam machinery. The first was for 'Certain Improvements in the Construction and Arrangement of Steam-engines,' and the second was for an improvement in the mode of driving the screw-propeller by the application of a large wheel with internal teeth. Though oppressed with fits of melancholy as regards the Millwall works, Fairbairn struggled bravely on, determined not to be driven into the Bankruptcy Court. He avoided this alternative, but he felt compelled at last to wind up this branch of the business, and the works were disposed of for £12,000, although they had cost upwards of £50,000. It seems that the total loss sustained by the Millwall works was upwards of £100,000.

Fairbairn was engaged from 1861 to 1865 in aiding the Government on an official investigation respecting the application of iron to defensive purposes in warfare. For a long time the Government authorities were opposed to iron vessels, but they were at last borne down by the force of scientific opinion, which Fairbairn assisted materially in moulding. He made a series of important experiments on the mechanical properties of iron and steel plates, their strength, ductility, resistance to punching force, etc. Some of the results obtained he communicated to the British Association, the Royal Institution, and the Institution of Naval Architects. The official Iron Armour Committee aided in the work, and eventually iron triumphed over wood in the construction of ships of defence.

In the year 1850 Fairbairn visited the North of Europe. He was received at St. Petersburg by the Czar, and at Stockholm was greeted with a warm welcome by the populace, while King Oscar awarded him a special medal of distinction. At the Great Exhibition of 1851, in London, Fairbairn acted as a juror in the machinery department. In 1853 he was appointed President of the Mechanical Section of the British Association, which met that year at Hull, and he delivered the opening address 'On the Progress of Mechanical Science.' In 1853-54 he formed one of a committee of the British Association appointed to consider the best means for cooling air in tropical climates. In 1854 he was elected President of the Institution of Mechanical Engineers, and was re-elected to the office in the ensuing year. During the former year (1854) he visited Paris. He was introduced to the Academy of Sciences, and honoured with an interview by the Emperor Napoleon, who presented him on leaving with a handsome gold snuff-box set with diamonds. Chosen one of the English jurors at the Paris Exhibition of 1855, he was nominated by the French Imperial Commission as Chairman of one of the mechanical sections. After the close of the Exhibition, he addressed to the President of the Board of Trade, Lord Stanley of Alderley, an elaborate report 'On the Machinery of the Paris Universal Exhibition, 1855.' For his services in France, the Emperor Napoleon awarded him the Legion of Honour in 1855. When in 1857 a public statue was raised in Manchester to the great engineer James Watt, Fairbairn delivered the inaugural address as President of the Literary and Philosophical Society and Chairman of the Watt Memorial Committee. He also contributed a note on Watt to the memoir of him by Arago. We further find Fairbairn generously interesting himself at this time on behalf of the family of Henry Cort, an inventor who had contributed largely to the improvement of the iron manufacture.

At the close of 1857 Fairbairn left England in order to make a tour through Italy. He went by way of Paris, Marseilles, Nice, and Genoa, and then visited the most important cities of Italy, including Naples, Rome, Florence, Bologna, Milan, and Turin. Shortly after his return he read a paper before the Manchester Literary and Philosophical Society 'On the Comparative Temperature of the Climates of England and some parts of Italy.' The writer demonstrated that, although Italy had the credit of possessing a warm and agreeable climate in the winter season, this only applied to the districts which lay south of the Apennines. In the northern cities he found the cold much greater than in England, and almost Russian in its severity. From 1859 to 1865 Fairbairn took a keen interest in the laying of the Atlantic Cable. He was a member of the Permanent Consulting Scientific Committee, to whom mechanical questions as to the construction and laying of the cable were referred from time to time. He declined to join the Company, however, on account of his advancing years. He drew up several papers and reports on the practicability of the scheme, and the best methods for carrying it into effect. Fairbairn was for a number of years President of the Manchester Literary and Philosophical Society, which owed much of its success and efficiency to his efforts. In 1860 he was awarded the Gold Medal of the Royal Society for his various experimental enquiries into the properties of the materials employed in mechanical construction—which enquiries were duly set forth in the *Philosophical Transactions* and in the publications of other scientific societies.

In 1861 Fairbairn acted as President of the British Association, whose meetings that year were held in Manchester. The retiring President, Lord Wrottesley, on this occasion passed the following eulogium on Fairbairn: 'We may derive important instruction from the career of Mr. Fairbairn, whether we view him as the successful engineer or as the distinguished man of science. In the former capacity he is one who has by perseverance, combined with talent, risen from small beginnings to the summit of his profession, and he forms one of that noble class of men—the Stephensons, the Brunels, the Whitworths, the Armstrongs—who have conferred such important services on their country, and some of whom, unfortunately for that country, have perished, alas! too soon, exhausted by their arduous toils. Mr. Fairbairn, therefore, is one of the many examples of what can be done in England by such men who resolve, undaunted by the difficulties and obstructions that beset their path, to struggle gallantly onward till success crown their efforts. Again, if we look at Mr. Fairbairn's claims to scientific distinction, they read to us an important lesson, for they show what can be done by zeal and energy, and the exercise of a strong and resolute will, fully determined to carry out objects in which the public is deeply interested. It is extraordinary that any man should have been able, during the few leisure hours that can be snatched from an important and engrossing business, to accomplish for science what Mr. Fairbairn has done: and not only has he been a most successful contributor to mechanical science, but his liberality has been unbounded in placing all his great mechanical resources at the disposal of his fellow labourers in the same field. Such a man is one whom all should delight to honour, and to such a man I resign with great satisfaction the chair which I now vacate.'

Fairbairn delivered a comprehensive and searching inaugural address on the recent triumphs of science, especially in the branch of mechanics as applied to engineering and to machinery, and was afterwards warmly complimented upon it by Lord Brougham, Prof. Sedgwick and John Rennie. An offer of knighthood arose out of the British Association Meeting, but Fairbairn respectfully declined the honour. He accepted, however, the honorary degree of LL.D. conferred upon him by the University of Edinburgh, and he afterwards received the same degree from Cambridge University. His biographer describs the latter degree as that of D.C.L., but that of course is a mistake. In connection with the great International Exhibition of 1862, Fairbairn was appointed President of the Jury for machines and tools employed in the manufacture of wood and iron. Owing to his long experience in engineering matters, he was frequently consulted by the Admiralty during the last twelve or fifteen years of his life on questions connected with iron shipbuilding and naval construction. In the year 1869, when he was in his eightieth year, the dignity of a baronetcy was conferred on Fairbairn. He did not seem to care for the honour on his own account, but he was pleased for his family's sake, and gratified by this recognition of the services he had rendered to science.

Between the years 1850 and 1873, Fairbairn was a voluminous writer on his special subjects. References have already been made to some of his papers, but others may now be mentioned. To the Institution of Civil Engineers he contributed a paper in 1850 on 'Tubular Girder Bridges,' and to the Royal Society in the same year a paper entitled 'An Experimental Enquiry into the Strength of Wrought-iron Plates and their Riveted Joints, as applied to Shipbuilding and Vessels exposed to Severe Strains.' At the meeting of the British Association in 1853, he read a contribution 'On the Mechanical Properties of Metals as derived from repeated Meltings, exhibiting the Maximum Point of Strength, and the Causes of Deterioration.' In the succeeding year he published a volume *On the Application of Cast and Wrought Iron to Building Purposes*, which was dedicated to Sir David Brewster, and passed through three editions. For the eighth edition of the *Encyclopædia Britannica* he rewrote in 1856 the article on 'Iron.' A work which he brought out the same year was entitled '*Useful Information for Engineers*, being a Series of Lectures delivered to the Working Engineers of Yorkshire and Lancashire. Together with a series of appendices containing the results of experimental enquiries into the strength of materials, the causes of boiler explosions, etc.' A short memoir presented to the British Association in 1859 was entitled 'Experiments to determine the Efficiency of Continuous and Self-acting Brakes for Railway Trains'; but this was afterwards greatly elaborated, and submitted to the Institution of Civil Engineers. 'The Strength of Iron Ships' was the title of an important paper read before the Institution of Naval Architects in 1860, and the same year saw the appearance of a second series of *Useful Information for Engineers*. To the Oxford meeting of the British Association in 1860, Fairbairn contributed a 'Report of Experiments to determine the Effect of Vibratory Actions and long continued Changes of Load on Wrought-iron Girders.' At the Manchester meeting in the ensuing year he confirmed and supplemented these experiments. The whole results were afterwards embodied in a paper read before the Royal Society. His next undertaking was an important work in two volumes, being a *Treatise on Mills and Millwork*, the first part of which appeared in 1861 and the second in 1863. In 1865 was published Fairbairn's *Treatise on Iron Shipbuilding*, dedicated to the Duke of Somerset, First Lord of the Admiralty; and in 1866 a third series of *Useful Information for Engineers* appeared. For Thomas Baines's valuable work, *Lancashire and Cheshire*, Fairbairn wrote a whole section—forming a quarto volume of 260 pages—on 'The Rise and Progress of Manufactures and Commerce, and of Civil and Mechanical Engineering, in Lancashire and Cheshire.' This task occupied him from August, 1867, to July, 1869. Fairbairn's last literary production was a paper read before the Royal Society in 1873 —when the author was eighty-four years of age—'On the Durability and Preservation of Iron Ships, and on Riveted Joints.' The above is a long category of literary labours, and it appears all the more remarkable when we remember that for a considerable part of the time during which the works were written Fairbairn was engaged in business as a practical captain of industry.

For a few years before his death Fairbairn's health had been failing, and indeed he was never quite the same after the death of his eldest son John in 1867. In October, 1873, he somewhat imprudently attended the opening of the new buildings of Owens College, Manchester. A severe bronchial attack followed, which for a time completely prostrated him. He visited Brighton and London in June, 1874, and Sir William Gull recommended absolute rest. In July he wrote a cheery letter on the marriage of his granddaughter, and then went down to the country seat of his son-in-law, Mr. Bateman, Moor Park, near Farnham, Surrey. Here, after a last brief painful attack of illness, he expired on the 18th of August, 1874. His remains were conveyed to Manchester, and interred in the burial-ground of Prestwich Parish Church. The funeral was attended by upwards of fifty-thousand persons. A statue was raised to him, and other honours paid to his memory, by the citizens of Manchester.

It is interesting to find that Fairbairn and his wife had been spared to each other for eight years beyond their golden wedding-day. They had nine children, seven sons and two daughters. Fairbairn lived at the Polygon, Ardwick, Manchester, for thirty-four years, namely, from 1840 to 1874. 'The Society at the Polygon during the last fifteen or twenty years of his life was of an unusually intellectual, refined, and attractive character, and brought together guests of singularly varied acquirements and talents. Among them were the Chevalier Bunsen, Sir David Brewster, Mr. Wm. Hopkins, Dr. Prince Lee, Bishop of Manchester, Lord Rosse, Lord Wrottesley, the Rev. Vernon Harcourt, Dr. Robinson of Armagh and his gifted wife, Sir Edward and Lady Sabine, the Earl of Derby, Earl Granville, Lord Brougham, Mr. Leonard Horner, Mrs. Gaskell, Lord Houghton, Lord Shaftesbury, the several eminent Professors of Owens College, and many others, whose names are well known in science, literature, and the public service. It was his custom to invite groups of visitors regularly every autumn; his invitations were gladly responded to, and these annual pleasant gatherings of choice spirits were thoroughly enjoyed by those who had the good fortune to be present at them.'

Fairbairn was for more than fifty years an attendant at the Cross Street Unitarian Chapel, Manchester, and a white marble tablet, executed by Woolner, placed above his pew, records this fact. One of the ministers of this chapel was the Rev. W. Gaskell, husband of the friend and biographer of Charlotte Brontë, and herself a charming novelist, in whose works Fairbairn took a deep interest.

The great scientific merits of Fairbairn were attested by the ablest of his contemporaries. As to his personal character, Mr. Pole supplies some interesting illustrations of its many-sidedness, and yet its intensity. No difficulty daunted him, and he was gifted with great intuitive powers. He was indefatigable and earnest in his work, and possessed an indomitable perseverance and a determination to excel. His correspondence was prodigious, yet he found time for reading—Goldsmith,

B B

Washington Irving, and Prescott being his favourite writers, though late in life he warmly appreciated George Eliot, Mrs. Craik (Dinah Mulock), and Mrs. Gaskell. He had no tastes for field sports, but was deeply interested in farming He was of most regular habits, was fond of companionship, was famed for his high-mindedness and integrity, and he hated all shams. He was liberal in thought, feeling, and action; he sympathised with suffering and distress, was simple in his tastes and wants, and never made mere money-getting his object. He was a modest, courteous gentleman, a most faithful friend, and an affectionate and indulgent parent. The moral he drew from his own career was that industry and perseverance must in the nature of things lead to success; and the records of English enterprise teem with examples in support of this.

I must now briefly follow the fortunes of other members of the Fairbairn family, who were, or are, identified with British industry. Sir Thomas Fairbairn, Sir William's son, and the present holder of the baronetcy, was born in 1823. He was educated privately. We learn that a long residence in Italy afforded him opportunities for the study and appreciation of art, and induced him to make efforts for its encouragement in England, especially in connection with education. He is a strenuous advocate of art teaching in schools. Sir Thomas is something more than the son of his father; he has always had a distinct individuality of his own, which won for him a reputation upon his own merits. We have seen that he entered his father's business, and he rendered valuable aid in the solution of many mechanical problems which arose in connection with the important undertakings of the firm. During the great contest of 1852 between the leading engineering machinist firms and their workmen—when upwards of 100,000 hands were out of employment for four months, Sir Thomas was one of the most prominent figures in the struggle. He contributed to *The Times* a long series of letters under the signature of 'Amicus.' These letters excited the widest interest and comment, the whole newspaper press entering into the controversy. Even by such friends of the working-classes as Lord Shaftesbury, it was felt that the men were on this occasion in the wrong, but they exhausted their savings in the vain hope of compelling their masters to give way. For many years after this 'Amicus' was a frequent contributor to *The Times* on questions of social, industrial, and political interest.

Sir Thomas Fairbairn has stated that he was taken away from an intended University career in 1840, and was engaged at Millwall until the final closing of the works. He acted as Chairman of the Exhibition of the Art Treasures of the United Kingdom at Manchester in 1857, and on Her Majesty's visit in June was offered the honour of knighthood, which he declined. He was one of Her Majesty's Commissioners for the Exhibition of 1851, and took an active part in the organisation of the Great Exhibition of 1862 in a similar capacity. In 1870 he was appointed High Sheriff of Hampshire, in which county he has a residence, and he is a magistrate and deputy-lieutenant for that county, as well as for his native county of Lancashire. Of the two other surviving sons of Sir William Fairbairn, one, William Andrew, left the engineering firm and became a private gentleman, while the other was a clergyman, the Rev. Adam Henderson Fairbairn, M.A., Vicar of Waltham St. Lawrence, Berks.

The Leeds branch of the Fairbairn family is of equal importance with the Manchester branch. Its founder was Sir Peter Fairbairn, Sir William's youngest brother. Peter was born in 1799, and like his brother he was compelled early to learn the valuable lesson of self-reliance and independence. His educational advantages were few in number, and at eleven years of age he was sent to work at the Percy Main Colliery. Here he remained for three years, and in 1814 he was apprenticed to Mr. John Casson, a millwright and engineer at Newcastle. Owing to his intelligence and diligence, he soon began to make his mark, and to gain the confidence and esteem of his employers. He was never ashamed of his origin, and the little breakfast-can which he always carried with him on his journeys between the farm-house at Percy Main and the millwright's shop in Newcastle, was preserved by him as a precious relic in the days of his prosperity. Mr. Holdsworth, a maker of cotton machinery at Glasgow, having seen Peter, and accurately read his capabilities, engaged him as his foreman. The experience he gained during his residence on the Clyde, and afterwards as traveller for the firm, proved invaluable to him in after years. In 1821 he left his service, and was for a brief period with his brother in Manchester. Then he was for a short time with Rennie, after which he had a year's experience with engineering firms in France. In 1823 he again entered his brother's service, but left it this time to accept a position as partner in the firm of Holdsworth & Co., of Glasgow.

Peter Fairbairn remained in Glasgow until 1828, and then went to Leeds, where he started business for himself as a machine maker. From this time forward until his death his name was associated with the enterprising Yorkshire town. Fairbairn played no insignificant part in the rapid development of Leeds during the second quarter of the nineteenth century. He first devoted himself to the improvement of flax-spinning machinery, and having, after almost insuperable difficulties, constructed the model of a new machine, he exhibited it to a large employer of labour, Mr. Marshall. The latter was so struck with it, that he ordered him to begin the manufacture of the new machine forthwith, promising to replace his old machines with them as fast as they could be made. 'It will be impossible for me to do that without assistance,' replied the inventor, 'for I have neither workshop nor money.' 'Never mind that,' said Mr. Marshall; 'the Wellington Foundry at the New Road end is to let; go and take it at once—I'll see that you're all right.' What followed is thus described by a writer in *Fortunes made in Business*:—

'Elated by this encouragement, Peter Fairbairn lost no time in following the advice given by his new patron, and was soon installed, with his models and machines, in the Wellington Foundry, which at that time was but an extremely humble and unpretentious establishment. In this quiet way was founded the giant concern which to-day covers some seven or eight acres of ground, and finds employment for from 2,000 to 3,000 work-people. From the time of his entering upon the tenancy of the Wellington Foundry, Peter Fairbairn's progress was rapid in the extreme. For a while Barney Calvert (his clerk) had to go to Mr. Marshall's counting-house at the end of every week for the money wherewith to pay the wages of the handful of mechanics employed; but this condition of dependence did not endure long; the establishment prospered so well that the proprietor was soon in a position to run alone. Orders poured in upon Peter Fairbairn fast, and each new improvement that he introduced secured him an accession of customers. He applied himself to the making of woollen as well as of flax machinery, and was successful with both. He is generally credited with being the first to substitute iron for wood in the construction of woollen machinery. It is not too much to say that by his achievements in the way of simplifying the mechanical processes in connection with the manufacture of flax, he gave great impetus to the trade, and was largely instrumental in preserving to Leeds its supremacy in this branch of the industrial arts.'

Though not an inventor of the highest order, Peter Fairbairn was undoubtedly an inventor of repute, but it was chiefly as an improver of machinery that his name became known all over the world. His improvements in flax- and hemp-preparing machinery in particular were invaluable, and greatly lessened the cost of production. He also effected a very serviceable improvement in the roving machine, and, together with Henry Houldsworth, he adapted what is known as the 'differential motion' to that machine, thereby greatly extending its power and simplifying its action. He further introduced the 'rotary gill,' which proved of great utility in the manufacture of tow. Among other services which he rendered to the manufacturing interest were the machines he introduced for preparing and spinning silk waste, and his improvements in the machinery for the making of rope-yarn. This indefatigable worker 'continued for several years to devote himself to the making of flax and woollen machinery; but as time wore on he began to turn his attention more to the art of constructing engineering tools, and of late years Wellington Foundry has been very largely employed in this branch of machine making. On the breaking out of the Crimean War his firm were requested by the Government to construct certain special tools to be used in the manufacture of implements of war; and since that time the Wellington Foundry has always been more or less engaged in turning out heavy work of this description. In the gun factories of Woolwich and Enfield may be seen in operation a variety of huge machines for cutting, twisting, boring, and tearing iron and steel, many of which machines are supplied by this firm. Machines for the manipulation of textiles are often very large; but machines for making machines are Brobdingnagian in comparison. Cannon-rifling machines, milling machines, boring machines, planing machines, and slotting machines are amongst the formidable mechanical contrivances which the Fairbairns have now occupied themselves in constructing for many years; and a walk through their foundry of eight acres is enough to suggest to the uninitiated the age of mammoths, so forcibly do the machines seem to typify the strength, size, and power of things gigantic.'

Like his brother, Peter Fairbairn was a man of indomitable perseverance, and although he was of a genial temperament in private life, and given to hospitality, he was a man of decided opinions, which he firmly held and expressed. He never had but one serious trade dispute with his men, and in this his determined character brought him off victorious. It was during the strike of 1833, when trade was in a critical condition. Having taken up what he considered to be a just position, and finding his work-people to be intractable, he engaged a number of untrained hands, whom he proceeded to teach their trade. His men retaliated by violent outbreaks, and on one occasion they attacked his house, smashed the dining-room window to atoms, and fired a pistol into the house to the imminent peril of his son and daughter. But Fairbairn held on, and eventually won the day.

In 1827 Fairbairn married a daughter of Mr. Robert Kennedy of Glasgow, by whom he had one son and two daughters. Elected to the Town Council of Leeds in 1835, Fairbairn continued to serve on that body for seven years. He was again elected in 1854, and made an alderman. He was next appointed to the magistracy, and in 1857 was elected mayor. His term of office was a memorable one, as the Queen and the Prince Consort visited Leeds in 1858 for the purpose of opening the new Town Hall. During the same year the British Association held its meetings in Leeds. Fairbairn presented to the town a marble statue of Her Majesty, executed by Noble at a cost of £1,000, and it was erected in the Town Hall. Fairbairn placed his mansion, Woodsley House, at the disposal of the Queen and her distinguished party during the Royal visit. His enterprise and munificence during his two years of office led Her Majesty to confer upon him the honour of knighthood. Sir Peter was a liberal supporter of the local charities, and of all movements for the encouragement of art and science; he likewise took a keen and intelligent interest in music and the drama, and was president of the Yorkshire Choral Union. To mark their appreciation of his public spirit, his fellow-townsmen subscribed for his portrait, which was executed by Sir Francis Grant, P.R.A., and hung in the Council

Chamber of the Town Hall, and they likewise commissioned a bronze statue of him by Noble. Sir Peter retired from municipal life in 1859, and died on the 4th of January, 1861. His first wife had died in 1843, and he was survived by his second wife, a daughter of Mr. R. W. Brandling, whom he married in 1855. By his energy, clear-headedness, and perseverance, Sir Peter Fairbairn succeeded in building up a great fortune, and establishing one of the largest industrial concerns in the North of England. On hearing of his death Sir Charles Phipps wrote to the son expressing the regret with which the Queen and the Prince Consort had heard of the decease of so excellent a man, and Sir Charles added, 'I had, I am happy to say, seen a good deal of your poor father, and it was impossible to be thrown into his society without respecting and valuing the sterling qualities of his truly English character.'

Andrew Fairbairn, Sir Peter's only son, was born at Anderston, Glasgow, on the 5th of March, 1828. He was educated at Leeds, and afterwards at Geneva, and with his tutor at the latter place, Professor Rodolphe Töpffer, he made several tours on foot through Switzerland. On one occasion they also went from Geneva to Venice and back. In 1842 he returned to England, and was sent to the High School of Glasgow. In October, 1846, he became a pensioner at Christ's College, Cambridge, but migrated to Peterhouse in January of the following year. He graduated in 1850, coming out as thirty-seventh wrangler, and in 1853 he took his M.A. degree. On leaving Cambridge he began to study for the Bar at the Inner Temple. He was called in 1852 and attended the West Riding Sessions and the Northern Circuit until 1856. He then relinquished practice, and after a visit to Germany he returned to Leeds and entered his father's business. 'Possessing the family instinct for industrial pursuits, he entered very heartily into the work which his father committed to his charge, and soon proved a valuable aid to the extension of the firm's connections. His educational training and knowledge of the world gave him considerable advantage in his subsequent dealings with spinners and manufacturers abroad, and year by year the productive capacity of the Wellington Foundry had to be enlarged. Sir Peter Fairbairn despatched his son in the first instance to Germany, where the firm had already many business friends; and Sir Andrew travelled over a great part of Bohemia, Moravia, Silesia, and Prussia, acquiring, as he went on, a close acquaintance with the practical working of the flax mills of Germany. He subsequently made similar journeys to France, Belgium, Switzerland, and Italy, and in the two latter countries obtained an insight into the waste-silk spinning trade. In 1858 Sir Andrew made a business tour to Russia, going from Grimsby to Cronstadt; and after visiting Moscow, Narva, and other centres of trade, returned to England by way of Warsaw and Vienna.'

Having acquired a knowledge of the various branches of mechanical engineering, Andrew Fairbairn was taken into partnership, and on the death of his father in the following year he succeeded to the entire business. In 1863, however, he took into partnership his cousin, Mr. T. S. Kennedy, and Mr. J. W. Naylor, who had been in the works since his fifteenth year, and who had risen through all the grades of the business. The firm thus constituted has since carried on the work of mechanical invention begun by Sir Peter Fairbairn, while the number of persons employed has increased three or fourfold. Andrew Fairbairn was even more deeply interested in the municipal affairs of Leeds than his father, and in 1866 he was elected mayor. Re-elected in 1867, he acted in May, 1868, as a Commissioner of the Leeds Exhibition of Fine Arts. The Prince of Wales inaugurated the exhibition, being a guest of the Mayor, and in the ensuing August Andrew Fairbairn received from the Queen a patent of knighthood. Sir Andrew resigned his mayoralty in September, 1868, in order to stand as Liberal candidate for Leeds, but he was unsuccessful at the polling-booths. He was again unsuccessful when he contested

Knaresborough in 1874. In 1880, however, he was elected for the Eastern Division of the West Riding, and when the Division was split up into six sub-divisions in 1885 he was chosen as the first representative of the Otley Division. He only represented this constituency, however, until the following year, and since 1886 he has not sat in Parliament.

From 1870 to 1878 Sir Andrew Fairbairn was chairman of the Leeds School Board. He retired in the latter year on the ground of the excessive expenditure of the board. In 1877 he was appointed a member of the Royal Commission for the Paris Exhibition; 'and in watching after the special interests of Leeds, and securing as far as possible the efficient representation of its machinery and manufactures, he displayed great zeal and energy.' Appointed to the Engineering and Agricultural Committee presided over by the Duke of Sutherland, he resided in Paris from March to the end of June, 1878. In 1885 Fairbairn was appointed Vice-President of the Railway Congress at Brussels, and was made a Knight Commander of the Order of Leopold by the King of the Belgians. Sir Andrew Fairbairn married in 1862 Clara Frederica, daughter of Sir John Lambton Loraine, Bart.

From this record of the principal members of the Fairbairn family, it will have been apparent how great must have been the impression they left upon the industries of the country. For some eighty years or so the brothers and their descendants have assisted in developing the resources of England, and in materially aiding its prosperity. Nor can the good they achieved be measured by their personal labours, for their example has stimulated many to the exercise of inventive skill and the advancement of science.

SIR WILLIAM SIEMENS.

SIR WILLIAM SIEMENS.

CHARLES WILLIAM SIEMENS—or, as his name was given before his naturalisation in England, Carl Wilhelm Siemens—was the fourth son of Christian Ferdinand Siemens, who was born at Wasserleben, on the northern edge of the Harz Mountains, in 1789. Ferdinand married early Eleonore Deichmann, a lady belonging to a North German family residing near Hanover. The young couple settled down at a small place called Lenthe, a few miles from Hanover, and here Ferdinand Siemens farmed and cultivated certain Government lands which had been assigned to him. William Siemens has left it on record that his father was healthy in body; of an energetic and restless disposition; passionate, yet tender-hearted; fond of historical studies and gifted with a receptive mind; independent in judgment; distinguished for a high moral standard, and his hatred of humbug and formalism; a fair classical scholar, but with no bias towards those scientific branches of enquiry in which his sons became so famous. Madame Siemens is described as having been of somewhat delicate health; possessed of a high-minded and self-sacrificing nature; gentle and amiable in character; strongly devoted to her children; refined and poetical in her tastes; and imbued with deep religious principles.

Ferdinand and Eleonore Siemens had no fewer than fourteen children—eleven sons and three daughters, of whom three sons and one daughter died in infancy. Ernst Werner von Siemens, the eldest son, was the founder of the fortunes of the family.

Born at Lenthe in 1816, he was educated at the Lübeck Gymnasium, and entered first, in 1834, the Prussian Artillery Service at Magdeburg, proceeding in the following year to the Military School of Berlin. Here he studied closely chemistry, mechanics, and mathematics. He gained his commission as lieutenant in 1838, and, after some experience in other capacities, in 1844 he was appointed Superintendent of the Artillery workshops at Berlin. He had already developed scientific tastes, and taken out his first patent for galvanic silver and gold plating. He rendered valuable service in developing the telegraphic system in Prussia, and discovered the important insulating property of gutta-percha for underground and submarine cables. Being somewhat hampered by his duties as a military officer, he left the army in 1849, and shortly afterwards quitted the service of the state altogether. He now devoted himself to the construction of telegraphic and chemical apparatus of all kinds. The eminent firm of Siemens & Halske was established at Berlin in 1847; and branches were subsequently formed at St. Petersburg, London, Vienna, and Tiflis—these being managed by Werner's younger brothers. In addition to devising various useful forms of galvanometers and other electrical instruments of precision, Werner von Siemens was one of the discoverers of the principle of the self-acting dynamos. He further made valuable determinations of the electrical resistance of different substances, one of his discoveries being known as the Siemens Unit. Scientific and technical papers by Siemens were published in the *Proceedings* of the Berlin Academy, in Poggendorff's *Annalen*, in Dingler's *Polytechnische Journal*, etc., and these papers were republished in collected form in 1881. The munificent sum of 500,000 marks was given by Siemens in 1886 in order to found an imperial institute of technology and physics. The University of Berlin made Werner von Siemens a Doctor in 1860; in 1874 he was elected a Member of the Royal Academy of Sciences of Berlin; in 1886 he was created a Knight of the Prussian Order of Merit; and finally, in 1888, the Emperor Frederick III. conferred upon him a patent of nobility.

Hans Siemens, the second son, born in 1818, after pursuing various avocations, established a large glass factory at Dresden, where he successfully applied in his undertakings the regenerative furnace invented by his brothers Frederick and William. He died nearly thirty years ago. Ferdinand, the third son, eventually settled as an agriculturist on a large estate which he purchased near Königsberg, in East Prussia. Passing by for the present William, the fourth son, we come to Friedrich, the fifth son. He was born in 1826, and became famous as an inventor, etc. In early life he was a sailor, but in 1848 he joined his brother William in England, studying under him, and remaining in this country for some years. On the death of his brother Hans, he became manager of the glass-works at Dresden, and so great was his success that he was able to found similar factories in Bohemia and Saxony, which ultimately gave employment to 2,000 workmen. Friedrich Siemens invented a continuously working glass furnace, and also discovered a new method of cooling which produced toughened glass of extraordinary resistance. He further constructed gas-burners with a greatly increased power of illumination. Upon the death of his brother William, Friedrich succeeded him in the management of that portion of the business associated with furnaces and heat applications. Carl Heinrich Siemens, the sixth son, born in 1829, was more known for his practical than inventive skill, and he had much to do with the success of the commercial undertakings founded by the brothers. In 1855 he took charge of a large branch factory established at St. Petersburg, which had the great telegraphic system of Russia within its control. He proceeded to London in 1869, and some years afterwards was engaged in the laying of the Direct United States Cable; but in 1880 he returned to Russia, where he continued to reside. Walter Siemens, the seventh son, born in 1832, was Prussian Consul at Tiflis. From here also he directed the extensive mining works in the Caucasus belonging to his brothers Werner and William. He likewise assisted in the management of the telegraph manufactory works at Tiflis, and in the establishment of the Indo-European Telegraph. Unfortunately, to the great grief of his family, he was killed by the kick of a horse in 1868. Otto Siemens, the eighth son, born in 1836, succeeded to his brother Walter's position, but he died prematurely in 1871. Two daughters of Ferdinand and Eleonore Siemens lived to the age of maturity. One, Mathilde, the eldest of the family, married in 1838 Herr Himly, Professor of Chemistry at the University of Göttingen, and afterwards at the University of Kiel. She died in 1876. The other daughter, Sophie, married Dr. Carl Crome of Lübeck, who in 1875 was called to be one of the Reihsgerichtstrath, or Supreme Court of Appeal, in Leipsic.

It will be seen from this brief summary, that the Siemens family has been gifted as well as numerous. I now turn to the main subject of this biographical sketch, Sir William Siemens, who was born at Lenthe, on April 4, 1823. Although after his naturalisation in England he retained the names of Charles William, he preferred to be known as William only. It is said that as a child he was fairly strong, though of a delicate and sensitive organisation. He was a great pet, and made music in the house; but when he was supplanted by the birth of a new baby his song was heard no more. He gave no indication in youth of a bias towards those pursuits which rendered his name famous. Educated first by a resident tutor at Menzendorf, he was next sent to a commercial academy at Lübeck. In 1838 he went to an industrial school at Magdeburg, where he was under the eye of his brother Werner, and where he studied the principles of natural science. In the early morning hours, before beginning his school duties, he studied mathematics under Werner's tuition. Young William had a severe trial in 1839, when he lost his mother, whom he passionately loved. Soon afterwards—in January, 1840—came the death of his father, upon which Werner, who was only then twenty-three years of age, assumed with noble courage and devotion the guardianship of the family.

At Easter, 1841, William Siemens left the Magdeburg School, with an excellent record in algebra, geometry, trigonometry, and physical and technical subjects. He had a fluent command of his own language, and some knowledge of French. The opportunities for real scientific training at Magdeburg, however, had been very limited. Siemens now went for a year's study at Göttingen University, where he attended lectures on physical geography and technology, the higher mathematics, and theoretical and practical chemistry and physics. He seems to have worked very earnestly during this short university experience. In the year 1843, being then only twenty years of age, young Siemens visited England, and succeeded in introducing a process for electro-gilding invented by his brother Werner and himself. It was in Birmingham that he did this, and thirty-eight years afterwards he described the circumstances in his inaugural address as President of the Midland Institute. That address was delivered in the Town Hall, Birmingham, on October 28th, 1881, and I quote from it the following autobiographical passages, as being both interesting and instructive :—' That form of energy known as the electric current was nothing more than the philosopher's delight forty years ago ; its first application may be traced to this good town of Birmingham, where Mr. George Richards Elkington, utilising the discoveries of Davy, Faraday, and Jacobi, had established a practical process of electro-plating in 1842. It affords me great satisfaction to be able to state that I had something to do with that first practical application of electricity ; for in March of the following year, 1843, I presented myself before Mr. Elkington with an improvement on his processes which he adopted, and in so doing gave me my first start in practical life. Considering the moral lesson involved, it may interest you, perhaps, if I diverge for a few minutes from my subject in order to relate a personal incident connected with this my first appearance amongst you.

'When the electrotype process first became known it excited a very general interest; and although I was only a young student of Göttingen, under twenty years of age, who had just entered upon his practical career with a mechanical engineer, I joined my brother, Werner Siemens, then a young lieutenant of artillery in the Prussian service, in his endeavour to accomplish electro-gilding, the first impulse in this direction having been given by Professor C. Himly, then of Göttingen.

'After attaining some promising results, a spirit of enterprise came over me so strong that I tore myself away from the narrow circumstances surrounding me, and landed at the East End of London with only a few pounds in my pocket and without friends, but an ardent confidence of ultimate success within my breast.

'I expected to find some office in which inventions were examined into, and rewarded if found meritorious, but no one could direct me to such a place. In walking along Finsbury Pavement I saw written up in large letters "So-and-So," (I forget the name), "Undertaker," and the thought struck me that this must be the place I was in quest of; at any rate I thought that a person advertising himself as an "Undertaker" would not refuse to look into my invention, with the view of obtaining for me the sought-for recognition or reward. On entering the place I soon convinced myself, however, that I came decidedly too soon for the kind of enterprise there contemplated, and finding myself confronted by the proprietor of of the establishment, I covered my retreat by what he must have thought a very lame excuse.

'By dint of perseverance I found my way to the Patent Office of Messrs. Poole & Carpmael, who received me kindly, and provided me with a letter of introduction to Mr. Elkington. Armed with this letter, I proceeded to Birmingham to plead my cause with your countryman.

'In looking back to that time, I wonder at the patience with which Mr. Elkington listened to what I had to say, being very young, and scarcely able to find English words to convey my meaning. After showing me what he was doing already in the way of electro-plating, Mr. Elkington sent me back to London in order to read some patents of his own, asking me to return if, after perusal, I still thought I could teach him anything. To my great disappointment I found that the chemical solutions I had been using were actually mentioned in one of his patents, although in a manner that would hardly have sufficed to enable a third person to obtain practical results.

'On my return to Birmingham I frankly stated what I had found, and with this frankness evidently gained the favour of another townsman of yours, Mr. Josiah Mason, who had just joined Mr. Elkington in business, and whose name as Sir Josiah Mason will ever be remembered for his munificent endowment for education. It was agreed that I should not be judged by the novelty of my invention, but by the results which I promised, namely, of being able to deposit with a smooth surface thirty pennyweights of silver upon a dish cover, the crystalline structure of the deposit having theretofore been a source of difficulty.

'In this I succeeded, and I was able to return to my native country and my mechanical engineering a comparative Crœsus. By dint of a certain determination to win, I was able to advance step by step up to this place of honour, situate within a gunshot of the scene of my very earliest success in life, but separated from it by the time of a generation. But notwithstanding the lapse of time, my heart still beats quick each time I come back to the scene of this, the determining incident of my life.'

A patent was taken out by the Elkingtons on the 25th of May, 1843, in the name of Moses Poole, embodying the discovery. The title was for 'Improvements in the deposition of certain metals, and in apparatus connected therewith.' The invention consisted in the employment of certain new solutions of gold, silver, and copper, for the purposes of electrical deposition, and in the application of a thermo-electrical battery for depositing the same. This battery was also included in the patent, and it was described as being used 'for the purpose of generating electrical currents applicable to the deposition of metals.' Mr. Pole, Siemens's biographer, states that Messrs. Elkington paid the young inventor the sum of £1,600 for his rights, less £110, the cost of the patent. Not bad that for the first work upon which he was engaged. When the triumphant inventor returned to Germany he was looked upon by his family as quite a Crœsus.

The brothers Werner and William now took a third person into their confidence, a clever mechanic named Leonhard, who assisted them in perfecting their inventions. In 1844 William Siemens paid a second visit to England, and patented his differential governor. In describing this new invention, Mr. Pole remarks that 'steam-engines for turning machinery have always been liable to irregularities in their velocity of motion, arising partly from variations in the steam-pressure, and partly from variable resistances in the work done.' Various contrivances were tried at different times to equalise the motion, Watt's governor up to this period having been the most successful. Siemens's invention, however, was a great advance. Its novel feature, 'the added uniform motor, acted as a timekeeper, with which the motion of the engine could be compared, and this gave to the invention the name of the Chronometric Governor.' In bringing it forward Siemens associated with himself a civil engineer of repute named Joseph Woods. An attempt to dispose of the patent for a large sum failed, and it became necessary for the inventors to supply the manufacturers with machines for the purpose of trying them. Mr. Woods read a paper on the Governor before the Institution of Civil Engineers, and Robert Stephenson, John Penn, and others spoke warmly of its merits. A model of the machine was exhibited at the International Exhibition of 1851, and it was awarded a prize medal.

Another invention introduced by Siemens in 1844 was that of anastatic printing. Its originator was a Mr. Baldamus of Erfurt, but the brothers Siemens took it up and perfected it, and William produced the first roller quick printing press that had been used in the trade. A patent was taken out for the new process, entitled, 'Improvements in producing and multiplying copies of designs and impressions of printed or written surfaces.' The patent embraced two objects: first, a mode of obtaining on metallic surfaces reversed facsimiles of typography, engravings, designs, writings, etc.; and secondly, mechanical presses for printing impressions from such reversed facsimiles. Great efforts were made to push the invention, and Faraday lectured upon it at the Royal Institution; but the experiments proved so costly and unremunerative that Siemens abandoned the thing altogether, and it was ultimately superseded by other processes.

Meantime, even the inventions of proved value already described caused William Siemens great concern. Large sums of money subscribed by his family and others, as well as amounts of his own, kept going out in a constant stream, while no return came in. This led in time to recriminations and dissensions, so that the future which had once seemed so bright began to wear another hue. But by the aid of some railway work, Siemens was able to return to Germany in 1845, and settle certain urgent private affairs. In 1846 the brothers resolved to abandon the joint working of the patents. William relieved his brother of all responsibility, and took the whole matter upon his own shoulders. His difficulties just at this time were enough to crush almost any man. Yet he went on inventing, and brought out an improvement in the manner of exhausting air by mechanical power. Although it did not yield him any profit, it was used afterwards with success.

Having paid a visit to the manufacturing districts of Lancashire in the autumn of 1846, Siemens took a place in Manchester early in the following year. He entered upon various engineering matters, and had also an engagement at the large print works of Messrs. Hoyle & Sons, but his main investigations were into the nature of steam-power. He had already studied the theory of heat and the conservation of energy, and had kept up with all the recent discoveries in connection therewith. As the result of experiments now made by Siemens, he was enabled to take out a patent in December, 1847, for 'Improvements in engines to be worked by steam and other fluids.' Negotiations were set on foot with an eminent manufacturing firm, Messrs. Fox, Henderson & Co. of Smethwick, near Birmingham. Trial was made of a new engine constructed by Siemens, and in the end the inventor entered the manufactory of Fox, Henderson & Co., receiving not only his interest in the patents, but a fixed salary of £400 per annum. He was now relieved from pecuniary anxiety, and forthwith took up his residence in one of the suburbs of Birmingham. His brother Frederick afterwards joined him as assistant under the same firm. The chief engineering manager of the firm, Mr. Edward Cowper, remained the firm friend of William Siemens all through life, 'and gave him essential support in his later heat-inventions.'

This regenerative steam-engine, as Siemens's machine was called, was ingenious and remarkable, but the difficulties attending the invention prevented its commercial introduction. In 1850, however, the Society of Arts awarded Siemens a gold medal for his regenerative condenser. In a paper read before the Institution of Mechanical Engineers in 1851, the inventor gave a short historic sketch of the steam-engine condenser generally, explaining his new arrangement, and its mode of application to different forms of engine. At the close of 1852 Siemens's relations with Fox, Henderson & Co. were terminated, the losses and difficulties sustained by the firm having led to friction with the inventor. William Siemens now took up the electrical work which afterwards developed so rapidly. He began by making known in England the telegraphic inventions of Siemens & Halske, whose works in Germany had already become of an extensive character. In 1849 he read a paper at the Society of Arts descriptive of his brother's telegraphic achievements, and in the following year an English agency was successfully established. An agreement was signed between the two brothers. In March, 1850, William Siemens introduced his brother's gutta-percha wire-covering to the British Electric Telegraphic Company, and soon afterwards he carried out an arrangement for working the manufacture in Great Britain. He next induced Fox, Henderson & Co., to take up the work, and under his direction large contracts were executed by that firm and Siemens & Halske for the Lancashire and Yorkshire Railway Company, etc.

In March, 1852, Siemens went to London, establishing himself as a civil engineer in John Street, Adelphi. He undertook this year an important series of experiments on the total heat of steam, and its expansion when in an isolated state. But improvements in his regenerative steam-engine soon began to occupy him once more, and to carry out these he returned to Birmingham, the old firm with which he had been connected still taking an interest in the work. Shortly afterwards he wrote an elaborate treatise with the object of explaining the scientific principles on which his invention was based, as well as expounding the doctrines and practice affecting heat as a source of mechanical power. This composition, entitled 'On the Conversion of Heat into Mechanical Effect,' was read at the Institution of Civil Engineers on May 17, 1853. The paper was divided into three sections, which dealt respectively with the Relations between Heat and Mechanical Effect, the Performances of Actual Engines, including Heated-Air Engines, and the Necessary Characteristics of a Perfect Engine. This paper gained for Siemens the Telford premium and silver medal awarded by the Institution. It was subsequently translated into Italian. The inventor undertook to produce one of his improved engines, and this was finished in March, 1854. It was of fifteen horse-power, and had a satisfactory trial in January, 1855. Several engines were afterwards constructed for England, France, and Germany, which varied in size from five to forty horse-power. Two were shown and worked at the Paris Exhibition of 1855, where the invention was awarded a first class medal. The inventor claimed by this machine to provide a motive force at one-third or one-fourth part of the cost and encumbrance of the existing steam-engine. A company was formed in Genoa for the purpose of manufacturing the engine, and it had branches in Paris, Vienna, Liège, and other continental cities. Accidents and ill-fortune, however, attended the construction of the machines, and the enterprise was abandoned in 1859.

Siemens continued to make further experiments in heat, but the practical difficulties in connection with his machines ended in discouragement. This was also the case with his invention for regenerative evaporation. Mr. Pole observes with regard to these experiments: 'The regenerative principle was undoubtedly sound, and he had devoted ten or twelve of the best years of his life to its application, during which time he had the support of many eminent engineers, the practical aid of two of the best manufacturing firms in the country, and the funds of a powerful commercial association. Neither theoretical knowledge, nor practical experience, nor ingenuity, nor skill, nor money, nor perseverance, nor influence, was wanting. But in spite of their promised advantages, the regenerative steam-engine would not supplant the simple machine of Watt, nor would the regenerative evaporator supersede the old-fashioned sugar and salt pans.

'It is hard now to explain these failures. Probably they arose from the aims being too high, and from the introduction of more complication than the nature of the machines would bear.

'In the steam-engine, for example, instead of the simple plan of evaporating and re-condensing water, in which the most ordinary machine could hardly go astray, there was substituted the alternate heating to a very high temperature, and re-cooling, with the aid of the regenerator, of a permanent elastic fluid, which introduced not only a more elaborate construction, but new difficulties in the management, in consequence of the more intense heat applied in the working parts of the machine.

'And with the regenerative evaporator the more complex arrangements required larger outlay of capital, with greater trouble in working, and sometimes endangered the quality of the manufactured article.

'These difficulties were courageously attacked by Mr. Siemens's inventive ingenuity, and there is no doubt that in many cases satisfactory results were attained by the new machines; but on the whole the long and repeated trials showed that the complications and difficulties introduced were not commercially compensated for by the advantages gained in the saving of fuel.'

But all these preliminary labours were not to prove abortive. A happy thought occurred to Frederick Siemens that the regenerative principle to which his brother had given so much attention 'might be made available in a much more simple manner by applying it directly to the ordinary furnaces in which the fuel was consumed. It was well known that in the working of powerful furnaces, the smoke and gases resulting from the combustion passed away into the atmosphere at a very high heat, while the air supplying the fire was drawn in at the ordinary atmospheric temperature. All therefore that the inventor here proposed to do, was to apply the regenerative principle by means of a "respirator," so arranged as to intercept and absorb the superfluous heat from the escaping gases, and to give it out again in heating the air used to feed the fire. In this way not only would waste be prevented, but the intensity of action of the furnace might be much increased.' Working upon these lines, William perfected the idea by experiments, and a patent was taken out in December, 1856, in the name of Frederick Siemens, for an 'Improved arrangement of furnaces; which improvements are applicable in all cases where great heat is required.' The principal object of the invention was thus described: 'Constructing furnaces in such manner that the heat of the products of combustion is absorbed by passing the same through chambers containing refractory materials so arranged as to present extensive heat-absorbing surfaces; and is communicated to currents of air or other gases by passing the latter currents alternately over the same heated surfaces.' The invention excited deep interest when it was described by William Siemens in a paper read before the Institution of Mechanical Engineers on the 24th of June, 1857.

Experiments were soon set on foot, and furnaces were erected on the new principle at Sheffield and Wednesbury—in the former case the application being to the melting and re-heating of steel; and in the latter case to the re-heating of iron. At length Siemens had his triumph, for the furnaces succeeded, and the saving of fuel was much greater even than had been expected. There were still formidable difficulties to overcome in finding materials sufficiently refractory to withstand the more intense heat produced, but these were ultimately surmounted. Mr. E. A. Cowper next made an important and successful application of the furnace to the heating of the air for hot-blast iron-smelting furnaces. This was patented, and later Siemens gave Cowper his assistance in regard to further improvements, and several patents were taken out in their joint names. The invention was soon extensively used in all iron-making countries, its advantages including great saving of fuel, no leakage, no wear and tear of pipes, and an increased make of iron. In the course of twenty or thirty years, the savings in the iron trade by the process amounted to £500,000 per annum.

Among William Siemens's other early inventions were,

improvements in calico printing, the introduction of a double-cylinder air-pump, and a new refrigerating machine. But none of these achieved such a remarkable success as his new meter for measuring water, brought out in 1851. This instrument, which was called a 'Fluid Meter,' was patented in 1852. Its characteristics were thus described: 'Various arrangements of screws or helices, which are caused to revolve by the passage of water or other fluid through them, and of fixed guides and channels in connection with such screws or helices to regulate and direct the current of the fluid, together with various contrivances for registering the number of revolutions of the screws.' Although the instrument was simple, the preliminary experiments were arduous. In 1853 a second patent was taken out by Siemens in conjunction with Mr. Joseph Adamson, a Leeds engineer, who had suggested improvements in various points. The new patent proved to be so simple and efficient in character that a hundred meters were soon ordered, and the demand continued to increase. The machine was adopted extensively in England, Europe, and the United States. Its principle was explained at the Institution of Mechanical Engineers in July, 1856, when Siemens claimed to have been the first to bring into use a meter which would work with a high water-pressure. When the patent had only been in operation for a year, it was already beginning to secure Siemens a handsome income. For many years, the royalties in Great Britain alone amounted to upwards of £1,000 a year. The Siemens water-meter proved to be one of the most useful hydraulic machines ever invented. By the close of 1885 nearly 130,000 meters had been sold by the inventor's English firm of agents alone.

The great question of telegraphic submarine cables next engaged Siemens's attention, and it was not long before the business assumed enormous proportions. As early as 1847 an English telegraph engineer named Brett obtained a provisional concession from the French Government for a cable between

England and France, but on account of the supposed impracticability of the project the concession was allowed to lapse. In August, 1850, as the result of experiments by Mr. C. V. Walker, an electrical engineer, a submarine cable was actually laid across the Strait from Dover to Cape Grisnez. It consisted of a copper wire only, covered with gutta-percha, but with no other protection. Nevertheless, a few messages were successfully transmitted, but as the wire refused to act on the following day, when the French official engineers arrived to test it, the concession was cancelled. It appears that a French fisherman had cut a piece out of the cable, and exhibited it in triumph at Boulogne as a rare specimen of seaweed with its centre filled with gold! A third concession was obtained in 1851, a Submarine Telegraph Company was formed, and owing to the efforts of Mr. Thomas Crampton, a shareholder of the Company, a cable was successfully laid across the Channel in September of the above year. 'It was twenty-four miles long, consisting of four copper wires, insulated by gutta-percha, covered with tarred yarn, and protected by an outer covering of galvanised iron wires. It has remained perfect to the present time, and still forms one of the communications between the two countries.' Other cables now followed in quick succession. Messrs. Newall & Co., of Gateshead, large wire rope makers, seeing the great demand springing up, laid out works for the construction of submarine cables on an extensive scale. They engaged Siemens & Halske as their electrical and consulting engineers, and William Siemens carried out the tests. During 1858-1859 the following cables were laid down under the auspices of Messrs. Siemens: from Bona, in Algeria, to Cagliari, in Sardinia, for the French Government; from Cagliari to Malta and Corfu, for the Mediterranean Extension Company; from the Dardanelles to Scio and Candia, for the Levant Company; from Syra to Scio, for the Greek Government; from Singapore to Batavia, for the Dutch Government; from Weymouth to the Channel Islands; from Suez to Suakim and Aden, and from

Aden to Kurrachee, for the Red Sea and India Telegraph Company. Siemens likewise devoted himself to electrical work on his own account, and between 1854 and 1859 took out four patents for his own and Werner Siemens's improvements of various kinds in telegraphic detail. William Siemens further set up a London workshop for the manufacture of telegraph materials. It was capable of employing about 100 workmen, and was situate in Millbank Row, Westminster—a central position, which was also favourable for carrying on experiments in other fields.

Speaking of Siemens's domestic life, Mr. Pole says that in 1852 he entered the family of Mr. William Hawes, a well-known professor of music, and father of the celebrated contralto Maria B. Hawes. Their house was in Adelphi Terrace, and during his residence here he was tenderly nursed by the Hawes family through a severe attack of typhus fever. In 1855, he rented a house in Kensington Crescent, taking his brothers Frederick and Otto to reside with him. He was now able to receive friends, and was well acquainted with many of the eminent foreigners who sought refuge in this country after the political convulsions of 1848. Among them were Semper, the renowned architect, Richard Wagner, Bucher (with whom he was intimate, although not agreeing with his political views), Kinkel, whose son he at a later period took into his employment, and the brothers Luigi and Alphonso Scalia, with whom he formed a true friendship that never flagged, even after the brothers left for Italy to join the ranks of Garibaldi. He visited at the houses of many friends, where he occasionally met men eminent in literature, art, or science, and in this way he became personally intimate with many of the leading men among his professional brethren. Siemens was thrown much into contact with Mr. Lewis Gordon, Professor of Engineering in the University of Glasgow, who had married a Hanoverian lady, and a family connection of Siemens. An attachment sprang up between Siemens and Miss Anne Gordon, the youngest sister of the Professor. It was at this time that Siemens formally naturalised himself in England, 'and on the 19th March, 1859, as he used amusingly to say, he took oath and allegiance to two ladies in one day—the Queen, and his chosen partner in life.' Miss Gordon was an excellent singer, having studied under Manuel Garcia. Her marriage with Siemens took place on the 23rd of July, 1859, and the honeymoon was spent in Germany. The union was a thoroughly happy one.

In December, 1860, Siemens was elected a full member of the Institution of Civil Engineers. He was then put up for the Royal Society, his nomination paper being signed by Hawkshaw, Bateman, Airy, Faraday, Percy, Thomson, Wheatstone, Rennie, Joule, and others. On the 5th of June, 1862, he was elected a Fellow. Siemens was at this time carrying forward his experiments with the regenerative furnace, the object being to provide such materials, and to arrange such a construction of furnace, as should in practical use withstand the great heat produced. Many of the early failures to achieve this resulted in the destruction of the furnace itself, or of its accessories. 'In the course of these trials,' remarks Mr. Pole, 'a modification suggested itself to the two brothers, of such a character as to amount to a most important new invention. It was found that the use of solid fuel, in the body of the furnace, offered obstacles to the favourable working of the system, and the idea arose of substituting *gaseous* fuel, the solid fuel being converted into combustible gases in a separate construction called a "gas producer."

'This was patented 22nd January, 1861, in the names of the two brothers jointly. The patent said: "It is an essential part of our invention that the solid fuel should be decomposed in a separate apparatus, so that the introduction of solid fuel into the furnace may be altogether avoided; and independently of the advantage that results from heating the gaseous fuel prior to its entering into combustion, there is a great advantage derived from the absence of any solid carbon or ashes in the working chamber of the furnace, by which we are enabled to carry on operations in the furnace which it has only been possible hitherto to conduct in covered vessels or pots." The specification described various modifications of furnaces having "gas generators" of this kind.

'The new invention was described by William Siemens in a second paper read to the Institution of Mechanical Engineers on 30th January, 1862. After alluding to this original form of the furnace, he said :—

'" In attempting, however, to apply the principle to puddling and other larger furnaces, serious practical difficulties arose, which for a considerable time frustrated all efforts, until by adopting the plan of volatilising the solid fuel in the first instance, and employing it entirely in a gaseous form for heating purposes, practical results were at length attained surpassing even the most sanguine expectations previously formed.

'" The fuel employed, which may be of a very inferior description, is separately converted into a crude gas, which being conducted to the furnace has its naturally low heating power greatly increased by being heated to nearly the high temperature of the furnace itself, undergoing at the same time certain chemical changes whereby the heat developed in its subsequent combustion is increased. The heating effect is still further augmented by the air necessary for combustion being also heated separately to the same high temperature."'

A patent was secured, and gas furnaces were constructed, some of which saved fifty per cent. of fuel. Messrs. Chance, the large glass manufacturers near Birmingham, speedily had thirteen of the furnaces in use, together with a special one for optical lighthouse lenses, a manufacture requiring special care and perfection. Siemens explained the furnace to Faraday, who lectured upon it at the Royal Institution, his address on that occasion being the last he ever delivered. Siemens frequently spoke afterwards of the great delight with which he had spent two days in the company of Faraday. The regenerative gas furnace soon became a pecuniary success from its enormous saving of fuel. The furnace was awarded a Grand Prize at the Paris Exbibition of 1867.

Siemens now sought to apply his regenerative furnace to the process of puddling—that is, the formation of malleable iron from the pig, or cast, iron produced by smelting the ore. He constructed a puddling furnace, which he described in a paper read before the British Association. The communication was deemed so important that the Council ordered it to be published *in extenso*, an honour rarely accorded. Siemens stated in this paper that, after a careful scientific analysis, he had come to the conclusion that the process of puddling, as then practised, was extremely wasteful in iron and fuel, immensely laborious, and that it yielded a metal only imperfectly separated from its impurities. The inventor could not do much with the furnace as regards iron, but with regard to steel he made a very remarkable and successful application of the regenerative furnace. As his biographer notes, this proved to be one of the most important labours of his life. In 1722 Réaumur, the eminent French philosopher, had devised a method for making steel by fusing malleable iron with cast steel. Some time later a practical steel-maker named Heath, of Sheffield, made experiments on the same lines. At length the Bessemer process, introduced between 1856 and 1860, enabled steel to be produced on a large scale and at a cheap rate. But the process required a peculiar and cumbersome apparatus. Siemens Brothers contemplated the application of the gas furnace to steelmaking by the terms of their patent of January, 1861. Describing the furnace, the patent said it might be employed with advantage for smelting iron, for making steel, or for roasting copper and other ores. It appears that the general opinion of practical men was opposed to the idea, but William Siemens resolutely set himself to prove its feasibility. Messrs. Martin, steel and iron manufacturers, of Sireuil, in the Department of the Charente, succeeded under Siemens's direction not only in melting steel already made, but in effecting the production of the metal itself by his process. Siemens himself took premises in Birmingham, and succeeded in perfecting his experiments for making steel. In 1868 the Landore Works, near Swansea, were opened for the manufacture of steel by the Siemens process. By the year 1881 the annual production of steel in England under Sir William's process was upwards of 340,000 tons.

Among minor matters, Siemens was requested by the Government in 1867 to give his advice with regard to checking the recoil in gun-carriages. He recommended hydraulic compression; but, although his suggestion was adopted, no acknowledgment was made of his services in the matter. In 1866 he extended the scope and usefulness of his chronometric governor, which he asserted was capable of securing a really uniform rotation in mechanism. He demonstrated that it would apply to clocks and other things, and took out a patent for his improved governor. It was eventually used for a purpose he had not contemplated. 'It had been remarked that in regulating the speed of an engine, the machine acted to some extent as an absorber of surplus power, and this suggested the idea of applying it as a substitute for the treadmill or crank, in forced prison labour. It was thus used in the gaols of Liverpool, Manchester, Leicester, Stafford, and elsewhere, giving every satisfaction.' In 1861 the firm of Siemens & Halske acted as electricians for the Government in the laying down of the Malta and Alexandria Cable. The cable was divided into three sections, viz., Malta and Tripoli, Tripoli and Benghazi, and Benghazi and Alexandria, and the total length was about 1,350 miles. Werner and William Siemens wrote a joint paper about this time for the British Association, embodying their studies of the 'Principles and Practice involved in dealing with the Electric Conditions of Submarine Electric Telegraphs.' They recommended india-rubber as an insulator, and devised an ingenious machine for applying it to cables. William Siemens contributed to the Institution of Civil Engineers an elaborate paper 'On the Electrical Tests employed during the Construction of the Malta and Alexandria Telegraph, and on Insulating and Protecting Submarine Cables.' At the International Exhibition of 1862 Siemens & Halske exhibited a great variety of electrical apparatus of various kinds, appearing both as British and as foreign exhibitors. The collection attracted wide notice, and was awarded three separate medals. William Siemens wrote an article in the *Practical Mechanic's Journal*, giving a full description of the collection, as well as a history of the electric telegraph. In 1860 he gave evidence before a Committee appointed by the Board of Trade on the best form for the composition and outer covering of submarine telegraph cables.

In 1863 William Siemens, with the aid of the Berlin firm, established large works at Charlton, near Woolwich, for the manufacture of all kinds of telegraph instruments, apparatus, and materials, including submarine cables, which could thus be shipped from the River Thames for direct transport. At the close of the following year Mr. Halske retired from the London firm, and it was reconstituted at the beginning of 1865 under the name of Siemens Brothers. The partners were Werner Siemens, William Siemens, and Carl Siemens. The Berlin firm retained its old name of Siemens & Halske. The works at Charlton grew so rapidly as to necessitate the employment of some 3,000 men. The Algerian Cable was the first work undertaken by the new firm. It was laid between Oran, on the Algerian coast, and Carthagena, in Spain, and was about 140 miles long. Werner and William Siemens personally superintended the laying of the cable. After it had been successfully completed, under great difficulties, the cable unfortunately broke ten miles from Carthagena, upon the edge of a precipice which descends almost perpendicularly from comparatively shallow water to 2,800 metres. The contract involved the Siemens firm in legal proceedings and financial loss, and the disaster affected William Siemens keenly. No considerable portion of the cable was ever recovered, and the French Government laid down an alternative line.

However, in 1868-69, the Berlin and London firms 'executed jointly a work of great national importance and of high responsibility, namely, the establishment of a line of land telegraphs forming a direct communication between England and India, and afterwards known by the name of the Indo-European Telegraph.' Messrs. Siemens obtained concessions from the Prussian, Russian, and Persian Governments, and the Indo-European Telegraph Company was formed in alliance with the Electric and International Telegraph Company. Half the capital was subscribed before the issue of the prospectus, and the rest immediately afterwards. The construction of the line was begun in June, 1868, and completed by the 10th December, 1869. The total length of the various sections was no less than 2,750 miles. The line went through Russian and Persian territory, from the Prussian frontier to Teheran, so connecting the existing Prussian system—and through it the British Islands—with the lines of the Indian Government. 'The complete line from England to India, as worked by the Company, passes from London to Lowestoft, thence by submarine cable to Norderney, then by Emden and Berlin to Thorn, on the eastern frontier of Prussia, and thence by Messrs. Siemens's new line to Teheran, and so by the Indian Government lines to all parts of India. In order to give the Company complete control over the communication, the Prussian Government agreed that there should be laid down, for their exclusive use, two additional wires, with separate posts, and under separate management, through their district, from Norderney to Thorn. By this arrangement, therefore, the whole communication from England to India is kept in British hands.' Serious obstacles were encountered in laying the cable, especially that portion of it crossing the Caucasus and the Black Sea. The following interesting passage is from Mr. Pole's description:—

'The construction of the line involved great difficulties, partly by physical obstacles, but chiefly by the fact of the line passing through an uncommercial and unsettled country, peopled in some parts by only semi-civilized races.

'In the first place, it was not an easy matter to get the necessary apparatus delivered upon the ground. The materials for the Persian portion of the line, consisting of 11,000 iron posts, 33,400 insulators, and 900 miles of wire of large section, were shipped to St. Petersburg, whence they were transported on the Neva and the Volga to Astrakhan, and again shipped across the Caspian for Lenkoran, Astara, and Recht, the northern parts of Persia. At these ports it was found difficult to get beasts of burden to distribute the materials in the interior of the country within the prescribed time.

'Then, when the materials were on the ground, their fixing met with new obstacles of a strange and unusual nature. The Circassians, who were often roaming about armed, and who had but little respect for law and order, used to find amusement in firing at the insulators, upsetting the posts, and damaging the wires; and until they could be brought to good behaviour, the workmen and inspectors were obliged often to work and go about under a guard of Russian soldiers.

'Then some curious difficulties were found from the effects of great cold in winter, combined with some peculiar conditions of moisture in the air. Occasionally the wires would become surrounded with envelopes of frozen dew, increasing to some inches in diameter, which would weigh down the wires, or would break up into separate beads, hanging like huge necklaces between the poles. These conditions rendered necessary either extra strong wires, or short bearings, where they were found likely to occur.

'Then there were other evils. At some periods large

numbers of the men were invalided by fever or other diseases, and one of the best German members of the staff died. There also occurred frequent quarrels with the natives, sometimes carried to bloodshed. In one instance a good native servant was beheaded by swift native law, on a groundless charge of shooting a villager.

'But the good temper and spirit of the officers carried them through their difficulties, which, indeed, they often viewed on the amusing side.'

Besides taking out several patents at this time for improvements in the details of electrical apparatus, Siemens devised a new form of the Electrical Resistance Measurer—one of singular practical utility for cheapness and simplicity of construction, ease of manipulation, portability, and capability of employment with exactness by unskilled and inexperienced operators.

Siemens's principal recreation was in travelling, and on his excursions abroad—with the exception of a business journey to the Black Sea—he was accompanied by his wife. In the autumn of 1860 they visited Germany, and were present at a great meeting at Coburg on behalf of German unity. At Dresden they examined the fine glass-works of Hans Siemens. In August, 1862, they again made a tour in Germany, which was extended to Austria and Styria. Many interesting cities were visited, the travellers returning by Salzburg and the Salzkammergut, Dresden, and Berlin. During this same year Siemens found it necessary to reside permanently in London, so he took a house called Aubrey Lodge, on Campden Hill, the highest point of Western London. Here he resided until 1870, and he would frequently entertain, with his wife, distinguished representatives of science, art, and literature. During this period Siemens delivered many lectures and addresses to the members of scientific and other institutions, and on one occasion he gave great delight to the boys of the City of London School by a series of interesting experiments. In the spring of

1866 Mr. and Mrs. Siemens travelled through Italy, and subsequently visited Berlin, the occasion being made memorable by the meeting in the Prussian capital of the five brothers—Werner, William, Frederick, Carl, and Walter Siemens. Later in the year William Siemens was seized with serious illness, but a long stay at Bonchurch, in the Isle of Wight, restored him to comparative health. In March, 1867, he was called upon to attend the funeral of his brother Hans at Dresden. Fifteen months later he sustained another severe loss by the death of his brother Walter, who met with a violent end in the manner already indicated. In September, 1868, Siemens took a holiday in Switzerland, but the rough climbing over glaciers, etc., caused him much fatigue and subsequent suffering.

By the year 1870 Siemens had achieved both a reputation and a competence, and as the accumulation of money had never been his chief object, he was now glad to have the opportunity of enjoying the delights of intellectual life, and of mingling in literary and scientific gatherings and labours. At the same time, the next ten years of his life, while not so arduous as the preceding ten years, were as active as any period in his life, and marked by the perfecting of many miscellaneous inventions. In 1873 the Landore Steel Works were making about 1,000 tons of steel weekly, the fourth largest output in the world. The Chief Constructor of the Royal Navy having expressed his belief that vessels could be made of steel instead of the heavy plated iron, Siemens conducted a series of experiments with this object, producing a light steel of superior quality. The result was that he obtained a contract from the Admiralty for the production of the plates, angles, and beams to be used in the construction of two armed despatch vessels, the *Iris* and the *Mercury*, to be built at Pembroke Dockyard. The work was satisfactorily executed, and the steel stood the most stringent tests. Although the Landore Works acquired great fame, however, for the character of their manufactures, they were anything but prosperous from the commercial point of view. Difficulties of management, a ruinous fall in prices, and other causes, led to serious losses, Siemens himself being the principal sufferer. Yet the production of high-class steel went on. Siemens estimated that the quantity of steel which had been made by his processes in various places to the end of 1882 amounted to 4,000,000 tons. Six years later the production in Great Britain alone was nearly 1,000,000 tons per annum. Siemens made many experiments for the direct production of iron and steel from the ores, and, while he did not live to accomplish this, he never ceased to express his belief that it would ultimately be done. When the Shah of Persia visited England in 1873, his apartments were placed in direct communication, through the Indo-European Telegraph, with his own palace. His Majesty sent for Dr. Siemens, and highly complimented him on the great achievements of his Company, and he likewise conferred upon the inventor the Imperial Order of the Lion and the Sun.

The most important telegraphic work executed by Siemens Brothers was the laying of the Direct United States Cable in 1874, for which work the steamship *Faraday* was specially constructed after designs by William Siemens. The steamer was 5,000 tons register, and 360 feet long, and in her interior were three enormous tanks, capable of stowing under water 1,700 miles of cable. She was propelled by twin-screws so arranged as to give great facility in manœuvring. The line of the Direct United States Cable was to be 3,060 nautical miles in length, to extend from Ballinskellig Bay in Ireland to Torbay in Nova Scotia, from whence it was continued, also by submarine cable, to Rye Beach in New Hampshire, there joining the American land lines. The eventful voyages of the *Faraday* in the laying of this cable are thus detailed by Mr. Pole:—

'She sailed, to commence the laying of the Direct Atlantic Cable, on the 16th May, 1874. The expedition was in charge of Mr. Carl Siemens, and the manager of the firm, Mr.

Loeffler, was also on board. She carried on this occasion the cable for the American sections and shore ends. She arrived off the American coast early in June, and was there joined by the *Ambassador*, a ship also sent out by Messrs. Siemens to assist in the laying. The work was much delayed by foggy weather; and on the 2nd July there appeared in *The Times* the following startling announcement, communicated by Reuter's telegrams:—

'"The steamer *Faraday* has struck on an iceberg off Halifax, and is a total wreck."

'The consternation caused by such an announcement may well be imagined, but not a moment was lost; Messrs. Siemens sent telegraphic messages in all directions to gather information. After some hours of suspense impossible to describe, everything pointed to the explanation that the rumour was a mere Stock Exchange panic. Messrs. Siemens obtained the assurance that the report was without foundation, and they authoritatively announced this in *The Times* of the next day. But not till news came, as it did soon afterwards, from Carl Siemens, did the family feel relieved of the load of anxiety. The *Faraday* arrived safely at Woolwich on the 6th of August, having completed all the work she had then to do.

'On the 26th of August, 1874, she again left Charlton, with the main cable on board, to be laid under the superintendence of Mr. Carl Siemens. She arrived at Ballinskellig Bay on 1st September, and having attached the cable to the shore end, she commenced paying out on the 6th September, accompanied by two tenders, the *Ambassador* and the *Dacia*.

'She had laid about 500 or 600 miles when Dr. Werner Siemens, who was testing the cable from the shore at Ballinskellig Bay, found that a very slight fault had passed overboard. Hitherto it had not been customary to stop operations for faults of so trifling a character, as being too unimportant to interfere with the proper working of cables. But the brothers were determined that this cable should be as perfect as human skill could make it, and they therefore agreed to haul back and cut out the fault. In doing this the cable broke, but it was picked up again within forty-eight hours in 2,680 fathoms of water, successfully spliced, and the laying proceeded with. This picking up of the cable out of a depth of nearly three miles is noteworthy, as being the first time that such a feat was successfully accomplished.

'Owing to severe weather, to the loss of grapnels which had been broken in consequence of the rocky bottom upon which the operations were being carried on, and to the supply of coal running short, the *Faraday* and her two tenders were eventually obliged to put into Queenstown to effect some repairs, and to obtain coals and supplies. William Siemens visited them there on the 10th October, and the *Faraday* left again on the 23rd.

'The principle of eliminating even the smallest faults was rigidly adhered to, although the completion of the cable was much delayed thereby; but since it has been handed over to the proprietors, it has proved to be one of the most satisfactory cables ever laid, and its rate of transmission is far superior to that of cables in which minute faults have been allowed to remain.'

Another large undertaking carried out by Siemens Brothers in 1874, was the laying of the Brazilian Cable. The line lay between Rio de Janeiro and the coast of Uruguay, near the Brazilian frontier, in all 1,130 nautical miles of sea cable and 50 statute miles of land line. The work was successfully carried through, but not until two terrible disasters had occurred. The steamship *Gomos*, which went out with stores and materials, laid in due course one of the sections of the cable, but on the night of the 25th May, 1874, she struck on a sand-bar at Rio Grande do Sul, and became a total wreck, losing about 240 nautical miles of cable. In the following November another steamer, the *La Plata*, was sent out with stores and 184 nautical miles of cable. Three days after her departure, however, she foundered during a violent gale in the Bay of Biscay, and fifty-eight lives were lost. This painful disaster seemed inexplicable, for the *La Plata* was a fine iron screw-steamer of 968 tons register. The captain was experienced and the vessel was well found in every respect. All kinds of rumours were bruited abroad, and as the loss occurred at the time when the agitation against unseaworthy ships was at its height, reports were even circulated to the prejudice of the owners and charterers. Altogether there was considerable public excitement. The affair was a serious one for Siemens Brothers, as they lost the whole of their cable staff, including the chief of the expedition, Mr. Ricketts, and six skilled assistants accompanying him.

The Board of Trade ordered an enquiry, which was held at Greenwich by Mr. Balguy, police magistrate, assisted by Captain Oates and Captain Pryce, as nautical assessors, and by Mr. Traill, chief surveyor of the Board of Trade, as engineering assessor. The investigation lasted eleven days, and it was proved that Dr. Siemens had even voluntarily increased the means of safety and comfort for the crew and passengers. The Report was duly issued, and Mr. Balguy found—(1) That the *La Plata*, when she left Gravesend, was a strong ship, and in a seaworthy condition. (2) She was not overladen, and her cargo was properly stowed. (3) She was in proper trim. The assessors made a separate report. While substantially agreeing with the magistrate, they differed on some minor points, and in particular pointed out that 'the trim of the vessel (for which the captain was responsible) was not quite safe under such contingencies as a heavy head-sea or a violent gale. All the judges completely exonerated the Messrs. Siemens from blame. Sir William Siemens's biographer says of this disaster, and of its effects upon Siemens himself:—

'The immediate cause of the disaster was judged to be the

entrance of water into the engine-room; it was at first thought that a leak arose from some damage to the hull when the boat-davits were carried away, but this was disproved. No sufficient cause for the leakage could be shown, and there was reason to believe that it arose from some derangement of the water-passages connected with the engine, which it was quite within the power of the engineers to control. The magistrate, therefore, expressed his opinion "that the disaster originated in the stoke-hole";—the assessors, going into more detail, agreed that there was "gross negligence in the engine-room department," and they also attributed mismanagement to the captain. The evidence, however, was conflicting, and many of the facts were obscure.

'The Queen manifested the deepest sympathy for the sufferers, and directed special enquiries to be made after the widow of Captain Dudden, who, it was reported, behaved with the greatest courage.

'Besides providing for the widows and families of the principal members of their own staff who had been lost, Messrs. Siemens gave £500 to the public fund raised in aid of the widows and orphans of the men lost in the ship. Similar sums were given by Mr. Henley and by Messrs. Grant Brothers (from whom the contract for the cable was obtained), and the total of the fund was raised to about £4,650, which was distributed by a committee formed principally of officials of Messrs. Siemens and Mr. Henley.

'Dr. Siemens felt this calamity very deeply: it aged him perceptibly, and its effects on him were visible for years afterwards. Indeed, it is doubtful whether he ever regained the bright buoyant spirits he had before the catastrophe.'

A third ship, the *Ambassador*, was sent out, which successfully completed the laying of the Brazilian Cable. Dr. Siemens not only showed the deepest sympathy with those who suffered from the *La Plata* disaster, but he was also the recipient of sympathy himself.

The late Emperor of the Brazils visited England in 1871. He was a very able man, and took a keen interest in scientific matters. Siemens went over the works at Charlton with his Majesty, to whom he explained the various manufacturing processes. Two years afterwards, the Emperor conferred upon him the Imperial Order of the Rose, subsequently advancing him to the rank of a dignitary of the same Order.

Siemens Brothers laid the French Atlantic Cable in 1879 for the *Compagnie Française du Télégraphe de Paris à New York*. The line was from Brest, *viâ* St. Pierre Miguelon, to Cape Cod in Massachusetts, the length being about 2,250 nautical miles. Although the order was only given in March, 1879, the cable was finished by the 17th of June, and successfully laid by the *Faraday* by the 26th of October following. It was in perfect working order, and such an example of rapidity of production is probably unmatched.

Electric lighting is another branch of science with which the name of Siemens is indelibly associated. Faraday produced the electric spark when lecturing at the Royal Institution in 1831 on the 'Evolution of Electricity from Magnetism'; and he then predicted that others would follow in his steps who would make this power available for very important purposes. Wheatstone and other discoverers soon justified his words. Werner and William Siemens began to labour in the same field about 1854, and two years afterwards the former made an important advance towards aggregating magneto-electric currents. He constructed an armature resembling in section the letter H, into the hollows of which the insulated wires were wound longitudinally. The armature was so mounted as to secure a rapid rotation and a succession of currents, and the invention was adopted and largely used by Siemens & Halske in their magneto-electric machines—especially in one called a *Zeiger*, an alphabetical indicating instrument. The Siemens armature was used in constructing the electric lights off Dungeness, the South Point, the South Foreland, etc.

But a greater discovery was to follow. By the close of 1866 the Siemens Brothers had discovered, and clearly established, the principle of electro-magnetic augmentation and maintenance of a current without the aid of steel or other permanent magnets. Experiments were carried out at Berlin by the two brothers, in the presence of Professors Dove, Magnus, Du Bois Reymond, and other leading physicists. The value of the discovery was demonstrated, both practically and scientifically, and it was decided to lay the matter before the Academy of Berlin and the Royal Society of London. The new electro-dynamic inductor revealed extraordinary powers, even in the smallest of the machines, and it solved the problem of exploders for mines and quarries, as well as of exploding cartridges. William Siemens explained the discovery before the Royal Society on the 14th of February, 1867, in his important paper entitled 'On the Conversion of Dynamical into Electrical Force without the Aid of Permanent Magnetism.' He described the apparatus, and demonstrated beyond doubt that permanent magnetism was not requisite in order to convert mechanical into electrical force. The most powerful electrical or calorific effects could be produced without the aid of steel magnets, which were open to the objection of losing their permanent magnetism in use. Strangely enough, the discovery was made simultaneously, and without concert, by Professor Wheatstone and Mr. Alfred Varley, and the latter had already applied for a patent, depositing, in a sealed document, a provisional specification. Three scientists, therefore, made, independently of each other, this great discovery in connection with the principle of electricity. Siemens's patent was dated January 31st, 1867. 'The nature of the invention was thus described in the first claim :—

'" Developing powerful electric currents in electro-magnetic apparatus by causing the poles of a rotating electro-magnet or keeper to be forcibly approached successively to the similar poles, and forcibly severed from the dissimilar poles of stationary electro-magnets or coils, the currents being directed by means of a commutator or of current changers, so as to produce the above effect, and thereby cause an accumulation of magnetism and of the currents produced by the apparatus."

'The application to marine lights is mentioned as follows:—

'"Lighthouses have in some cases been illuminated by means of electric lamps. . . . As the powerful batteries, such as would be requisite for these electric lamps, are exceedingly perishable and expensive to maintain, magneto-electrical machines have been employed for producing the requisite electrical currents; but even these machines are apt to lose their efficiency, owing to a gradual decrease of the permanent magnetism of the steel bars employed. The present invention consists, first, in obtaining powerful electric currents without the aid either of large batteries or of permanent magnets by the following method."

'The method is then described, and the patent also goes on to state how lights may be transmitted through wires to lights, beacons, and buoys out at sea.'

Mr. Pole points out that the immediate result of this discovery was the production of one of the most wonderful of modern instruments, the dynamo-electric machine, or, as it is now more briefly called, the dynamo. 'If mechanical agency be applied to it in the form of muscular force, or water or steam power, the machine will convert this into its proper equivalent (minus certain necessary losses) of energy in the shape of an electric current; or, by a reverse operation, if an electric current be introduced into it, it may be changed into a corresponding equivalent of mechanical power, which will do work that might be done by muscles, or by water, or by steam.' Very important improvements were afterwards effected in the Siemens machine by Dr. Werner Siemens and Friedrich von Hefner-Alteneck, and a patent was taken out in 1873, entitled 'Improvements in apparatus for producing and regulating electric currents, such apparatus being particularly applicable to electric lighting.' Hefner-Alteneck had the chief share in the invention, and the machine was called sometimes the 'New Siemens,' and at others the 'Hefner-Alteneck.' Many later machines have been introduced for producing large electric currents, including those of Edison, Hopkinson, Gramme, Gordon, Sawyer, the Brush Company, etc. In 1878 Messrs. Siemens constructed the electrical apparatus for the Lizard Light on their principle. In a lecture given at the Royal Institution in February, 1879, Professor Tyndall detailed the progress of electric lighting; and Dr. Siemens supplemented this account in March, 1880, by lecturing on the dynamo-electric current generally. The electric transmission of power was Siemens's favourite study. It had strongly impressed him in the autumn of 1876, when visiting the Falls of Niagara; and when in the spring of 1877 he gave the opening address as President of the Iron and Steel Institute, he startled his audience by stating that 'a copper rod three inches in diameter would be capable of transmitting 1,000 horse-power a distance of, say, thirty miles, an amount sufficient to supply one-quarter of a million candle-power, which would suffice to illuminate a moderately-sized town.'

Other inventions by Siemens included the following:—An improved pyrometer, or thermometer for very high temperatures, acting by electricity; the bathometer, for measuring ocean depths without the sounding-line, the means employed being variations in the attraction exerted on a delicately suspended body; and the deep sea electrical photometer, by which investigations could be carried on by the penetration of light into deep water. Siemens's proposal for the conveyance of force from waterfalls like Niagara was received with a good deal of incredulity, but he adhered to his view. There was more belief, because there was complete demonstration, in regard to his ingenious experiments for ripening fruit under electricity, and his labours in the direction of applying electricity to illumination, and in constructing a combined gas and coke stove, by which the air required for combustion is heated in passing to the burner, so that the warmth usually wasted below the grate and up the chimney is brought forward, and radiation of heat increased. In 1882 Siemens published a work on the *Conservation of Solar Energy*, which was an ingenious endeavour to explain certain phenomena in solar physics on the principle of his own regenerative furnace.

Besides being elected on the Council of the Royal Society, Siemens was admitted to those select societies, or inner circles, called the Royal Society Club and the Philosophical Club. He also served on the Council of the British Association and the Institution of Civil Engineers. For two years he held the office of President of the Institution of Mechanical Engineers, and he acted as President and Member of Council of the Iron and Steel Institute. In 1875 the Institute presented him with the Bessemer gold medal, 'in recognition of the valuable services he had rendered to the iron and steel trades by his important inventions and investigations.' He was likewise elected first President of the Society of Telegraph Engineers and Electricians. He made an offer of £10,000 to the Iron and Steel Institute for the erection of a Hall of Applied Sciences, but difficulties arose as to the mode of carrying out the scheme, and it consequently fell through. In the Society of Arts—which was the first Society he ever joined—he took a profound interest, and at the time of his death he was Chairman of the Council. He was awarded the gold medal of the Society in 1875. At the Chemical Society, the Royal Institution, and the United Service Institution, he made frequent appearances. He was elected into the Athenæum Club under the special rule admitting distinguished men. In June, 1870, he received the honorary degree of D.C.L. at Oxford, the other recipients of the honour at the same time being Sir Edwin Landseer, Sir Francis Grant, Sir William Armstrong, Mr. Robert Lowe, and Mr. Matthew Arnold.

Between 1870 and 1879, Dr. and Mrs. Siemens paid several

visits to the Continent. In 1870 Carl Siemens and his family removed to London, and Dr. Siemens took one of the Palace Houses opposite Kensington Gardens, to accommodate his own family and his brother's, and they occupied the same dwelling until 1881, domestic happiness doing much to mitigate the inventor's many business anxieties. In 1874 Siemens also took a country seat, Sherwood House, near Tunbridge Wells, which he found to be a charming and beautiful retreat. In this establishment 'electricity played every part, from cooking the dinners to calling the servants, ripening the peaches and brushing the boots.' In June, 1878, Siemens was made an Honorary Member of the Cambridge Philosophical Society, and in 1879 the University of Glasgow conferred upon him the degree of LL.D.

During the last few years of his life, Siemens devoted a great deal of attention to such questions as smoke abatement, an improved house stove, and London fogs. In 1883, Sir William Thomson was asked, 'Can you scientific people not save us from these black and yellow City fogs?' Sir William's instant answer was, 'Sir William Siemens is going to do it; and I hope, if we live a few years longer, we shall have seen almost the last of them.' Alas! Siemens passed away within a few days, while the London fogs still remain. Siemens had great faith in gas as a heating agent, and he made numerous experiments to test his ideas. He went so far as to anticipate the time when, by means of some arrangement analogous to his gas producer, gas might be made in the coal districts, and supplied by a gigantic system of distribution to the public generally as fuel. In the year 1880 the firm of Siemens Brothers at Charlton was turned into a limited company, the brothers Werner, William, and Carl still remaining as directors, however, together with a new director, Mr. Loeffler. Among important electric light undertakings carried out by the firm were those at the British Museum, the Royal Albert Dock, and the Savoy Theatre, while they also lighted the *Austral* steamship and the town of

Godalming on the same principle. They further applied electricity to the propulsion of railway trains, and to the system of haulage in mines. Werner Siemens proved the feasibility of an electric railway in 1879, and two years later a permanent electric tramway was laid down in Berlin. Lines of electric railway have been open for ten years past in Ireland and the United States, and it remains to be seen what developments electric traction is capable of in the future. Siemens predicted the use of electric propulsion in long tunnels and on underground lines, where steam locomotion has the great disadvantage of fouling the air. Electrical power has been used in a great variety of ways during the last few years, in addition to those above cited.

Dr. Siemens gave one of a course of six lectures delivered at the Institution of Civil Engineers, in the year 1883, demonstrating the practical applications of electricity. The particular subject he chose was 'The Electrical Transmission and Storage of Power.' He had before this taken out a patent for 'Improved means and apparatus for producing light and heat by electricity.' His achievements in electric horticulture and fruit-growing, and in gardening by electric light—thus taking the place of the sun,—were very remarkable, and were made known in papers read before the Royal Society and the British Association. Dr. Siemens was one of the Board of Visitors in connection with the Indian Engineering College at Cooper's Hill, and he was able to initiate reforms there which were of real practical service to those who were being educated for his own profession of civil engineering. In Sept. 1882, Dr. Siemens delivered an able address, as President of the British Association, on the practical applications of Science. In July, 1883, he represented the British Government—together with Lord Sudeley, Sir W. Thomson, and Sir F. Abel—at the great Exhibition of Electric Apparatus held in Vienna, and he delivered the introductory lecture of a series given on electrical subjects. The following November he was awarded the Howard Quinquennial Prize by the Institution of Civil Engineers. During this and several preceding years he was elected a member of numerous learned societies in France, Germany, America, and Russia; and he received the degree of LL.D. from the University of Dublin, and that of Ph.D. from the University of Göttingen. In 1882 Siemens founded a Science Prize at King's College, London, and the same year he gave evidence before the Royal Commission on Technical Education—a class of education which he desired to see broadened and extended. He also still continued to give lectures at various places on scientific subjects.

Among English honours conferred upon Siemens, and which he much prized, were the Freedom and Livery of the Goldsmiths' Company and the Freedom and Livery of the Turners' Company. Then, in April, 1883, he was awarded a still higher distinction, when the Queen personally conferred upon him the honour of knighthood at Osborne, in recognition of the services which he had rendered to the cause of science. Congratulatory addresses and messages poured in upon Sir William and Lady Siemens, and *Punch* gave a clever fancy portrait of Sir William, with the whimsical inscription, 'The Electric Knight-Light.'

Early in November, 1883, Siemens was seized with illness. He still moved about, however, but on the 14th of that month he took a chill which affected his lungs. For five days he lingered, and then passed peacefully away on the 19th of November, in his sixty-first year. A post-mortem examination revealed that there had been long-standing disease of the heart, which was aggravated by a fall he had about a fortnight before his death. The sad news of his decease brought messages of regret and sympathy for Lady Siemens, from the Empress of Germany, Prince William of Prussia, and the Crown Prince Rudolph of Austria. There was a public funeral service in Westminster Abbey on the 26th of November. The Royal Society and other scientific societies and institutions were represented, and among the pall-bearers were Professor Huxley,

Sir Frederick Bramwell, Sir James Brunlees, Sir William Thomson, and Professor Tyndall. The body was conveyed after the service to Kensal Green Cemetery for interment. A simple monument was subsequently erected over the grave, with a medallion portrait of Sir William by Mr. Bruce Joy; and a magnificent memorial window was erected by his brother engineers in Westminster Abbey. This window was unveiled in November 1885, when Sir F. Bramwell delivered an eloquent eulogium upon Siemens.

Tributes continued to be paid to Sir William Siemens, at home and abroad, long after his death. Full justice was done to his career as a man of science, an engineer, an inventor, and a man of business. He undoubtedly made his mark upon the age, and gave a great impetus to several branches of scientific industry. He gained considerable wealth, but he used it wisely and creditably. He was liberal by nature, and indulged his scientific and artistic tastes. He had no mean powers of literary expression, and he had great intensity of application in whatever he undertook. He was of active habits, with a receptive and imaginative mind; was of a sanguine temperament, independent in judgment, and animated by an irresistible desire to realise objects in applied science when once conceived. His religion he himself described as Liberal Protestantism. Unqualified praise has been given to all his relations in private life, and a man is known nowhere better than in his own home.

THE RENNIES.

THE RENNIES.

The science of engineering owed many of its finest and most enduring developments to the genius of the Rennie family. The works of John Rennie and his two sons not only testify to their fame to-day, but must continue to do so for many generations. Some of the greatest mechanical enterprises and achievements ever witnessed in Great Britain are associated with their names; and this volume of sketches of industrial leaders may well and fitly close with a record of their labours.

John Rennie, the father, was born at the farm of Phantassie, in East Lothian, on the 7th of June, 1761. His father, like many other members of the family before him, owned the small farm which he cultivated. Farming was not an enviable occupation in the Lothians in the middle of last century, for roads were bad and communication difficult, and blackmailing and cattle-lifting were prevalent. Phantassie was on the old post-road between London and Edinburgh, but that did not benefit it much. In 1763, when Rennie was two years of age, the first stage-coach between London and Scotland began to run. It only went once a month, however, and the journey from Edinburgh to London occupied from twelve to eighteen days. As young Rennie grew up he had aspirations beyond the quiet monotonous life which was a characteristic feature of the Scottish Lowlands. For a time he worked for Andrew Meikle, a farmer and millwright in the Phantassie district. Meikle was of an ingenious turn of mind, and invented a threshing-mill, which was capable of being worked by water, wind, or horses. Meikle took out a patent for the machine, and it proved to be a valuable boon to the husbandman, effecting an immense saving of labour as well as of corn. In course of time the threshing-mill was generally adopted in Great Britain, and, indeed, throughout the civilised world. It was Meikle who first stirred in John Rennie his love for mechanics and the science of engineering.

Old Rennie died in 1766, leaving nine children—four sons and five daughters. George, the eldest, managed the farm and acted as head of the family, though he was but seventeen years of age. William, the second son, went to sea, and died in America; and James, the third son, studied medicine in Edinburgh, went out to India, and was killed whilst dressing the wounds of his commanding officer at Seringapatam. John, being only five years old at the time of his father's death, was brought up under the care of his excellent mother. He was educated at the parish school of Prestonkirk, and was put to work, as we have seen, at Andrew Meikle's, where he remained for two years. Next he was sent to the Dunbar High School, where he showed such proficiency in mathematics, etc., that a visitor of the school said 'One would have imagined him a second Newton.' Then he returned home and to the workshop of his friend Meikle, whom he assisted in his plans and inventions. At the early age of nineteen he was employed in fitting up new mills at Invergowrie, near Dundee. Subsequently he executed repairs at Aitcheson's flour-mills at Bonnington, near Edinburgh, employing cast-iron pinions instead of the wooden trundles formerly used. Dr. Smiles, in his *Lives of the Engineers*, states that he made quite an original mark as a country millwright. But he was already aiming at something much higher than this. Determined to acquire a thorough scientific training, he matriculated at Edinburgh University in 1780, and entered the classes of Dr. Robison, Professor of Natural Philosophy, and Dr. Black, Professor of Chemistry. In addition to studying strictly scientific works, Rennie acquired a knowledge of the French and German languages. Music also beguiled his hours of recreation. Having closed his college training in 1783, Rennie set forth upon a tour through the English manufacturing districts. By easy stages he reached Birmingham, and sought out James Watt, to whom he had a letter of introduction from Dr. Robison. Watt took to him at once, and remained his firm friend through life. Returning after some months to Phantassie, Rennie threw himself into mill and machinery work, and likewise constructed his first bridge. It was built for the Trustees of the County of Midlothian, across the Water of Leith, about two miles west of Edinburgh. But though he was full of work, he accepted an invitation from Watt to return to Birmingham, and early in 1785 he entered the famous works of Boulton & Watt at Soho. Here his mechanical genius soon manifested itself; and Watt thought so highly of Rennie that he committed to him the sole direction of the construction and fitting up of the machinery of the Albion Mills, London. This important undertaking was successfully completed; and the ingenious improvements effected in the connecting wheel-work were so striking that Rennie at once rose into general notice, and abundance of mill-work speedily flowed in upon him. Watt was delighted with his young assistant's success; and the great Smeaton, who visited the Albion Mills, 'pronounced them to be the most complete in their arrangement and execution which had yet been erected in any country.' Rennie's system of wrought- and cast-iron wheels was soon generally adopted in all large machinery. The Albion Mills were unfortunately destroyed by fire in 1791, but upon part of the ground Rennie obtained leave to erect a workshop, in which he continued all through life to carry on the business of a mechanical engineer.

In 1792 Rennie undertook and completed his first work of civil engineering in England—the Kennet and Avon Canal, which extends from Newbury to Bath. The total length of the canal is fifty-seven miles. Many difficulties were experienced in cutting it, but all were effectually surmounted, and the various bridges, aqueducts, culverts, etc., successfully built. 'Among the finest architectural structures forming part of the canal is the aqueduct over the river Avon, about a mile from Limpley Stoke and six miles from Bath, which is greatly admired for the beauty of its elevation; and, indeed, wherever there is an aqueduct or a bridge upon the line of this canal, it will be found excellent in workmanship and tasteful in design. As a whole, the navigation was pronounced to be of the best executed in the kingdom, and the works have stood admirably down to the present time. In a commercial and national point of view the undertaking was of great importance, connecting as it did the navigation of the metropolis with that of Bristol and St. George's Channel, as well as opening up an extensive intermediate district; and it eventually proved highly remunerative to the proprietors.'

Rennie's next important undertaking, the Rochdale Canal, was even more difficult than the first, cuttings having to be made through hard rocky regions. This canal opened a direct water communication between the manufacturing districts of West Yorkshire and South Lancashire. Locks, reservoirs, strong bridges, and embankments were all necessary, and it is stated that George Stephenson encountered no more formidable difficulties in constructing his railway through the same district than Rennie did in constructing his waterway. But Rennie persevered, the canal was duly opened, and the engineer's sterling workmanship endures to this day. He further constructed the Lancaster Canal, and superintended the execution of the Grand Western Canal in Somerset, the Polbrook Canal in Cornwall, and the canal between Arundel and Portsmouth. He made elaborate reports on various other canals, and was extensively consulted as a canal engineer.

Fen drainage was another work in which Rennie achieved great and beneficial results. He first turned his attention to

South Lincolnshire, and reclaimed the whole of that extensive district which extends along the south verge of the Wolds, from near the City of Lincoln eastward to the sea. Included therein were Wildmore Fen, West Fen, and East Fen, which comprised about 75,000 acres of land that for the greater part of the year lay under water, thus being rendered comparatively useless either for pasturage or tillage. Rennie was next consulted as to the draining of the Cambridgeshire Fens, and he conceived a grand scheme for the drainage of the Great Level, by means of more effectual outfalls and a system of intercepting catch-water drains. Unfortunately, however, the only part of the scheme executed during his lifetime was the Eau Brink Cut, for the purpose of securing a more effectual outfall of the river into the Wash near King's Lynn. In 1807, Rennie reclaimed 23,000 acres of fertile land in the district of Holderness, near Hull; in 1812 he was engaged in embanking lands exposed to the sea, when he succeeded in effectually protecting the thirty miles of coast extending from Wainfleet to Boston, and thence to the mouths of the rivers Welland and Glen; and in 1814 he produced a plan, which was carried out, for protecting the Earl of Lonsdale's valuable marsh-land on the south shore of the Solway Firth. 'It has been said of Mr. Rennie,' remarks Dr. Smiles, 'that he was the greatest "slayer of dragons" that ever lived—this title being given in the Fens to persons who, by skill and industry, have perfected works of drainage, and thereby removed the causes of sickness and disease, typified in ancient times as dragons or destroyers. In this sense, certainly, Mr. Rennie is entitled, perhaps more than any other man, to this remarkable appellation.'

Rennie's most widely-accepted claim upon posterity, however, is as one of the greatest bridge-builders of the world. We have already seen that he began his noble series of structures with the bridge over the Water of Leith, near Edinburgh, and it now remains to consider his more important works in this category. The first of these was the bridge across the Tweed at Kelso, designed in 1799 and opened in 1803. It consists of five semi-elliptical arches of 72 feet span, each rising 28 feet, and 4 piers, each 12 feet thick, with a level roadway 23 feet 6 inches wide between the parapets, and 29 feet above the ordinary surface of the river. It was one of the first bridges constructed with a level roadway, and was succeeded by the engineer's new bridge over the Esk at Musselburgh. Rennie's earliest English bridge, and the first of his cast-iron bridges, was that thrown over the Witham at Boston, Lincolnshire, in 1803. Like all Rennie's bridges, it is elegant in appearance, and consists of a single arch of iron ribs, forming the segment of a circle, the chord of which is 80 feet. During the next fifteen or twenty years Rennie was called upon to construct a great number of minor bridges, and while erecting one at Newton Stewart, across the Cree, he nearly lost his life during a heavy flood, which swept down the valley with great fury.

The finest and most celebrated of Rennie's bridges—to return to his greater works—is the Waterloo Bridge over the Thames. It was commenced in 1811, and finished in less than six years, at a cost of upwards of £1,050,000. Mr. D. K. Clark, in describing the bridge, says it 'has a level roadway, carried on nine equal semi-elliptical arches, of 120 feet span each, and 32 feet rise, leaving a clear height of 30 feet above high-water spring tides. It was built of granite, in a style of solidity and magnificence previously unknown. Inverted arches were built between the elliptical arches in order to counteract the lateral pressure. The elliptical arch was carried to a greater extent of flatness than in bridges previously built. Isolated coffer-dams upon a great scale, in a tidal river, with steam-engines for pumping out the water, were employed in the building of this bridge, for the first time, it is believed, in Britain. The length of the bridge between the abutments is 1,380 feet, and the width between the parapets is 42 feet 4 inches. The long inclined approach on the Surrey side is formed by a series of 39 semi-circular arches of 16 feet span, besides an elliptical arch, of

26 feet span, over the Narrowwall Road, and an embankment of 165 yards long, on an inclination of 1 foot rise in 34 feet of length. The total length of the bridge, with approaches, is 2,456 feet, or nearly half a mile.'

Waterloo Bridge was opened on the 18th June, 1817, by the Prince Regent. The Duke of Wellington and many other distinguished personages were present at the imposing ceremony. Originally called the Strand Bridge, its name was changed to that of Waterloo, in honour of the Iron Duke. The Prince Regent offered to confer the honour of knighthood upon Rennie, but the engineer declined it, being content to remain a simple citizen. He wrote afterwards to a friend, 'I had a hard business to escape knighthood at the opening.' As Dr. Smiles justly remarks, 'Waterloo Bridge is indeed a noble work, and probably has not its equal for magnitude, beauty, and solidity. Dupin characterized it as a colossal monument worthy of Sesostris or the Cæsars; and what struck Canova most during his visit to England was, that the trumpery Chinese bridge, in St. James's Park, should be the production of the Government, whilst Waterloo Bridge was the enterprise of a private company. Like all Rennie's works, it was built for posterity. That it should not have settled more than a few inches—not five in any part—after the centres were struck, is an illustration of solidity and strength probably without a parallel. We believe that to this day not a crack is visible in the whole work.'

Southwark Bridge was Rennie's next undertaking. It extends from Queen Street, Cannon Street, to Bridge Street, Southwark, and consists of three cast-iron arches, with two stone piers and abutments. The arches are flat segments of circles, the centre one being not less than 240 feet span, rising 24 feet, and springing 6 feet above high-water of spring tides. The two side arches are of 210 feet span, each rising 18 feet 10 inches, and springing from the same level. The two piers are 24 feet wide each at the springing, and 30 feet at the base. The first stone was laid by Admiral Lord Keith early in 1815, and the bridge was opened for traffic in March, 1819. In constructing this bridge, great precautions had to be exercised in securing the foundations of the piers, as the Thames was here at its narrowest and deepest point. The coffer-dams were consequently made of unusual strength and depth, and were constructed in the form most capable of resisting external pressure. The stone and iron work were alike splendid; and Robert Stephenson, in describing the structure in his article on 'Iron Bridges' in the *Encyclopædia Britannica*, said that 'as an example of arch-construction, it stands confessedly unrivalled as regards its colossal proportions, its architectural effect, and the general simplicity and massive character of its details.'

Rennie's achievements in dock and harbour construction are almost equally famous. The London Docks, the East and West India Docks at Blackwall, the Hull Docks, the Prince's Dock at Liverpool, and those of Dublin, Greenock, and Leith were all designed by him, and wholly or partially executed under his own superintendence. When the London Docks were constructed, it was determined to limit the access in the first instance to the Middle River entrance at Bell Dock, 150 feet long and 40 feet wide. The entrance lock communicated with the Wapping Basin, which covered a space of 3 acres, and this again led to the great basin called the Western Dock, 1,260 feet long and 960 feet wide. The bottom of the dock was laid 20 feet below the level of high water of an 18 feet tide; and the quays next to the river were 5 feet above high water, increasing to 9 feet at the great dock. Other docks were subsequently constructed, communicating with each other and with a larger and deeper entrance lower down the river at Shadwell. Rennie began the work of making the docks early in 1802, and they were completed in January, 1805. Some time after the docks were opened, Rennie suggested that the whole of the lifting cranes should be worked by the power of a steam-engine instead of by human or by horse labour. Yet although he estimated the saving at £1,500 a year, while greater regularity and despatch would also be secured, the innovation was regarded as too bold a one to be attempted. He further suggested the adoption of tramways all round the quays, provided with trucks, but this labour-saving process was likewise in advance of the time. The East India Docks, constructed solely for vessels of the East India Company ranging from 1,000 to 1,800 tons burden, were opened in August, 1806. They had an entrance lock into the Thames 210 feet long and 47 feet wide. The Export Dock was 760 feet long and 463 feet wide, covering a surface of 8⅓ acres; and the Import Dock was 1,410 feet long and 463 feet wide, covering a surface of 18⅔ acres. The depth of the basins was 22 feet below high-water mark of ordinary spring tides; and the total surface of dock room, including quays, sheds, and warehouses, was about 55 acres. The docks were eventually united to the West India Docks, under the joint directorate of the East and West India Dock Company. Among improvements introduced by Rennie in these docks were iron roofings for the sheds and a new description of iron cranes. It is stated that his machinery for transporting immense blocks of mahogany by a system of railways and locomotive cranes effected in six months a saving in men's wages more than sufficient to defray their entire original cost. Another excellent work effected by Rennie was the improvement of the Clyde by a system of dredging and by the erection of numerous jetties, etc., which rendered this important waterway a splendid navigable river. He also greatly improved the Grimsby Dock walls, and invented the system of curved walls for resisting the pressure of water.

The original Holyhead Harbour works were the construction of Rennie. They were begun in 1810 and finished after his death. The works consisted of a pier 1,150 feet long, and terminating at a depth of about 14 feet at low-water of spring tides; at 80 feet distance from the extremity of the main pier there was a jetty 60 feet long, carried out at right angles to its inner face, to check any swell which might come round the pier-head from entering the harbour, and to throw it upon the opposite shore. The roadway was 50 feet wide, and 8 feet above the level of high-water of spring tides, the parapet being 7 feet higher. The harbour was laid out with a view to further extensions, and the engineer made some valuable suggestions in this respect, but they were not adopted. An entirely new harbour was constructed by the Government in 1847-73, at an enormous expense. This was subsequently extended, and the quay lengthened to 4,000 feet. Rennie constructed the Howth and Kingstown harbours, but the latter was still incomplete when he died, and the original design was afterwards departed from. He further constructed the Hull Docks. The principal one, the Humber Dock, begun in 1803 and finished in 1809, was 900 feet long by 370 wide, covering a surface of 7½ acres. It was while constructing these works that Rennie invented the dredging-machine, as now used, for the purpose of clearing the basins of mud and silt. A list is given of no fewer than fifty harbours and docks which this indefatigable engineer constructed wholly or in part, or greatly improved. Rennie himself thus described the broad principles upon which harbours should be constructed: 'Every harbour should be so constructed as to have its mouth as much exposed as possible to the direction from whence vessels can most conveniently enter in stormy weather when they are least manageable; but the heads should be made of such a form as to admit of the least sea entering it, or so as to occasion as little swell within the haven as possible. This cannot by any practicable construction be *entirely* avoided; but means should be provided within the harbour so as to reduce the recoil of the waves to a minimum,—for it is the undertow or retiring sea, after the breaking of a wave, that renders vessels most unmanageable by making the helm lose its effect. At such a time the mariner is at a loss what to do, or how to manage his vessel; and for the want of due attention to these particulars many of the most artificial harbours in the kingdom are exceedingly difficult of access, and some of them are most unsafe even when entered.'

That useful accessory in harbour-building, the diving-bell, was vastly improved by Rennie while he was engaged upon extensive repairs in the Ramsgate Harbour works in 1813. His biographer states that 'he proceeded to design and construct a bell of cast-iron, about 6 feet in height, 4½ feet wide, and 6 feet long, having one end rather thicker and heavier than the other, that it might sink lower, and thus enable the exhausted or breathed air more readily to escape. At the top of the bell eight solid bull's-eyes of cast glass were fixed, well secured and made water-tight by means of leathern and copper collars covered with white lead, and firmly secured by copper screw bolts. To the top of the inside were attached two strong chains for the purpose of fastening to them any materials that might be required for the work, and flanges were cast along the sides of the bell, on which two seats were placed, with footboards, for the use of of the men while working. In the centre of the top was a circular hole, to which a brass-screwed lining was firmly fixed, and into this a brass nozzle was screwed, having a leathern water-tight hose fastened to it, 2½ inches in diameter. The hose was in lengths of about eight feet, with brass-screwed nozzles at each end, so that it could be lengthened or shortened at pleasure, according to the depth of water at which the men in the bell were working. For the purpose of duly supplying the machine with air, a double air-pump was provided, which was worked by a sufficient number of men. The air-pump was connected with the hose referred to, and was either placed on the platform above or in a boat which constantly attended the bell while under water. Two stout wrought iron rings were fixed on the top of the machine, to which ropes or chains were attached for the purpose of lowering or raising it. The whole weighed about five tons; and it was attached to a circular frame-work of timber, strengthened by iron, erected over where the intended new circular pier-head was to be built, and so fixed to a pivot near the centre of the work, that it was enabled easily to traverse its outer limits. On the top of the framework was a truck, made to move backwards or forwards by means of a rack on the frame, and a corresponding wheel provided with teeth, worked by a handle and pinion. On the truck were placed two powerful double-purchase crabs or windlasses, one for working the diving-bell suspended from it, and the other for lowering stone blocks or other materials required for carrying on the operations at the bottom of the sea. By these ingenious expedients the building apparatus was so contrived as to move all around the new work, backwards and forwards, upwards and downwards, so that every part of the wall could be approached and handled by the workmen, no matter at what depth, whilst the engineer stationed on the pier-head above could at any time ascertain, without descending, whether the builders were proceeding in the right direction, as well as the precise place at which they were at work.'

The Ramsgate Harbour improvements were so expeditiously and successfully completed, that the trustees caused a memorial stone to be fixed in the centre of the new pier-head, bearing a bronze plate on which were recorded the details of Rennie's ingenious labours, as well as their own obligations to the engineer; and they also presented him with a handsome piece of plate.

The Bell Rock, or Inchcape, Lighthouse, was a fine work executed by Rennie and Robert Stevenson, the Scotch engineer. It was begun in 1807 and finished in 1810, at a cost of £61,000. The site is a reef of Old Red Sandstone rocks in the German Ocean, twelve miles south-east of Arbroath, and nearly opposite the mouth of the Tay. The reef is 2,000 feet long; at high-water of spring tides it is covered to a depth of 16 feet; at low-water it is partly uncovered to a height of 4 feet; and for a hundred yards around, the sea is only three fathoms deep. This dangerous reef was formerly a fruitful cause of shipwreck, and according to tradition, the Abbot of Aberbrothock, or Arbroath, placed a bell on it, 'fixed upon a tree or timber, which rang continually, being moved by the sea, giving notice to the saylers of their danger.' Southey has enshrined the legend in one of his best ballads. Many plans were suggested for a lighthouse on the Bell Rock before Rennie examined the spot and made a report to the Commissioners of Northern Lights, recommending a substantial stone lighthouse, similar to that on the Eddystone, as being the only kind of structure calculated to meet the necessities of the case. The report was adopted, and the works authorised, and carried out as stated. The lighthouse was 127 feet high, and the plan of construction generally followed was that of Smeaton with the Eddystone Lighthouse, one of the few deviations consisting in the substitution of dove-tailed pieces of stone for chain-bars in the joints both of the walls and the floors. Rennie designed the structure and was chief engineer, and the works were practically executed by Robert Stevenson, the resident engineer. Dangers and difficulties attended the accomplishment of the task, but in 1810 the Bell Rock Lighthouse shed its friendly light across the tempestuous ocean for the benefit of the imperilled mariner.

Rennie was employed by the Government on many public works. He advised the Navy upon the improvement of their flour-mills at Rotherhithe, which were worked by the rise and fall of the tide; and when there was great alarm in England in 1803, owing to the possible descent of Napoleon upon our shores, he devised means for the sudden flooding of the valley of the Lea round London, in order to check the approach of a hostile army from that quarter. He further laid out and constructed the Hythe Military Canal on the coast of Kent, which was defended by earthworks, and protected by a breastwork on the land side. He next fixed moorings in the tideways of the royal harbours, improved the machinery of the Waltham Powder Mills, cleared the Thames in front of Woolwich

Dockyard of its immense accumulation of mud, erected a quarantine establishment in the Medway, provided wet docks for the Royal Navy, and introduced improved machinery at the various dockyards. The Royal Dockyards—Portsmouth, Plymouth, Deptford, Chatham, etc.—were not only far apart, but some of them were ill-adapted to their purposes. Having been commissioned by the Admiralty to find a site on the Thames for a great naval arsenal and harbour, Rennie recommended Northfleet as possessing every advantage that could possibly be wished for in a naval station. He was not allowed to carry out his design, however, but was instructed instead to construct extensive dockworks at Sheerness, that spot being chosen by the authorities as commanding the entrance both to the Thames and the Medway. We learn that 'the plan finally decided upon was that of a river-front, extending from the Garrison Point to near the Old Town Pier of Sheerness, of the length of 3,150 feet, including the entrances, and enclosing within it three basins : one to the north, 480 feet long and from 90 to 200 feet wide, containing a surface of about two acres, 4 feet below low-water of spring tides, with two frigate docks and a building-slip and boat-slips ; a central tidal basin 220 feet square, of the depth of 2 feet below low-water, with storehouses around it for the reception and delivery of victualling and other stores ; and on the west end of the dockyard a basin 520 feet long and 300 feet wide, covering a surface of nearly four acres, provided with dry docks for ships of the line on the south side, with their sills and the bottom of the basin laid 9 feet below low-water of spring tides, westward of which were the mast-ponds, mast-locks, and workshops. In the rear, on the south of these works, were placed saw-pits, timber-berths, and the officers' houses. The total surface of the dockyard was 64¾ acres. The foundation-stone of the docks was laid by the late Lord Viscount Melville in 1815, and the works were then commenced and continued without interruption until the year 1826, when the whole were completed.

'Their execution was attended with many difficulties, and necessarily required a great deal of Mr. Rennie's care and attention. The foundations were a soft running sand, extending to an almost fathomless depth. The strong currents flowing past the place rendered it necessary to adopt an entirely new system of operations, which were carried out to an extent never before attempted in so exposed a situation. The form of sea-wall was devised which should most effectually resist the strong pressure of the current and the heavy swell beating upon its outer side, without yielding to the lateral pressure or thrust of the water of the basins and the earth by which it was backed. At the same time, the weight necessary to ensure stability must not be such as to sink vertically. Mr. Rennie adopted the means to secure these objects which he had employed with such success at Grimsby Docks in 1797, namely, to take the like quantity of materials as would have been necessary for an ordinary wall, and dispose of them in such a form, that the same weight should be distributed over a greater surface, thus diminishing the vertical pressure. In the foundations of the walls he also adopted the method employed by him in similar works, of driving the piles and cutting off their heads at an angle inclining inwards, or towards the land side, laying the courses of stone at the same angle ; by which a greater resistance was offered to the pressure of the earth, and the building was prevented from being pushed outwards, as was more or less the case in most of the walls built on the old construction. The entrance gates to the basin were also planned and executed with great skill, Mr. Rennie carrying into effect the same simple but correct principles laid down by him in his report on the Northfleet Docks, making the direction of the entrance suitable to the current in the Medway, from which the ships entered the port.'

Other branches of dockwork executed by Rennie included a new river wall, with ship-basin and two building-slips, at Woolwich ; the new dockyard, building-slips, and dry dock, at

Pembroke; the new entrance to Deptford Basin; and various improvements at Chatham, Portsmouth, and Plymouth.

But one of his most gigantic undertakings was the famous Plymouth Breakwater. It is the best known of all engineering works of the kind. In their article on 'Breakwaters' in *Chambers's Encyclopædia*, Messrs. D. and T. Stevenson describe the Plymouth Breakwater as follows: 'The sound or harbour, being open to the south, was so much exposed to storms that, early in the present century, it was determined to construct a breakwater across its mouth, with openings between it and the shore, on either side, for the ingress and egress of shipping. The works were commenced in 1811, from designs by Rennie, and were estimated to cost £900,000. The operations consisted in transporting along a tram-road large blocks of limestone got from a neighbouring quarry, shipping them in vessels fitted with trap-doors, and by means of these depositing them in the shape of a huge mound in the required situation. The design was to carry the rubble mound to a height of ten feet above low-water, to give the seaward face a slope of 3 to 1, and the inner face $1\frac{1}{2}$ to 1, and the width on top 30 feet. As soon as the stones began to appear above water, a perceptible benefit resulted in the relative calmness of the sound during the prevalence of storms; but the structure was frequently very roughly handled by the waves, which altered and flattened its shape. A severe storm in November, 1824, overthrew a length of 796 yards of the finished work; after this the breakwater was raised 10 feet higher, the seaward slope made 5 to 1, and the top width 45 feet, the top and slopes paved with masonry, and the top protected with expensively dressed granite blocks, joggled together and bedded with cement. It was not until 1841 that the works were finally completed by the deposit of more than 3,000,000 tons of stone, and an expenditure of nearly £1,500,000. The breakwater is nearly a mile long, the central portion is 1,000 yards; and two wings, of 350 yards each, extend from the ends of this at a slight angle. The open channels at each end, between the breakwater and the shore, are each about half a mile wide, and their depth is respectively 40 and 22 feet at low-water. The breakwater is 400 feet wide at the base, and 45 at the top—the two sides being made very sloping for the security of the stones. The slopes and top are faced with masonry. The water-space protected by this breakwater comprises 1,120 acres, and it is generally admitted that the money has been well spent on the work. The breakwater requires constant repair.'

Dr. Smiles states that the actual amount of rubble deposited for the Plymouth Breakwater to the end of 1848—when the work may be said to have been completed—was 3,670,444 tons, besides 22,149 cubic yards of masonry, or an amount of material at least equal to that contained in the Great Pyramid. The breakwater 'may in all respects be regarded as a magnificent work, worthy of a great maritime nation.'

Other labours of Rennie remain yet to be mentioned. He cut the Crinan Canal, and reported on the water-supply of Manchester, Edinburgh, Leeds, Bristol, Doncaster, and many other large towns at home and abroad. He erected the anchor-forge at Woolwich Dockyard, advised the Bank of England on its machinery for the manufacture of bank-notes, and supplied the Dutch with designs of dredging-machines for clearing the mud out of the rivers and canals. He constructed the machinery for making ropes according to Captain Huddart's patent. He urged the introduction of steam-power into the Royal Navy, and constructed a small steamboat called the *Comet*, which was the precursor of other royal ships of vaster dimensions. The last of his great engineering works, New London Bridge, he did not live to complete. His design consisted of five semi-elliptical arches, the centre one 150 feet span, the two side arches 140 feet each, and the two land arches 130 feet each, making a total lineal waterway of 690 feet; the height of the soffit, or underside, of the central arch being 29 feet 6 inches above the level of Trinity high-water mark. The design was generally approved, and a Bill carried through Parliament, but—as we shall presently see—his son John carried through the work.

Rennie rarely took any rest from his labours, which extended over a period of forty or fifty years; but in September, 1816, he visited France with his friend, James Watt, jun. At Cherbourg he examined the famous breakwater then in course of construction, and he also took notes of the building-yards and docks of other towns and cities. In 1820 his health began to fail, but he persisted in going about for some twelve months after that. He was in the midst of designs for new enterprises, when he expired somewhat suddenly on the 4th of October, 1821. His remains were interred in St. Paul's Cathedral, near to those of Sir Christopher Wren. At the age of twenty-nine Rennie had married an Inverness lady named Miss Mackintosh, with whom he had ever lived happily until her death, which occurred a few years before his own decease. They had nine children, six of whom survived their parents. One who knew Rennie well thus wrote of him in the *Gentleman's Magazine*, shortly after his death :—

'Every part of the United Kingdom possesses monuments of his glory, and they are as stupendous as they are useful. They will present to our children's children objects of admiration for their grandeur and of gratitude to the author for their utility. Compare the works of Rennie with the most boasted exploits of the French engineers, and remark how they tower above them. Look at the breakwater at Plymouth, in comparison with the caissons at Cherbourg—any one of his canals with that of Ourke, and his Waterloo Bridge with that of Ruilly. Their superiority is acknowledged by every liberal Frenchman. He cultivated his art with the most enthusiastic ardour, and instead of being merely a theorist, he prepared himself for practical efficiency by visiting and minutely inspecting every work of magnitude in every country that bore similitude with those which he might be called on to construct; and his library abounded in a richer collection of scientific writings than that of almost any individual. The loss of such a man is irreparable. Cut off in the full vigour of his mind, his death seems to suspend for a time the march of national improvement, until the just fame of his merit shall animate our rising artists to imitate his great example, and to prepare themselves by study and observation to overcome, as he did, the most formidable impediments to the progress of human enterprise, of industry, and of increased facility in all the arts of life. The integrity of Mr. Rennie in the fulfilment of his labours was equal to his genius in the contrivance of his plans and machinery. He would suffer none of the modern subterfuges for real strength to be resorted to by the contractors employed to execute what he had undertaken. Everything he did was for futurity, as well as present advantage. An engineer is not like an architect. He has no commission on the amount of his expenditure, if he had, Mr. Rennie would have been one of the most opulent men in England, for many millions have been expended under his eye. But his glory was in the justice of his proceedings, and his enjoyment in the success of his labours. It was only as a millwright that he engaged himself to execute the work he planned, and in this department society is indebted to him for economising the power of water, so as to give an increase of energy, by its specific gravity, to the natural fall of streams, and to make his mills equal to four-fold the produce of those which, before his time, depended solely on the impetus of the current. His mills of the greatest size work as smoothly as clockwork, and by the alternate contact of wood and iron, are less liable to the hazard of fire by friction. His mills, indeed, are models of perfection.

'If the death of such a man is a national loss, what must it be to his private friends and to his amiable family? Endeared to all who knew him by the gentleness of his temper, the cheerfulness with which he communicated the riches of his mind, and forwarded the views of those who made useful discoveries or improvements in machinery or implements, procured him universal respect. He gave to inventors all the benefits of his experience, removed difficulties which had occurred to the author, or suggested alterations which adapted the instrument to its use. No jealousy nor self-interest ever prevented the exercise of this free and unbounded communication; for the love of science was superior in his mind to all mercenary feeling.'

Rennie was a man of punctual and systematic habits, with a great love of order. All the reports he drew up were model documents. He declined to speculate in enterprises in which he was concerned, even when he knew such speculations would prove profitable. In person he was commanding of stature, and possessed of Herculean strength. He was eminently truthful, honest, and upright; was profound in mind, sagacious and serene in character; and his modesty was as conspicuous as his genius.

George Rennie, the eldest son of John Rennie, was born in 1791, and educated at Edinburgh University. When twenty years of age he began the study of practical engineering under his father in London. Appointed superintendent of the machinery of the Mint in 1818, he at the same time assisted in the planning and execution of several of his father's later works. Upon his father's death he entered into partnership with his younger brother John as engineers and machinery constructors; and during the existence of the firm it carried on an immense business, including the execution of most of the works which had been designed by his father, and the completion of those which he had left unfinished. The undertakings of the two brothers embraced the construction of bridges, harbours, docks, shipyard and dredging machinery, steam-factories both in Great Britain and on the Continent, and marine engines for warships. They built ships both of wood and iron, drained large tracts of land in the midland counties of England, and superintended the construction of several continental railways. George Rennie died in 1866.

Sir John Rennie, John Rennie's youngest son, claims fuller attention as being the most widely-known member of his family. In the interesting *Autobiography* which he left behind him, he states that he was born in Stamford Street, Blackfriars, London, on the 30th August, 1794. He was sent to Dr. Greenlaw's school at Isleworth, where the most remarkable pupil at this time was the poet Shelley, of whom he gives a striking picture. Rennie afterwards went to the school of the celebrated Dr. Charles Burney, at Greenwich. Here he became a tolerable proficient in the classics. When the days of tuition were over, the elder Rennie would not send his son to Oxford or Cambridge, as he intended to bring him up to the profession of a civil engineer, and he held that a young man could not bend himself to the practical part of the work after he had been to the University. At the close of his preliminary training, Rennie was invested with some amount of independent responsibility, and helped his father in the construction of the Vauxhall, Southwark, and Waterloo bridges. In 1813 he was despatched to Aberdeen and Peterhead to secure stone for the works. In 1814 he gained great experience in following the surveys made by Francis Giles in various parts of the country. Rennie made a tour in France and Belgium in August, 1815, and visited the scene of the sanguinary Battle of Waterloo. After his return he was closely engaged in the works connected with the Waterloo and Southwark bridges, the latter of which was almost entirely under his direction. But he managed in the evenings to study mathematics, and to attend Sir Humphry Davy's lectures at the Royal Institution.

Having received a tolerably good education, theoretical and practical, as a civil engineer, young Rennie was sent forth on his travels before beginning business fully on his own account. His father considered that he should study what had been done in ancient and modern times, both in architecture and engineering. Accordingly, in June, 1819, he left England—in company with his cousin, General Sir J. Aitchison, and Lord Hotham—for a tour through Switzerland, Italy, Greece, Asia Minor, Turkey, and Egypt. He gives graphic descriptions of Milan, Venice, Bologna, Rome, and other cities, always keeping his eye on those works—harbours, canals, roads, and bridges—which especially appealed to him as a civil engineer. At Rome he made the acquaintance of Canova and Thorwaldsen, and saw Lawrence, Chantrey, and Turner, whom he had known in England. He attended the splendid receptions given by the beautiful Princess Borghese, the Duchess of Devonshire, and others. Naples, Corfu, Zante, Patras, Corinth, Athens, Argos, Mycenæ, were all visited in turn; and at Athens the travellers saw and conversed with Byron's beautiful Maid of Athens. Then came Smyrna, Ephesus, Miletus, Broussa, Constantinople, Alexandria, and Cairo. In the last-named city Rennie had an audience of the celebrated Pasha Mehemet-Ali. He was seized with fever at Cairo, and had a renewal of it in Italy on his return voyage. Florence, Leghorn, and Genoa he subsequently visited, and he was struck by the magnificent site which the Gulf of Spezzia afforded for a naval arsenal. This idea has since been partially realised.

Rennie reached England in September, 1821, and in less than a fortnight after his landing he was called upon to mourn the loss of his father. The sad event prostrated him for a time, but as soon as he recovered from the shock he was stimulated to earnest labour by the brilliant example of his father. His first ambition was to succeed him in his numerous great works then being carried on by the Admiralty, such as the Plymouth Breakwater, and the new Chatham and Woolwich Dockyards. Although he was only twenty-seven years of age, he was at once appointed by the Lords of the Admiralty to succeed his father as their engineer. Next, he was appointed drainage engineer to the Eau Brink Commissioners, who had been chosen to carry into effect the Eau Brink Cut, for the improvement of the drainage of the great level of the fens, called the Bedford Level, amounting to about 300,000 acres of valuable land. This scheme consisted of a cut for altering the channel of the Ouse, by means of which nearly two miles of the navigation of that river would be saved, and an additional fall for the drainage of five feet perpendicular would be gained. This great work had been planned nearly a century before, but had always been opposed by the inhabitants of the fens as being inadequate. At length it was resolved to proceed with the scheme, but so many difficulties arose that the whole of the funds subscribed, amounting to about £80,000, were expended in litigation and in the cost of obtaining the Act of Parliament. A second Act of Parliament was subsequently obtained, and the Commissioners elected to carry out the undertaking were Lord William Bentinck, Sir Andrew Hammond, Bart., Sir Charles Browne, M.D., and Mr. Thomas Hoseason. Messrs. Jolliffe & Banks received the contract for the works, and, as already stated, John Rennie was appointed drainage engineer.

'The effect of this work,' says Rennie, 'greatly exceeded the most sanguine expectations of its supporters. Immediately after it was opened, the low-water mark at the upper end of the cut fell five feet, and the drainage waters were carried off with a degree of rapidity which astonished the whole country. The autumn and winter of 1821-22 was characterised by an unusual quantity of rainfall, and if it had not been for the opening of the Eau Brink Cut the whole, or the greater part, of the level of the fens would have been under water, and therefore the fenmen were very well pleased with the result. At this time I was appointed to succeed my father as chief drainage engineer, and the late Mr. Telford had been previously appointed chief engineer for navigation. Immediately after my appointment, which was in the month of December, 1821, I went to Lynn to examine the works, and was much astonished to find the great effects which had been produced by the Eau Brink Cut. Instead of the circuitous old shallow course, full of shoals and obstructions of every kind, there was a fine, straight, deep channel, two miles shorter than the old one, of the proper width, bordered by strong banks of the full height; the floods passed off without difficulty, and the navigation was so much improved that the lighters and barges going up the river from Lynn saved several tides. It is true, that upon examining the country between Denver Sluice and Cambridge, there was a great deal of water out in several places, but this was attributed to the interior drains and rivers not being properly defended and embanked, so that they could carry off the water to the main outfall below. I also examined the new steam pumping apparatus, which had lately been erected for draining Soham and other fens. This, although proposed by my father in 1786, was the first of the kind that had been erected. It consisted of a scoop wheel, with a perpendicular lift, worked by a condensing engine. It answered its object completely, and has since been imitated by numerous others with equal success in different parts of the fen and lowland districts.'

Rennie's next appointment was as engineer-in-chief to Ramsgate Harbour, again succeeding his father. This harbour was established by special Act of Parliament for the purpose of affording shelter to vessels of 300 tons lying in the Downs during south-west gales. In short, the harbour was made for clearing the Downs of small vessels, so that large ones might ride in safety, and this purpose was successfully answered. Hitherto, the heavy seas, and the proximity of the Goodwin Sands, had proved very dangerous for craft of all kinds. Further business flowed in rapidly upon Rennie, and he succeeded his father at Sunderland, Donaghadee, Port Patrick, and Kingstown Harbours, the West India Docks, and other places. But the most difficult and anxious work in progress at this time was the new dockyard at Sheerness, which Rennie now completed from his father's designs, the work also having been partially executed by the latter. Rennie went down to Plymouth in March, 1825. Difficulties had arisen in connection with the breakwater, and there was a difference of opinion between Rennie and Joseph Whidbey, the superintendent of the breakwater, as to how they should be met. The Admiralty accepted Rennie's plans in preference to Whidbey's, and on the latter resigning his position, Rennie was appointed chief engineer. He was not long in erecting outer works which effectually broke the force of the waves before they reached the main body of the breakwater. Soon afterwards Rennie was ordered to erect a new Victualling Establishment for the Navy at Cremill Point, near Devonport, and he was further directed to report to the Admiralty on the feasibility of applying the Cornish system of high-pressure engines to the Admiralty steam-vessels.

Then came the greatest of the legacies left him by his father, viz., the building of new London Bridge. This was a most arduous undertaking. 'New London Bridge,' observes Mr. Clark, 'was built 180 feet higher up the river than the old bridge. It consists of five semi-elliptical arches, the least of which is wider than any other elliptical arch ever before erected. The centre arch has $152\frac{1}{2}$ feet span, with $37\frac{1}{2}$ feet rise; the next two arches are of 140 feet, and the two abutment arches are of 130 feet span. The roadway is 52 feet wide. The clear waterway at all times of the tide is 692 feet, or 60 feet more than the old bridge afforded at high-water. The whole length of the bridge is 1,005 feet. At the City side the bridge is carried over Thames Street on a dry arch. At the Borough or south side the approach is formed on an inclined plane, supported on a series of brick arches, with a large dry arch facing Tooley Street. This bridge deserves further remark for the difficulty of the situation in which it was built, above the old bridge, in a depth of from 25 feet to 30 feet at low-water, on a soft alluvial bottom, covered with large loose stones, scoured away by the force of the current from the foundations of the old bridge. The whole of these stones had to be removed by dredging before the coffer-dams for the piers and abutments could be commenced; otherwise it would have been extremely difficult, if not impracticable, to have made them watertight. The difficulty was further increased by the old bridge being left standing, to accommodate the traffic, whilst the new bridge was building, and the restricted waterway of the old bridge occasioned such an increased velocity of the current as materially to retard the operations at the new bridge. At times the tide threatened to carry away all before it; and it was found expedient that two of the small arches of the old bridge on each side should be thrown into one, to compensate for the additional obstruction which the water occasioned to the navigation. The piers and abutments stand upon platforms of timber, the floors of the coffer-dams resting upon piles about 20 feet long. The masonry is from 8 feet to 10 feet below the bed of the river. The great magnitude and extreme flatness of the arches, of which the key-stones are 4 feet 9 inches long, demanded unusual care in the selection of the materials, which were of the finest blue and white granite from Scotland and Devonshire, as well as great accuracy of workmanship. The new bridge was opened for traffic in August, 1831, the period occupied in its erection, from the time of driving the first pile for the dam of the south pier, being seven years, five months, and thirteen days.

'The centering employed for the new London Bridge is worthy of notice. It consisted of trussed timber girders, supported at the piers. The striking plates and wedges, by which the centre was lowered after the completion of the arch, were strong beams suitably notched, one of which, the wedge, was kept in its place by cross wedges. When the centre was to be lowered, the cross wedges were knocked out, and the main wedge driven back.'

William IV. opened the new London Bridge with great state. His Majesty walked over the whole of the bridge, accompanied by the Ministers of State, the Lord Mayor and Corporation, and the Bridge Committee. The Tower guns volleyed at intervals, and as the day was remarkably fine, the Thames was crowded with boats filled with gaily-dressed people. The original London Bridge, which in its first form dated back to 1176, was removed in 1834, under Rennie's supervision, at a cost of £10,000. After the opening of the new bridge, Rennie received the honour of knighthood for his services.

In order to make worthy approaches to new London Bridge, Rennie, and his brother-in-law, Cockerell, who was an excellent authority, submitted designs to a Committee of Taste appointed by Parliament for the beautifying of London. Their designs were rejected, however, and the Committee authorised the late Sir Robert Smirke, then one of the Crown architects, to design the present buildings on both sides of the bridge, as far as King William Street on the north, and the old Town Hall of Southwark on the south. It is generally admitted, as Rennie has remarked, that 'a more unworthy set of buildings was never designed.' A rare opportunity was lost of constructing handsome and appropriate buildings to adorn one of the greatest thoroughfares in the world.

Drainage works next occupied Rennie's attention. The Eau Brink Cut was enlarged under his direction, for the damage done by its overflow, in consequence of the channel being too narrow, had involved the Commissioners in large amounts as compensation to the Lynn Harbour Trustees and others. He then, in conjunction with Telford, improved the River Nene, so as to render it a good outfall for the drainage of the extensive low fenlands bordering it, which, on account of their bad drainage, were frequently subject to floods, and comparatively valueless. It was necessary to stop up the old channel and to divert the river through the new outfall. Rennie gives this interesting and amusing account of how the work was accomplished :—

'When everything was ready, we went down and met the contractors, Messrs. Jolliffe and Banks, and immediately gave them orders to commence filling up the old channel; they had about thirteen hundred men, and horses, carts, and materials, and appliances of all kinds, and set to work in right good earnest. The Corporation of Wisbech, who had always opposed the measure, although they were compelled by the Act to contribute £30,000 towards it, which was perhaps the cause, offered every obstruction in their power, and said that the new outfall was not excavated deep enough according to the Act, and came down in their barge with their law officers, giving us official written notices to stop all proceedings. At this critical moment the contractors were rather taken aback; Mr. Telford and I, however, nothing daunted, ordered the men to proceed stopping the channel, and to take no notice of the Corporation. We further told them that if they did not go away their barge and all in it would be swamped, and that the responsibility would rest entirely with them. Seeing that we were in earnest, they turned tail, and, leaving their protest, returned to Wisbech. The third day afterwards the old channel was completely closed, and the Nene diverted to its new outfall. It should be observed here that Mr. Telford and myself, calculating upon the loose nature of the soil, which was silt, and which we felt confident would scour when fairly acted upon by the current, only made the contract for the excavation to the level of low-water of spring tides; and therefore it would have wasted money to have excavated that which we knew the current would do for nothing. The current at first appeared to have very little effect; and the Duke of Bedford's manager, the late excellent and talented Tycho Wing, a school-fellow of mine at Dr. Burney's, became much alarmed, and was sadly afraid that the outfall would be a failure. Telford and I knew better, and assured him that our only doubt was whether the current would not be too strong, and render it necessary to protect the sides with stone. This we considered to be no disadvantage—on the contrary, a great benefit; for, making the cut small in the first instance, we should always be able to regulate the scour whenever it might have a tendency to enlarge the cut beyond the size necessary to discharge the drainage water effectually, at the same time preserving a sufficient depth for navigation; but, if it had been too large in the first instance, it could not have been properly adjusted afterwards. Mr. Wing was comforted by our assurances; still, he had his doubts, and two months elapsed before any sensible scour appeared to take place. The fact was, the fall in the bottom was so little, that the current had to remove the obstacles to its progress, which it could only do by degrees, when it had accumulated sufficient fall or head; having done this, its progress was most rapid, and increased daily, so that within six months after it had been opened it had scoured out the bottom to nine feet below low-water of spring tides; the sides also had been regularly scoured away, and the area of the cut was increased to three times its original size. Spring tides, which had scarcely exceeded a few feet at Wisbech, and not much more at Cross Keys, rose remarkably at both places, so that vessels of considerable tonnage could reach Wisbech even at neaps, whereas before they could only get up there at spring tides. The trade of the port increased so rapidly that they were soon enabled to pay off the £30,000 which they had been previously obliged to borrow to contribute to the cost of the outfall.'

Another undertaking in connection with the Nene is thus described by Rennie: 'It had long been a favourite idea with the late Lord William Bentinck and his friend Mr. Thomas Hoseason, of Banklands, to make a bridge across the Nene estuary, at Cross Keys, in order to shorten the distance between the south of Lincolnshire and Norfolk. The bridge over the lower end of the Eau Brink had been completed, and another had been made at the Fossdyke Wash by my father, for the Welland; so that it was only necessary to make another across the Nene estuary, at Cross Keys, to complete this desirable line of communication. A company was accordingly formed for this purpose, of which Lord William Bentinck was the head. An Act was obtained at the same time as the Nene Outfall Act, and I was appointed the engineer. The Nene Outfall Commissioners obtained a clause in the Bridge Act compelling the Company to build the bridge over the Nene Outfall Cut at the same time; this I told them was very unwise, for as the bridge was to be built of wood, with a drawbridge opening in the centre to allow vessels to pass, it would be impossible to drive the great piles forming the piers of the bridge sufficiently deep to be below the scour in the outfall; the better plan would be to wait until the outfall had been scoured to its full depth, and then build the bridge. My opinion was overruled; the bridge was built; and it was impossible, as I expected, to drive the piles to the requisite depth. Where the full effect of the scour had taken place, it was found necessary to secure the piles of the bridge by throwing a great mass of stone round them. This materially obstructed the current through the bridge, until at length there was a fall through it of from two to three feet, which greatly injured the drainage, so that the Nene Outfall Commissioners ultimately got an Act to make a new bridge for the Company at the Commissioners' expense. All this might have been avoided if the bridge had been built as I originally recommended. The spot where this bridge and line of embankment is made is the same place where King John's army was lost, and where my father was nearly drowned some years before my time, crossing in his carriage, being overtaken by the tide. Six thousand acres of this Wash have been reclaimed from the sea by myself; and, where once the tides used to ebb and flow, fields are now under culture producing the finest crops.'

Rennie next drew up a plan for draining Whittlesea Mere, and all the low fenny country around it, to the extent of 55,000 acres. He showed that by improving the Nene from Peterborough to the outfall, by making a main drain to Whittlesea Mere to connect it with the Nene, and by making a catchwater drain round the base of the surrounding hills, so as to discharge the highland water into the Nene at Peterborough and the Ouse at Hermitage Sluice, the whole country would be thoroughly well drained, and the navigation greatly improved, while there would be an ample supply of fresh water at moderate cost. Although this plan was approved by Robert Stephenson also, it was not adopted. The Middle Level Corporation, in whose district lay the greater part of the lowlands to be drained, would not listen to it, but insisted on draining these lands by the Ouse, ten miles farther distant. This measure was carried out at double the cost of Rennie's plan, and a minor plan was substituted for the improvement of the Nene, which cost a great deal more than any benefits derived from it. But the sands below Lynn, at the mouth of the Ouse, accumulated to such an extent that the navigation up to that town was seriously obstructed. Rennie was consequently requested by a Committee to enquire into and report upon the whole subject. Rennie thus states what followed: 'I accordingly employed nearly twelve months in surveying and levelling the Great Wash and the mouths of the Ouse, Nene, Welland, and Witham, which are the principal rivers discharging their waters into the Great Wash, and which drain all the adjacent fenlands, amounting to nearly a million of acres, besides the highlands. I found that by improving all the mouths of these rivers, an additional fall of seven feet might be gained for the Ouse, two feet for the Nene, and a similar amount for the Welland and the Witham, and recommended that all these rivers should be united and made to discharge their waters into one great main channel in the centre of the Great Wash, and that the main and minor channels should be properly embanked. By this means, not only would all these rivers be much improved, and the drainage and navigation rendered as perfect as they could be made, but, in addition to this, from 150,000 to 200,000 acres of land would be gained from the Wash, or, in other words, a new county, of most valuable land, would be added to the kingdom. This project was so vast and important that it took the world by surprise. It was impossible to deny the soundness of the principles or data upon which it was founded, or the vast importance of it in a national point of view, if means could be found to carry it into effect; but here was one of the great difficulties, and another still greater presented itself, viz., that of uniting together the vast number of conflicting interests concerned, so that they might combine together as one whole body for the completion of the undertaking.'

When the plan was promulgated, all kinds of objections were raised against it and attacks made upon it. The affair remained in abeyance for several years, and then it was decided that it would be better to divide the scheme into two parts, one comprising the Ouse and Nene, the other the Welland and Witham. It was next resolved to form a company for the Norfolk half, including the Ouse and Nene, and to reclaim 35,000 acres of land from the Great Wash. Plans were prepared, and in 1846 a Bill authorising the works was carried through Parliament, entitled the Norfolk Estuary Act. But the Company were saddled with so many pecuniary responsibilities that they could not undertake to execute the scheme alone. Consequently the Middle Level Commissioners and the Lynn Corporation, who represented the drainage and navigation interests, agreed to contribute the sum of £60,000 each towards the completion of the new channel for the Ouse, on condition that Robert Stephenson and John Rennie should be joint engineers. This was agreed to; a Bill was obtained, and the works were begun in 1850. They were satisfactorily executed, and the effect on the port of Lynn was so marked that the Corporation were soon enabled to pay off their contribution of £60,000 towards the Norfolk Estuary works. The Estuary

Company next turned their attention to reclaiming from the Wash the 35,000 acres which had been allotted to them by the Crown. By slow stages a portion of this large tract of submerged land was recovered, but by no means so much as might have been the case had Rennie's recommendations been followed.

Rennie was next employed by the Corporation of Boston to improve the outfall of the river between the Grand Sluice at the upper end of the town and Hobhole, near the mouth of the river, a distance of nearly four miles. The Witham and Black Sluice Commissioners would not join in the work, however, but as the outfall of the Witham became worse and worse, the Boston Corporation determined to do what they could single-handed. Rennie recommended two reforms which would shorten the navigation quite half a mile, and admit and discharge the tidal and fresh waters more readily, thus deepening the water-line and bed of the river all the way up to the Grand Sluice above Boston. The Corporation acted upon Rennie's advice, and the engineer remarks: 'The effect of this work exceeded my most sanguine expectations; in a short time it improved the channel upwards to Boston to such an extent that spring tides rose at Boston Bridge 14 feet, and neaps 10 feet, and the bed of the river was deepened from 3 to 4 feet below low-water springs, so that vessels drawing 15 feet and 16 feet could come up to the town at springs, and vessels drawing 12 to 13 feet could come up at neaps; moreover, all the silt was scoured away from the front of the Maudfoster Sluice, so that it discharged the highland water from the fens, which it had not done for years before, and improved also the discharge of the waters from the Grand and Black Sluices. I must confess that I was not a little elated at this successful result, as it most completely established the correctness of my father's opinion as well as my own, and demonstrated the fallacy of my friend Telford's judgment. The cost of the above works was £33,000, which was very small compared with the advantage obtained. The Corporation of Boston were so much pleased with the success that they determined to carry into effect the remainder of the improvement in the old channel to Boston, which was afterwards done by confining the channel by degrees to a proper width by means of fascines and loose stone and clay properly combined together up to the level of half tide, so that the flow and ebb always acted to the greatest advantage in one and the same channel without materially diminishing the quantity of tidal water.

'The effect of these additional works was to still further deepen the bed of the river and increase the flow of the tide by lowering the low-water mark, which improved the navigation and drainage still further, so that the trade of Boston revived and increased in prosperity, and all this was effected by the resources of Boston alone ; and it is only to be regretted that the drainage interests, who derived so much benefit, were not compelled to contribute their just proportion.'

Rennie further executed minor works for the improvement of the Witham near Lincoln. Also, at the request of the Commissioners of the Ancholme Level—consisting of about 50,000 acres of low fenlands, bordering upon the Ancholme in North Lincolnshire—he drew up a series of recommendations for improving the drainage of the lands, as well as the navigation of the river. All these works were successfully executed, and they answered so completely that the Ancholme district is as well drained as any level in the kingdom, while the navigation is complete of the kind.

Railways naturally attracted Rennie's attention as soon as they began to be mooted. He was offered the post of engineer to the Manchester and Liverpool Railway, and with him were joined his brother George and Mr. Charles Vignoles. They made the requisite surveys, choosing the route over Chat Moss. When the Bill for the works was carried through Parliament after great difficulty, Rennie and his co-engineers prepared working drawings and estimates, and naturally expected to be appointed executive engineers. Rennie and his brother were passed over, however, and Stephenson was appointed chief engineer, with Vignoles as resident engineer. The Rennies had designed that the width of gauge should be 5 feet 6 inches from centre to centre of the rail, but Stephenson adopted the old colliery waggon gauge of 4 feet 8½ inches. It was only after enormous litigation and expense that the 4 feet 8½ inch gauge was acknowledged to be as much too narrow as Brunel's gauge of 7 feet on the Great Western Railway was too wide. In 1826 Rennie projected a railway from London to Birmingham, and his brother and Messrs. Jessop and Chapman proposed another from Birmingham to Liverpool, thus connecting three important places, but the scheme was in advance of the time. John Rennie likewise devised plans for two lines from London to Brighton, as well as a coast-line from Brighton westwards, but the period for these also was not yet ripe. Robert Stephenson's line from London to Birmingham was ultimately preferred to Rennie's.

In the year 1822 Rennie was elected a member of the Travellers' Club, and in the following year was elected a Fellow of the Royal Society. He was one of the original members of the Athenæum Club, and one of the original Fellows of the Royal Geographical Society and the Zoological Society. Some time after the opening of new London Bridge, Rennie went on a short Continental tour. He was in bad health, and still suffering from the effects of a fall into the coffer-dam while engaged in constructing London Bridge. From London he went to St. Petersburg, and visited the Government establishment at Kolpnau for the cotton, gun, and general iron manufactures. He was much interested in finding the latest mechanical improvements adopted here. He also examined the great naval arsenal at Cronstadt, and made suggestions for improvements, some of which were adopted. With his brother, he afterwards built four iron steamboats, with their engines, for the Caspian Sea, which were the first ever afloat there. They further made the iron gates for the docks of Sebastopol, together with several vessels of war, worked by the screw, for the Baltic and Black Seas. Rennie visited Novgorod, Moscow, and Warsaw, and then returned to England by way of Germany. At this time he lived in a house in Whitehall Place, with his two younger brothers, Matthew and James. Although he was a bachelor, he saw a good deal of society, and was on more or less intimate terms with all the leading authors, painters, sculptors, and men of science of the day.

By the year 1833 Rennie had completed the London, Hyde Park, Staines, and Cramond bridges; the great naval works at Sheerness, Woolwich, and Chatham; the Victualling Department, or Royal William Yard, and a large portion of the breakwaters at Plymouth, Sunderland, Port Patrick, Donaghadee, and Port Rush; a considerable portion of Kingstown Harbour, the Eau Brink Cut, the Nene Outfall, the Witham Outfall, the Ancholme Drainage, and several other minor works. Rest was consequently necessary again, so he went on a tour through Spain. His party had an encounter with brigands near Cordova, but they reached that city without harm, and then proceeded to Seville. From thence they went to Madrid, and found the capital in a state of the greatest excitement, owing to the vigorous rising of the Carlists under Zumalacarregui. Toledo and Barcelona were next visited, and Rennie returned home by way of Toulouse, Bordeaux, and Paris. On another occasion Rennie visited Austria and South Germany, and at Vienna made the acquaintance of the famous Prince Metternich and the Archduke Charles, Commander-in-Chief of the Austrian armies, who was the first general who defeated the great Napoleon at Aspern.

Rennie examined three alternative routes for a ship canal from London to Portsmouth, and he regarded the canal as perfectly practicable, though it was doubtful whether it would ever have made a sufficient return upon the capital. The undertaking was not carried through, and railways have since rendered it unnecessary. The machinery manufactory founded by the elder Rennie was carried on by John and George Rennie, who constructed the rolling mills for the Calcutta and Bombay mints; machines for Deptford, Portsmouth, and Cremill Point; locomotive engines for railways, steam-engines and machinery for English and foreign vessels, etc., etc. In 1832 Rennie made complete hydrographical surveys of all the harbours in the Isle of Man, and suggested plans for the best way of improving them, some of which were carried into effect. He further improved the port of Hartlepool, and the mouth of the Coquet, near Warkworth, and constructed the piers of Sunderland Harbour. During 1837-38 he was again occupied with the Brighton railway scheme, which he carried through, as well as the Blackwall Railway. All through the time of the railway mania his labours were most arduous, as his advice and aid were sought in connection with a multitude of schemes. His alternative plan for the Great Northern line, which was acknowledged to be superior to that adopted, was unfortunately thrown out of Parliament. Another important line lost was the Bristol and Chepstow, which would have materially shortened the distance between Bristol, Birmingham, and Liverpool, and have enabled the South Wales Railway also to shorten materially their distance to London. A scheme for a Central Kent Railway line likewise fell through, though the South-Eastern Company admitted it to be better than theirs for Kent and the sea-coast, and the landed proprietors who opposed it subsequently repented of their action. The South-Eastern were compelled to expend nearly £700,000 to cut off the angle between London and Tunbridge, all of which might have been saved by the adoption of Rennie's plan, while under the same plan there would have been no necessity for that expensive line, the London, Chatham, and Dover.

On three occasions Rennie visited Sweden with the object of constructing railways. He made elaborate surveys, but the Swedish Government were apathetic, and they would give no guarantee, although they had made a concession to Count Adolphe Rosen, who offered half of it to Rennie for his services. 'Accordingly,' says Rennie, 'the Swedish railways remained in abeyance until the year 1852; by this time the Swedish Government had considered the subject maturely, and felt that, as every other European nation had adopted them, Sweden, if she desired to keep pace with other countries, must either make the railways herself, for which at the time the Government had not the money, or she must encourage others to make them by guaranteeing a sufficient interest for the capital expended. Accordingly I went there again, and was as usual very kindly received by the King and his Ministers, and I saw that they were becoming more anxious than ever that the railways should be made. I had been there in October, 1848, and had the honour of being invited to dine at the palace in Stockholm, as I had previously the honour of dining with their Majesties at the summer palace of Hoga, near Stockholm. Upon arriving at the palace, I was most courteously received by King Oscar, who did me the honour of presenting me to his handsome, graceful, and intelligent Queen. When her Majesty heard that the railways were to be commenced, she said that she heard so much talk about them and nothing had been done, that she feared they never would be made, "therefore talk no more about them, but set to work and make them." The dinner-party consisted of about thirty. I had the honour of sitting next the Lord Chancellor, a very agreeable, intelligent person, who sat next to the Royal Family. We had an excellent dinner, without the least restraint, and the common topic of conversation seemed to be, who would be elected President of the French Republic, Cavaignac or Louis Napoleon, and everybody seemed in favour of Cavaignac as the proper person; they all spoke disparagingly of Louis Napoleon. It seems curious to think how little the world knew of that extraordinary man, and how completely he disappointed all previous expectations.

'When at Stockholm I was presented to his present Majesty,

King Charles XV., then Prince Karl, a very handsome, intelligent young man. Since his accession to the throne he has done me the honour of conferring upon me the order of Knight Commander of the Order of Wasa, for what his Majesty was pleased to term the great services which I had rendered Sweden. This was the more agreeable, as it was sent to me through my personal friend Count Platen, then the Swedish representative at the Court of London.'

In 1852 the concession for the Swedish railways was renewed, with a Government guarantee of four per cent. on the amount of capital required, viz., £420,000, with power to raise £167,000. Rennie went over to Sweden again : the works were begun, and everything was going on well, when the Chairman of the Company, the notorious John Sadleir, M.P., committed suicide, and his fearful mismanagement of the Swedish railway and other undertakings was fully exposed. Rennie resigned his post of engineer, and it was well he did so, for things were carried on in a discreditable manner, and as a man of honour he would have nothing whatever to do with the whole concern. In the hands of an honest body of directors the Swedish lines would have paid well.

In 1852 Rennie acted as engineer to a Belgian and English company formed for the reclamation of tracts of land on the Scheldt. He had here to complain of the enormous waste of money and labour, some 1,300 men being engaged at from 3s. to 4s. per day, who were not doing half the work they were engaged for. The scheme also of endeavouring to reclaim 3,000 acres of land at once he saw to be impossible, and after great difficulty he persuaded the contractors to reclaim by smaller portions, which was successfully done. Rennie was strongly of opinion that the whole of the sea-board of Holland required to be re-modelled. If all the superfluous channels were filled up, and the islands which they surround were united to the mainland, a great quantity of valuable land would be gained to the State.

Rennie went to Portugal in 1855, at the request of the Government, to make arrangements for a general system of railways and other works. He was cordially received by Dom Fernando, husband of the late Dona Maria, Queen of Portugal, and brother to the late Prince Consort. Rennie inspected the great aqueduct of Lisbon, which he regarded as a grand and magnificent work, the finest of the kind in Europe. He was also much interested in the Castle and Cathedral of Belem, the latter of which buildings was erected in honour of Prince Henry, the Portuguese navigator. At the request of the Government he prepared plans for docks or landing jetties for the port of Lisbon. He thought the harbour the finest and most spacious in Europe, always excepting that of Vigo. Next he went to Oporto, where he carefully examined the port, and found that, owing to a variety of causes, the harbour of Oporto was hermetically sealed for three-fourths of the year. Vessels had been known to go to the Brazils and back, while others were waiting in the offing for a favourable opportunity to cross the bar. Then the mails for Oporto, the second city in the Kingdom, had frequently to be delivered at Vigo, sixty miles further north, and to be thence transported by land. To remedy the defects, Rennie drew up a plan for erecting two piers at a cost of £400,000—one on the ridge of rocks on the south side, and another on the north—in such a direction that the entrance between them, which was to be 500 feet wide, should be least exposed to the prevailing storms. These works would have been a great improvement, and well worth the money, but as the bar would still be unapproachable on certain occasions, the engineer cast about for a site for a new harbour, and found an excellent one at Mattozenhas. As fine granite was cheap and plentiful, he considered that for a sum of £500,000 an admirable harbour might be made here with a double entrance. He therefore strongly recommended it in preference to expending £400,000 on the old entrance. The King and the Government approved the plans, and the Finance Minister

Fontes gave orders for the works to be begun immediately. Shortly afterwards, however, there was a change of Ministry, and the whole arrangements fell to the ground. Rennie afterwards examined the harbours of Viana and Figuera, and reported upon them. When Dom Pedro had attained his majority, and ascended the throne, he invited Rennie to visit Lisbon again, feeling convinced that until her railways, harbours, and docks were placed on a proper footing, Portugal could never take her proper place among the nations. Rennie accordingly went over with his harbour plans and reports, and made further surveys through Portugal with a view to the construction of railways. Several important lines were begun, including one for a better and more direct communication with Spain; but disputes arose between Messrs. Peto, Betts & Co., the contractors, and the Portuguese Government, which terminated in the abandonment of what would have been for Portugal a great national work. Rennie subsequently visited Tunis in company with one of Messrs. Peto & Betts's agents, to examine into the feasibility of constructing a railway from the Goletta to the city. The requisite survey was made, but owing to the imprudent action of the contractors' agent, the French Consul became alive to the whole situation, and in an audience with the Bey threatened him with the vengeance of France if the concession were granted. The Bey was obliged to submit, and the project was abandoned.

I may pause here to note Rennie's chief contributions to the literature of engineering. He wrote a pamphlet on the *Drainage of Lombardy* which attracted the practical attention of the Italian Premier, Signor Sella. One of his papers contributed to the Institution of Civil Engineers upon the 'Harbour of Ostia' was full of instructive practical facts relating to the effect of the action of tides and of rivers in the formation of deltas, shoals, and bars at the entrances of harbours. His presidential address to the Institution of Civil Engineers in 1846 was practically a condensed history of the rise and progress of engineering science in modern times. In 1847 he published a monograph on Plymouth Breakwater. But his most important contribution to professional literature was his work on *The Theory, Formation, and Construction of British and Foreign Harbours*. It was dedicated to the Queen, and was published in two volumes in 1854. In addition to being a survey of larger engineering works, this treatise included descriptions of the docks constructed by Rennie at Whitehaven for Lord Lonsdale, and the extension of the Cardiff Docks which he carried out for the Trustees of the Marquis of Bute. Rennie was admitted to be the highest authority on all matters connected with hydraulic engineering, harbours, canals, drainage, irrigation, the storage of water, and the management of rivers. It may be added that he greatly contributed to the introduction of Sir Francis Pettitt Smith's invention, the screw-propeller, into the Royal Navy.

Rennie was called upon to make an official report on the condition of the city of Odessa, which seems to have been the worst city in the world as regards paving and sewers. There was, in fact, neither one nor the other, and people living only one mile from the food supplies and the butchers' shops were practically starved at certain seasons of the year. The engineer's recommendations had a salutary effect. Then he was asked to examine the water-supply of Vienna, which he found to be most defective. He made investigations in the vicinity, and having found a source whence a good water-supply could be obtained, he drew up a report to the municipality of Vienna. That sage body thanked him for it, and then spent many years in fruitless discussions as to whether they should carry out his recommendations. In 1861 Rennie constructed for the Portuguese Government the harbour of Ponta Delgada, the chief town in St. Michael's, the principal island of the Azores. He next carried out additional improvements in Ramsgate Harbour, in regard to which he occupied the post of principal permanent engineer. After the harbour was transferred to the

Board of Trade, he still continued in his old post, and at the same salary, viz., £315 per annum and travelling expenses. He then turned his attention to constructing the Dagenham Dock, on the left bank of the Thames, utilising the Dagenham Lake, a fine sheet of water, for the purpose. He made considerable progress with the works, and something was done towards converting the lake into a great dock establishment, but although several Acts of Parliament were obtained, the works could not be completed under Rennie's plans, and they fell into abeyance.

Sir John Rennie took a high view of his profession. Here is what he wrote on this subject towards the close of his *Autobiography:* 'The real object of the civil engineer is to promote the civilization of the world, by the proper application of the great mechanical means at his command, and to take a high independent position as a scientific man, thoroughly versed in his profession both theoretically and practically, and wholly independent of contractors, and all sinister influences. Unless he can do this, he never will be held in that esteem and respect, or take that high position without which no professional man can properly discharge the duties that he owes to himself and to the public.

'Against what I have said it may perhaps be urged that I assign too high a place to the profession to which my father and myself have had the honour to belong; but I think that when the subject has been calmly and fairly considered it will be generally admitted that I have not done so without reason. Without wishing for a moment to depreciate the merits of any other body of men, I think it will be conceded that the objects proposed by the engineer, and the acquirements, knowledge, and experience that he must possess before he can practise successfully, are at least equal to those of any other profession, particularly after the practical examples exhibited to the world of the great benefits that engineering has already conferred upon mankind. Therefore are we entitled to be ranked amongst the most learned professions, and to receive all the honours they have most justly earned; and I trust the time is not far distant when this justice will be accorded to them.'

With regard to the proper training for a civil engineer, Rennie observes: 'Let him first get a sound elementary education in the several departments of arithmetic, algebra, geometry, natural philosophy, geography, geology, astronomy, chemistry, land and hydrographical surveying, as well as grammar, English composition, history, French, German, and Latin, according to the improved system of modern education; every youth of ordinary talents has a tolerably fair knowledge of these at seventeen or eighteen. What then should be the training for an engineer? First let him go through the best course of modern education at his command, including the elements of geometry, mathematics, and the physical sciences, not excluding Latin and Greek, in spite of the prejudice against them now frequently expressed. Then let him be apprenticed for two or three years to some good steam-engine and machinery manufacturer, where he should learn to make drawings and calculations, handle tools, make models, steam-engine machinery, and put machinery together. By this means, if he applies his mind to it properly, he may become a practical as well as theoretical mechanician, which is the soundest basis for good engineering; indeed, without this it is impossible for an engineer to be thoroughly successful, but being well grounded in this most important knowledge, all the others will become comparatively easy. Having gone through this apprenticeship, let him bind himself for three or four years to some well-known civil engineer, of large practice in railways, docks, harbours, waterworks, canals, drainage, rivers, etc. In this office the pupil will learn everything connected with these departments, and as they are founded more or less upon practical mechanics, he will soon find that from his previous mechanical education he has already acquired considerable knowledge of them, and it will only be necessary to apply those principles, modified according to the particular circumstances required; in fact, the principles are the same, although applied upon a larger scale.'

The practical instructions which Rennie gives to civil engineers in concluding his *Autobiography* are invaluable, even in the light of the advances which the science of engineering has made since they were written. They range over such topics as the construction of harbours and canals, drainage, the water-supply of towns, the storage of inflammable goods, docks and warehouses, embankments, breakwaters, bridges, etc.

It is cheering to find a veteran writing as follows, after an experience of human life extending over a period of upwards of seventy years: 'The motto of life should be, "Forward!" We must expect to be checked, thwarted, and baffled in our endeavours to obtain success; but these obstacles, instead of totally arresting our progress, should serve only to increase our energy. Like a river, impeded in its course, in silence waits till its accumulated strength sweeps the obstruction from its path, and it flows on majestically as before—so should we make every difficulty we encounter add to our strength, instead of increasing our weakness. Nevertheless, since "'tis not in mortals to command success," we may sometimes struggle in vain; and fortune ever against us, we may be overcome at the last; but even then we have this satisfaction—we have fought a good fight; we have done the best we could; we have done our duty to the best of our ability, and this is all that can be required of us. To do my duty has been my endeavour through life; and probably if I had adhered to it more strictly I might have done a great deal better. Nevertheless, little as I have done, I should not have accomplished half so much had I not kept that one object in view, as far as my physical and mental powers would permit; and this is no small consolation. The old motto, "*Nil desperandum,*" should be constantly on our lips, and should act like the spur on a jaded steed. Affairs are never so bad but they might have been worse, and they may generally be mended by energy and perseverance, and a determination to make the best of everything. We may not be able to accomplish all we desire to achieve; nevertheless, by refusing to yield to misfortune we shall escape the reproach of cowardice and faintheartedness. When we suffer a defeat, let us calmly consider the cause of it, and nine times out of ten we shall find it is through our own fault; these lessons of experience should be carefully laid to heart, and serve for our future guidance.

'I have never deemed wealth desirable for mere personal gratification, but only in so far as it would have enabled me to help others, to promote the advancement of science and the well-being of my fellow-creatures; this would have conferred the greatest happiness upon me, but it has been denied by the Almighty Disposer of events, and most probably with justice, that it might be done better by other hands. I therefore humbly bow to the Almighty's decision; and if I have done the best I could in His sight, I am amply rewarded. I, however, most deeply regret that I have not done more. I return my most fervent thanks to the Almighty that He, out of His great mercy, has allowed me to do the little I have done; and I most devoutly hope that He through His Son Jesus Christ will pardon my shortcomings; and I say with all reverence, Bless the Lord for all His mercies.'

Sir John Rennie contemplated writing a history of engineering—enlarged from his address to the Institution of Civil Engineers—as well as a Life of his revered father, but he did not live to accomplish either of these works. After the year 1866, he undertook scarcely any professional labours, though he lived for eight years beyond this time. He had just completed his eightieth year, when he passed away, on the 3rd of September, 1874. Rennie's was a full, useful, and valuable life, and it worthily carried forward the traditions he inherited from his father. In both these men there was a lofty spirit of enterprise and an indomitable will, and we can give equal honour to both for those magnificent works which have added so much to the material prosperity and glory of England.

THE END.

INDEX.

AMERICAN WAR, Wedgwood on the, 281.
Anecdotes of George Stephenson, 4, 5, 7, 8, 22, 31, 50, 60; Robert Stephenson, 9, 10, 41, 67, 71; Charles Knight, 81, 82, 83, 94, 98, 113, 129; Sir George Burns, 143, 146, 148, 150, 159, 161, 179, 184, 186; Edward Irving, 144; Sir Josiah Mason, 197, 200, 217, 219; Dr. Priestley, 202; Michael Faraday, 211; Josiah Wedgwood, 240, 261, 265, 267, 270, 272; Thomas Brassey, 314, 319, 320, 321, 322; William Fairbairn, 339, 341; B. R. Haydon, R.A., 348; Peter Fairbairn, 372; Sir William Siemens, 386.
Ardrossan steamers, The, 161.
Argentine Railway, The, 329.
Arnold, Dr., on railways, 52; on newspapers, 120.
Assyrian and Babylonian pottery, 234.
Atmospheric pressure on railways, 56.

BARBERINI VASE, The, 287-289.
Bedford Level, The, 445.
Bell Rock Lighthouse, The, 434.
Bentley, Thomas, the friend and partner of Wedgwood, 250, 262, 265, 270-273, 282.
Berwick, Royal Border Bridge of, 63.
Blenkinsop's locomotive, 12.
Books and Library Series, Increase of, 120, 121.

Booksellers and publishers, Eminent, 77.
Book trade, Great increase of the, 122.
Brassey, Thomas, his birth and ancestry, 303; education and early occupations, 304; begins to tender for railways, 305; his marriage, 306; character as a contractor, 307; foreign undertakings, 308-314; his activity, 314; takes the Great Northern Railway contract, 315; his financial method, 316; pecuniary difficulties, 317; his Austrian contract, 318; summary of his important contracts, 320; Italian lines, 321, 322; the Grand Trunk Railway, 323, 324; other undertakings, 327; Australian works, 328; the Argentine Railway, 329; Indian railways, 330; Brassey's last labours and death, 331; his character, 332.
Bridgewater, The Duke of, 257.
Brindley, James, the engineer, 247, 254, 279.
Britannia Tubular Bridge, 65, 349.
British pottery and porcelain, 236.
Brougham, Lord, and popular education, 95, 99.
Brunel, the engineer, 47, 57, 71.
Burns, James (Sir George's brother), 146, 183.
Burns, Dr. John (Sir George's brother), 142, 162.
Burns, John (Sir George Burns's grandfather), 141.

INDEX.

Burns, John (Sir George's father), 142, 151.

Burns, John (Sir George's son), 162, 168, 175, 177, 178, 179.

Burns, Sir George, the typical merchant prince, 135; his ancestry, 141; his birth, 142; begins a business career, 143; acquainted with Chalmers and Irving, 144; enters into partnership with his brother, 146; marries, 146; his shipping ventures, 147; he co-operates with MacIver, 150; loses his father, 151; founds with Samuel Cunard and David MacIver the Cunard Company, 152-154; character of its fleet, 155; voyage of the *Britannia*, 156; his personal friends, 158; conveys the Queen through the Crinan Canal, 159; new business enterprise, 161; loss of the *Orion*, 161; family bereavements, 162; opposition of the Great Western Company, 163; and of the Collins line, 165; new Cunard steamers, 166; he retires from business, 166; arrangements of the Cunard Company, 167; various ocean steamer lines, 171; Burns at Wemyss Bay, 174; his philanthropic enterprises, 175; his personal character 177; member of the Gaiter Club, 178, 179; his friends, 180, 181; celebrates his golden wedding, 183; his political opinions, 184; is created a baronet, 185; his death, 186.

Byerley, Thomas, Wedgwood's nephew, 258, 267, 281.

CANTERBURY and Whitstable Railway, 42.

Catherine, The Empress, and the famous Wedgwood service, 275.

Cavour, Count, and Thomas Brassey, 321, 322.

Chalmers, Dr., and George Burns, 143, 145.

Chinese porcelain, 233.

Clanny's safety-lamp, Dr. W. R., 15.

Collins line of steamers, The, 165; its disastrous collapse, 166.

Colombian Mining Association, The, 40.

Conway Tubular Bridge, 68.

Coroners' inquests and boiler explosions, 357.

Cugnot, N. J., makes the first practical working engine, 11.

Cunard Company, Founding of the, 152-154; its first triumph, 156; its magnificent vessels, 164; provisioning of its fleet, 169; number of its vessels, 172.

Cunard, Sir Samuel, 153-156, 168, 183.

DARWIN, ERASMUS, 252, 258, 264.

Davy, Sir Humphry, and the safety-lamp, 15.

Dickens, Charles, 118, 157.

Drainage works, Rennie's, 449-456.

Dynamo-electric machine, 414.

EGYPTIAN POTTERY, 234.

Electro-plating, The process of, 209-217.

English and foreign workmen compared, 312.

English railways, 52, 55.

Erdington Orphanage, The, 220.

Etruria works, Opening of Wedgwood's, 270; description of, 278.

Evans, Oliver, constructs a steam dredging-machine, 11.

FAIRBAIRN, ANDREW (William's father), 337, 339, 340, 348.

Fairbairn, Sir Andrew (Sir Peter's son), his birth and education, 376; travels, 377; enters into business, 377; is knighted, 377; his public services, 378.

Fairbairn, Sir Peter (William's brother), 339; his birth and early life, 371; begins business as a machine maker at Leeds, 372; his inventions and improvements, 373, 374; his public services, 375; is knighted, 375; his death and character, 376.

Fairbairn, Sir Thomas (Sir William's son), 359; his birth and education 370; public services, 371.

INDEX.

Fairbairn, Sir William, and George Stephenson, 6.
Fairbairn, William, his birth, 337; early life and education, 338, 339; apprenticed to a millwright, 340; his experiences in London, 341; marries Dorothy Mar, 342; first inventions, 342; becomes partner with James Lillie, 343; constructs water-wheels, 344; builds the *Lord Dundas*, 345; dissolves partnership, 346; opens works at Millwall, 346; invents the riveting machine, 347; visits Turkey, 347; assists Robert Stephenson with the Britannia Bridge, 349; patents wrought-iron girder bridges, 349; advises on the Rhine bridge at Cologne, 350; honours conferred upon him, 351; his improvements in steam-boilers, 352; founds the Association for the Prevention of Steam-boiler Explosions, 353; various scientific researches, 356-358; iron shipbuilding and engine manufacture, 359; great work in mill construction, 360; course of the Fairbairn firm, 361; the shipbuilding yard at Millwall, 362; honours to Fairbairn, 363-364; he visits Italy, 364; president of the British Association, 365; created a baronet, 366; his voluminous writings, 366-368; his death, 368; his character, 369.
Flaxman models for Wedgwood, 280, 285.
Follett, Sir William, and George Stephenson, 61.
Furnace, The regenerative steam, 394, 398-400.

GAUGES, The battle of the, 57
George III. at the Windsor Theatre, 81.
Gladstone, Mr., on Wedgwood, 292-296.
Grand Junction Railway, The, 49.
Grand Trunk Railway of Canada, 323.
Grecian pottery, 235.

Great Western Company's steamers, The, 163.
Great Western Railway, The, 57-59.

HAWKSHAW, SIR JOHN, on unskilled labour, 313.
Hedley, William, constructs the *Puffing Billy*, 12.
Hetton Railway opened, 20.
Holyhead Harbour, 431.
Hudson, George, 'the Railway King,' 53.
Huskisson, Mr., his lamentable death, 38.

JAPANESE POTTERY, 234.
Jerrold, Douglas, and Charles Knight, 129.

KEAN, EDMUND, at Windsor, 85.
Knight, Charles, 75; his birth and education, 79; studies business, 82; founds the *Windsor & Eton Express*, etc., 83; early reminiscences, 84; promotes popular education, 85; publishes *The Plain Englishman*, 88; Knight's *Quarterly Magazine*, 90; prosecuted for libel, 93; concerned in the Byron memoirs, 94; meeting with Lord Brougham, 95; connection with the Society for the Diffusion of Useful Knowledge, 96-99; its important works, 101-110; he opposes the paper duty and newspaper stamp, 111; his *Pictorial Bible*, 111; *History of England*, 112; *Pictorial Shakespeare*, 113; miscellaneous works, 114-117; his interest in Shakespeare, 118; *The Penny Magazine*, 119; *English Cyclopædia*, 123; *Popular History of England*, 124, 125; *Passages of a Working Life*, 126; his literary friends, 128; last years and death, 130; his services to the people, 131.
Knowledge, Charles Knight on, 87.

LANDORE STEELWORKS, The, 401, 406.

Leicester and Swannington Railway, The, 42.
Leopold, King, and the Stephensons, 51.
Liverpool and Manchester Railway projected, 27; is strongly opposed, 28; the Bill rejected, 32; new Bill carried, 33; construction of the line, 34, 36; opening of the railway, 37; its success, 39.
Locomotive experiments and improvements, 11, 12, 13, 35, 43.
London and Birmingham Railway begun, 44,; difficulties in its construction, 45; its successful completion, 47.
London and West India Docks, etc., 430.
London Bridge, New, 445.

MacIver, David, 149, 150, 154, 168.
Manchester Steam-users' Association founded, 354.
Mason Science College founded, 222.
Mason, Sir Josiah, 191; his birth, 197; education and early employments, 198; settles in Birmingham, 199; a split-ring maker, 200; takes up the pen trade, 202; its progress, 207; his connection with the electro-plating trade, 209; enters the firm of Elkingtons, 215; establishes a copper industry, 218; his accumulating wealth, 219; he founds the Erdington Orphanage, 220; erects the Mason Science College, 222; speech in laying the foundation stone, 223; the college opened, 227; honours to Mason, 229; his death and character, 230.
Midland Railway, The, 49.
Multitubular boiler, The, 13.
Murdoch, William, 11.

Newcastle High Level Bridge, 63.
Newspaper and periodical press, Great development of the, 112.

Ocean traffic between 1850-90, 171.

Palmerston, Lord, in Scotland, 179.
Paris and Rouen Railway, The, 308.
Peel, Sir Robert, and George Stephenson, 60, 62.
Pen, History of the, 191-195.
Pen trade of Birmingham, The, 203-205; the trade abroad, 207.
Penny Cyclopædia, Story of the, 103-110.
Penny Magazine, The, 119.
Pitt and Wedgwood, 286.
Plymouth Breakwater, 438.
Popular History of England, Knight's, 123.
Popular publications, Spread of, 78.
Post-office reform, 111.
Pottery, History of ancient and modern, 233-236.
Praed, Winthrop Mackworth, 90, 92.
Priestley, Dr., 202, 250, 258.
Printing industry, The, 75; its earlier developments, 76.
Prize system in literature, The, 116.
Pyrometer, Wedgwood's invention of the, 283.

Queen Victoria in her youth, 98.

Railway Act, The first public, 21.
Railway passenger carriage, The first, 27.
Railways, Progress of English, 52, 55.
Railways ridiculed, 24.
Ramsgate Harbour, 433.
Rennie, George, 442.
Rennie, John, the elder, his birth, 423; his education, 424; his earliest engineering works, 425; construction of canals, 426; fen drainage, 426; his first great bridge, 427; Waterloo Bridge, 428; Southwark Bridge, 429; London and East and West India Docks, 430; Holyhead Harbour, 431; Ramsgate Harbour, 433; the Bell Rock Lighthouse, 434; further works of Rennie, 435; Royal Dockyards, 436; other dockyards, 437; Plymouth Break-

water, 438; miscellaneous works, 439; Rennie's death and character, 440-442.
Rennie, Sir John, his birth and education, 443; his travels, 444; succeeds his father as Admiralty engineer, 444; drains the Bedford Level, 445; engineer for Ramsgate Harbour, etc., 446; completes new London Bridge, 447; is knighted, 449; his great drainage works, 449-456; railway schemes, 456; visits Russia, 457; summary of his works, 458; he visits Spain and Sweden, 458-460; reclaims land from the Scheldt, 461; designs Portuguese harbours and railways, 462, 463; his literary labours, 463, 464; later works, 464; views of his profession, 465, 466; admirable survey of his own life, 467, 468; his death, 468.
Rhine bridge at Cologne, The, 350.
Rouen and Havre Railway, The, 310.
Royal Dockyards, etc., 436, 437.

SAFETY-LAMP, Stephenson's, 15; Davy's, 15; Clanny's, 15.
Saltaire, The great works at, 360.
Shaftesbury, Lord, 181, 183.
Shakespeare's house at Stratford, 118.
Shipping Industry of Great Britain, 135; its rise and progress, 136-141; later developments, 173.
Siemens, Carl Heinrich, 383, 406, 407, 417.
Siemens, Ernst Werner von, 381, 382, 406, 414, 417, 418.
Siemens, Ferdinand, and his family, 381.
Siemens, Ferdinand, the younger, 383.
Siemens, Friedrich, the inventor, 383, 390, 393.
Siemens, Hans, 383, 406.
Siemens, Otto, 384.
Siemens, Sir William, Birth of, 381; his education, 384; visits England, 385; his remarkable experiences, 385-387; his first patent, 388; the differential governor, 388; anastatic printing, 389; engineering improvements, 390; heat experiments, 391-394; various inventions, 395; submarine cables, 396; Siemens's home life, 397; his marriage, 398; the regenerative furnace, 398-400; steel-making, 401; the chronometric governor, 401; the Malta and Alexandria Cable, 401; Siemens's works at Charlton, 402; the Indo-European Telegraph, 403; travels in Germany, Italy, and Switzerland, 405, 406; the Landore Steel Works, 406, 407; the Direct Atlantic Cable, 407, 408; the Brazilian Cable, 409-411; experiments in electric lighting, 412, 413; the dynamo, 414; Siemens's other inventions, 415; honours awarded to him, 416, 417; further electrical achievements, 418; knighthood for Siemens, 419; his death and character, 419-20.
Siemens, Walter, 383, 406.
Society for the Diffusion of Useful Knowledge, 95-111.
Southwark Bridge, 429.
Stanhope and Tyne Railway, The, 48.
Steam-blast, Invention of the, 14.
Steamboat, The first successful, 139.
Steam-boilers, Improvements in, 352, 358.
Steam-engine, The regenerative, 390.
Steam passage across the Atlantic, The first, 140.
Stephenson, George, his birth, 3; early life, 4; marriage, 5; friendship with William Fairbairn, 6; birth of his only son, 6; loss of his wife, 7; his struggles, 7; appointed enginewright at Killingworth, 8; studies the locomotive, 11; makes his first travelling engine, 12; waste steam and the steam-blast, 13; invents the 'Geordie' safety lamp, 15; the

Davy-Stephenson controversy, 15; he receives a public testimonial, 16; introduces steam machinery underground, 17; his locomotive experiments, 18; lays down the Hetton Railway, 20; marries Elizabeth Hindmarsh, 21; appointed engineer for the Darlington and Stockton line, 22; establishes a locomotive manufactory at Newcastle, 23; at the opening of the Darlington Railway, 24; appointed engineer of the Liverpool and Manchester Railway, 28; examined before a Parliamentary Committee, 30; the Bill carried, 33; beginning of the line, 34; he constructs the *Rocket*, 35; opening of the railway, 37; triumph of the improved locomotive, 43; he is overwhelmed with railway projects, 48; personal glimpses of him, 50; railways constructed under his superintendence, 52; visits Belgium and Spain, 59; illness, 60; anecdotes concerning him, 60; his last public appearance, 62; death, 62; and character, 63.

Stephenson, George, and Thomas Brassey, 305.

Stephenson, Robert (father of George Stephenson), his life at Wylam, 3; love for birds and animals, 4.

Stephenson, Robert, birth of the great engineer, 6; his education and early years, 9; reminiscences of his youth, 10; at Edinburgh University, 21; chief engineer in Robert Stephenson & Co., 23; at the opening of the Liverpool and Manchester Railway, 37; visits Spanish America, 40; his meeting with Trevithick, 41; his marriage, 42; early railway projects, 42; constructs the London and Birmingham Railway, 44; recognition of his success, 47; his loss with the Stanhope and Tyne line, 48; engineer for the North Midland Line, 49; visits the Continent, 49; decorated by the King of the Belgians, 51; his railway projects in the North, 53; loses his wife, 53; beginning of his fame, 54; conduct during the railway mania, 56; the battle of the gauges, 57; begins to construct his magnificent bridges, 63; the Royal Border Bridge of Berwick, 63; the High Level Bridge at Newcastle, 63; the Britannia Tubular Bridge, 65; the Conway Tubular Bridge, 68; the Victoria Railway Bridge at Montreal, 68; Stephenson in Parliament, 69; his social gatherings, 69; at the zenith of his fame, 69; honours and rewards, 70; his sad loneliness, 70; his death, 71; and character, 72.

Stockton and Darlington Railway, Opening of the, 24.

Story of railway enterprise, 318.

Stratford de Redcliffe, Lord, 81.

Submarine cables, 395, 401, 403, 407-411.

Surrey Iron Railway, The, 21.

Sweden, King of, and Robert Stephenson, 70.

Symington, William, 11.

TAYLOR, TOM, on Charles Knight, 131.

Trevithick, Richard, 11, 41.

Trotter, Captain, and George Burns, 180.

VESSELS, Improvements in, 137-140.

Victoria, Queen, in her youth, 98; visit to Scotland, 159.

Victoria Railway Bridge, Montreal, 68, 324.

WARRINGTON RAILWAY, The, 42.

Waterloo Bridge, 428.

Wedgwood, John (Josiah's brother), 262.

Wedgwood, Josiah, his ancestry, 237; his birth, 238; early life, 238; education, 239; apprentice-

ship, 241; enters into business, 242; his discoveries in pottery, 243; his partner Wheildon, 243; establishes himself at Burslem, 245; growth of his business, 246; his fame spreads, 249; he meets with Thomas Bentley, 250; marries his cousin, 251; improves the engine-lathe, 253; promotes the Grand Trunk Canal, 254; makes interesting experiments, 256; meets with royal and aristocratic patrons, 257; his friendship with Erasmus Darwin, 258; is received by the Queen, 260; is joined by his cousin, Thomas Wedgwood, 261; Bentley becomes his partner, 262; Wedgwood's leg amputated, 264; his designs in cream-ware, 267; his only patent, 268; opening of the Etruria works, 270; Wedgwood's audience with George III. and the Queen, 273; his works pirated, 274; commission from the Empress Catherine of Russia, 275; description of Etruria, 277, 278;
new designs and wares, 280; he mourns the loss of Bentley, 282; his address to the workmen in the Potteries, 283; agitates for free trade, 286; reproduces the Barberini Vase, 287; retires from business, 289; his life at Etruria Hall, 290; last illness and death, 291; characteristics of Wedgwood and his works, 292-299.

Wedgwood Memorial Institute founded, 292; its opening, 298.

Wedgwood, Thomas (Josiah's brother), 256, 279.

Wedgwood, Thomas (Josiah's cousin), 261, 289.

Wedgwood, Thomas (Josiah's son), 275.

Wharncliffe, Lord, and Robert Stephenson, 44.

Wheatstone, Professor, 52.

Wheildon and Wedgwood, 243.

Windsor Express, Actions against the, 93.

Wrottesley, Lord, on Sir William Fairbairn, 365.

www.ingramcontent.com/pod-product-compliance
Lightning Source LLC
Chambersburg PA
CBHW022059300426
44117CB00007B/513